Cognitive Models and Spiritual Maps

Interdisciplinary Explorations of Religious Experience

edited by

Jensine Andresen
and
Robert K.C. Forman

IMPRINT ACADEMIC

Cover Illustration

Harappan Seal, Mohenjo-daro © J.M. Kenoyer
Reproduced courtesy of the Department of Archaeology and Museums,
Government of Pakistan

This figure is seen on an Harappan seal found in Mohenjodaro, part of the Indus Valley, located in what we know today as Pakistan and western India. Hymn XXVII, 5 of the Rig Veda mentions 'Hariyupiyah', perhaps Harappa, causing scholars to speculate that the Harappan seals also were composed by the authors of the Vedas. Wearing seven bangles on his left arm and six on his right, the male figure is depicted with three faces and sports an elaborate headdress that includes two outward projecting buffalo-style curved horns. Because he is seated in cross-legged yogic posture, his heels are pressed together under his groin, and his feet project beyond the edge of the short platform, some speculation that meditation practice may have been part of human culture as long as 4500 years ago.

For more on this topic, see:
www.harappa.com/indus/33.html

Published in the UK by Imprint Academic
PO Box 1, Thorverton EX5 5YX, UK

Published in the USA by Imprint Academic
Philosophy Documentation Center, Bowling Green State University,
Bowling Green, OH 43403-0189, USA

ISBN 0907845 13 4

British Library Cataloguing in Publication data
A catalogue record for this book is available from the British Library
Library of Congress Card Number available.

ISSN: 1355 8250 (*Journal of Consciousness Studies*, **7**, No. 11–12, 2000)

JCS is indexed and abstracted in *PsycINFO*® and *The Philosopher's Index*.

Journal of Consciousness Studies
controversies in science & the humanities

Vol. 7, No. 11–12, November/December 2000

SPECIAL ISSUE 'COGNITIVE MODELS AND SPIRITUAL MAPS'
Edited by Jensine Andresen and Robert K.C. Forman

Jensine Andresen (Boston University STH, 745 Commonwealth Avenue, Boston, MA 02215, USA) received her PhD from Harvard University, where she concentrated on Indo-Tibetan Buddhism, and is now assistant professor of theology at Boston University. Her current focus is on bioethics, and she also pursues research on cognitive science and religious experience. In addition to the present volume, she has edited *Religion in Mind* (Cambridge University Press, 2001)

James Austin (3890 Moscow Mount Road, Moscow, ID 83843-8113, USA) 'retired' as emeritus professor of neurology from the University of Colorado Health Sciences Center in Denver, Colorado, and is now affiliate professor of philosophy at the University of Idaho. He has long been interested in the creative process in biomedical research (*Chase, Chance and Creativity*, 1978) and in the inter-relationships between experiential neurology and meditative training (*Zen and the Brain*, 1998).

Eugene D'Aquili was a clinical associate professor of psychiatry at the University of Pennsylvania until his death in 1998. He wrote several books and numerous papers relating on biogenetic structuralism to philosophy of science, religious phenomenology and neuroepistemology. He received his MD from the University of Pennsylvania in 1966, having been awarded the Priestley Prize for Original Scientific Research, and went on to get a PhD in anthropology.

Christian de Quincey (Institute of Noetic Sciences, 475 Gate Five Road, Suite 300, Sausalito, CA 94965-2835, USA) is a science writer and researcher specializing in the history, science and philosophy of consciousness. He holds degrees in psychology and consciousness studies from John F. Kennedy University, California, and has been studying and writing about consciousnes and human potential for over twenty-five years. He edits the *Noetic Sciences Review*.

Arthur Deikman (15 Muir Avenue, Mill Valley, CA 94941, USA) is clinical professor of psychiatry, University of California, San Francisco. He divides his time between research into the mystical traditions and the nature of consciousness, and the practice and teaching of psychotherapy. His published works include *The Observing Self: Mysticism and Psychotherapy* (1982) and *The Wrong Way Home: Uncovering the Patterns of Cult Behavior in American Society* (1990).

Robert Forman (The Forge Institute, 383 Broadway, Hastings on Hudson, NY 10706, USA) is an associate professor of religion at Hunter college, CUNY, having served on the faculties of Vassar College, Union Theological Seminary and the New School for Social Research. He is a co-founder and executive editor of *The Journal of Consciousness Studies* and founder and executive director of the Forge Institute for Spirituality and Social Change. Dr Forman has authored and edited a number of books including *The Problem of Pure Consciousness: Mysticism and Philosophy* (1990) and *The Innate Capacity: Mysticism, Psychology, and Philosophy* (1998).

Stanley Krippner (Saybrook Graduate School, 450 Pacific, 3rd floor, San Francisco, CA 94133-4640, USA) received a PhD in educational psychology from Northwestern University. Prior to joining the Saybrook faculty in 1972, Dr. Krippner directed the Dream Laboratory at Maimonides Medical Center in New York and was director of the Child Study Center at Kent State University. At Saybrook he is currently responsible for developing and teaching courses in the area of consciousness studies. He has written over 500 articles and several books, including *Human Possibilities* and *Song of the Siren*.

Brian Lancaster (Liverpool JMU, Henry Cotton Campus, Webster Street, Liverpool L3 2ET, UK) is principal lecturer in psychology at Liverpool John Moores University, where he is a director of the Consciousness and Transpersonal Psychology Research Unit. He is also a research fellow of the Centre for Jewish Studies at the University of Manchester and an associate of the Academy of Jerusalem. He has undertaken research on the interface between neuroscience, psychology and religion and has taught Jewish mysticism and meditation for over 25 years both in the UK and in Israel. He is author of *Mind, Brain and Human Potential* (1991) and *The Elements of Judaism* (1993).

Andrew Newberg (University of Pennsylvania, 110 Donner Building, 3400 Spruce Street, Philadelphia, PA 19104, USA) received his MD from the University of Pennsylvania School of Medicine in 1993 and is a fellow of the Division of Nuclear Medicine at the Hospital of the University of Pennsylvania. His research has focused on neurophysiology and human ritual, religion, and neuroimaging techniques to study the effects of meditation on the central nervous system. He is the associate director of Neurobiological Studies for the Conference on Scientific Progress in Spiritual Research and the director and co-founder of the Institute for the Scientific Study of Meditation. He has published widely in journals such as *American Psychologist*, *Zygon*, and *Anthropology of Consciousness*.

Robert Sharf (Department of Asian Languages and Cultures, 3070 Frieze Building, Ann Arbor, MI 48109-1285, USA) is associate professor of Buddhist studies at the University of Michigan. He specializes in East Asian Buddhism and is author of *Coming to Terms with Chinese Buddhism: A Reading of the Treasure Store Treatise* and co-editor of *Living Images: Buddhist Icons in Context* (both forthcoming).

Phillip Wiebe (Trinity Western University, 7600 Glover Road, Langley, BC, V2Y 1Y1, Canada) received his PhD from the University of Adelaide, Australia. He is currently professor and chair of the philosophy department at Trinity Western University and also director of the MA Program in Religion, Culture and Ethics. He is the author of *Visions of Jesus: Direct Encounters from the New Testament to Today* (1997).

Ken Wilber (6183 Red Hill Road, Boulder, CO 80302, USA) is a prolific writer whose recently published *Collected Works* includes some seventeen books, most recently *Integral Psychology: Consciousness, Spirit, Psychology, Therapy* (2000) and *A Theory of Everything: An Integral Vision for Business, Politics, Science, and Spirituality* (2000).

Publisher's Note

We apologize to authors, editors and readers for problems with typesetting software, which have made it impossible to include diacritic marks in this volume.

Jensine Andresen and Robert K.C. Forman[*]

Methodological Pluralism in the Study of Religion

How the Study of Consciousness and Mapping Spiritual Experiences Can Reshape Religious Methodology

This special issue of the *Journal of Consciousness Studies* throws down a methodological challenge to the field of Religious Studies. Over the last half century, the academic study of religion has developed a variety of angles and approaches: structuralist, Eliadian, Marxist, feminist, and so on. Recently, approaches popular in many institutions and departments have centred on linguistic and cultural analysis, notably the postmodern and deconstructivist approaches championed by Derrida and others. With the dawn of the interdisciplinary field of the study of human consciousness, and with this issue of the *Journal of Consciousness Studies*, we challenge this prevailing approach by presenting readers with articles analysing religion, spirituality, and spiritual experience, not solely as cultural phenomena, but as phenomena that can be related to human physiology, and a kind of pan-human technology of human spiritual development.

This issue offers new and exciting approaches whereby our understanding of religion and religious experiences may be enhanced by reference to methods stemming from cognitive science, neuropsychology, developmental psychology, philosophy of mind, anthropology, and the myriad other fields that have joined together to investigate the phenomenon of consciousness. Because consciousness plays such a central role in the creation of human experience, and because the field of consciousness studies is growing more mature by the year, it only makes sense that we should learn what we can about the functioning of consciousness from the myriad disciplines that have deigned to place it under their scopes. It is time for religious studies to draw upon neuropsychology, cognitive neuroscience, artificial intelligence, artificial life, psychology, and other disciplines. It is time for religious studies to explore how consciousness functions and how it may play

* Our thanks to Rajiv Malhotra, whose thoughts, insights and energy contributed significantly to this introduction.

a role in the constitution of reality, in spiritual experience, in the generation of doctrine, and in ritual and meditative life.

Also constructively, this volume attempts to forge a truce in the twenty-years' methodological war that has been waging between constructivists and perennialists in the study of religion. To summarize each side's historical position briefly, constructivists (i.e., Katz, Proudfoot) presented religious experience as wholly constructed from the fabric of pre-existing materials. Perennial psychologists (i.e., Forman, Barnard, Rothberg, etc.) claimed that mystical experiences, regardless of the tradition involved, share certain common underlying experiential cores, notably the so-called Pure Consciousness Event and several more advanced mystical states.

As in any just war, both constructivists and perennial psychologists made some good points, and we hope this volume sheds light on both sides of the debate. By drawing upon evidence from a range of disciplines other than the study of religion *per se*, this volume may help systematize how the constructivist and perennial psychologist positions about religious experience can be seen as complementary in a way that may help illuminate the broader relationship between subjectivity and objectivity. This is what Wilber calls, in this volume, the right and left quadrants. As Varela, Thompson, and Rosch (1993) already have proposed in the context of ontology, and as generations of Buddhist philosophers have articulated before them, 'consciousness' stands as the mediating term between the qualia, or felt experience, of the subjective, and the 'hard' reality we refer to as 'the external world'. Since our perceptual systems translate between the two continuously, defining what we colloquially understand to be 'life', it is time to recognize their complementarity.

The Exploding Field of Consciousness Studies

The *Journal of Consciousness Studies*, and the regular meetings in Tucson and elsewhere on the study of consciousness, have become the principle venues for the incredibly dynamic study of consciousness and its relationship to human phenomena. One of the reasons that these debates are so vital is that they have made it a point to include *both* the full range of externally measurable phenomena that impact consciousness, *and* the role of the subjective aspect of consciousness on those phenomena.

Insofar as there is a majority report in the field of religious studies, it is that formation goes from the past to the present, from the background of social training to the interpretative models, from the cognitive set to the experience, from the linguistic training to the construction of experience. This has been an enormously valuable model. But it portrays the vector of influence as solely unidirectional: the concrete influencing the abstract. In portraying the causal vector as aiming only one way, the American Academy of Religion is in danger of painting itself into a methodological corner.

This journal and recent conferences have examined how physics, biology and neurobiology, sociology, religion, philosophy, psychology, cognitive psychology, animal behaviour, and even art and poetry all may impact and be impacted by consciousness, intuition, psychological leanings, and direct, non-dual experiences. For example:

- Several articles, including two by one of the present authors, have explored what mysticism might teach us about consciousness;
- Many thoughtful people are exploring the role of consciousness in shaping cultures;
- Scientific studies have been conducted on distance healing and the effects of prayer on medical treatment;
- Scholars have begun to explore the role and impact of consciousness, not only apophatic and non-dualistic experiences, but also in visions of God, Christ and other divine forms; and
- The present issue of the *Journal of Consciousness Studies* offers the analyses of several noted authors on a variety of spiritual experiences.

That the field is so open-minded seems right and proper. After all, if there is one thing that is certain about consciousness studies, it is that we do not know the answers. We do not know how to think about consciousness, how it relates to the body, or how it might connect to anything beyond the body. We do not know if the final theory of consciousness will look like a formula, a brain diagram, a sentence, some combination of the three, or something entirely different. We do not even know the correct questions to ask. Clearly, this field is in a formative stage.

But one thing is clear. The interplay between subjectivity and objectivity must be part of any complete answer, and this examination can benefit greatly from studies of culture and general research on the nature of consciousness. On the one hand, subjectivity and intentionality clearly are influenced by a range of cultural and linguistic contexts and backgrounds. As Dr. Katz and others have pointed out, our background and training set up situations and influence our ability to have most experiences, including many mystical ones. The vector in this analysis goes from the objective realm of cultural and social influence, to our subjective ability to have such experiences.

On the other hand, consciousness itself can influence culture and society — its language, theology and belief, conceptual systems, etc. Similarly, religious experiences can influence one's belief system, and, if one writes or speaks persuasively, the belief systems of an entire tradition. The direct experiences of Buddha, Patanjali, Muhammad, Paul and Uddalaka clearly played a role in the formation of their respective traditions. So this vector of influence goes from subjective consciousness to objective culture.

Culture and consciousness interact with, and reflexively influence, one another, and so do biology and consciousness. Biology and neurobiology clearly influence consciousness — change the brain chemistry, or change neural pathways, and you will change some aspect of consciousness. Electrically stimulate some aspect of the brain, and the subject will have some shift in conscious experience, be it a memory, a visual distortion, or a desire. Physiology clearly influences our ability to have a vision of the divine, or to experience a moment of non-dual emptiness.

Conversely, consciousness influences biology. If you have a thought or a fear, clearly the local chemistry of the brain will shift, however subtly. This is the whole point of the theory of a fight or flight mechanism: when I think I'm in danger, my heartbeat, blood pressure, epinephrine output and other physiological parameters will change. A long-term subjective shift in feelings or awareness, generated by a happy or unhappy marriage, stressful job or long-term meditation inevitably will cause long-term changes in body and brain physiology. Similarly, spiritual satisfaction will have its long-term physiological effects.

The study of religion will benefit greatly from a more interdisciplinary consideration of how consciousness and subjective experiences, including religious ones, may actively influence, and be influenced by, human physiology. To undergo a vision of any divine form, or even to believe that we are having such a vision, will no doubt effect our heart rate, our blood chemistry and pressure, our serotonin levels, etc. It is high time that we studied how, and how much.

It is time for scholars of religion to leap with both feet into the discussion of consciousness, spirituality, and the role of direct experience as important and creative elements of human religions. What will this mean? Many things. We must explore the nature of spiritual experiences in more detail by drawing more guidance from consciousness studies. We must learn how physiology connects with spiritual experiences by increasing research on the biology of religious experience. We must examine the implications of research on the biology of religious experience for views on the 'validity' of those experiences. We also must understand how significant conscious experiences may have shaped and redirected the world's religious traditions, as, for example, Spanish Catholicism shifted significantly as a result of Theresa's visions.

It is time for scholars of religion to open their conceptual doors to a fuller range of analyses and to embrace the total phenomenon of religions and religious experiences. It is time to develop alternative and more inclusive paradigms that include more than social and conceptual influences. There is a place for the analysis of the given, but also for the analysis of the experientially novel. There is a place for the analysis of dogma, but also of the ineffable. It is time to include more of human life in the study of religion.

Four Aspects of the Study of Religion

How might we typologize the different elements of a more complete study of religion? We suggest that there are four discrete but interrelated aspects to a thoroughgoing methodology for religion. Let's look at each one in turn.

A. Doctrinal Analysis — Understanding God's message as revealed through human language and concepts.

In much of the Graeco-Semitic religion of the West, the basic assumption has been that God reveals primarily through prophets, oracles and divine messengers. This view brought the study of texts and historical dogma to the fore, causing many theological seminaries and universities to emphasize this methodology. As

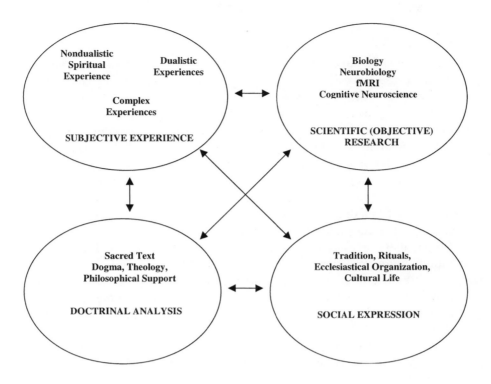

a result of this history, doctrinal analysis remains overemphasized in the field of religion as a whole.

Yet as Wiebe, Sharf, and Lancaster show in the pages below, a thoroughgoing methodology must *include* this doctrinal aspect. Insofar as it's focused on hermeneutics and the lived meaning of a text, it is the province of Wilber's lower left quadrant.

B. Social Expression — Understanding society's interpersonal, cultural and religious interactions.

This approach also emphasizes background analysis, except that the deconstructive method here primarily is focused on society, ritual, sociological, and interpersonal behavioural patterns. Too often, historians and sociologists of religion focus primarily on this approach to the exclusion of all others, as if to reduce the understanding of religion to anthropology and socio-political dynamics. This approach generally leaves out the 'felt experience' of the religious practitioner, which is similar to a deaf person's studying music through the analysis of written musical notes, or a reviewer of written recipes never tasting the cuisine. It tends to devalue the religious lives of others and the idiosyncracies of religious experience itself.

Krippner's fascinating study of shamans and primal culture delves into society's interpersonal, cultural and religious interactions.

C. Subjective Experience — A study of the felt character or peculiarities of religious experiences.

In our diagram we have separated two distinct kinds of religious experience, non-dualistic and dualistic, roughly apophatic and kataphatic forms of spirituality. We also recognize that some experiences, which we call 'complex experiences', may include elements of one or both, and thus that there is a continuum of religious experiences. Subjective experiences of any kind, we suggest, may influence dogma insofar as major religious leaders such as Paul, Theresa or Buddha try *to express* what it is that they have experienced. Experiences may effect tradition, ritual, and even politics, as in the case of Joan of Arc's remarkable experiences. And these experiences clearly will have their biological correlates, too.

The upper left quadrant of Wilber's model expressly encourages explorations of spiritual experiences, while the papers by Newberg and d'Aquili, Deikman, and Austin, also expressly include the subjective side of spiritual life.

Although some experiences, notably the non-dualistic and 'pure consciousness' varieties, seem largely, or perhaps even entirely, unconstructed by cultural language and background, other experiences seem more shaped by the background. What, then, is the relationship between formed and unformed experiences?

Here we can turn to the religious and spiritual traditions themselves. Because priests and practitioners have pondered such questions for centuries, the testimonies and sacred scriptures of individual traditions may have something to teach us. In our study of particular traditions, and in our own experiential lives, we have noticed a kind of continuum. One begins a spiritual practice, of course, utterly enmeshed in the historical world, or what Buddhists and Hindus would call *samsara*. This is the lowest level of Bonaventure's spiritual ascent, the first of the ten stages of Ox herding. As meditation slowly moves one away from sensation and thought, the formative role of background and context slowly slip away. One becomes less and less aware of one's surroundings, thinks with borders that are less and less clearly defined, and moves away from the cares of the world. The fourteenth century English text entitled *Cloud of Unknowing* calls this moving into the Cloud of Forgetting. And in some branches of Buddhism and Hinduism, practitioners are believed to have become less and less enmeshed in *samsara*, the cyclical mundane world.

D. Scientific (Objective) Research — A variety of objective studies performed on religious adepts and believers.

Just as intellectual and sociological processes are involved with some religious experiences, so, too, may a variety of physiological processes be correlated with them. As we see in the pages that follow, neuropsychology, biology, developmental psychology, cognitive neuroscience, fMRI, and other areas of research all may be used to understand religious experiences. It would be premature to identify 'causes' *per se*, but correlations may help us understand some parameters of religious consciousness at work.

Papers by Andresen, Newberg and d'Aquili, and Austin all provide examples of the use of science to examine religion, while Wilber's upper right quadrant also invites this methodological approach.

Consciousness and the Study of Religion

The study of religion brings into sharp focus a particular kind of consciousness — generally called 'religious experience'. Anthropologists and religionists alike have noted the surprising consistency with which people across many time periods and cultures have demarcated religious experience differently from other types of experience. That 'religious experience' is so commonly, and cross-culturally, set apart from other types of conscious experience should give us pause. Indeed, perhaps the domain of the religious reflects pan-human correlations at a deeper level than conceptuality — electrical activity in the frontal and temporal lobes of the brain, the stimulation of hormone flows, and the ceasing of random thought generation all may be seen as cross-cultural technologies of spiritual experience.

With studies from the field of cognitive science now readily available, it is time for religious studies to reach beyond its traditional disciplinary methods (e.g., historicism, textual exegesis, philology, and the like) if we really hope to fully understand ourselves and our religions. Textual religious sources reveal worlds about human psychology and sociology, and the historical study of religion helps us contextualize ourselves appropriately in the scheme of things. But if we want to understand how and why we tick *spiritually*, we are going to have to venture out of this box, probing first consciousness, and then its subcategory, religious consciousness (i.e., 'religious experience').

Of course, there are many ways to study religious consciousness, and this issue demonstrates that many different approaches can be valuable. We are arguing, therefore, for a species of methodological pluralism in the study of religious experiences that looks not only at a variety of conscious states, but also one that applies relevant findings from cognitive science, group dynamics theory, and a host of other domains to the task of understanding religion.

The Challenge

Our hope for this special issue is that the field of Religious Studies may take guidance from the field of Consciousness Studies. This will entail a renewed emphasis on religious experience in the study of religion, which seems only appropriate considering the significant degree to which traditions themselves stress the importance of these experiences. The meditative schools of Hinduism, Buddhism and Taoism, not to mention Kabbalah and mystical Christianity, all stress direct experience of the profound. Figures such as Sankara, Meister Eckhart, Nagarjuna and countless others all have stressed the necessity of integrating experience along side conceptuality, and using it to sharpen one's views. To do justice to these traditions and inspirational figures, we must give full attention to the description and analysis of experiential realities.

It is time as a field of scholarship to remove the barriers that have constrained our vision. A range of approaches illuminate reality, which itself reflects interactive and reflexive causes, requiring a range of methodological glasses. It is time to look through all of them, and to see religion and human life in the richly complex hues that they are.

References

Varela, F.J., Thompson, E. and Rosch, E. (1993), *The Embodied Mind* (Cambridge, MA: MIT Press).

Experiential and Experimental Studies

Jensine Andresen

Meditation Meets Behavioural Medicine

The Story of Experimental Research on Meditation

This paper juxtaposes Asian spiritual narratives on meditation alongside medical and scientific narratives that emphasize meditation's efficacy in mitigating distress and increasing well-being. After proposing a working definition of meditation that enables it usefully to be distinguished from categories of similar practices such as prayer, I examine meditation's role in Mind/Body medicine in the West. Here, I survey a number of scientific studies of meditation, including the work of Dr. Herbert Benson and his colleagues who examine a meditational variant they call the 'Relaxation Response', to examine the breadth of efficacy claims made on behalf of the complex and multidimensional grouping of diverse practices we have come to as 'meditation'. Among other positive outcomes, meditation has been credited with reducing blood pressure, anxiety, addiction, and stress, while Relaxation Response has been shown to decrease sympathetic nervous system (SNS) activity, metabolism, pain, anxiety, depression, hostility, and stress. I conclude the paper by suggesting that findings from cognitive neuroscience on the subject of visual imagery can be used to elucidate genres of meditative practice that focus on internal visualization sequences, and I use practices from the Rnying ma tradition of Tibetan Buddhism to illustrate why certain integral aspects of meditation forever will remain beyond scientific grasp.

Meditation East and West

Although scholars are uncertain exactly what the Harappan figure on our volume's cover is doing, textual and other evidence suggests that the cross-legged practitioner probably had a spiritual objective in mind. Of course, although we can not be sure the extent to which such an objective was ritualistic and/or meditative, it certainly may be distinguished from the more contemporary Western, scientific mode of examining meditation and other forms of spiritual practice. Perhaps even more remarkable, however, is the fact that the ancient, Asian

Journal of Consciousness Studies, **7**, No. 11–12, 2000, pp. 17–73

understanding of meditation as a technique integrally connected to something spiritual and religious has survived industrialization and the Internet to remain the central force motivating most Asians, monastic and lay alike, to engage in meditation practice today. (This observation becomes less surprising, however, when one considers that many contemplative practitioners in Asia find meditation efficacious in catalysing phenomenological and soteriological experiences recognized as 'profound' in myriad Asian contexts.) Whereas 4500 years of political upheaval and socioeconomic transition have not significantly shifted this spiritual focus in Asia, meditation techniques needed only to cross an ocean to find themselves within the first few years of their arrival in the West contextualized in radically different frameworks.

Although the Asian narrative context in which meditation arose is explicitly more *spiritual* than the Western, scientific mode of engaging these techniques, some Asian researchers (e.g., Nagata *et al.*, 1990 [cited in Austin, 1998b]) have been interested in examining meditation scientifically. And on the other hand, it certainly would be false to contend that important contemplative traditions, with explicitly spiritual objectives, have not existed for many hundreds of years in the context of Western religions. Nevertheless, time spent in Asian Buddhist monasteries clearly demonstrates the ongoing power of spiritual agendas in motivating individuals to practise meditation in the East. Interestingly, health-related objectives relating to meditation have been in the past, and continue to be, shared by both Asian and Western meditation practitioners alike. Indeed, many Chinese people daily may be witnessed in parks throughout the country practising Mao-style T'ai Chi Ch'uan or various forms of Ch'i Kung in order to attain the health benefits of these meditational arts. Indeed, as Stone and Chang (1997) also point out, Ch'i Kung is increasingly popular in the West, too, where meditation classes have been sprouting up at local gymnasiums, health clubs, and community centres. Much of the pull, of course, has to do with meditation's perceived ability to help counteract high blood pressure, anxiety, depression, and other symptoms of an excessively stressed-out Western lifestyle.

Following upon Deikman's (this volume) thesis that spirituality involves an experience of the connectedness underlying reality, Asian meditators traditionally have sought to engage in meditative practice with their 'receptive consciousness', which involves a shift from the focus on a personal experience of self to one oriented towards the larger reality that contains it. In contrast, in our Western, scientific studies of meditation, we operate primarily out of an instrumental consciousness, which is unremarkable inasmuch as our science itself is based upon a relatively instrumental consciousness. As scientists, we prod meditation to grasp its physiological, psychophysiological, and cognitive correlates (e.g., Woolfolk, 1975; Davidson, 1976; Boals, 1978; Morse *et al.*, 1979; Delmonte, 1983; 1984f), to model it and construct theories about it (e.g., Delmonte, 1987a,b; Delmonte and Kenny, 1985), and to propose its clinical application (e.g., Delmonte, 1984c; 1986b; Benson, 1987a). Although researchers' own agendas may be more complex, the demands of people in funding agencies and the media who want to know why meditation research is important may encourage researchers to emphasize such potential clinical benefits (Newberg, 1999). It is not surprising that we find specific sociocultural agendas motivating scientific research on meditation (Griffith 1985 [1974]; also see Davidson *et al.*, 1984 for a helpful historical analysis of meditation).

Nevertheless, as a result of press coverage touting meditation's efficacy in improving health, many Western enthusiasts embark upon meditation regimes to facilitate an array of health-related benefits, with stress and blood-pressure reduction being particularly emphasized (e.g., Schneider *et al.*, 1995; Tianuru and Gitre, 1996).

What unifies spiritual, scientific, and health-related agendas regarding meditation is the notion of 'efficacy'. Meditation is a *technique* or *tool* designed to help someone accomplish something. In Asia and in some meditation communities in the West, people quest after spiritual goals such as immortality, seen variously as union with *Isvara,* attainment of the 'deathless', reunion with Siva, or the achievement of birth in Amitaba's Pure Land right here on earth. Hindu, Buddhist, and Taoist meditation manuals describe techniques believed to be especially efficacious in achieving these ends, and lineage reputations often were, and are, made or broken over the perceived efficacy of the group's concatenation of meditation techniques.

Some Western researchers and practitioners also find themselves becoming heavily invested in a meditation community's spiritual efficacy claims, as is evidenced by a simple visit to a Buddhist dharma centre in the United States. Scores of Americans genuinely set out on the path to enlightenment frequent these centres, sometimes to the consternation of family and friends more acclimated to traditional membership in Judaeo-Christian worship communities. While I do not intend to argue that any particular meditation agenda, be it spiritual, scientific, or health-related, inherently is better than any other, it is instructive to examine how our choice of a border serves to change the phenomena we are framing. In short, the 'meditation' we monitor by EEG, fMRI, PET, and other techniques may not be the same beast as the meditation engaged in by solitary practitioners in remote Himalayan caves. Indeed, a study comparing such differences in objective and pursuit could prove extremely enlightening.

If the term 'meditation' does not refer to one, singular and monolithic entity, to what, exactly, does it refer? How should we define this phenomena, if, indeed, we should define it at all? Over twenty years ago, Brown (1977, pp. 236–7), wrote a particularly cogent article addressing the definitional dilemma as it applies to meditation, in which he made the following points:

> In the experimental literature, meditation has many meanings. It has been defined in terms of certain physiological variables, for example, as a certain meditation pattern, measured by EEG (Akishige, 1973; Anand *et al.*, 1961[a]; Banquet, 1973; Kasamatsu & Hirai, 1966 [reprinted as Kasamatsu & Hirai, 1969a,b]); by certain changes in arousal (Fischer, 1971); by more specific autonomic variables (Wallace, 1970; Walrath & Hamilton, 1975); and by a certain pattern of muscular tension/relaxation (Ikegami, 1973). Others have defined meditation more in terms of attention deployment (Davidson & Schwartz, 1976; Deikman, 1966; Van Nuys, 1973) [also see DiNardo and Raymond, 1979], related cognitive control

mechanisms (Silverman, 1968), or ego control mechanisms (Maupin, 1965). Still others have defined meditation more as a process of therapy, with resultant significant changes in affective and trait variables (Davidson & Goleman, 1975; Davidson, Goleman, & Schwartz, 1976; Goleman, 1971).

There is little agreement on: how to define meditation, what should be measured, and what the most useful measuring instruments may be. Research on meditation is still in an embryonic state. No doubt, the slow process of data accretion will advance our knowledge of meditation so that some day we may better know what sort of data to collect. Yet, the present state of meditation research is largely wasteful; some consensual criteria must be used to establish which kinds of data are most useful to collect. The two most fundamental questions in meditation research should be: (a) What are the most important variables of meditation and how may they be operationally defined and measured? (b) How are these variables related to each other?

Over twenty years after Brown made these comments, we still find ourselves in the midst of this same conundrum — given the phenomenological richness of the practices involved, what constitutes a good working definition or understanding of practices we group into the category of meditation? Personally, I shy away from definitions, which appear to me transient at best, contrived at worst, and, as Lakoff and Johnson (1999) have shown, smell suspiciously of the human body/mind/brain's 'Container Image Schema'. Nevertheless, some containers actually do hold water. Perhaps, then, it is not too bold to claim that in its broadest sense, meditation is associated with the process of increasing self-awareness (Ferrari, 1998; see Natsoulas, 1997 for a discussion of self-awareness as it relates to consciousness and Smythies, 1997 for an examination of the neuroanatomy of awareness in general).

A caveat should be raised, however. Although research on meditation may necessitate a working definition of sorts, attempts to craft a precise definition of meditation threaten to limit the phenomena artificially and to obscure the subtlest nuances of its practice. Indeed, similar definitional risks apply to the practice of prayer, which often is tailored to individual disposition and temperament, and, hence, eludes a single, precise definition. Everything considered, however, to make research possible at all, we do need to distinguish categories such as meditation and prayer, while we also may find it useful to distinguish 'scholarly' definitions (e.g., 'meditation is a process of increasing self-awareness') from experimentally-driven, operational definitions (e.g., 'meditation results in different EEG patterns;' and 'meditation is accompanied by increasing scores on such and such awareness index', McNamara, 2000). Additionally, despite the context in which we are considering meditation, we must strive to remain sensitive to how indigenous traditions themselves describe or define their own practices, above and beyond what fantasies we may happen to project onto the techniques from the vantage of our own social locatedness.

Heuristically, is it more useful to distinguish categories such as 'meditation' and 'prayer' in terms of method, or in terms of goal? To avoid pitting, for example, Buddhist meditators hell-bent on enlightenment against Christian pray-ers hell-bent on Heaven, we should eschew those frameworks that focus too myopically on practitioners' goals. Such a convention obliterates important *commonalities* between religious practices in many of the world's religious traditions. Instead, we (author and Smith, 2000) propose here a framework for distinguishing religious practices in terms of method, namely whether they are 'discursive' or 'non-discursive'. By discursive, we refer to mental states that entertain multiple objects serially; by non-discursive, we refer to mental states that entertain only a single object serially. In other words, we classify practices according to attentional focus, i.e., whether the practitioner assumes a single versus multiple object focus. Discursive practices, be they recitative (as in invocations and homages to deities), gestural (as in ritual gestures and movements in groups), or mental (as in guided contemplations and confessions of sin), are characterized by the mind being focused upon a series of thoughts and images. Non-discursive practices, be they recitative (as in *mantra* practice or the Jesus prayer), gestural (as in *mudra* practice or religious dance), or mental (as in single-pointed meditation in Hinduism, Buddhism, Taoism, etc.), are characterized by the mind being focused upon a single object (with *mantras* such as *Om Mani Padme Hum* being treated as a single object) without voluntary discursion or involuntary distraction towards other objects.

According to the discursive/non-discursive schema, the crucial difference between meditation and prayer is that the former is non-discursive while the latter is discursive. Buddhists are not juxtaposed against Christians, nor Muslims against Jews, because it is obvious that many different traditions include examples of both discursive and non-discursive techniques within their repertoire of religious practices. By employing a method-based, as opposed to outcome-based framework, scientific researchers are able to engage in fruitful interreligious studies of religious practices, thereby demonstrating why our world's religions commonly find a particular genre of techniques efficacious in effecting a particular genre of spiritual experience.

To recap, in both East and West, various spiritual, scientific, and health-related agendas employ the rhetoric of 'efficacy' when referring to meditation practice, though Eastern narratives tend to focus on spiritual efficacy while Western descriptions tend to focus on scientific efficacy (both Eastern and Western traditions discuss health-related goals). Like the term 'prayer', the term 'meditation' itself eludes a precise definition, yet the recitative, gestural, and mental dimensions of this type of non-discursive practice all may be grouped under the same general category. In the remainder of this essay, I leave aside the question of both Eastern and Western spiritual agendas relating to meditation in order to focus on how the notion of 'efficacy' is employed in health-related and scientific meditation studies in the West.

Meditation's Role in Mind/Body Medicine

From the late 1950s to the present, we have witnessed in the United States the growing popularity of meditation (Ramaswami and Sheikh, 1996). Asian meditation groups also are increasing in number, which Gussner (1987) attributes to the reduction of esoteric and mystical religious options in the West after 1500 CE. Sampling 327 respondents from ten mainline Asian-based meditation groups, Gussner and Berkowitz (1988) found that members are drawn predominantly from the upper-middle class of the American mainstream and have substantially higher education and occupational attainment than the population as a whole (also see Delmonte, 1987b). The increasing visibility of Asian meditation groups in the U.S. occasionally incites criticism, as we can see when Jones (1980) uses theology to critique Transcendental Meditation (TM). Ironically, however, while *Asian* meditation traditions are threatening to many people, meditation itself has been an important feature of the Western tradition in general (Scopen and Freeman, 1992) and specifically of Christianity itself (Main, 1979).

The popular, intellectual press in the U.S. (e.g., Laborde, 1997; Gawler, 1987; 1996) emphasizes meditation's health-related benefits, thereby reflecting the aims of the general wellness movement in the United States. Deepak Chopra heralds meditation as part of his alternative-medicine revolution (e.g., Chopra, 1985; 1987; 1989; 1990; 1991; 1993; 1994; Friedman, 1994), while other writers (e.g., Beck, 1976; Benson *et al.*, 1991; Guidano and Liotti, 1983; Gentry *et al.*, 1986; Childre, 1996; Childre and Cryer, 1998; Borysenko, 1987; Wright, 1997; Burns, 1999 [1980]; Gordon, 1996) have increased our awareness concerning alternative paths to wellness in general. Alternative therapies comprise the elements of a larger 'behavioral medicine' revolution in the U.S. (Domar *et al.*, 1993; Friedman and Benson, 1994; Friedman *et al.*, 1994), one with significant implications for the economics of health-care reform (Friedman *et al.*, 1995; Benson and Friedman, 1996a; Friedman *et al.*, 1997).

From the 1970s to the present, many scientific studies of meditation mirrored general American concerns about heart disease, hypertension, stress, behavioural coping, substance abuse, and lifestyle by claiming meditation's efficacy in alleviating the negative states associated with these conditions (Bradley and McCanne, 1981; see Engel, 1997 for descriptions of meditative experience and a summary of empirical studies on meditation.) Like yoga (Taimni, 1961; Benson, 1969; Tulpule, 1971; Joshi, 1984; Patel, 1984; Ebert, 1988; Taylor, 1995), biofeedback (Kiefer, 1972; Raskin and Bali, 1976), and yoga and biofeedback studied together (Patel 1973; 1975), meditation has been discussed within a scientific context and credited with improving health outcomes in many specific ways — by reducing heart rate and blood pressure (Benson, Rosner and Marzetta, 1973; Taylor and Farquher, 1977; Hafner, 1982; Delmonte, 1984g; Muskatel and Woolfolk, 1984; Lukoff *et al.*, 1995; Wenneberg *et al.*, 1997; for popular press accounts, see 'Naturally Healthy', 1996; 'Can We Think About', 1996; 'Transcendental Meditation', 1996; 'Transcending Hypertension', 1996), lowering systolic and diastolic blood pressure more than in a group taught progressive muscle relaxation (Kinsman and Staudenmayer, 1978; Warrenburg *et al.*, 1980; Kamen, 1978; Schneider *et al.*, 1995); and significantly improving exercise tolerance and reducing exercise-induced myocardial ischemia in patients with known coronary artery disease (Zamarra *et al.*, 1996). Further, TM proponents claim that TM is a cost-effective way of addressing hypertension, since, according to their calculations, the annual average cost of TM is $286, while antihypertensive medications range from $375–$1051 per year (Herron *et al.*, 1996; for a similar analysis of medical expenditure savings and TM, see Orme-Johnson and Herron, 1997).

Meditation also has been credited with increasing nonrenal, nonhepatic blood flow, probably due predominately to increased cerebral blood flow (CBF) (Jevning, Wilson, Smith, and Morton, 1978; Jevning *et al.*, 1996), increasing blood flow in the forearm area (Levander *et al.*, 1972), increasing basal skin resistance and decreasing respiratory rate (Allison, 1971; Elson *et al.*, 1977; also see Janby, 1977; Laurie, 1977; Curtis and Wessberg, 1975), influencing the autonomic nervous system (Orme-Johnson, 1973; Orme-Johnson *et al.*, 1977; Parker *et al.*, 1978) and heart rate variability (Sun *et al.*, 1986); decreasing arousal (Fenwick, 1983), helping to control depression (Carlin and Lee, 1997), furthering rehabilitation (Poulet, 1996), treating asthma (Honsberger and Wilson, 1973; Wilson, 1975), alleviating stuttering (McIntyre and Silverman, 1974), reducing insomnia (Miskiman, 1977a,b; Jacobs, Benson, and Friedman, 1993; Jacobs, Rosenberg, Friedman *et al.*, 1993), increasing plasma prolactin and growth hormone levels (Jevning Wilson, and VanderLaan (1978); serving as an effective tool in palliative care (Cole, 1997), assisting in cancer recovery (Gross, 1994; Simon, 1999), assisting during the grieving process (Edwards, 1997), improving psychological health (Linden, 1971; Hjelle, 1974; Ferguson, 1980 provides an overview of psychological studies on meditation; also see Jung, 1943; Noble, 1987; Parry and Jones, 1986; Shaffi, 1973), and reducing anxiety (Girodo, 1974; Otis, 1974; Daniels, 1975; Puryear and Cayce, 1976; Dillbeck, 1977; Lazar *et al.*, 1977; Schwartz *et al.*, 1978; 1984; Bahrke and Morgan, 1978; Boswell and Murray, 1979; Goleman *et al.*, 1979; Lintel, 1980; Delmonte, 1985c; Eppley *et al.*, 1989; Sakairi, 1992; Miller *et al.*, 1995), including the anxiety associated with public speaking (Kirsch and Henry, 1979) and, more recently, that associated with magnetic resonance imaging (MRI) testing (Thompson and Coppens, 1994; Lukins *et al.*, 1997; Quirk *et al.*, 1989). Interestingly, however, meditation and other selected interventions such a hypnosis, imagery, and relaxation have not been demonstrated to be effective in reducing stress responses in anxious, recreational scuba divers (Morgan, 1995).

Meditation's impact has been tested on elementary school students (Abrams, 1977), juvenile offenders (Childs, 1974), and prisoners (Bassett *et al.*, 1977; Orme-Johnson *et al.*, 1977) alike. As a technique, meditation specifically is credited with reducing domineering tendencies (Fehr, 1996), reducing inflammation (Klemons, 1977); influencing age-correlated physiological variables (e.g., Wallace *et al.*, 1982), modifying strenuous physical stress' suppressive influence on the immune system (Solberg *et al.*, 1995), reducing chronic pain (Kabat-Zinn, 1982; 1990; Kabat-Zinn *et al.*, 1985; Collura and Kabat-Zinn, 1997), and inducing an improved sense of well-being (Berman, 1995). Furthermore, while Delmonte (1985a) states that the results of studies on the biochemical responsivity to meditation are inconclusive, he (1985a,b) also claims that the intentional fostering of positive expectations during meditation is associated with lower physiological arousal in terms of diastolic and systolic blood pressure, heart rate, and skin conductance. Many authors also have written on meditation in connection with expectations (Delmonte, 1985b; 1986a), self-report (Delmonte, 1984i; 1985d), 'self-actualization' (Dice, 1979; Alexander *et al.*, 1991), behavioural self-control (Shapiro and Zifferblatt, 1976), and personality (Fehr, 1977; Delmonte, 1980; 1984h; West, 1980b).

Although meditation has been extensively credited with decreasing autonomic arousal, disagreements sometimes ensue over how to compare data between experiments that focus on different facets or types of meditation. Experimental protocols often drive data in particular ways, making it difficult to know which characteristics one can attribute to 'meditation' per se and which more likely are artifacts of experimental design. For example, Corby *et al.* (1978) examined Hindu Tantric Yoga meditators, grouping them into three levels based on meditation proficiency and measuring their skin resistance, heart rate, respiration, autonomic orienting responses, resting EEG, EEG alpha and theta frequencies, sleep-scored EEG, averaged evoked responses (ERPs), and subjective experience. Methodologically, this study is important because its design incorporates different groupings based on meditation proficiency. In contrast to studies on TM meditators, Corby and his colleagues claim that proficient meditators in the Tantric Yoga tradition demonstrated increased autonomic activation during meditation; alternatively, inexperienced meditators demonstrated autonomic relaxation. Proficient Tantric Yoga meditators also demonstrated increased alpha and theta power, minimal evidence of EEG-defined sleep, and decreased autonomic orientation to external stimulation in this study. One meditator even displayed an episode of sudden autonomic activation as he approached an ecstatic state of intense concentration, leading Corby and the other researchers to conclude that their findings challenge the '"relaxation" model of meditative states' (also see Cauthen and Prymak, 1977).

Elson (1979) challenged Corby *et al.*'s finding, stating that both Elson *et al.* (1977) and Ghista *et al.* (1976) showed that 'a state of wakeful relaxation and decreased metabolic activity was present during meditation'. Whereas Corby *et al.*'s study divided meditators into three groups, claiming that proficient meditators demonstrated increased autonomic activation while unexperienced demonstrated autonomic relaxation, and also that proficient meditators demonstrated increased alpha and theta activity, Elson *et al.* focused on meditators with an average of 1.8 years of experience, roughly analogous to Corby *et al.*'s middle group. McNamara (2000) observes that this difference in methodology between the two studies, namely the degree to which the levels of meditative proficiency of the subjects were differentiated, could account for some of the discrepancies in the findings. Elson (1979) himself suggests that the difference in the two studies may be linked to different experimental conditions — Corby *et al.*'s study involved tones, noise bursts, and white noise, and Elson claims that these conditions may have caused greater distraction for experienced meditators than for controls — i.e., that meditation proficiency may be accompanied by a heightened sensitivity to environmental stimuli. Although Corby (1979) could have countered this claim by showing that meditators differed from non-meditators in their autonomic nervous system (ANS) arousal to environmental stimuli, he instead replied that 'a progressive decrease in cardiovascular and electrodermal orienting responses' occurred as proficient subjects practiced meditation, findings similar to those of Das and Gastaut (1955) and Anand *et al.* (1961a).

The extent to which meditation influences arousal is central to its perceived health benefits. Some researchers claim that meditation decreases arousal more than does rest (e.g., Jevning, Wilson, Smith, and Morton, 1978; Morrell, 1986), but a survey of the literature by Holmes (1984) and a study he conducts with colleagues (Holmes *et al.*, 1983; Holmes, 1987) in which the arousal-reducing effects of meditation are compared to those of rest, both show no consistent evidence that meditating subjects attain lower levels of physiological arousal than do resting subjects. Benson and Friedman (1985) criticize this finding, however, as does Morrell (1986); Dillbeck and Orme-Johnson (1987) also differentiate TM and rest in terms of physiological variables.

Additionally, not all studies use language claiming that meditation reduces arousal. A recent study by Peng *et al.* (1999) challenges the traditional understanding of meditation as a psychologically and physiologically quiescent state. Observing both Chi and Kundalini yoga practitioners, Peng and his colleagues found prominent and intermittent heart rate oscillations associated with slowing breathing. Perhaps more instructive than this finding, however, is the extent to which researchers apply a broad net in labeling the phenomena under their microscope 'meditation'. Here, researchers are studying Chinese Ch'i Kung alongside Indian Kundalini practice, and yet they group their findings under the umbrella term 'meditation'. Given the unique historical and cultural trajectories in the development of these two practices, coupled with their significant divergence from other kinds of, for example, Tibetan or Zen meditation, it would be inaccurate to go away from this study with the idea that something truly unusual had been discovered. The only thing that is necessarily unusual here, in the context of preexisting meditation studies, is the actual practices being examined.

Despite the categorical imprecision that attends grouping a wide variety of practices under the header 'meditation', and our foray into the debate over meditation's impact on arousal complete, a continued survey of literature on meditation provides evidence that this technique also is credited with decreasing substance abuse (e.g., Robbins, 1969; Marzetta *et al.*, 1972; Benson and Wallace, 1972b; Shafii *et al.*, 1974; 1975; Lazar *et al.*, 1977; Marlatt and Pagano, 1984; Alexander, Robinson, and Rainforth, 1994; also see Klajner *et al.*, 1984, who discuss the impact of relaxation training in general on substance abuse), decreasing alcohol intake (Benson, 1974a; Brautigam, 1977; Alexander, Robinson, and Rainforth, 1994), and reducing tension, self-blame, and addiction (Carrington, 1987; also see Carrington, 1977; 1978; 1979; 1984a,b). It also is credited with reducing violent deaths in a community (Assimakis and Dillbeck, 1995), and, conversely, with improving shooting performance (Solberg *et al.*, 1996)! Delmonte (1984a) claims that meditation can help reverse retarded ejaculation, though more than a few tantric *yogis* might cite in opposition to this finding a myriad of ancient texts describing the use of *Vajrayana* meditation techniques to

prevent ejaculation! Finally, in an unrestrained, serenade on the benefits of meditation, Venkatesh *et al*. (1997) employ a 'Phenomenology of Consciousness
Inventory' to conclude that the long-term practice of meditation appears to produce more intense experiences of 'joy', 'meaning', 'time', 'love', and 'awareness'. To illustrate the range of opinions gracing this field, one may juxtapose
these specific claims with Delmonte's (1988) finding that short-term compliance
with a new meditation regime during the first three months correlates with intro-
version, suggestibility and neuroticism, while long-term compliance of six
months to two years correlates with repression and extroversion.

Many Western researchers (e.g., Goleman and Schwartz, 1976; Michaels *et al*.,
1976; Kanas and Horowitz, 1977; Delmonte, 1984d; Kaplan *et al*., 1993; Barnes
et al., 1997) credit meditation with reducing stress. For example, MacLean *et al*.
(1997) assert that TM counters the effects of stress by reducing basal cortisol and
average cortisol levels (also see Michaels *et al*., 1979). Claiming that previous
efforts to reduce stress-related symptomatology and to help patients cope with
chronic pain were limited by a lack of an adequate control, Astin (1997) conducted an eight-week stress reduction programme based on training in mindfulness meditation. When compared to controls, subjects who had been trained in
meditation exhibited reductions in overall symptomatology; increases in domain-
specific senses of control in their lives; and higher scores for spiritual experiences, causing Astin to conclude that mindfulness meditation, with its emphasis
on developing detached observation and awareness, may be a powerful cognitive
behavioural coping strategy and may help prevent relapse in the case of affective
disorders (also see Johnson and White, 1971; Brown *et al*., 1984a,b; Delmonte,
1989). Furthermore, given its success in combating stress, mindfulness meditation recently was employed to reduce stress in the inhabitants of a bilingual,
inner-city neighbourhood in Meriden, Connecticut (Roth and Creaser, 1997).

The Relaxation Response

A specific species of meditation — the 'Relaxation Response' — occupies a
central role in Western behavioural medicine, in large part because of the
well-publicized work of Dr Herbert Benson and his colleagues at Harvard Medical School and at the Mind/Body Medical Institute in Boston. Dr Benson and his
colleagues use the term 'Relaxation Response' to refer to 'a set of integrated
physiological changes that are elicited when a subject assumes a relaxed position
in a quiet environment, closes his or her eyes, engages in a repetitive mental
action, and passively ignores distracting thoughts' (Hoffman *et al*., 1982, p. 190).
(For general reading on the Relaxation Response, see Benson 1975; 1982b;
1983c; 1984a; 1987b; 1993; Benson, Beary, and Carol, 1974; Benson, Greenwood, and Klemchuk, 1975; Benson, Kotch, Crassweller, and Greenwood, 1977;
Benson and Goodale, 1981; Friedman, Steinman, and Benson, 1996; Friedman *et
al*., 1998; 1999; Myers *et al*., 2000. For a discussion of nine world approaches to
relaxation, see Borkovec, 1985.)

After writing on pneumonia (e.g., Benson, Akbarian, Adler, and Agelmann, 1970) and the pharmacologic induction of hypertension in the squirrel monkey (Benson, Herd, Morse, and Kelleher, 1970), Herbert Benson began writing on yoga and Transcendental Meditation in the early 1970s. Within a decade or so, he had shifted his emphasis to Tibetan meditation. By the late 1980s, and continuing until the present, Dr Benson has been addressing spirituality and health issues (e.g., Kass *et al.*, 1991; Friedman and Benson, 1997; Benson and Dusek, 1999; Benson and Myers, 2000b), and, one can assume, tenure secured, he found himself increasingly comfortable in claiming that the Relaxation Response was a 'bridge between medicine and religion' (Benson, 1988; see Elias, 1997 for coverage of Benson's early difficulty convincing Harvard colleagues of the relevance of his work). Indeed, similar claims, namely that spirituality and religiosity have health-related implications, characterize the burgeoning area of 'spirituality and health' research in the United States, which is founded on the 'power and biology of belief' (Benson, 1996) and its medical aspects (Benson and Myers, 2000a).

Over the years, Benson and his colleagues (e.g., Benson 1983d; 1987a) have demonstrated the Relaxation Response's broad clinical applicability, thereby illustrating the manner in which meditation research can be included positively in health-oriented agendas. For example, the Relaxation Response — an essentialized meditation practice stripped of soteriological implications — has been shown to reduce blood pressure levels significantly (e.g., Benson *et al.*, 1971; Benson and Wallace, 1972a; Benson, Marzetta, and Rosner, 1974; Benson, Rosner, Marzetta, and Klemchuk, 1974; Benson and Greenwood, 1976; also see Bali, 1979, who discusses the long-term effects of relaxation on blood pressure and anxiety). Benson (1976; 1977) alone, and together with his colleagues (Peters, Benson, and Peters, 1977; Lehmann and Benson, 1982; 1983; Stainbrook *et al.*, 1983; Benson and Caudill, 1984; Barr and Benson, 1985; Caudill *et al.*, 1987; Stuart *et al.*, 1987; Leserman, Stuart, Mamish, Deckro, *et al.*, 1989; Friedman *et al.*, 1992; Stuart *et al.*, 1993; Friedman, Myers, Krass, and Benson, 1996), has written copiously on the Relaxation Response's usefulness in treating hypertension and cardiovascular disease (Benson, Alexander, and Feldman, 1975; Barr and Benson, 1985), including cardiovascular diseases related to stress (Benson, Kotch, and Crassweller, 1976; 1978).

Some studies show that the Relaxation Response, and certain forms of meditation in general, decrease sympathetic nervous system (SNS) activity (Wallace *et al.*, 1971; Wallace and Benson, 1972; Beary and Benson, 1974; Benson, 1975; Hoffman *et al.*, 1982). This find at least partially explains how these techniques are efficacious in treating medical disorders caused or exacerbated by SNS arousal (Jacobs *et al.*, 1996), such as hypertension (e.g., Benson, Marzetta, and Rosner, 1974), headaches (Benson, Malvea, and Graham, 1973; Benson, Klemchuk, and Graham, 1974), pediatric migraine (Fentress *et al.*, 1986), anxiety and pain in individuals undergoing stressful medical procedures (e.g., Mandle *et al.*, 1990; Herod, 1995), premenstrual syndrome (Goodale *et al.*, 1990), insomnia (Jacobs, Benson, and Friedman, 1993; Borkovec, 1982), and infertility (Domar *et al.*, 1990; Domar and Benson, 1993). Benson (1983a,b) discusses the mechanisms mediating the relationship between norephinephrine levels and the Relaxation Response, though, as Hoffman *et al.* (1982) report, earlier studies measuring plasma norepinephrine levels during the practice of the Relaxation Response show it to be unchanged (Michaels *et al.*, 1976) or variable (Lang *et al.*, 1979). Also, as McNamara (2000) points out, because plasma norepinephrine is a poor measure of brain norepinephrine, however, it is not surprising that null results are found.

In addition to being credited with treating medical conditions associated with SNS arousal, the Relaxation Response also has been used preoperatively with ambulatory surgery (Domar *et al.*, 1987) and cardiac surgery (Leserman *et al.*, 1989a) patients. The technique also has been employed successfully as an element in behavioural therapies designed to alleviate chronic pain (Kutz *et al.*, 1983) and pain in general (Benson, Pomeranz, and Kutz, 1984). Indeed, according to Caudill *et al.* (1991), chronic pain sufferers who had experienced behavioural medicine intervention showed decreased clinic use.

Other studies claim that the Relaxation Response and meditation result in decreased oxygen consumption (metabolism) (e.g., Wallace *et al.*, 1971; Beary and Benson, 1974; Benson, Steinert, *et al.*, 1975; Benson, Dryer, and Hartley, 1978a; Anand *et al.*, 1961b; Sugi and Akutsu, 1968; Dhanaraj and Singh, 1977; Fenwick, 1974; also see Corey, 1977). In one of the most sophisticated experimental studies directed at understanding meditation's impact on metabolism, Benson *et al.* (1990) tested three Tibetan Buddhist monks in Rumtek monastery in Sikkim. These monks engaged in several different meditative practices, including *gTum-mo* yoga (or *Gtum mo*, according to the current Tibetan transliteration system), which is intended to create 'heat' in practitioners. Benson and his colleagues found that their Sikkimese subjects could raise resting metabolism up to 61% and could lower it down to 64%, a feat undoubtedly of relevance for high-altitude dwelling monastics. Unlike some earlier studies of meditation's impact on arousal, Benson *et al.*'s paper clearly acknowledges that there exist many different forms of meditative practice, some of which decrease metabolism in striking ways, and some of which increase it. In an earlier study, Benson *et al.* (1982) showed that *gTum-mo* practitioners were able to increase the temperature of their fingers and toes by as much as 8.3 degrees Celsius (see Benson, 1982a; Pasachoff *et al.*, 1982).

The Relaxation Response promises mental health benefits, too. Since it has been shown to be efficacious in combating symptoms of psychophysical imbalance (Hellman *et al.*, 1990), the Relaxation Response also has been called a 'bridge' between psychiatry and medicine (Benson, Kotch, and Crassweller, 1977), thereby reflecting more general relationships between behavioural medicine and psychiatry (e.g., Friedman *et al.*, 1994) and between meditation and psychiatry/mental health (e.g., Keefe, 1975; Lesh, 1970; Epstein, 1986; Goleman, 1997). Eliciting the Relaxation Response has been associated with fewer symptoms of anxiety (Benson, Frankel, *et al.*, 1978; Benson, 1984b; 1985a; 1986), depression, and hostility (Kase, 1997). The technique also has proven effective in treating stress and improving well-being in working people (Carrington *et al.*,

1980; Peters, Benson, and Porter, 1977), and it has been described as a technique for combating stress in general in the *Harvard Business Review* (Benson, 1974c), the *Harvard Medical Alumni Bulletin* (Benson, 1986), and elsewhere (Benson 1985a,b; Everly, Jr. and Benson, 1989; also see Broussard, 1994). In one study on stress, Hoffman *et al.* (1982) demonstrate that subjects exposed to graded orthostatic and isometric stress during monthly hospital visits and then trained in the Relaxation Response showed higher concentrations of plasma norepinephrine during subsequent graded stresses, while controls showed no such elevated concentrations. Consistent with the results of an earlier study (Michaels *et al.*, 1976), Hoffman *et al.*'s results suggest that subjects who elicit the Relaxation Response are less responsive to stress; the authors also mention Cryer's (1980) suggestion that the Relaxation Response may reduce adrenergic end-organ responsivity, though the mechanism is unclear.

Given the success of the Relaxation Response and other forms of meditation in treating stress-related disorders, it is not surprising that psychiatrists and psychotherapists have begun to reflect upon and integrate these techniques into their practices (Kretschmer, 1962; Ornstein, 1971; Curtin, 1973; Shafii, 1973a,b; Carrington and Ephron, 1975a,b; Deatherage, 1975; Glueck and Stroebel, 1975; Smith, 1975; 1976; 1978; Carpenter, 1977; Shapiro and Giber, 1978; Welwood, 1980; Welwood, 1983; Vassallo, 1984; Kutz *et al.*, 1985a,b; Wolman, 1985; Russel, 1986; Bogart, 1991). Further demonstrating how disease is a reflection of the psyche (Williams, Jr. *et al.*, 1985), researchers also have introduced the Relaxation Response into a high-school setting, in which students trained in the Relaxation Response showed positive psychological characteristics (Benson *et al.*, 1994).

Researchers, doctors, and laypersons use the term 'Mind/Body medicine' to describe a form of behavioural medicine that sometimes finds itself integrated with spirituality (Benson, 1979; Benson and Friedman, 1995; Friedman and Benson, 1996; Benson and Dusek, 1999; Benson and Myers 1999; 2000b; Goleman and Gurin, 1993; United States Congress, 1999; Watkins, 1997). The placebo effect, more recently dubbed 'remembered wellness' (Benson, 1995; Benson and Friedman, 1996b; Benson and Myers, 1999), plays an important role in this enterprise. Mind/Body medicine increasingly is well-accepted by the Western medical community (e.g., Eisenberg *et al.*, 1993; Friedman *et al.*, 1993; Czaharyn, 1996; D'Antoni *et al.*, 1995; Hassed, 1996; Keegan and Cerrato, 1996), and in 1996, the National Institute of Health even urged doctors to accept meditation as an effective treatment for chronic pain, anxiety, panic attacks, insomnia, premenstrual syndrome, and infertility (Carlin and Lee, 1997). Additionally, the Relaxation Response and meditation have distinguished themselves from similar techniques, as, for example, when the Relaxation Response is compared favourably with 'progressive relaxation' in effecting systematic desensitization (Greenwood and Benson, 1977; for comparisons involving TM, see Davies, 1977; Alexander, Robinson, Orme-Johnson, and Schneider, 1994; see Wilkins, 1971 for a discussion of muscle relaxation training and desensitization). Just as meditation itself has been compared to hypnoidal states (Delmonte,

1984b,e; Earle, 1981), Benson, Arns, and Hoffman. (1981) and Benson (1989) compare the Relaxation Response and hypnosis, while Van Nuys (1973) and Spanos *et al.* (1979) discuss the connection between meditation and hypnotic susceptibility. Furthermore, Brown *et al.* (1982) discuss differences between mindfulness meditation and self-hypnosis, while von Kirchenheim and Persinger (1991) show that deep relaxation does not cause time distortions to the same extent as does hypnosis (also see Morse *et al.*, 1977; Paul and Trimble, 1970).

The aforementioned research studies and articles overwhelmingly attest to the successful incorporation of meditation generally, and the Relaxation Response more specifically, into the wellness regimes of many Westerners. The following pages detail agendas present in scientific studies of meditation, focusing especially on those studies that employ sophisticated technological gadgetry to demonstrate meditation's impact on the body/mind.

The Scientific Pursuit of Meditation

Exotic and mysterious, meditation has inspired much scientific research and commentary, mostly by Western researchers who want to know what is happening in the bodies and brains of meditators to cause them to manifest decreased sympathetic nervous system (SNS) activity and to report pronounced subjective states of well-being (see Shapiro 1983; Shapiro and Walsh, 1984; Kohr, 1978; Lang *et al.*, 1979). Some theoretical attempts have been made to understand meditation — Kaplan (1978) and Watts (1979) consider meditation in the context of psychological theory, Lancaster (1993) uses neuropsychology to understand states of 'no-self', and others discuss contemplative practice within the context of 'biogenetic structuralism' (e.g., Laughlin, Jr. *et al.*, 1993; Ashbrook, 1993) and 'neurophenomenology' (Varela, 1996). Furthermore, d'Aquili and Newberg (1993a,b; 1998) and Newberg and d'Aquili (1994) provide theoretical models of complex brain activation relating to meditative practice and mystical experience (also see Short, 1995; Fenwick *et al.*, 1985). Following Sperber's (1996) admonition to attend to the dynamics of micro-level processes, I examine here the specific micro processes that have contributed to the temporal stability of methodological design in scientific research on meditation.

In the West, social factors (e.g., the dominance of techno-medical explanatory paradigms) and psychological factors (e.g., the American objective of feeling good) have worked together to stabilize what I call here 'techno-medical' studies of meditation. More general encounters between Tibetan Buddhists and Western scientists under the auspices of various 'Mind and Life' gatherings in Dharamsala, India (e.g., 'Mind and Life I', 1991; deCharms, 1993; Hayward and Varela, 1992) have supported this trend, as has the desire of Asian researchers to use scientific rhetoric to validate their own culture's archaic practices (e.g., Kripalvanandji, 1977). A clear progression, indicating the increasing 'technologization' of scientific studies on meditation, exists in the literature, demonstrating Western reliance on techno-medical forms of validation.

In the early 1970s, around the time that general attention was being paid within the discipline of anthropology to phenomena such as shamanic trance and altered states of consciousness (e.g., Ludwig, 1966; Forman, 1990; Tart, 1975; for later discussions, see Tart 1990; Forman, 1998), Gellhorn and Kiely (1972) wrote an article claiming that meditation causes practitioners to experience various 'altered states' of awareness (also see Shapiro, 1980; Schuman, 1980; Istratov *et al.*, 1996; Goleman, 1996). To explain why this might be so, the authors adopted Hess' (1925) autonomic nervous system (ANS) model of an energy-expanding or ergotrophic system and an energy-conserving or trophotropic system operating in a complementary fashion. According to d'Aquili and Laughlin (1975), the ergotropic system includes the sympathetic nervous system, which governs arousal states and fight or flight responses, while the trophotropic system includes the parasympathetic peripheral nervous system, which governs basic vegetative and homeostatic functions.

Consistent with the dearth of nuanced phenomenological typologies of varieties of meditative and yogic activity in much of the experimental literature on meditation, Gellhorn and Kiely (1972) crudely differentiated 'Asian meditation' from 'yogic ecstasy'. The authors also hypothesized that reduced muscle tone during meditative relaxation leads to the loss of the ergotropic tone of the hypothalamus, a situation followed by trophotropic-system dominance. In the autonomic nervous system, stimulation of the ergotrophic system leads to augmented sympathetic discharges, while stimulation of the trophotropic system leads to augmented parasympathetic discharges (Gelhorn, 1970). In their study, Gellhorn and Kiely interpreted EEG (electro-encephalography) patterns as indicating that trophotropic dominance during meditation is compatible with full awareness, but the authors also commented that some ergotropic influence still appears to be exerted upon the cerebral cortex and is correlated with subjects' heightened perceptual sensitivity. In contrast to meditation, during ecstatic yogic experiences, Gellhorn and Kiely claimed that ergotrophic dominance prevails.

Somewhat analogous to Gellhorn and Kiely's (1972) study, Fischer (1972; 1975) placed mystical ecstasy at one end of the ergotropic scale (also see Govinda, 1972) and yogic *samadhi* at the opposite extreme of the trophotropic scale, connecting rapture and *samadhi* in an figure-eight loop intended to represent the trophotropic rebound observed in response to intense ergotropic hyperarousal. Also similar, Wulff (1992) described the pairing of meditation practice with a form of group practice that produces ergotropic arousal, the antithesis of the calm inwardness usually associated with meditation itself. Austin (1998b, p. 287) criticizes Gellhorn and Kiely's study for basing evidence on destructive lesions too large and electrical stimulations too intense to lead to clear cut explanations. Mills and Campbell (1974) also criticize Gellhorn and Kiely's model, rightly arguing that it obliterates basic differences within and among the various meditative traditions and claiming that the model is ambiguous with regard to the way the opposing ergotropic and trophotropic systems may affect the individual (Kiely, 1974 poses a rejoinder).

Let's Go Techno!

While early studies of meditation focus more on macro-scale physiological phenomena such as arousal, newer studies, in conjunction with advances in cognitive neuroscience, tend to focus on more micro-scale correlates of meditative experience (Brown & Engler, 1980). Meditation researchers, myself included, find themselves fascinated with the issue of what brain-level processes may contribute to the profound sense of well-being described by many meditators. In some cases, data derived from technological studies helps us answer this question, but in others, inconsistent and opaque data shifts attention away from what could be an interesting discussion of *qualia* to technological debates on instrumentation. Nevertheless, it seems that every time a new neuropsychological tool arrives on the market, it is quickly deployed to help researchers scrutinize meditation.

Our techno story begins in 1955 and continues to the present, during which time meditation has found itself both prodded and poked by means of a variety of technological apparati, with inconclusive results. Many studies fail to utilize controls, studies follow their own unique protocols, and, often, entirely different meditation traditions are examined in the context of a single study. As a result, the data that we do have from EEG studies, for example, only appears to show a consistent pattern when novices are separated from proficient meditators. Meditating assuredly is a dynamic skill, and, like any other skill such as tennis playing ability, basketball prowess, or skiing agility, people may go through stages in their acquisition of meditative proficiency. (Of course, there will be the Michael Jordans of the meditation world, e.g., Milarepa, an 11th-century Tibetan practitioner, and, hence, some novice meditators simply may be capable of catalysing brain-level changes and of experiencing interesting phenomenological states quite early in their practical careers.)

In 1955, Western researchers first used EEG measurements to evaluate brain amplitude changes and electrical coherence in the brain during meditation. Das and Gastaut (1955) found that beta frequencies characterize Indian yogic meditators at the time they believe they are entering *samadhi,* though Anand *et al.* (1961a) claim that Das and Gastaut's finding may reflect an artifact caused by excess tension in the scalp muscles picked up by the surface EEG electrodes (also see Cooper *et al.*, 1965). A second EEG study of meditation soon followed (Bagchi and Wenger, 1958).

Unfortunately, EEG rhythms are very blunt indicators of underlying brain activity resulting from the synchronization of large pools of cells, and their patterns reflect diffuse, non-specific regulatory processes. In other words, any EEG picture will have multiple causes, and many different states can lead to a similar EEG. According to Fenwick (1987, pp. 104–5), the EEG is the spatial average of activity generated by the cells in the superficial layers of the cortex, and it would sum to zero if certain groups of cells were not linked together and did not fire synchronously. Scalp EEGs report a spatial average of small cortical areas, and the larger the cortical area involved in synchronized activity, the higher the amplitude of the EEG (also see Ehrlichman and Weiner, 1980; Elbert and Rockstroh, 1987).

As Austin (1998b, p. 88) succinctly remarks, 'We know that people's EEGs differ, that an individual's EEGs vary, and that meditation is not one state but a series of dynamic physiological changes. So it comes as no surprise to find that many different EEG changes have been recorded during meditation, and that most studies are open to criticism.'

Nevertheless, some generalities in EEG data on meditation do pertain. Meditation appears to be comprised of different stages (Brown and Engler, 1980), and, in general, many *early* EEG studies of meditators show that alpha rhythms increase in amplitude to 11–12 Hz and then slow in frequency by 1–3 Hz before spreading forwards into the frontal channels. (Later studies call this finding into question, however, as I discuss below.) Alpha waves are brain waves of 8 to 13 cycles per second that normally accompany states of relaxed wakefulness (Wulff, 1992, p. 174; Markand, 1990; Oken and Salinsky, 1992; Kiefer, 1985). Next, theta activity increases, in the range of 6–7 Hz, though some of these waves may be consistent with drowsiness. In some meditators, bursts of theta activity are seen bitemporally, and still other patterns occur for longer periods at higher amplitudes. Later, initial short theta bursts are followed by longer, rhythmic theta trains lasting ten seconds to several minutes. Increasingly-rhythmic theta trains become synchronized in both the anterior and posterior EEG leads, and TM subjects show rhythmic theta patterns that sometimes continue even after the subjects have stopped meditating (for an early article on EEG patterns in posterior cerebral regions, see Walter and Rhodes, 1966).

Additionally, some meditators display beta activity of 20 cycles per second after they have passed beyond their rhythmic theta stage of meditation, and, in a state described as 'deep' or 'transcendent', fluctuating beta, no chin muscle activity, reduced EEG responses to sensate stimuli from the outside, and the ability to remain alert enough to signal out all are displayed. When exposed to intermittent photic stimulation, experienced meditators exhibit significantly smaller reductions in alpha activity and alpha blocking, with alpha induction occurring earlier and more frequently for the meditators than for a control group of non-meditators (Babb *et al.*, 1981). Finally, bursts of theta activity may alternate with a recurrence of the alpha rhythm. Generally, then, brain amplitude changes during meditation involve enhanced, rhythmic, synchronous theta activity. In the deeper stages of meditation, low-voltage fast beta ripples, also described as bursts of beta spindling, sometimes are superimposed on slower waves. Indeed, regular meditation may freeze the hypnagogic process (a drowsy interval between sleeping and wakefulness, according to Austin, 2000), first in the predominantly alpha wave stage, and, later in the predominantly theta wave stage (Banquet, 1972; 1973; Austin, 1998b, pp. 88–92; Fenwick, 1987; Wulff 1992, pp. 172–184; Elson *et al.*, 1977; Herbert and Lehmann, 1977).

While some scientific studies of meditation focus on experienced or long-term meditators (e.g., Kornfield, 1979; Stigsby *et al.*, 1981; Williams and West, 1975; Benson *et al.*, 1982; Benson *et al.*, 1990; Herzog *et al.*, 1990–91; Shapiro, 1992; Lazar *et al.*, 1999), other studies separate short- and long-term meditators, as we have seen in the earlier study by Corby *et al.* (1978). For example, in studies on

TM, researchers (e.g., Wallace *et al.*, 1982; Mason *et al.*, 1997; Delmonte, 1984g; Jevning *et al.*, 1992) claim that long-term meditators perform better than do novices on particular measures. Experience, or the length of time one has practised meditation, is an important variable that should be included in future, empirical research on meditation, since traditions themselves often emphasize improvements in proficiency

Topographic EEG mapping methods show that theta predominates during the Japanese meditational practice called *zazen*, or 'just sitting', with alpha and theta activity predominating throughout the frontal and parietal regions, and with alpha activity continuing to occur diffusely throughout the occipital and temporal areas (Austin 1998b, p. 89, citing personal communication with T. Hirai concerning studies done in 1985 on Reverend Ashibe). Kasamatsu *et al.* (1957) also report on the EEGs of Zen and yoga practitioners (also see Akishige, 1968; Hirai, 1974; 1975). According to Austin (1998b, pp. 88–9), because alpha waves persist during tasks that can be accomplished easily and/or automatically, experienced Soto Zen monks engaging in walking meditation show a 50% alpha record, while inexperienced monks show only about a 20% record, and the non-meditating, graduate-student control group exhibits no alpha waves at all during walking.

Having conducted an EEG study of meditation, Banquet (1973) concedes that his own data is difficult to interpret, since not all faster EEG frequencies in the beta and gamma range have the same significance. Initially, their fast activity took the form of intermittent spindle-like bursts of beta activity interspersed between alpha or theta rhythms, but later, beta activities continuously rippled over the surface of the larger, slower waves, which took over and became the slow, ongoing, background activity. The amplitude of this beta activity fluctuated, reaching relatively high levels and tending to appear first over the left hemisphere. Predominating anteriorly, it extended back to include all leads. A special method of computerized analysis, called compressed spectral array, showed that even faster activities also were present, reaching gamma frequencies of 40 cycles per second. Furthermore, in contrast to the TM meditators in Banquet's study, when control subjects developed faster frequencies, they occurred at several different rates and were not as rhythmic or regular.

Counteracting generalizations on EEG findings from meditation research, Tebecis (1975) contends that EEG changes during TM are not as pronounced or consistent as previously reported. Considerable variation is displayed between subjects, according to Tebecis — some subject show no EEG changes during TM compared to equal periods of non-meditation, and the changes that do occur in particular individuals are not necessarily repeated in a subsequent session. Although trends towards increased theta and decreased beta activity during meditation do appear, no significant differences are found in a comparison of mean EEG parameters of an experimental group between periods of meditation and non-meditation.

EEG findings from meditation studies have prompted Austin (this volume) to remark that meditation may help access alternate states during certain transition periods in the sleep/waking cycle. Wallace *et al.* (1971) assert that there is no evidence of sleep in practitioners of TM, while Younger *et al.* (1973, p. 99) state that in a group of eight meditators, seven of whom were trained in TM, an average of approximately half of the meditation period was spent in waking alpha, 'slightly less asleep and the remainder alert' (also see Younger *et al.*, 1975). Furthermore, Pagano *et al.* (1976, p. 308) claim that five 'experienced' TM practitioners spent significant time during their meditation sessions 'in sleep stages 2, 3, and 4', though this seems very unlikely. Commenting on the abovementioned findings, Elson *et al.* (1977, p. 56) claim that their own study provides evidence that stage 1 sleep is a transitional phase, unlike full wakefulness and unlike straightforward sleep, and that, with training, meditators learn to hold this stage — 'If the normal process of falling asleep involves a sequential series of neurophysiological events, as postulated by Freemon (1972), then meditation might be seen as stimulating earlier events, while inhibiting the occurrence of later ones'. Elson *et al.* also claim that Younger *et al.*'s subjects did not fall asleep, but rather, that they entered the non-descending theta state typical of advanced meditation.

In Fenwick *et al.*'s study (1977), almost all meditators showed the slow, rolling eye movements indicative of drowsiness. These eye movements were combined with jerking of the head and body similar to movements observed in transitional periods when individuals are falling asleep. Like Elson *et al.*, these authors, too, suggest that meditators are able to hold themselves at the transitional level between sleeping and wakefulness. A study by Stigsby *et al.* (1981) claims that some experienced meditators do learn to enter and remain in a stable EEG condition between wakefulness and drowsiness. Finally, Mason *et al.* (1997) conducted standard ambulatory night sleep EEGs on eleven long-term TM practitioners who claimed to experience 'higher states of consciousness' during sleep as compared to nine short-term practitioners and eleven non-practitioners. When compared to the short-term practitioners, the TM practitioners showed theta-alpha activity simultaneously with delta activity and decreased chin electromyograph (EMG) during deep sleep; when compared with the combined control groups, the TM practitioners also showed greater theta wave strength (Berwick and Oziel, 1973).

Perhaps acting counter to the claim that meditation induces a hypnogogic state, many studies find that strong and sustained alpha coherence distinguishes meditators from non-meditating subjects, who lose EEG coherence when they begin to drop off to sleep (also see Haynes *et al.*, 1977; Austin 1998b, p. 89). Apparently refuting the hypnogogia hypothesis, coherence indicates the uniformity of EEG activity over the entire cerebral surface, specifically how many EEG peaks and valleys are in synchrony at many different electrode sites. Periods of increased EEG coherence can last for over forty seconds and involve the alpha, theta and beta frequencies (Freeman and Skarda, 1985). Furthermore, increased alpha coherence is more evident frontally, and it tends to correlate both with the clarity of ongoing experience, and also with the suspension of respiration. This strong, sustained alpha coherence distinguishes meditators from non-meditators, who lose EEG coherence when they begin to drop off to sleep. (Interestingly, according to Williams and West, 1975, increased alpha activity also occurs during prayer, especially when accompanied by crying, and also during Sufi meditation involving the free flow of tears).

Paty *et al.* (1978) report that during a period of extended meditation, surface EEG findings can become dissociated from behaviour, a phenomenon known as 'noncorrespondence'. Because one of their subjects could perform the simple task of checking his watch while registering delta brain waves, the authors suggest that behaviour has other correlates of its own, and that these mechanisms lie much deeper in the brain than the surface EEG can reach. According to Austin (1998b, pp. 92–3), noncorrespondence may provide hints concerning how the surface EEG may miss moments when meditation opens up quickly into brief, alternate states of consciousness, which Austin refers to as episodes of 'microawakening' and 'microsleep'. In a person's topography of awareness, such micro events set up sharp cliffs or plunge into deep valleys, which may indicate that the meditator rises up abruptly, or drops down, through many physiological layers. While ordinarily, the cliff edges are rounded off, correlating with gradual transitions, Austin claims that if the brain passes suddenly through its transition periods, more opportunities may arise for the shearing off of adjacent aggregates of functions. In this manner, meditation may enable unstable fragments of physiological mechanisms to be briefly 'loosened', making them available to recombine in new ways.

Drawing generalizations from meditation research is confusing for many reasons, not least of which is the myriad methodological approaches employed by researchers. As Wulff (1992) observes, many meditation studies betray little methodological reflection concerning choice of dependent and independent variables, and whereas ideally, control subjects should differ significantly from experimental subjects on only one independent variable — meditation practice — in reality, they differ along other dimensions as well. Furthermore, researchers may choose measures such as EEGs because they are current in scientific research or because they have used them before in other studies. Furthermore, states Wulff (p. 182):

> However impressive the EEG may be, its application in meditation research is roughly akin to using a half-dozen microphones to assess life in New York City. In either case, we can detect trends in general activity — the shift, say, from early evening to early morning — but the subtleties of the innumerable components that make up the global measures still lie beyond the capacities of these instruments.

Further confusion arises from confounding meditation with similar activities. For example, Taneli and Krahne (1987) study TM meditators who are engaged in thinking about their *mantra*, noting that they show the abrupt onset of desynchronized EEG activity, with increased beta frequencies, lasting for one to two minutes. Because subjects are asked to think about their *mantra* as an example of 'meditation', however, and because *mantra* recitation involves the processing of linguistic elements, it likely represents a different form of non-discursive practice than does single-pointed focus on a non-linguistic object (also see Bormann, 1996; Lee *et al.*, 1997).

Based on a broad literature review of EEG studies of meditation, Fenwick (1987, p. 115) concludes that many early studies were conducted

> by naïve experimenters who had little conception of the normal range of changes that occur in ordinary physiological and pathological states. There was initially a tendency to attribute differences, either between controls and meditators, or between pre- and post-meditation sessions for same subject experiments, to an effect of meditation rather than to the non-specific changes in alertness, arousal, and attention which occur in the meditation session. As mentioned by numerous reviewers, subject selection, type of meditation, and control procedures were poorly thought out, making interpretation of the experimental results difficult. It has never been possible in EEG work to argue from alterations in EEG pattern or spectral profile to changes in mental state, as patterns and profiles are non-specific, and may occur with a variety of different sets of brain functioning, each of which can support a different cognitive state.

Having sounded these warnings, however, Fenwick does draw some tentative generalizations from EEG studies of meditation, as we have done here. In brief, most types of meditation lead to alterations in alpha frequency and to an increase in theta activity with a change in scalp distribution. Beta spindling also occurs, though such spindling is not limited to meditation and may occur generally in the population. And while meditation has been shown to alter cerebral rhythms on a long-term basis, it is difficult to discern the extent to which these alterations may result from general lifestyle modifications or from meditation itself.

Some methodological problems associated with EEG studies of meditation have been corrected by more recent research conducted by Herbert Benson and his colleagues, e.g., Jacobs, Benson *et al.* (1990) study Tibetan Buddhist monks using EEG analysed with Fast Fourier transform and power analysis, finding marked asymmetry in alpha and beta activity between the hemispheres and increased beta activity in general. During two subjects' practice of *gTum-mo* yoga, right mean percentage total power for beta was greater than for left, while for alpha, left was greater than right. These findings are consistent with earlier research (Das and Gastaut, 1955; Banquet, 1973; West, 1980a) claiming that increased beta or fast EEG activity occurs during deep states of meditation.

Jacobs *et al.* (1996) also attempt to correct for methodological problems in previous meditation research, 'including lack of empirically sound experimental designs (self-selection bias, non-random assignment, no pretesting prior to training), reliance on visual analyses of a few channels of EEG activity, and failure to assess CNS effects in novice subjects' (p. 122), problems they claim are evident in studies by Delmonte (1984b) and West (1980a). In their own study of the central nervous system (CNS) effects of the Relaxation Response in twenty, novice subjects, Jacobs *et al.* use a controlled, within-subjects design and topographic EEG mappings as the dependent measure. EEG measures from fourteen scalp locations show that the Relaxation Response condition produces greater reductions in frontal EEG beta activity relative to the control condition, while no significant differences are observed for any other frequency or scalp region. This suggests that the Relaxation Response reduces cortical activation in anterior brain regions in novice subjects. Contrary to earlier studies reporting increased alpha during relaxation, this study's observation of reduced alpha power during practice of the Relaxation Response is consistent with more recent studies (e.g., Jacobs and Lubar, 1989; Pagano and Warrenburg, 1983) using power spectral analyses that show how relaxation reduces alpha power and increases theta power.

Some researchers wonder whether meditation preferentially activates the right hemisphere of the brain. Fenwick (1987) finds more right hemisphere brain activity during meditation, which he believes probably is associated with the suppression of left hemisphere activity. On the other hand, Pagano and Warrenburg (1983) claim that meditation does not shift the way the brain processes information from a mode that is primarily 'linear' and left-hemispheric to an approach that is more holistic and right-hemispheric. Indeed, Bennett and Trinder (1977) report that TM meditators activate their left hemisphere more during analytic tasks and their right hemisphere more during spatial tasks, although simple relaxation with the eyes closed yields similar findings. Moreover, for long-term meditators, there is no evidence that meditation improves performance on right-hemisphere tasks, nor does there exist evidence that it interferes with performance on left hemisphere tasks (Pagano, 1981). (For a report on hemisphere asymmetry during altered states of consciousness in general, see Wescott, 1974).

Given the current popularity of Tibetan and Zen meditation in the West, the ubiquitous reliance on TM meditators in early meditation studies (e.g., Boudreau, 1972; Seeman *et al.*, 1972; Kanellakos and Lukas, 1974; McCuaig, 1974; Bloomfield *et al.*, 1975; Blackwell *et al.*, 1975; 1976; Candelent and Candelent, 1975; Avila and Nummela, 1977; Block, 1977; Borland and Landrith, 1977; Besseghini and Witterberg, 1977; Dillbeck and Bronson, 1981; Pelletier, 1977; Pirot, 1977; Rimol, 1977; Simon and Oparil, 1977; Tjoa, 1977; Barmark and Gaunitz, 1979; Beiman *et al.*, 1980; Becker and Shapiro, 1981; Badawi *et al.*, 1984) may strike some readers as anachronistic. In the early 1970s, Tart (1971) recommended TM practice, and Benson (1974b) defended it from suspicion. By the 1980s, however, Persinger (1980; 1987; 1988) openly attributed cult-like tendencies to TM.

Despite Benson's more recent turn towards Tibetan meditation, not all attention has departed from TM, as one can see by consulting the web site of the Maharishi School of Management in Fairfield, Iowa (www.mum.edu). The University was founded in 1971 by Maharishi Mahesh Yogi, and it was called the Maharishi International University until 1995, when it underwent a change of name to the somewhat counterintuitive Maharishi School of Management. The site surveys a number of studies that use science to validate TM, appearing to distance TM from the explicitly religious context in which many meditative techniques evolved (though other sources, e.g., Alexander *et al.*, 1990, recognize Maharishi's debt to the Indian Vedic tradition). However, certain studies conducted by researchers associated with the Maharishi University of Management actually project fundamental categories onto the data that is collected. For example, Travis and Wallace (1997; 1999) report that a meditative state of 'transcendental consciousness' is marked by skin conductance responses and heart rate deceleration (also see Bakker, 1977; Farrow and Herbert, 1982; Travis and Pearson, 2000).

Another methodological quandary relates to 'demand characteristics' — subjects who believe meditation is efficacious may perform better during meditation studies in order to bear out researchers' hypotheses (West, 1987, pp. 19–20; Orne, 1962). It is not surprising that those individuals who write about meditation's efficacy sometimes have considerable vested interests, and that the rhetorical strategy of imputing efficacy to meditation is particularly pronounced in studies conducted by researchers who actually practise meditation themselves. For example, Dr. Robert Keith Wallace was the President of the Maharishi International University when he authored the short booklet 'Neurophysiology of Enlightenment: Scientific Research on Transcendental Meditation' (Wallace, 1974), a publication claiming that TM leads to a new, hitherto undiscovered 'fourth' state of consciousness (also see Ramamurthi, 1995). Indeed, in some cases, researchers-*cum*-teachers actually choose their own students as subjects, increasing the demand pressure even more. Expectations and pressures both may distort research findings, since even when meditators are used during intervals of non-meditation as their own controls in order to eliminate the effects of personality differences, they often continue to harbour positive expectations concerning the results of meditation practice.

Given the vested interests of many meditation researchers, it is not surprising that so few meditation studies report on the drawbacks of meditation practice. Two exceptions are Lazarus (1976) and Otis (1984), who report on psychiatric problems precipitated by TM. Fenwick (1983) also raises questions about meditation, and Sifford (1988) reports on a lawsuit brought by a former TM practitioner against the community for defrauding him with false promises of mental bliss and neglecting to warn him about possible adverse side-effects from practising TM. Epstein and Lieff (1986) also discuss the psychiatric complications of meditation practice, while Kornfield (1989), himself an avid meditator and meditation instructor, acknowledges that practitioners often bring past issues with them to their meditation practice.

Indeed, many Indo-Tibetan meditation manuals warn against the risk of becoming addicted to meditation, an addiction to a deautomized state that may result in a distancing from family, an eschewing of responsibilities, and a vulnerability to manipulation and control by others whom one has been conditioned to accept as more spiritual or more advanced than oneself. (Following Deikman, 1969, 'automatization' refers to the mental process basic to human consciousness, whereby the repeated exercise of an action or a perception results in the disappearance from consciousness of its intermediated steps. 'Deautomatization', on the other hand, refers to the undoing of automatization by reinvesting actions and percepts with attention, leading to the breakdown of the psychological structures that organize, limit, select, and interpret perceptual stimuli. Also see Deikman, 1971; 1982. Further, Odanjnyk, 1988, describes meditation as a practice that induces deautomatized habitual responses, while Alexander, 1931 describes meditation as a form of 'catatonia'.)

As Deikman (this volume) recognizes, imagining oneself to be more advanced or more spiritual can reinforce the 'survival self' and be a barrier to the type of 'receptive consciousness' he describes as the real goal of mystical engagement. Indeed, in its more insidious manifestations, practitioners can become so manipulated by unscrupulous or delusional teachers that they begin to overlook their guru's most obvious and tawdry breaches of morality and conduct, explaining them away as 'enlightened' actions beyond the comprehension of lowly mortals — a sure recipe for the formation of cult-like communities. This problem, too, is raised in Asian meditation treatises (e.g., Upadhyaya, 1986), many of which warn neophyte practitioners about the dangers of selecting an immoral or self-serving guru who uses the rhetoric of spiritual superiority to revel in inappropriate behaviour.

Though his work is controversial and is frequently criticized on methodological grounds (Wulff, 1997, pp. 101–3; Brothers, 1998), Michael Persinger (1987) does recognize that religious practice in some cases has negative ramifications. Persinger believes that religious experiences are natural correlates of temporal lobe transients and, as such, that they can be detected by routine EEG measurements. He also asserts that meditative hallucinations and religious experiences in general are generated by endogenous, transient electrical stimulation with the deep structures of the temporal lobe (see Persinger, 1984a,b; 1995a,b; Persinger and Valliant, 1985; Persinger, 1996; 1997; Ross and Persinger, 1987). For example, Persinger (1984c) claims to have recorded a delta-wave-dominant electrical seizure in the temporal lobe of a TM teacher during a peak experience within a routine TM practice session. Persinger questions the efficacy of TM in promoting health, inciting Orme-Johnson (1995) to attempt to refute Persinger's claims.

In one of his experiments, Persinger (1992a) compared 221 university students who had learned to meditate (65–70% in the TM style) to 860 non-meditators, finding that the 'sensed presence', a transient intrusion of the right-hemisphere equivalent of the left-hemispheric, highly-linguistic sense of self, was significantly more prevalent in the meditators. He also claimed that variants of the sensed presence were more frequent in female as opposed to male meditators, and that these variants were particularly evident in left-handed meditators (also see Persinger, 1993b).

In a subsequent article, Persinger (1993a) compared the 'Personal Philosophy Inventories' of this same sample of 221 meditators and 860 non-meditators, claiming as a result of this comparison that meditation practice promotes 'cognitive kindling'. This 'cognitive kindling', says Persinger, causes meditators as compared to controls to display a significantly wider range of what he considers to be 'complex partial epileptic-like signs' (e.g., experiences of vibrations, hearing one's name called, paranormal phenomena, deriving profound meaning from reading prose and poetry, and religious phenomenology). According to McNamara (2000), while we should first note that the 'signs' mentioned by Persinger may not actually characterize epilepsy (also see Britten et al., 1984), we also should recognize that Persinger's use of the adjective 'cognitive' to describe 'kindling' is somewhat odd. Kindling does occur in the brain, usually deep in the temporal lobe and hippocampus, and it is similar to a seizure, in which a subliminal and repetitive signal starts to recruit larger and larger areas of brain tissue. Neuronal signaling from these recruited areas begins to fire in synchrony until it spills over into the motor system and eventuates in a seizure. Discovery of the kindling phenomena in the brain was associated with low-intensity electrical stimulation of the brain (i.e., hippocampus) of the experimental animal. Even though the experimenter kept the stimulus intensity constant, the stimulated area of the brain began to recruit larger areas. Although for some time kindling was taken to be a model of epilepsy, this idea never took firm hold. Researchers now recognize that the phenomenon is not well understood, and that its connections to cognition, if any, are even less well understood.

Halgren *et al.* (1978) do find that electrical stimulation of the human hippocampal formation and amygdala evoke mental phenomena. The hippocampal/amygdaloid complex is buried deep in the temporal lobes and is connected with myriad parts of the brain, the most import of which is the limbic circuit. The amygdala is important for emotion, fear, and aggression, while the hippocampus is crucial for memory formation and for spatial cognition. Some researchers believe that the hippocampus performs a kind of indexing function for long-term memories stored in the cortex, so that stimulation of the hippocampus could cause certain memories in the temporal lobes (and in other lobes) to be activated via the indexing function. Literature on the electrical stimulation of the brain (ESB) in humans usually refers to epileptics who need brain surgery. The brain is stimulated in order to map its functional geography so that tissue associated with language is not excised or cut out. Since it is carried out in diseased (epileptic) brains, researchers do not know whether ESB tells us anything reliable about the brain or cognition itself. Certainly, ESB produces reports of cognition, e.g., memories, confabulations, visual scenes, and emotions, but it is a leap to claim that 'transients', if they exist at all, themselves produce similar cognitions (McNamara, 2000).

Nevertheless, it is true that meditators in many traditions, in addition to practitioners of many world religions, often report experiencing the presences of other beings and entities such as spirits, angels, and gods. Cook and Persinger (1997) call this the 'sensed presence', a term mentioned earlier in this section. Cook and Persinger claim that experiences of the 'sensed presence' can be induced by bursts of complex magnetic fields, and that it is 'a right hemisphere homologue of the left hemispheric sense of "self"' (also see Persinger, 1983; Persinger and Richards, 1991; 1994). As McNamara (2000) notes, this alone is a problematic notion, since the sense of self is not limited to one hemisphere or another. Nevertheless, Persinger and his colleagues correlate the 'sensed presence' with right temporal-lobe theta activity (Munro and Persinger, 1992); with 'vectorial hemisphericity', described as the relative metabolic activity of synaptic patterns between the cerebral hemispheres at the time of transient interhemispheric intercalation (Persinger, 1992c, 1993b; Lavallee and Persinger, 1992); and with sensory deprivation, a technique used by meditators in many traditions to induce mystical experiences (Tiller and Persinger, 1994; also see Deikman, 1963; 1969; 1971). Furthermore, Persinger (1989b) claims that the visitor experience, a more intense form of the sensed presence, results from functions of deep temporal lobe structures and the use of right temporal lobe functions for the consolidation of memory, and that these experiences are precipitated by depression, stress, and exposure to the focal tectonic strain fields that accompany luminous phenomena (also see Persinger, 1989a; 1992b; Makarec and Persinger, 1985; Persinger *et al.*, 1988; Michon and Persinger, 1997. For a critical evaluation of Persinger's work, see Andresen, 2000).

The Newest Kids on the Block

The rhetoric of meditation's efficacy remains with us when we move from EEG studies to more recent technological studies of meditation, which employ evoked potentials, HMPAO-SPECT imaging, and PET imaging. 'Evoked potentials' have yet to be used fully to explore all of the electrical correlates of stimuli delivered during meditation. Notwithstanding, these potentials, which involve computer amplification of a series of weak brain signals vibrating with faint electrical potentials that have been converted into measurable physiological waveforms (Austin, 1998b, pp. 284–6), have been used to understand certain facets of meditative awareness. During a test of what happens when a person pays special attention to something ('selective attention'), electrodes that record from the right frontal region showed the most obvious evidence of extranegativity. This negative potential may have deeper, subcortical origins, since the interval is too short between stimulus and response for it to have arisen in the cortex alone. Austin recommends the lateral geniculate nucleus, the superior colliculus, and the pulvinar as possible subcortical sites that may work together as a system of several 'gates'. It also is possible that the right frontal lobe consults its own prior sets of attention or intention before acting to cause such gates to open more widely.

Commenting that prior EEG studies of meditation do not provide firm, objective evidence for neurophysiological changes that occur during meditation, Newberg *et al.* (1997) attempt to determine alterations in regional cerebral blood flow during meditation by subjecting six experienced meditators in the Tibetan Buddhist tradition to HMPAO-SPECT imaging. Marked changes in mean activity occurred in the right and left thalamus, right basal ganglia, right and left frontal, and right medial temporal, with a decrease in mean activity in the left posterior superior parietal region. Furthermore, a significant positive correlation was found between the right dorsolateral prefrontal cortex (DLPFC) and the right thalamus, while the left DLPFC showed a significant inverse correlation with the left posterior superior parietal area. The changes described, and the correlations, are the mean values for all the subjects. The researchers conclude that meditation involves several coordinated cognitive processes — changes in the inferior frontal lobe and the DLPFC suggest intense concentration, while decreases in the parietal lobe may be connected to meditators' subjective reports of alterations in the senses of space and time.

PET (positron emission tomography) imaging, the most recent addition to the brain-imaging line-up, also has been deployed in the attempt to understand meditation. PET scans measure brain function by providing a metabolic map of the living brain, and state-of-the-art machines containing numerous detector rings permit simultaneous scanning of multiple brain slices during a single examination (Heiss *et al.*, 1986). PET scans of meditators, which facilitate the examination of brain metabolism during meditation, are based on the principle that nerve cells burn glucose for energy, and that they use more energy when they fire actively. By tagging glucose, researchers localize the place in the brain where glucose is burned. The glucose is tagged with an element that emits a positron, so that during the study, the positron lights up in the most metabolically-active regions of the brain. With the assistance of computed x-ray tomographic techniques, these active sites then are refined into an anatomical image. In PET scans, metabolic images are projected on a transaxial section with the frontal lobes at the top.

Recently, Danish researchers (Kjaer *et al.*, 1997) at the John F. Kennedy Institute at the University of Copenhagen employed both EEG and PET protocols to study meditation, concluding that meditation may induce an experience of an altered level of consciousness with relaxation and loss of voluntary control but with increased subjective sensory and conceptual experience. Using seven adults with between four and fifteen years of meditation experience, all of whom perform yoga and meditation several hours daily at the Scandinavian Yoga and Meditation School where most are teachers, researchers monitored EEGs during sessions lasting ninety minutes. During one forty-five minute period, subjects performed meditative relaxation guided by an audiotape, and researchers then performed scans during subjects' non-meditative resting states. In this study, researchers found a relative decrease in frontal, stiatal and cerebellar r-cerebral blood flow (CBF) during meditation and an increase in occipital and parietal association cortices. The meditative state also showed a distinct difference between flow distribution in abstract and concrete conditions. ('Abstract conditions' occurred when the subject was asked to consider feelings of happiness and 'Who am I?' questions, while 'concrete conditions' occurred when the subject was instructed to meditate on body orientation and the experience of a summer day in the countryside.)

According to Kjaer and his colleagues, abstract meditation showed bilateral perisylvian activation, while concrete meditation showed the activation of sensory association areas. The theta activity at all leads increased significantly (11%), while alpha activity decreased only slightly (2%). This surprising result caused the Danish team to conclude that meditation is significantly different from light sleep and from the resting control condition, and that the relaxed meditative state also is accompanied by relative hypoactivity in frontal, striatal, thalamic and cerebellar regions, a change that may be explained by fronto-subcortical activity. Furthermore, the researchers claimed that concrete meditation is accompanied by a relative hyperactivity of the posterior association cortices. Finally, both abstract and concrete meditation protocols were shown to induce differential PET activation, which may indicate content-dependent activation dissociated from general consciousness. The researchers concluded that the state of meditative dissociation is a major component of consciousness, and that it may be correlated with changes in the distribution of cerebral activity (Morris, 1998 also discusses the work of the Danish team, noting that the researchers are interested in mapping the neural networks supporting different aspects of consciousness in order to understand the pathophysiology of disorders, e.g., schizophrenia, attention-deficit disorder [ADD], and obsessive-compulsive disorder [OCD], in which normal consciousness is disrupted).

In *Zen and the Brain*, Austin (1998b, pp. 281–3) displays a PET scan of his own brain taken while he was lying quietly with his eyes masked and ears plugged lightly with cotton. In this scan, red indicates those regions of highest metabolic activity, and blue represents inactive regions. (Austin, 1998a notes that in some PET scans, the standard scale is adjusted so that white indicates the region of highest activity.) When the PET scan was taken, Austin, who describes himself as trained in the Zen tradition of *zazen*, or 'just sitting', was resting and letting go of his thoughts while he concentrated on his abdominal breathing.

According to Austin (1998b, p. 282), prominent metabolic activity registered on his PET scan in the upper basal ganglia nuclei, the caudate and putamen, and in the thalamus. In the cortex, activity was prominent over the middle, inferior, triangular, and opercular regions of the frontal lobes, and also in the transverse and superior temporal gyrus. Still more posteriorly, metabolic activity was high in the deepest reaches of the parietal lobe, the precuneus, and in the cuneus, which lies farthest forward in the occipital lobe. Some activity also was shown in the hippocampus and in the posterior cingulate gyrus (see Austin, this volume, for more on the function of various brain regions). A right-sided preponderance of cortical activity appeared in each of the cortical regions and was evident especially in the deeper regions of the parietal and occipital cortex, a finding corroborated by the fact that the controls showed higher oxygen metabolism over most left cortical regions. (After both hearing and vision are blocked, controls tend to decrease metabolism most in the right hemisphere.) According to Austin, differences between the right and left sides on his PET scan are consistent with the existence of a nonverbal state of mental and physical relaxation during which external visual and auditory stimuli are blocked and awareness has become simplified (for a report on the effects of the inverse condition, namely auditory stimulation during meditation, see Piggins and Morgan, 1977).

According to Austin (1998a), three particular points about his PET scan bear emphasis. First, the PET scan was included in the book as a simple demonstration of functional brain anatomy. Second, it represents the average of brain metabolic activity for a long, two-hour meditation session, the actual PET scan being a summary of many minutes of activity. No willed intent was present, just 'letting go' with loose, open, abdominal breathing. Third, inclusion of the scan in the book was meant to highlight the right-sided preponderance of some of the activity during the 'just lying' session with vision and hearing reduced. Obtaining more rigorous quantitative data for each of the two sides of the brain at the time the study was completed would have required a trans-arterial line, an earlier radioactive injection, and another corresponding two-hour scan to establish the data for an appropriate baseline control period. As Austin comments:

> Only if data were available from such a baseline control period might one then begin to infer that meditation is efficacious in increasing metabolic activity posteriorly. In fact, while I was in Japan in 1988, we were surprised to see how much activity posteriorly the Headtome IV could reveal in normal control people, under baseline conditions.

Austin conscientiously limits his interpretation of his own PET scan to suggest only that his prolonged session correlates with a tendency toward a right-sided preponderance of cortical metabolic activity in certain specified regions. Interestingly, Austin (1998b) also mentions another set of PET scans from eight subjects engaged in yoga meditation (Herzog *et al.*, 1990–91), data in which reduced metabolism in the posterior regions of cortex is found but no differences are found between right and left hemispheres (Morse, 1979). (Tangentially, Petersen *et al.*, 1988 discuss PET studies on single-word processing, which may be relevant to the understanding of *mantra* practice during contemplative practice.)

To conclude this brief survey of EEG, PET, and other scientific studies of meditation, what deserves note is that any claims to efficacy automatically are constrained by the degree of ambiguity inherent in validating mechanisms themselves. As Austin (1998b, pp. 283–4) and Morris (1998) reflect, although PET scans do accomplish good general mapping of brain metabolism, researchers recognize that PET technology often overlooks small details. If metabolic activity increases in one location, a PET scan alone does not indicate whether the local increase derives from the activity of nerve cells that only serve excitatory functions. Instead, it may represent cells burning glucose while serving inhibitory functions. As mentioned above in reference to Austin's discussion of his own PET scan, to exclude the possibility that metabolic activity only seems greater on one side of the brain because metabolic activity on the opposite side is reduced, quantitative blood level measurements also are required. Unfortunately, these involve puncturing the wall of an artery to sample arterial blood, a procedure not many subjects would agree to lightly.

By following patterns of blood flow as they shift towards the most active parts of the brain, fMRI scans provide the fastest way to image brain activity over the course of several seconds. Unlike structural MRI techniques, which measure how much volume exists in a particular region of the brain, fMRI is similar to PET imaging in that it displays the vagaries of brain function itself (see Diamond, 1992 for more on a patient's personal experience of fMRI). For this reason, it seems likely that future studies utilizing fMRI certainly will contribute to our understanding of brain function during meditation.

Indeed, fMRI already has been employed by Cho *et al.* (1998) to examine correlations between points used in acupuncture and various brain cortices. In the realm of meditation research, Lazar *et al.* (1999) conducted functional brain mapping of the Relaxation Response using 3T fMRI (3T fMRI uses a 3 Tesla magnet instead of a 1.5 Tesla magnet). Defining meditation as 'a conscious mental activity that induces a distinct hypometabolic state termed the relaxation response', Lazar and his colleagues tested five subjects with a minimum of four years of meditation training. Scanning the subjects with fMRI during meditation and during a control task that involved generating a random list of animals, the researchers found a significant ($p < .00005$) signal increase in the amygdala and hippocampus in four of the five meditators. At least three subjects activated their pon, hypothalamus, basal forebrain, anterior cingulate, and insula, and three of the subjects also showed large global signal decreases during the Relaxation Response periods. For three subjects, upon whom concurrent physiological monitoring (end-tidal CO_2, O_2 saturation, and respiration rate) was performed, levels of O_2 saturation increased during meditation, while end-tidal CO_2 concentration and respiratory rate decreased. These measures returned to baseline at the end of the meditation period, indicating that, when compared to the control task, meditation activates neural structures involved in attention and arousal (anterior cingulate, amygdala, and the reticular activating system) and control of the autonomic nervous system (insula, hypothalamus, basal forebrain, and limbic system).

Reflections on Technological Investigation of Meditation

As a researcher actively interested in pursuing fMRI studies of meditation myself, I would be exceedingly un-self-reflexive were I not to ask *why* people would want to use brain imaging techniques to understand the neural correlates of contemplative activity. What agendas are served in conducting these types of experiments? And what changes can we make in research protocols to insure that we do not gloss over important phenomenological differences between different forms of meditation practice?

Undoubtedly, the popularity of techno culture in all its guises contributes to the vogue of high-tech studies of meditation using tools such as EEGs, PET scans, and fMRI. In advocating the continuance of such studies, I therefore assume that the application of these technologies actually tells us something useful about meditation itself. Let us take a few paragraphs to unpack this assumption. You will recall Morris' (1998) mention of research by Lou, Kjaer and colleagues (see pp. 43–4 above), who are interested in mapping the neural networks supporting different aspects of consciousness in order to understand the pathophysiology of disorders in which normal consciousness is disrupted (e.g., schizophrenia, ADD, OCD, etc.). By examining PET data on meditation alongside PET data in which brain regions are active during other states of consciousness (e.g., active, resting, sleep), Lou and his team employ meditation research to illuminate much broader questions concerning the complex nature of consciousness itself. Furthermore, this research may have important clinical applications for the tangible alleviation of suffering associated with various debilitating conditions.

Similarly, by using fMRI to study meditation, and, thereby, by gaining information on blood flow patterns in the brain during particular types of meditative practice, we may be able to learn how increasing blood flow to certain regions of the brain and decreasing it to others is efficacious in promoting subjective states of calmness and well-being. Obviously, it will be important to collect detailed phenomenological reports from subjects involved in meditation research in order to correlate particular brain states with positive affect. At a later stage, potential clinical applications could include directed attention training to help persons suffering from conditions such as anxiety and panic disorder, possibly reducing these persons' dependence upon pharmacological solutions. Although meditation already is being applied in psychiatric settings, data from fMRI studies on meditation potentially could improve our understanding of meditation's mechanisms of efficacy, thereby enabling us to be more specific when 'prescribing' meditation regimes.

While technological studies of meditation may direct our health agendas positively towards the alleviation of human suffering, it will remain important for researchers pursuing these studies to credit the indigenous traditions that bring us knowledge of meditation in the first place. Neither TM nor the Relaxation Response were invented out of thin air, since both techniques drew upon a long and rich tradition of indigenous practice and belief, the former in the context of Hindu traditions in India, and the latter in the context of Tibetan practice in the Himalayas. It is important to credit the people and cultures that honed these techniques over centuries of practice, correlating their internal states carefully with their ritualistic involvement, and distilling what were, and what were not, culturally-desirable results. Just as pharmaceutical companies who hire anthropologists to research indigenous, tribal medicinal solutions should return a portion of their profits to indigenous communities, meditation researchers and promoters also have an ethical obligation to return back to the communities from which they derived important wisdom a percentage of the proceeds they make marketing those techniques in the United States and elsewhere. As Singer (1993 [1979]) admonishes us, it is our moral obligation to give back — it is the least we can do.

Researchers who familiarize themselves thoroughly with the specifics of a certain tradition, including its language, before and during the process of studying the tradition have a far greater chance of improving the quality of their science than those who do not. If scientific researchers do not take the time to learn about their subjects' traditions in some depth, they simply will not be equipped to avoid reductionist pitfalls when it comes to understanding meditation. Meditation is a complex and multidimensional grouping of diverse practices — it could not be farther away from a monolithic entity than could Christian prayer. Although practitioners in different traditions may engage in what externally appear to be similar practices and/or postures, these practitioners often have wildly different narrative traditions in which they contextualize these techniques. Even this difference in narrative context may impact patterns of physiological arousal and brain function. For example, both Hinduism and Buddhism share in common *Vajrayana* (Tantric) ritual and meditative practices, though each tradition invokes a different cultural narrative in explaining these practices' goals and objectives. Our discussion of Tibetan Buddhist meditation practice in the next section demonstrates the necessity of methodological specificity when pursuing meditation research.

Revisiting Methodology in Meditation Research:
Thod rgal and *Khregs gcod*

Many scientific studies of meditation involve questionable methodologies. Many studies involve multiple subjects, each observed during the course of a single monitoring period. In some cases, the subjects purport to be engaged in the same kind of meditation practice, but in others, researchers explicitly acknowledge that the subjects are practising different techniques. Furthermore, even if the subjects in a given study all claim to be practising TM or some other form of meditation, or simply because researchers may give all the students in a given study the same set of instructions, there is no way to monitor whether or not these subjects are actually all doing the same thing. There are many different routes to Tipperary, and different meditators may have learned different sequences of internal steps, activating vastly different parts of the brain, to arrive at what they similarly, yet subjectively and in their own languages, describe as 'transcendent', 'ecstatic', and/or 'blissful' states of awareness.

We desperately need longitudinal studies of meditation practitioners, i.e., studies that monitor particular practitioners engaged multiple times in the same practice. Even in the late 1970s, Brown (1977, pp. 237–8) recognized the need for carefully-designed, controlled, and longitudinal protocols:

> One practical way to approach these questions [concerning the operational definition of meditation variables and their relationship to one other] is to research the important variables of meditation as defined by the classical meditation literature. For example, the Tibetan Buddhist tradition alone contains thousands of volumes written on the meditative experience. The phenomenologies of meditative experiences are reasonably consistent across texts, with consensus on the most important subjective experiences of meditation. These texts have a sophisticated technical language for most aspects of the meditative experience; beginning yogis are required to learn this language much in the same way an apprentice to a modern scientific discipline must learn the language of his research trade. The terminology for the major variables in the meditative experience is quite precise. There are technical categories, reasonably comparable with the psychological categories of attention, thinking processes, perception, information-processing, physiological parameters, affect, and time. . . .
>
> The most obvious theme in all the classical meditation literature is a longitudinal emphasis. The texts illustrate which variables of meditation are most likely to undergo change at certain definable stages of practice over time. In fact, the texts mention relatively few stable meditation variables across all stages of practice. It is difficult to speak of a single meditative state apart from the level of experience. Viewing the empirical research on meditation against the longitudinal emphasis in the classical meditation literature, one must seriously question whether physiological and cognitive measures of meditation, taken without careful specification of the level of practice, will ever be of great consequence. The obvious implication is that

meditation needs to be researched over time with the same subjects. To approach the question concerning how the variables of meditation relate to each other, it is important to consider how they interact over time, since no longitudinal studies of meditation are presently available.

Although experimental costs make longitudinal studies difficult to fund, and drop-out rates are higher than in cross-sectional studies, researchers from different institutions should be encouraged to collaborate together in the design and implementation of meditation research to reduce costs, and also to improve results.

While West (1979) did conduct a longitudinal study to examine the physiological effects of meditation, a longitudinal protocol applied to EEG, SPECT, PET and fMRI studies would correct for variation between individual subjects. It also would help us begin to understand whether or not an individual meditator him- or herself always uses the same pattern of internal sequences to achieve the same subjectively-recognized state. Only after such longitudinally-rich data on a particular meditator have been collected will we know that our research on contemplative practice is more than anecdotal, making it appropriate to compare one subject's repertoire of fMRI or PET scans to similar repertoires from other. Furthermore, we will need to collect statistically-significant data, meaning that our studies will need to include a large enough N (= subject pool). And finally, longitudinal data promises to increase researchers' phenomenological understanding of the myriad varieties of meditation practice.

A brief digression into the intricacies of the Indo-Tibetan Buddhism illustrates the diversity of meditative practices that exist, even within a single tradition. Indo-Tibetan Buddhism distinguishes, both heuristically and phenomenologically, two broad categories of meditative engagement, 'Sutra Vehicle' (Skt. *sutrayana*) meditation, and 'Adamantine Vehicle' (Skt. *vajrayana*) meditation (the latter often is referred to as 'tantric' meditation). The first category, strict meditation, is oriented towards the 'mind' (Skt. *citta*) and itself is comprised of two sub-divisions, 'stabilizing' (Skt. *samatha*) meditation, and 'analytic' (Skt. *vipassana*) meditation. In contrast, the second broad category of contemplative practice, tantric meditation, is preeminently body-oriented and focuses on subtle transformations within the psychophysical continuum. Two subdivisions of tantric meditation also are distinguished, 'generation stage' (Skt. *utpattikrama*; Tib. *bskyed rim*) practices, and 'completion stage' (Skt. *nispannakrama*; Tib. *rdzogs rim*) practices. Generation and completion stages often are undertaken for the purpose of physical and mental purification, and such practices are reported to induce spontaneous and controlled experiences involving sensations of light, expansiveness, and spaciousness. Proper sequence and repetition are deemed crucial to the success of these practices. Additionally, both broad categories of practice, stric and tantric, and indeed particular variations of practice within these categories, have different cognitive goals, result in different phenomenologies of experience, and likely activate different mechanisms in the body/mind/brain.

Contemplative practices within the Rnying ma tradition of Tibetan Buddhism, which have yet to be studied technologically, would provide an interesting candidate for scientific research. I have chosen the Tibetan tradition here because of my greater relative knowledge in this area, though one could as easily have selected Hindu Hatha Yoga, Japanese Zen, or another of the myriad meditative traditions that exist, including any one of the many other meditative traditions within Tibetan Buddhism. Nevertheless, the well-developed textual tradition of the Rnying ma lineage provides scholars familiar with the Tibetan language a tremendous corpus of materials from which to collate subjective reports on the phenomenology of Rnying ma practices. Brown's (1977) description of Indo-Tibetan *Mahmudr* practice, common to the Bka rgyus lineage, likewise illustrates this point.

Since at least the ninth century, Tibetan scholars in general have elaborated a well-mapped terrain of 'generation stage' and 'completion stage' practices that involve internal visual imagery. In the Rnying ma tradition, texts describing practices of internal imagery and resultant visionary experience include Klong chen pa's (1308–1363) corpus and the 'Four Central Potentials' (Tib. *Snying tig ya bzhi*). Sections from Volume I on 'great yoga' (Skt. *mahayoga*), 'further yoga' (Skt. *anuyoga*), and 'primordial yoga' (Skt. *atiyoga*) within 'Jam mgon Kong sprul Blo gros mtha' yas' (1813–1899) *Gdams ngag mdzod: A Treasury of Instructions and Techniques for Spiritual Realization* (Kong sprul, 1971) also describe mental visualization practices. All three heterogeneous collections include texts reported to date from the late-tenth to the mid-fourteenth centuries. Often utilizing rich metaphoric language, these texts describe a method to reverse 'the appearance of the ground' (Tib. *gshi nang*), i.e., the arising of relative phenomena out of their ultimate context. This reversal occurs during completion stage practices referred to as the 'four visions' (Tib. *snang ba bzhi*), the fourth of which describes the collapse of all previous visions. The 'four visions' belong to the 'skipping grades' (Tib. *thod rgal*) method of Rnying ma practice, which is included within the 'oral lineage' (Skt. *upadesa*; Tib. *man ngag*) aspect of 'Great Perfection' (Tib. *rdzogs chen*) practices. These texts also describe the process whereby subtle elements of practitioners' psychophysical continuums coalesce and transform into radiant light. Additionally, Klong chen pa describes visionary experiences — mirage, smoke, fireflies, blazing butter lamps, and a cloudless sky (Smith, 2000) — phenomena previously described in the *Chdogya Upaniad*, an early text probably dating to around the seventh or eighth century BCE (Sourcebook in Indian Philosophy, 1957).

Drawing on the Tibetan Rnying ma tradition also would allow researchers to consult members of a contemporary practitioner lineage claiming close historical connections to tantric *cultus* in seventh-century India. It is likely that members of this lineage, e.g., monastic and non-monastic practitioners in Bylacuppe, India, could be interviewed to learn more about phenomenological descriptions of particular Rnying ma contemplative practices, and textual descriptions of such experiences likewise could be collected. Indeed, to facilitate particular visionary experiences within the Rnying ma tradition, contemporary practitioners sometimes enter 'dark retreats' for as short a period as one day to as long a period as fifty-five years (Smith, 2000; also see Hood and Morris, 1981).

It is interesting to note that so-called Great Perfection practices within the Rnying ma tradition, especially *thod rgal* practices, describe visionary sequences strikingly familiar to 'entoptic' visions. Entopic means 'within the eye', and it refers to seeing the contents of the eyeball. Retinal blood vessels and 'floaters' — the faint squiggly lines that meander across the vision field (Roach, 1998) — may be the anatomic inspiration for the cultivation of four successive visions in the Rnying ma tradition (Smith, 2000). To achieve the first vision, one cultivates '*vajra* chains', those little circles, called *thig le* in Tibetan, that attach themselves in chains when one stares ahead into empty space. To achieve the second vision, one works on increasing the size of these circles until one sees various deities inside. For the third vision, one cultivates the spontaneous arising of these visions. And for the fourth vision, the *thig le* hopefully disappear, the idea being that one exhausts the karmic potential and underlying 'defilements' causing these visions to arise in the first place — a cultural narrative that may, medically-speaking, correspond to retinal cell death. Even within the Tibetan frame of reference, practitioners undertaking *thod rgal* practice are aware that their visions are not objective phenomena; instead, they believe these states correspond to what is called 'projective visions' (Tib. *nangs gsal*) (Smith, 2000).

If granted access to this esoteric tradition, what would be an effective way of studying Tibetan *thod rgal* practitioners? First, it is important to realize that *thod rgal* practitioners seek secluded practice sites where they assume extreme postures, called 'seer', 'elephant', and 'lion', corresponding to three gazes, called 'emanation body' (Skt. *sambhogikaya*), 'enjoyment body' (Skt. *nairmanikaya*), and 'reality body' (Skt. *dharmakaya*). The gazes are used in conjunction with light sources believed to stimulate visions emerging from the very subtle channels (Skt. *kati*) linking the retinas to the heart, and the corresponding postures are thought to cause the 'winds' (Skt. *prana*; Tib. *rlung*) pervading the body to become calm. Both secrecy and postural distortion would make it difficult to conduct fMRI and PET studies of *thod rgal*, since it would be virtually impossible to assume the 'elephant' posture, for example, in a scanning apparatus. Researchers could measure physiological variables (e.g., heart rate, respiration, O_2 consumption, etc.), however, and perhaps they also could perform EEGs (Smith, 2000).

Khregs gcod is another Rnying ma practice in the same family as *thod rgal*, though *khregs gcod* is unique inasmuch as it does not focus on a set of techniques *per se*. Instead, the 'state' of *khregs gcod* is said to result from two kinds of preliminary practice, the 'separation of *samsara* from *nirvana*' (Tib. *khor de ru shan*), and 'fixing the mind' (Tib. *sems gdzin*). Without going into details, both contain a retinue of techniques to cause awareness to recognize itself without the mediation of conceptual objects. This direct awareness, called 'self-aware primordial wisdom' (Tib. *rang gyis rig pa'i ye shes*), is believed to underlie, pervade, and be the source of all phenomena. It is also given the name 'pure and perfect mind' (Skt. *bodhicitta*; Tib. *byan chub sems*), which may be characterized as the phenomenological reduction of the mind and its contents to their intertwined nature of 'emptiness' (Skt. *sunyata*; Tib. *stong pa nyid*) and the mind's indwelling clarity. (The term 'emptiness' here refers to the lack of phenomenon's essential nature.) The techniques preliminary to *khregs gcod* are intended to cause the mind to 'unbind' (Tib. *gcod*) the 'bundle' (Tib. *khregs*) of conceptual fabrications through a recognition of its own nature. Having achieved recognition of self-aware primordial wisdom, the actual practice of *khregs gcod* is to stabilize this recognition in the midst of all ordinary cognitive processing until it is continuous, without interruption of any kind (Smith, 2000).

How can we study *khregs gcod* scientifically? We probably can't. Without distorting the practice to such an extent that we lose it, it would be impossible to monitor any one subject 24 hours a day seven days a week. So while the 'instrumental' study of meditation does yield a certain genre of results, it overlooks the kind of 'receptive consciousness' that Deikman (this volume) so well describes. *Khregs gcod* is a good practice to mention here, because it exemplifies a kind of mystical engagement with interconnectedness that literally never sleeps.

Supplementing Our Techno Studies of Meditation:
Contributions from Cognitive Science

Given the phenomenological diversity of meditative techniques, our quest to understand meditation should not be restricted to quantifying brain wave activity by means of EEGs, identifying metabolic correlates by means of PET scans, and following shifting patterns of blood flow by means of fMRI scans. Indeed, researchers can look to other areas of cognitive science to illuminate other features of meditation. For example, it could be useful to revisit van der Lans' (1985) discussion of three cognitive psychological approaches to the study of religious experience (i.e., attribution theory, the approach of Hjalmar Sundén and the Swedish school, and information-processing models), which relate religious experiences to the functioning of preexisting cognitive structures. van der Lans also discusses meditation, specifically how it causes specific cognitive structures to become active and dominant, thereby replacing the usual interpretive schemes that underlie daily experience.

More specifically, we can use research in cognitive neuroscience (e.g., Kosslyn, 1988; 1994; 1995; Kosslyn and Koenig, 1992) describing a general theory of visual mental imagery, its relation to visual perception, and its implementation in the human brain to elucidate genres of meditative practice that focus on internal visualization sequences. Using brain-scanning techniques, Kosslyn describes how quasi-pictorial events in the brain are generated, interpreted, and employed in cognition. The resultant theory on the nature of the internal representation of visual mental imagery contends that visual imagery depends on the same brain mechanisms and systems underlying visual perception itself. Such research is certain to shed light on the nature of internal psychophysical transformations wrought by contemplative protocols involving internal mental visualization, whether they be found in Tibetan Buddhism, Sufism, Kabbalah, or other esoteric and religious contexts.

To conclude, let us recognize that the so-called meditation Western researchers have been studying is, like Mary Shelley's Frankenstein, an entity of our own creation. It is best to dispel the myth of a monolithic 'meditation' and to replace it with awareness of a plethora of very specific contemplative sequences, undertaken by monks and laypersons in specific lineages and sub-lineages throughout the world. Greater specificity will help us design scientific studies of contemplative practice that identify particular practices and the steps undertaken by individual practitioners en route to their particular goals. Only after many specific studies have been undertaken, preferably utilizing a longitudinal design, will we be able to look across practices to make tentative comments about meditative practice in general. Furthermore, we would be wise, as responsible researchers, to state clearly our own investment in our research on meditation when we report our results. If we are reporting on practices in which we ourselves are engaged, or if we enter our research with a positive predisposition towards the phenomena we are investigating, we should consider how this influences our findings. Such a self-reflexive move will enable us to deepen our wisdom concerning both the subtleties of introspective traditions, and also the way in which human conceptualizations and expectations interact with science.

References

Abrams, A. (1977), 'The Effects of Meditation on Elementary School Students', *Doctoral Dissertation, University of California, Berkeley*, **37(9-A)**, p. 5689 (Dissertation Abstracts International).

Akishige, Y. (ed. 1973), *Psychological Studies on Zen* (Tokyo: Zen Institute of Komazawa University).

Akishige, Y. (1968), 'Psychological Studies on Zen', in *Bulletin of the Faculty of Literature of Kyushu University*.

Alexander, C.N., Davies J.L. and Dixon, C.A. (1990), 'Growth of Higher Stages of Consciousness: Maharishi's Vedic Psychology of Human Development', in *Higher Stages of Human Development: Perspectives in Adult Grades* (New York: Oxford University Press).

Alexander, C.N., Rainforth, M.V. and Gelderloos, P. (1991), 'Transcendental Meditation, Self-Actualization, and Psychological Health', *Journal of Social Behavior and Personality*, **6** (5), pp. 189–247.

Alexander, C.N., Robinson, P., Orme-Johnson D.W., Schneider R.H. and Walton K.G. (1994), 'The Effects of Transcendental Meditation Compared to Other Methods of Relaxation and Meditation in Reducing Risk Factors, Morbidity, and Mortality', *Homeostasis*, **35** (4–5), pp. 243–63.

Alexander, C.N., Robinson, P. and Rainforth, M. (1994), 'Treating and Preventing Alcohol, Nicotine, and Drug Abuse Through Transcendental Meditation: A Review and Statistical Meta-Analysis', *Alcohol Treatment Quarterly*, **11**, pp. 13–87.

Alexander, F. (1931), 'Buddhist Training as an Artificial Catatonia', *Psychoanalytic Review*, **18**, pp. 129–45.

Allison, J. (1971), 'Respiratory Changes During Transcendental Meditation', *Lancet*, **1** (7651), p. 883.

Anand, B.K., Chhina, G.S. and Singh, B. (1961a), 'Some Aspects of Electroencephalographic Studies in Yogis', *Electroencephalography and Clinical Neurophysiology*, **13**, pp. 452–6.

Anand, B.K., Chhina, G.S. and Singh, B. (1961b), 'Studies on Shri Ramanad Yogi During His Stay in an Airtight Box', *Indian Journal of Medical Research*, **49**, pp. 82–9.

Andresen, J. (2000), 'Religion in the Flesh: Forging New Methodologies for the Study of Religion', in *Religion in Mind: Cognitive Perspectives on Religious Belief, Ritual, and Experience* (Cambridge: Cambridge University Press).

Ashbrook, J.B. (1993), 'From Biogenetic Structuralism to Mature Contemplation to Prophetic Consciousness', *Zygon*, **28** (2), pp. 231–50.

Assimakis, P. D. and Dillbeck, M.C. (1995), 'Time Series Analysis of Improved Quality of Life in Canada: Social Change, Collective Consciousness, and the TM-Sidhi Program', *Psychological Reports*, **76** (3 Pt. 2), pp. 1171–93.

Astin, J.A. (1997), 'Stress Reduction Through Mindfulnes Meditation. Effects on Psychological Symptomatology, Sense of Control, and Spiritual Experiences', *Psychotherapy & Psychosomatics*, **66** (2), pp. 97–106.

Austin, J.H. (1998a), Personal Communication.

Austin, J.H. (1998b), *Zen and the Brain: Toward and Understanding of Meditation and Consciousness* (Cambridge, MA: The MIT Press).

Austin, J.H. (2000), Personal communication.

Avila, D. and Nummela, R. (1977), 'Transcendental Meditation: A Psychological Interpretation', *Journal of Clinical Psychology*, **33** (3), pp. 842–4.

Babb, T.L., Halgren, E., Wilson, C., Engel, J. and Crandall, P. (1981), 'Neuronal Firing Paterns during the Spread of an Occipital Lobe Seizure to the Temporal Lobes in Man', *Electroencephalography & Clinical Neurophysiology*, **51** (1), pp. 104–7.

Badawi, K., Wallace, R., Orme-Johnson, D. and Rouzere, A. (1984), 'Electrophysiologic Characteristics of Respiratory Suspension Periods Occurring during the Practice of the Transcendental Meditation Program', *Psychosomatic Medicine*, **46**, pp. 267–76.

Bagchi, B.K. and Wenger, M.A. (1958), 'Simultaneous EEG and Other Recordings During Some Yogic Practices', *Electroencephalography and Clinical Neurophysiology*, **10**, p. 193.

Bahrke, M.S. and Morgan, W.P. (1978), 'Anxiety Reduction Following Exercise and Meditation', *Cognitive Therapy and Research*, **2**, pp. 323–33.

Bakker, R. (1977), 'Decreased Respiratory Rate during Transcendental Meditation Technique: A Replication', in *Scientific Research on the Transcendental Meditation Program: Collected Papers*, ed. D.W. Orme-Johnson, and J.T. Farrow, Second edition (Weggis, Switzerland: Maharishi European Research University Press).

Bali, L.R. (1979), 'Long-term Effects of Relaxation on Blood Pressure and Anxiety Levels of Essential Hypertensive Males: A Controlled Study', *Psychosomatic Medicine*, **41**, pp. 637–46.

Banquet, J.P. (1972), 'EEG in Meditation', *Electroencephalography and Clinical Neurophysiology*, **33**, p. 454.

Banquet, J.P. (1973), 'Spectral Analysis of the EEG in Meditation', *Electroencephalography and Clinical Neurophysiology*, **35**, pp. 143–51.

Barmark, S.M. and Gaunitz, S.C.G. (1979), 'Transcendental Meditation and Heterohypnosis as Altered States of Consciousness', *International Journal of Clinical and Experimental Hypnosis*, **27**, pp. 227–39.

Barnes, V., Scheider, R., Alexander, C. and Staggers, F. (1997), 'Stress, Stress Reduction, and Hypertension in African Americans: An Updated Review', *Journal of the National Medical Association*, **89** (7), pp. 464–76.

Barr, B.P. and Benson, H. (1985), 'The Relaxation Response and Cardiovascular Disorders', *Behavioral Medicine Update*, **6**, pp. 28–30.

Bassett, J., Blanchard, E. and Estes, L. (1977), 'Effects of Instructional-Expectancy Sets on Relaxation Training with Prisoners', *Journal of Community Psychology*, **5**, pp. 166–70.

Beary, J.F. and Benson, H. (1974), 'A Simple Psychophysiologic Technique which Elicits the Hypometabolic Changes of the Relaxation Response', *Psychosomatic Medicine*, **36**, pp. 115–20.

Beck, A.T. (1976), *Cognitive Therapy and the Emotional Disorders* (New York: International Universities Press).

Becker, D. and Shapiro, D.H. (1981), 'Physiological Responses to Clicks during Zen, Yoga and TM Meditation', *Psychophysiology*, **18**, pp. 695–9.

Beiman, I.H., Johnson, S.A., Puente, A.E., Majestic, H.W. and Graham, L.B. (1980), 'Client Characteristics and Success in TM', *Journal of Clinical Psychology*, **36** (1), pp. 291–5.

Bennett, J. and Trinder, J. (1977), 'Hemispheric Laterality and Cognitive Style associated with Transcendental Meditation', *Psychophysiology*, **14**, pp. 293–6.

Benson, H. (1969), 'Yoga for Drug Abuse (Letter to the Editor)', *New England Journal of Medicine*, **281**, p. 1133.

Benson, H. (1974a), 'Decreased Alcohol Intake associated with the Practice of Meditation: A Retrospective Investigation', *Annals of the New York Academy of Sciences*, **233**, pp. 174–7.

Benson, H. (1974b), 'Transcendental Meditation — Science or Cult?' *Journal of the American Medical Association*, **227**, p. 807.

Benson, H. (1974c), 'Your Innate Asset for Combatting Stress', *Harvard Business Review*, **52**, pp. 49–60.

Benson, H. (1975), *The Relaxation Response* (New York: Morrow).

Benson, H. (1976), 'The Relaxation Response and Cardiovascular Diseases', *Chest, Heart, Stroke Journal*, **1**, pp. 28–31.

Benson, H. (1977), 'Systemic Hypertension and the Relaxation Response', *New England Journal of Medicine*, **296**, pp. 1152–6.

Benson, H. (1979), *The Mind/Body Effect* (New York: Simon and Schuster).

Benson, H. (1982a), 'Body Temperature Changes during the Practice of gTum-mo Yoga (Matters Arising)', *Nature*, **298**, p. 402.

Benson, H. (1982b), 'The Relaxation Response: History, Physiologic Basis and Clinical Usefulness', *Acta Medica Scandinavica*, **660** (Supplement), pp. 231–7.

Benson, H. (1983a), 'The Author Responds', *Integrative Psychiatry*, **1**, pp. 66–8.

Benson, H. (1983b), 'Relaxation Response and Norepinephrine: A New Study Illuminates Mechanisms', *Integrative Psychiatry*, **1**, pp. 15–9.

Benson, H. (1983c), 'The Relaxation Response: Its Subjective and Objective Historical Precedents and Physiology', *Trends in Neuroscience*, **6**, pp. 281–4.

Benson, H. (1983d), 'The Relaxation Response: Physiologic Basis and Clinical Applicability', in *Biobehavioral Bases of Coronary Hearth Disease*, ed. T.M. Dembroski, T.H. Schmidt, and G. Blumchen (Besel: Karger).

Benson, H. (1984a), *Beyond the Relaxation Response* (New York: Times Books).

Benson, H. (1984b), 'The Relaxation Response and the Treatment of Anxiety', in *Psychiatric Update: The American Psychiatric Association Annual Review, Volume III*, ed. L. Grinspoon (Washington: American Psychiatric Press).

Benson, H. (1985a), 'Stress, Anxiety and the Relaxation Response', in *Behavioral Biology in Medicine* (South Norwalk, CT: Meducation).

Benson, H. (1985b), 'Stress, Health and the Relaxation Response', in *Behavioral Medicine: Work, Stress and Health*, NATO Advanced Science Institutes Series D: Behavioral and Social Sciences, No. 19 (Dordrecht: Martinus Mijhoff).

Benson, H. (1986), 'The Relaxation Response: How to Lower Blood Pressure, Cope with Pain and Reduce Anxiety in 20 Minutes a Day', *Harvard Medical Alumni Bulletin*, **60**, pp. 33–5.

Benson, H. (1987a), 'The Physiology, History and Clinical Applications of the Relaxation Response', in *Encyclopedia of Neuroscience*, ed. W. Klump (Boston: Birkhauser).

Benson, H. (1987b), *Your Maximum Mind*, W. Proctor, collaborator (New York: Times Books/Random House).

Benson, H. (1988), 'The Relaxation Response: A Bridge between Medicine and Religion', *Harvard Medical School Letter*, **4**, pp. 4–6.

Benson, H. (1989), 'Hypnosis and the Relaxation Response', *Gastroenterology*, **96**, pp. 1609–11.

Benson, H. (1993), 'The Relaxation Response', *Mind–Body Medicine*, ed. D. Goleman, and J. Gurin (Yonkers: Consumer Reports Books).

Benson, H. (1995), 'Commentary: Placebo Effect and Remembered Wellness', *Mind–Body Medicine*, **1**, pp. 44–5.

Benson, H. (1996), *Timeless Healing: The Power and Biology of Belief* (New York: Scribner).

Benson, H., Herd, J.A., Morse, W.H. and Kelleher, R.T. (1970), 'Behaviorally Induced Hypertension in the Squirrel Monkey', *Circulation Research Supplement*, **1** (26–27), pp. 21–6.

Benson, H., Akbarian, M., Adler, L.N. and Agelmann, W.H. (1970), 'Hemodynamic Effects of Pneumonia. I. Normal and Hypodynamic Responses', *Journal of Clinical Investigation*, **49**, pp. 791–8.

Benson, H., Shapiro, D.H., Tursky, B. and Schwartz, G.E. (1971), 'Decreased Systolic Blood Pressure through Operant Conditioning Techniques in Patients with Essential Hypertension', *Science*, **173**, pp. 740–2.

Benson, H. and Wallace, R.K. (1972a), 'Decreased Blood Pressure in Hypertensive Subjects Who Practice Meditation', *Circulation*, **2** (45, Supplement), p. 516.

Benson, H. and Wallace, R.K. (1972b), 'Decreased Drug Abuse with Transcendental Meditation: A Study of 1,861 Subjects', in *Drug Abuse: Proceedings of the International Conference*, ed. C.J.D. Zarafonetis (Philadelphia: Lea and Febiger).

Benson, H., Rosner, B.A. and Marzetta, B.R. (1973), 'Decreased Blood Pressure in Hypertensive Subjects Who Practiced Meditation', *Journal of Clinical Investigation*, **52**, p. 8a.

Benson, H., Malvea, B.P. and Graham, J.R. (1973), 'Physiologic Correlates of Meditation and their Clinical Effects in Headache: An Ongoing Investigation', *Headache*, **13**, pp. 23–4.

Benson, H., Marzetta, B.R. and Rosner, B.A. (1974), 'Decreased Blood Pressure associated with the Regular Elicitation of the Relaxation Response: A Study of Hypertensive Subjects', in *Contemporary Problems in Cardiology, Volume I: Stress and the Heart*, ed. R.S. Eliot (Mt. Kisco, NY: Futura).

Benson, H., Rosner, B.A., Marzetta, B.R. and Klemchuk, H.M. (1974), 'Decreased Blood Pressure in Pharmacologically Treated Hypertensive Patients who Regularly Elicited the Relaxation Response', *Lancet*, **1** (852), pp. 289–91.

Benson, H., Beary, J.F. and Carol, M.P. (1974), 'The Relaxation Response', *Psychiatry*, **37**, pp. 37–46.

Benson, H., Klemchuk, H.M. and Graham, J.R. (1974), 'The Usefulness of the Relaxation Response in the Therapy of Headache', *Headache*, **14**, pp. 49–52.

Benson, H., Steinert, R.F., Greenwood, M.M., Klemchuk, H.M. and Peterson, N.H. (1975), 'Continuous Measurement of O* *Journal of Human Stress*, **1**, pp. 37–44.

Benson, H., Alexander, S. and Feldman, C.L. (1975), 'Decreased Premature Ventricular Contractions through the Use of the Relaxation Response in Patients with Stable Ischemic Heart Disease', *Lancet*, **2**, pp. 380–2.

Benson, H., Greenwood, M.M. and Klemchuk, H. (1975), 'The Relaxation Response: Psychophysiologic Aspects and Clinical Applications', *International Journal of Psychiatry and Medicine*, **6**, pp. 87–98.

Benson, H. and Greenwood, M.M. (1976), 'Behavioral Modifications of Blood Pressure in Man', in *Regulation of Blood Pressure by the Central Nervous System*, ed. G. Onesti, M. Fernandes, and K.E. Kim (New York: Grune and Stratton).

Benson, H., Kotch, J.B. and Crassweller, K.D. (1976), 'The Usefulness of the Relaxation Response in the Treatment of Stress-Related Cardiovascular Diseases', *Journal of the South Carolina Medical Association*, **72**, pp. 50–6.

Benson, H., Kotch, J.B., Crassweller, K.D. and Greenwood, M.M. (1977), 'Historical and Clinical Considerations of the Relaxation Response', *American Scientist*, **65**, pp. 441–5.

Benson, H., Kotch, J.B. and Crassweller, K.D. (1977), 'The Relaxation Response: A Bridge between Psychiatry and Medicine', *The Medical Clinics of North America*, **61**, pp. 929–38.

Benson, H., Dryer, T. and Hartley, L.H. (1978), 'Decreased VO-sub-2 Consumption during Exercise with Elicitation of the Relaxation Response', *Journal of Human Stress*, **4**, pp. 38–42.

Benson, H., Kotch, J.B. and Crassweller, K.D. (1978), 'Stress and Hypertension: Interrelations and Management', in *Hypertension: Mechanisms, Diagnosis and Treatment*, ed. G. Onesti, and A.M. Brest (Philadelphia: Davis).

Benson, H., Frankel, F.H., Apfel, R., Daniels, M.D., Schniewind, H.E., Nemiah, J.C., Sifneos, P. E., Crassweller, K.D., Greenwood, M.M., Kotch, J.B., Arns, P. A. and Rosner, B. (1978), 'Treatment of Anxiety: A Comparison of the Usefulness of Self-Hypnosis and a Meditational Relaxation Technique', *Psychotherapy and Psychosomatics*, **30**, pp. 229–42.

Benson, H., Arns, P. A. and Hoffman, J.W. (1981), 'The Relaxation Response and Hypnosis', *International Journal of Clinical and Experimental Hypnosis*, **29**, pp. 259–70.

Benson, H. and Goodale, I. (1981), 'The Relaxation Response: Your Inborn Capacity to Counteract the Harmful Effects of Stress', *Journal of the Florida Medical Association*, **68**, pp. 265–7.

Benson, H., Lehmann, J.W., Malhotra, M.S., Goldman, R.F., Hopkins, J. and Epstein, M.D. (1982), 'Body Temperature Changes during the Practice of gTum-mo Yoga', *Nature*, **295** (5846), pp. 234–6.

Benson, H., Pomeranz, B. and Kutz, I. (1984), 'Pain and the Relaxation Response', in *Textbook of Pain*, ed. P. D. Wall, and R. Melzack (London: Churchill Livingstone).

Benson, H. and Caudill, M.A. (1984), 'The Use of Relaxation Techniques in the Management of Hypertension', *Primary Cardiology*, **10**, pp. 137–44.

Benson, H. and Friedman, R. (1985), 'A Rebuttal to the Conclusions of David S. Holmes' Article: "Meditation and Somatic Arousal Reduction"', *American Psychologist*, **40**, pp. 725–8.

Benson, H., Malhotra, M.S., Goldman, R.F., Jacobs, G.D. and Hopkins, P. J. (1990), 'Three Case Reports of the Metabolic and Electroencephalographic Changes During Advanced Buddhist Meditation Techniques', *Behavioral Medicine*, **16**, pp. 90–5.

Benson, H., Stuart, E.M. and Staff of the Mind/Body Medical Institute of New England Deaconess Hospital Harvard Medical School (1991), *The Wellness Book: The Comprehensive Guide to Maintaining Health and Treating Stress-Related Illness* (Seacaucus, NJ: Carol Publishing Co.).

Benson, H., Kornhaber, A., Kornhaber, C., LeChanu, M.N., Zuttermeister, P. C., Myers, P. and Friedman, R. (1994), 'Increases in Positive Psychological Characteristics with a New Relaxation-Response Curriculum in High School Students', *Journal of Research and Development in Education*, **27**, pp. 226–31.

Benson, H. and Friedman, R. (1995), 'The Three Legged Stool: Mind/Body Medicine and Mainstream Medical Care', *Mind–Body Medicine*, **1**, pp. 1–2.

Benson, H. and Friedman, R. (1996a), 'Harnessing the Power of the Placebo Effect and Renaming it "Remembered Wellness"', *Annual Review of Medicine*, **47**, pp. 193–9.

Benson, H. and Friedman, R. (1996b), 'Behavioral Medicine and Health Care Reform', *The Leifer Report*, Spring-Summer.

Benson, H. and Myers, P. (1999), 'The Importance of the Placebo Effect in Alternative Therapies', *The Forum*, **19**, pp. 7–8.

Benson, H. and Dusek, J.A. (1999), 'Self-Reported Health, Illness and the Use of Conventional and Unconventional Medicine and Mind/Body Healing by Christian Scientists and Others', *Journal of Nervous and Mental Disease*, **187** (9), pp. 539–48.

Benson, H. and Myers, P. (2000a), 'Medical Aspects of Belief', in *God for the 21st Century*, ed. R. Stannard (Radnor, PA: Templeton Foundation Press).

Benson, H. and Myers, P. (2000b), 'Mind/Body Medicine and Spirituality', in *Ten Scientists Consider Humility Theology*, ed. R. Hermann (Radnor, PA: Templeton Foundation Press).

Berman, J.C. (1995), 'The Surprising Lesson of My Own Illness', *Medical Economics*, **72** (19), pp. 113–5.

Berwick, P. and Oziel, L.J. (1973), 'The Use of Meditation as a Behavioural Technique (Letter)', *Behaviour Therapy*, **4** (5), pp. 743–5.

Besseghini, I. and Witterberg, S. (1977), 'The Effects of the Transcendental Meditation Program on the Exercise Performance of Patients with Angina Pectoris', *Scientific Research on Transcendental Meditation*, **1**, pp. 270–80.

Blackwell, B., Haneson, I.B. and Bloomfield, S. (1975), 'Effects of Transcendental Meditation on Blood Pressure: A Controlled Pilot Experiment', *Psychosomatic Medicine*, **37**, p. 86.

Blackwell, B., Haneson, I.B. and Bloomfield, S. (1976), 'Transcendental Meditation in Hypertension: Individual Response Patterns', *Lancet*, **1**, pp. 223–6.

Block, B. (1977), 'Transcendental Meditation as a Reciprocal Inhibitor in Psychotherapy', *Journal of Psychotherapy*, **9** (1), pp. 78–82.

Bloomfield, H., Cain, M.P., Jaffee, D.T. and Kory, R.B. (1975), *TM: Discovering the Inner Energy and Overcoming Stress* (New York: Dell Publishing Press).

Boals, G.F. (1978), 'Towards a Cognitive Reconceptualization of Meditation', *Journal of Transpersonal Psychology*, **10** (2), pp. 143–82.

Bogart, G. (1991), 'Meditation in Psychotherapy: A Review of the Literature', *American Journal of Psychotherapy*, **45**, pp. 383–412.

Borkovec, T.D. (1982), 'Insomnia', *Journal of Consulting and Clinical Psychology*, **50**, pp. 880–95.

Borkovec, T.D. and Bernstein, D.A. (1985), 'Forward to Relaxation Dynamics', in *Relaxation Dynamics: Nine World Approaches to Self-Relaxation*, ed. J.C. Smith (Champaign, IL: Research Press).

Borland, C. and Landrith, G. (1977), 'Improved Quality of City Life through the Transcendental Meditation Program: Decreased Crime Rate', in *Scientific Research on the Transcendental Meditation Program: Collected Papers*, ed. D.W. Orme-Johnson, and J.T. Farrow, Second edition (Weggis, Switzerland: Maharishi European Research University Press).

Bormann, J.E. (1996), 'Passage Meditation and the Use of a Mantram', *Beginnings*, **16** (5), p. 11.

Borysenko, J., with Larry Rothstein (1987), *Minding the Body, Mending the Mind* (Reading, MA: Addison-Wesley Pub. Co.).

Boswell, P. C. and Murray, E.J. (1979), 'Effects of Meditation on Psychological and Physiological Measures of Anxiety', *Journal of Consulting and Clinical Psychology*, **47**, pp. 606–7.

Boudreau, L. (1972), 'Transcendental Meditation and Yoga as Reciprocal Inhibitors', *Journal of Behavior Therapy and Experimental Psychiatry*, **3**, pp. 97–8.

Bradley, B. and McCanne, T. (1981), 'Autonomic Responses to Stress: The Effects of Progressive Relaxation, The Relaxation Response, and Expectancy of Relief', *Biofeedback and Self-Regulation*, **6**, pp. 235–51.

Brautigam, E. (1977), 'Effects of Transcendental Meditation Program on Drug Abusers: A Prospective Study', in *Scientific Research on the Transcendental Meditation Programs: Collected Papers*, ed. D.W. Orme-Johnson, and J.T. Farrow, Second edition (Weggis, Switzerland: Maharishi European Research University Press).

Britten, N., Wadsworth, M. and Fenwick, P. (1984), 'Stigma in Patients with Early Epilepsy: A National Longitudinal Study', *Journal of Epidemiology & Community Health*, **38** (4), pp. 291–5.

Brothers, L. (1998), Personal Communication.

Broussard, L.A. (1994), 'Meditation is a Useful Tool in Reducing Stress', *Knight-Ridder/Tribune News Service*, 6 May.

Brown, D.P. and Engler, J. (1980), 'The Stages of Mindfulness Meditation: A Validation Study', *Journal of Transpersonal Psychology*, **12** (2), pp. 143–92.

Brown, D.P., Forte, M., Rich, P. and Epstein, G. (1982), 'Phenomenological Differences among Self-Hypnosis, Mindfulness Meditation, and Imaging', *Imagination, Cognition, and Personality*, **2**, pp. 291–309.

Brown, D.P., Forte, M. and Dysart, M. (1984a), 'Differences in Visual Sensitivity among Mindfulness Meditators and Non-Meditators', *Perceptual & Motor Skills*, **58** (3), pp. 727–33.

Brown, D.P., Forte, M. and Dysart, M. (1984b), 'Visual Sensitivity and Mindfulness Meditation', *Perceptual & Motor Skills*, **58**, pp. 775–84.

Brown, D.P. (1977), 'A Model for the Levels of Concentrative Meditation', *International Journal of Clinical and Experimental Hypnosis*, **25** (4), pp. 236–73.

Burns, D.D. (1999 [1980]), *Feeling Good: The New Mood Therapy*, Revised and Updated Edition (New York: Avon Books).

'Can We Think About the Dow While Meditating', (1996). *Forbes Magazine (Supplement)*, **158** (12), p. 105.

Candelent, T. and Candelent, D. (1975), 'Teaching Transcendental Meditation in a Psychiatric Setting', *Hospital and Community Psychiatry*, **26**, pp. 156–9.

Carlin, P. and Lee, K. (1997), 'Treat the Body, Health the Mind', *Health*, **11** (1), pp. 72–8.

Carpenter, J.T. (1977), 'Meditation, Esoteric Traditions — Contributions to Psychotherapy', *American Journal of Psychotherapy*, **31** (3), pp. 393–404.

Carrington, P. (1977), *Freedom in Meditation* (New York: Doubleday).

Carrington, P. (1978), *Clinically Standardized Meditation: Instructor's Kit* (Laurel, MD: Pace Educational Systems).

Carrington, P. (1979), *Clinically Standardized Meditation: Instructor's Manual* (Laurel, MD: Pace Educational Press).

Carrington, P. (1984a), 'Modern Forms of Meditation', in *Principles and Practice of Stress Management*, R.L. Woolfolk, and P. M. Lehrer (New York: Guilford Press).

Carrington, P. (1984b), *Releasing* (New York: Doubleday).

Carrington, P. (1987), 'Managing Meditation in Clinical Practice', in *The Psychology of Meditation* (Oxford: Clarendon Press).

Carrington, P. and Ephron, H.S. (1975a), 'Meditation and Psychoanalysis', *Journal of the American Academy of Psychoanalysis*, **3**, pp. 43–57.

Carrington, P. and Ephron, H.S. (1975b), 'Meditation as an Adjunct to Psychotherapy', in *New Dimensions of Psychiatry: A World View*, ed. S. Arieti, and G. Chrzanowski, Volume 1 (New York: Wiley).

Carrington, P., Collings (Jr.), G.H., Benson, H., Robinson, H., Wood, L.W., Lehrer, P. M., Woolfolk, R.L. and Cole, J.W. (1980), 'The Use of Meditation-Relaxation Techniques for the Management of Stress in a Working Population', *Journal of Occupational Medicine*, **22**, pp. 222–31.

Caudill, M., Friedman, R. and Benson, H. (1987), 'Relaxation Therapy in the Control of Blood Pressure', *Bibliotheca Cardiologica*, **41**, pp. 106–19.

Caudill, M., Schnable, R., Zuttermeister, P., Benson, H. and Friedman, R. (1991), 'Decreased Clinic Utilization by Chronic Pain Patients: Response to Behavioral Medicine Intervention', *Clinical Journal of Pain*, **7**, pp. 305–10.

Cauthen, N.R. and Prymak, C.A. (1977), 'Meditation versus Relaxation: An Examination of the Psychological Effects of Relaxation Training and Different Levels of Experience with Transcendental Meditation', *Journal of Consulting and Clinical Psychology*, **45**, pp. 496–7.

Childre, D. (1996), *Freeze-Frame: Inner Fitness System* (Boulder Creek, CA: Planetary Publications).

Childre, D. and Cryer, B. (1998), *Freeze-Frame: One Minute Stress Management: A Scientifically Proven Technique for Clear Decision Making and Improved Health*, Second edition (Boulder Creek, CA: Planetary Publications).

Childs, J. (1974), 'The Use of the Transcendental Meditation Program as a Therapy with Juvenile Offenders', *Dissertation Abstracts International*, **34** (8-A, Pt. 1), pp. 4732–33.

Cho, Z.H., Chung, S.C., Jones, J.P., Park, J.B., Park, H.J., Lee, H.J., Wong, E.K. and Min, B.I. (1998), 'New Findings of the Correlation Between Acupoints and Corresponding Brain Cortices Using Functional MRI', *Proceedings of the National Academy of Sciences USA*, **95**, pp. 2670–3.

Chopra, D. (1985), *Creating Health: The Psychophysiological Connection* (New York: Vantage Books).

Chopra, D. (1987), *Creating Health: Beyond Prevention, Toward Perfection* (Boston: Houghton Mifflin).

Chopra, D. (1989), *Quantum Healing: Exploring the Frontiers of Mind/Body Medicine* (New York: Bantam Books).

Chopra, D. (1990), *Perfect Health: The Complete Mind/Body Guide* (New York: Harmony Books).

Chopra, D. (1991), *Creating Health: How to Wake Up the Body's Intelligence* (Boston: Houghton Mifflin).

Chopra, D. (1993), *Ageless Body, Timeless Mind: The Quantum Alternative to Growing Old* (New York: Harmony Books).

Chopra, D. (1994), *Journey Into Healing: Awakening the Wisdom Within You* (New York: Harmony Books).

Claxton, G.L. (1986), *Beyond Therapy: The Impact of Eastern Religions on Psychological Theory and Practice* (London: Wisdom Publications).

Cole, R. (1997), 'Meditation in Palliative Care — A Practiced Tool for Self-Management', *Palliative Medicine*, **11** (5), pp. 411–3.

Collura, J. and Kabat-Zinn, J. (1997), 'The Zen of Pain Control: Learning to Let Go of What Ails You', *Vegetarian Times*, **233**, pp. 28–30.

Cook, C.M. and Persinger, M.A. (1997), 'Experimental Induction of the 'Sensed Presence' in Normal Subjects and an Exceptional Subject', *Perceptual & Motor Skills*, **85** (2), pp. 683–93.

Cooper, R., Winter, A.L., Crow, H.J. and Walter, W.G. (1965), 'Comparison of Subcortical and Scalp Activity using Chronically Indwelling Electrodes in Man', *Electroencephalography and Clinical Neurophysiology*, **18**, pp. 217–28.

Corby, J.C. (1979), 'Ananda Marga Meditation: In Reply', *Archives of General Psychiatry*, **36** (5), p. 606.

Corby, J.C., Roth, W.T., Zarcone, J., V.P. and Kopell, B.S. (1978), 'Psychophysiological Correlates of the Practice of Tantric Yoga Meditation', *Archives of General Psychiatry*, **35** (5), pp. 571–7.

Corey, P.W. (1977), 'Airway Conductance and Oxygen Consumption Changes associated with Practice of the Transcendental Meditation Technique', in *Scientific Research on the Transcendental Meditation Program: Collected Papers*, ed. D.W. Orme-Johnson, and J.T. Farrow, Second edition (Weggis, Switzerland: Maharishi European Research University Press).

Cryer, P.E. (1980), 'Physiology and Pathophysiology of Human Sympathoadrenal Neuroendocrine System', *New England Journal of Medicine*, **303** (8), pp. 436–44.

Curtin, T.G. (1973), 'The Relationship between Transcendental Meditation and Adaptive Regression', *Dissertation Abstracts International*, **34** (4a), p. 1973.

Curtis, D.W. and Wessberg, H.W. (1975), 'A Comparison of Heart Rate, Respiration, and Galvanic Skin Response among Meditators, Relaxers, and Controls', *Journal of Altered States of Consciousness*, **2**, pp. 319–24.

Czaharyn, A.G. (1996), 'A Simple Form of Meditation for Use in Clinical Practice (Letter)', *American Family Physician*, **53** (8), pp. 2440–2.

Daniels, L.K. (1975), 'The Treatment of Psychophysiological Disorders and Severe Anxiety by Behavior Therapy, Hypnosis, and Transcendental Meditation', *American Journal of Clinical Hypnosis*, **17**, pp. 267–9.

Das, N.N. and Gastaut, H. (1955), 'Variations de l'Activité Électrique due Cerveau, Du Coeur et des Muscles Squelletiques au Cours de la Méditation et de l'Extase Yogique', *Electroencephalography and Clinical Neurophysiology*, **6** (Supplement), pp. 211–9.

Davidson, J. (1976), 'The Physiology of Meditation and Mystical States of Consciousness', *Perspectives in Biology and Medicine*, **19**, pp. 345–79.

Davidson, R.J. and Goleman, D.J. (1975), 'The Role of Attention in Meditation and Hypnosis: A Psychobiological Model of Transformations of Consciousness', Altered States of Consciousness and

Hypnosis: A Symposium Presented at the 27th Annual Meeting of the Society for Clinical and Experimental Hypnosis (Chicago).

Davidson, R.J. and Goleman, D.J. (1976), 'Attentional and Affective Concomitants of Medicine: A Cross-sectional Study', *Journal of Abnormal Psychology*, **85**, pp. 235–8.

Davidson, R.J., Goleman, D.J. and Schwartz, G.E. (1976), 'Attentional and Affective Concomitants of Meditation: A Cross-Sectional Study', *Journal of Abnormal Psychology*, **85**, pp. 235–8.

Davidson, R.J. and Schwartz, G.E. (1976), 'The Psychobiology of Relaxation and Related States: A Multi-Process Theory', in *Behavior Control and Modification of Physiological Activity*, ed. D.I. Mostofsky (Englewood Cliffs, NJ: Prentice-Hall).

Davidson, R.J., Goleman, D.J. and Schwartz, G.E. (1984), *Meditation: Classic and Contemporary Perspectives* (Wyoming: Aldine Publishing Company).

Davies, J. (1977), 'The Transcendental Meditation Program and Progressive Relaxation: Comparative Effects on Trait Anxiety and Self-Actualization', in *Scientific Research on the Transcendental Meditation Programs: Collected Papers*, ed. D.W. Orme-Johnson, and J.T. Farrow, Second edition (Weggis, Switzerland: Maharishi European Research University Press).

Deatherage, G. (1975), 'The Clinical Use of Mindfulness Meditation Techniques in Short-term Psychotherapy', *Journal of Transpersonal Psychology*, **7** (2), pp. 133–43.

deCharms, C. (1993), 'An Interchange between the Tibetan Understanding of Mind and the Western Science of Brain: Interview with His Holiness the XIVth Dalai Lama', *The Tibet Journal*, **18** (1), pp. 2–14.

Deikman, A.J. (1963), 'Experimental Meditation', *Journal of Nervous and Mental Disease*, **136** (3), pp. 329–43.

Deikman, A.J. (1966), 'De-automatization and the Mystic Experience', *Psychiatry: Journal for the Study of Interpersonal Processes*, **29** (4), pp. 324–38.

Deikman, A.J. (1969), 'Experimental Meditation', in *Altered States of Consciousness*, ed. C. Tart (New York: Doubleday).

Deikman, A.J. (1971), 'Bimodal Consciousness', *Archives of General Psychiatry*, **25**, pp. 481–9.

Deikman, A.J. (1982), *The Observing Self* (Boston: Beacon Press).

Delmonte, M.M. (1980), 'Personal Characteristics and Regularity of Meditation', *Psychological Reports*, **46**, pp. 703–12.

Delmonte, M.M. (1983), 'Some Cognitive Aspects of Meditation Practice', *Perceptual & Motor Skills*, **57** (3 Pt. 2), pp. 1160–2.

Delmonte, M.M. (1984a), 'Case Reports on the Use of Meditative Relaxation as an Intervention Strategy with Retarded Ejaculation', *Biofeedback & Self Regulation*, **9** (2), pp. 209–14.

Delmonte, M.M. (1984b), 'Electrocortical Activity and Related Phenomenon Associated with Meditation Practice: A Literature Review', *International Journal of Neuroscience*, **24**, pp. 217–31.

Delmonte, M.M. (1984c), 'Factors Influencing the Regularity of Meditation Practice in a Clinical Population', *British Journal of Medical Psychology*, **57** (Pt. 3), pp. 275–8.

Delmonte, M.M. (1984d), 'Meditation Practice as Related to Occupational Stress, Health and Productivity', *Perceptual & Motor Skills*, **59** (2), pp. 581–2.

Delmonte, M.M. (1984e), 'Meditation: Similarities with Hypnoidal States and Hypnosis', *International Journal of Psychosomatics*, **31** (3), pp. 24–34.

Delmonte, M.M. (1984f), 'Physiological Concomitants of Meditation Practice', *International Journal of Psychomatics*, **31** (4), pp. 23–36.

Delmonte, M.M. (1984g), 'Physiological Responses During Meditation and Rest', *Biofeedback & Self Regulation*, **9** (2), pp. 181–200.

Delmonte, M.M. (1984h), 'Psychometric Sources and Meditation Practice: A Literature Review', *Personality and Individual Differences*, **5** (5), pp. 559–63.

Delmonte, M.M. (1984i), 'Responses to Meditation in Terms of Physiological, Behavioral and Self-Report Measures', *International Journal of Psychosomatics*, **31** (2), pp. 3–17.

Delmonte, M.M. (1985a), 'Biochemical Indices Associated with Meditation Practice: A Literature Review', *Neuroscience & Biobehavioral Reviews*, **9** (4), pp. 557–61.

Delmonte, M.M. (1985b), 'Effects of Expectancy on Physiological Responsivity in Novice Meditators', *Biological Psychology*, **21** (2), pp. 107–21.

Delmonte, M.M. (1985c), 'Meditation and Anxiety Reduction: A Literature Review', *Clinical Psychology Review*, **5**, pp. 91–102.

Delmonte, M.M. (1985d), 'Response to Meditation in Terms of Physiological, Behavioural and Self-Report Measures: A Brief Summary', *Psychological Reports*, **56** (1), pp. 9–10.

Delmonte, M.M. (1986a), 'Expectancy and Response to Meditation', *International Journal of Psychosomatics*, **33** (2), pp. 28–34.

Delmonte, M.M. (1986b), 'Meditation as a Clinical Intervention Strategy: A Brief Review', *International Journal of Psychosomatics*, **33** (3), pp. 9–12.

Delmonte, M.M. (1987a), 'Constructivist View of Meditation', *American Journal of Psychotherapy*, **41**, pp. 286–98.

Delmonte, M.M. (1987b), 'Meditation: Contemporary Theoretical Approaches', in *The Psychology of Meditation*, ed. M.A. West (Oxford: Clarendon Press).

Delmonte, M.M. (1987c), 'Personality and Meditation', in *The Psychology of Meditation*, ed. M.A. West (Oxford: Clarendon Press).

Delmonte, M.M. (1988), 'Personality Correlates of Meditation Practice Frequency and Dropout in an Outpatient Population', *Journal of Behavioral Medicine*, **11** (6), pp. 593–7.

Delmonte, M.M. (1989), 'Meditation, the Unconscious, and Psychosomatic Disorders (Review)', *International Journal of Psychosomatics*, **36** (1–4), pp. 45–52.

Delmonte, M.M. and Kenny, V. (1985), 'Models of Meditation', *British Journal of Psychotherapy*, **1** (3), pp. 197–214.

Dhanaraj, V.J. and Singh, M. (1977), 'Reduction in Metabolic Rate during the Practice of the Transcendental Meditation Technique', in *Scientific Research on the Transcendental Meditation Programs: Collected Papers*, ed. D.W. Orme-Johnson, and J.T. Farrow, Second edition (Weggis, Switzerland: Maharishi European Research University Press).

Diamond, M. (1992), 'Re: A Patient's MRI Experience [letter]', *Journal of Otolaryngology*, **21** (4), p. 304.

Dice, M.L. (1979), 'The Effectiveness of Meditation on Selected Measures of Self-actualization', *Dissertation Abstracts International*, **40** (5A), p. 2534.

Dillbeck, M. (1977), 'The Effect of the Transcendental Meditation Technique on Anxiety Level', *Journal of Clinical Psychology*, **33**, pp. 1076–8.

Dillbeck, M. and Bronson, E. (1981), 'Short-term Longitudinal Effects of the Transcendental Meditation Technique on EEG Power and Coherence', *International Journal of Neuroscience*, **14**, pp. 147–51.

Dillbeck, M. and Orme-Johnson, D.W. (1987), 'Physiological Differences Between Transcendental Meditation and Rest', *American Psychologist*, **42** (9), pp. 879–81.

DiNardo, P. and Raymond, J. (1979), 'Locus of Control and Attention During Meditation', *Journal of Consulting and Clinical Psychology*, **47**, pp. 1136–7.

Domar, A.D., Noe, J.M., Ransil, B. and Benson, H. (1987), 'The Preoperative Use of the Relaxation Response with Ambulatory Surgery Patients', *Journal of Human Stress*, **13**, pp. 101–7.

Domar, A.D., Seibel, M. and Benson, H. (1990), 'The Mind/Body Program for Infertility: A New Behavioral Treatment Approach for Women with Infertility', *Fertility and Sterility*, **53**, pp. 246–9.

Domar, A.D. and Benson, H. (1993), 'Application of Behavioral Medicine Techniques to the Treatment of Infertility', in *Technology and Infertility: Clinical, Psychological, Legal and Ethical Aspects*, ed. M.M. Seibel, A.A. Kiessling, J. Bernstein, and S.R. Levin (New York: Springer-Verlag).

Domar, A.D., Friedman, R. and Benson, H. (1993), 'Behavior Therapy', in *Principles and Practice of Pain Management*, ed. C.A. Warfield (New York: McGraw-Hill).

D'Antoni, M.L., Harvey, P. L. and Fried, M.P. (1995), 'Alternative Medicine: Does it Play a Role in the Management of Voice Disorders?' *Journal of Voice*, **9** (3), pp. 308–11.

d'Aquili, E.G. and Laughlin Jr., C.D. (1975), 'The Biopsychological Determinants of Religious Ritual Behavior', *Zygon*, **10** (1), pp. 32–58.

d'Aquili, E.G. and Newberg, A.B. (1993a), 'Liminality, Trance, and Unitary States in Ritual and Meditation', *Studia Liturgica*, **23** (1), pp. 2–34.

d'Aquili, E.G. and Newberg, A.B. (1993b), 'Religious and Mystical States: A Neuropsychological Model', *Zygon*, **28** (2), pp. 177–99.

d'Aquili, E.G. and Newberg, A.B. (1998), 'The Neuropsychological Basis of Religion: Or Why God Won't Go Away', *Zygon*, **33** (2), pp. 187–201.

Earle, J.B. (1981), 'Cerebral Laterality and Meditation: A Review of the Literature', *Journal of Transpersonal Psychology*, **13**, pp. 155–73.

Ebert, D. (1988), *Physiologische Aspekte Des Yoga* (Leipzig: VEB Georg Thieme).

Edwards, M. (1997), 'Being Present: Experiential Connections between Zen Buddhist Practices and the Grieving Process', *Disability & Rehabilitation*, **19** (10), pp. 442–51.

Ehrlichman, H. and Wiener, M. (1980), 'EEG Asymmetry during Covert Mental Activity', *Psychophysiology*, **17**, pp. 228–35.

Eisenberg, D.M., Kessler, R.C., Foster, C., Norlock, F.E., Calkins, D.R. and DelBanco, T.L. (1993), 'Unconventional Medicine in the United States: Prevalence, Costs and Patterns of Use', *New England Journal of Medicine*, **328**, pp. 246–52.

Elbert, T. and Rockstroh, B. (1987), 'Threshold Regulation — A Key to the Understanding of the Combined Dynamics of EEG & Event-Related Potentials', *Journal of Psychophysiology*, **4**, pp. 317–33.

Elias, M. (1997), 'Clear Link Between the Head and Healing', in *USA Today*, 31 March.

Elson, B.D. (1979), 'Ananda Marga Meditation: Letter to the Editor', *Archives of General Psychiatry*, **36**, pp. 605–6.

Elson, B.D., Hauri, P. and Cunis, D. (1977), 'Physiological Changes in Yoga Meditation', *Psychophysiology*, **14** (1), pp. 52–7.

Engel, K. (1997), *Meditation*, Two volumes (New York: P. Lang).

Engler, J., 'Therapeutic Aims in Psychotherapy and Meditation', in *Transformations of Consciousness* (Boston: Shambala).

Epply, K.R., Abrams, A.I. and Shear, J. (1989), 'Differential Effects of Relaxation Techniques on Trait Anxiety', *Journal of Clinical Psychology*, **45** (6), pp. 957–42.

Epstein, M. (1986), 'Meditative Transformations of Narcissism', *The Journal of Transpersonal Psychology*, **18** (2), pp. 143–58.

Epstein, M.D. and Lieff, J.D. (1986), 'Psychiatric Complications of Meditation Practice', in *Transformations of Consciousness: Conventional and Contemplative Perspectives on Development*, ed. K. Wilber, J. Engler, and D.P. Brown (Boston: Shambala Publications Inc.).

Everly (Jr.), G.S. and Benson, H. (1989), 'Disorders of Arousal and the Relaxation Response: Speculations on the Nature and Treatment of Stress-related Diseases', *International Journal of Psychosomatics*, **36**, pp. 15–21.

Farrow, J.T. and Herbert, J.R. (1982), 'Breath Suspension during the Transcendental Meditation Technique', *Psychosomatic Medicine*, **44** (2), pp. 133–53.

Fehr, T.G. (1977), 'A Longitudinal Study of the Effect of the Transcendental Meditation Program on Changes in Personality', in *Scientific Research on the Transcendental Meditation Program: Collected Papers*, ed. D.W. Orme-Johnson, and J.T. Farrow, Second edition (Weggis, Switzerland: Maharishi European Research University Press).

Fehr, T.G. (1996), 'Therapeutische relevante Effekte durch transzendentale Meditation? (Therapeutically Relevant Effects of Transcendental Meditation?) (German)', *Psychotherapie, Psychosomatik, Medizinische Psychologie*, **46** (5), pp. 178–88.

Fentress, D.W., Masek, B.J., Mehegan, J.E. and Benson, H. (1986), 'Biofeedback and Relaxation-Response Training in the Treatment of Pediatric Migraine', *Developmental Medicine and Child Neurology*, **28**, pp. 139–46.

Fenwick, P. (1974), 'Metabolic and EEG Changes during Transcendental Meditation', *Psychophysiology Group Newsletter*, **1**, pp. 24–5.

Fenwick, P. (1983), 'Can We Still Recommend Meditation? (Editorial)', *British Medical Journal (Clinical Research Edition)*, **287** (6403), p. 1401.

Fenwick, P. (1987), 'Meditation and the EEG', in *The Psychology of Meditation*, ed. M.W. West (Oxford: Clarendon Press).

Fenwick, P., Donaldson, S., Gillis, L., Bushman, J., Fenton, G.W., Perry, I., Tilsley, C. and Serafinowicz, H. (1977), 'Metabolic and EEG Changes during Transcendental Meditation: An Explanation', *Biological Psychology*, **5** (2), pp. 101–18.

Fenwick, P., Gallino, S., Coate, M., Ripere, V. and Brown, D. (1985), 'Psychic Sensitivity, Mystical Experience, Head Injury, and Brain Pathology', *Journal of Medical Psychology*, **58**, pp. 35–44.

Ferguson, P. (1980), 'An Integrative Meta-Analysis of Psychological Studies Investigating the Treatment Outcomes of Meditation Studies', *Dissertation Abstracts International*, **42** (4-A), p. 1547.

Ferrari, M. (1998), 'Begin and Becoming Self-Aware', in *Self-Awareness — Its Nature and Development*, ed. M. Ferrari, and R.J. Sternberg (New York: Guilford Press).

Fischer, R. (1971), 'A Cartography of the Ecstatic and Meditative States: The Experimental and Experiential Feature of a Perception–Hallucination Continuum are Considered', *Science*, **174**.

Fischer, R. (1972), 'On Creative, Psychotic and Ecstatic States', in *The Highest State of Consciousness*, ed. J. White (Garden City, NY: Doubleday & Company).

Fischer, R. (1975), 'Cartography of Inner Space', in *Hallucinations, Behavior, Experience, and Theory*, ed. R. Siegel, and L. West (New York: Wiley).

Forman, R.K.C. (ed. 1990), *The Problem of Pure Consciousness: Mysticism and Philosophy* (New York: Oxford University Press).

Forman, R.K.C. (ed. 1998), *The Innate Capacity: Mysticism, Psychology, and Philosophy* (New York: Oxford University Press).

Freeman, W. and Skarda, C. (1985), 'Spatial EEG Patterns, Non-Linear Dynamics and Perception: The Neo-Sherrington View', *Brain Research Reviews*, **10** (3), pp. 147–75.

Freemon, F.R. (1972), *Sleep Research* (Springfield, IL: Charles C. Thomas).

Friedman, M. (1994), 'A Tide that Cannot be Stopped: Deepak Chopra's Mind–Body Medicine is a Hit with the Masses', *Vegetarian Times*, **203**, p. 112.

Friedman, R., Stuart, E.M. and Benson, H. (1992), 'Essential Hypertension: Nonpharmacologic Adjuncts to Therapy', in *Current Management of Hypertensive and Vascular Diseases*, ed. J.P. Cooke, and E.D. Frohlich (St. Louis: Mosby–Year Book).

Friedman, R., Zuttermeister, T. and Benson, H. (1993), 'Letter to the Editor', *New England Journal of Medicine*, **329**, p. 1201.

Friedman, R. and Benson, H. (1994), 'Behavioral Medicine: A Retrospective and a Look Forward', *Behavioral Medicine*, **19**, pp. 143–4.

Friedman, R., Vasile, R.G., Gallagher, R.M. and Benson, H. (1994), 'Behavioral-medicine and Psychiatry: Difference and Areas of Collaboration', *Directions in Psychiatry*, **14**, pp. 1–8.

Friedman, R., Sobel, D., Myers, P., Caudill, M. and Benson, H. (1995), 'Behavioral Medicine, Health Psychology and Cost Offset', *Health Psychology*, **14**, pp. 509–18.

Friedman, R. and Benson, H. (1996), 'Mind/Body Medicine and Diversity', *Mind–Body Medicine*.

Friedman, R., Steinman, M. and Benson, H. (1996), 'The Relaxation Response: Physiological Effects and Medical Applications', in *Comparative and Psychological Studies on Meditation*, ed. Y. Haruki (Tokyo: Waseda University Press).

Friedman, R., Myers, P., Krass, S. and Benson, H. (1996), 'The Relaxation Response: Use with Cardiac Patients', in *Heart and Mind: The Practice of Cardiac Psychology*, ed. R. Allen, and S. Scheidt (Washington: American Psychological Association Press).

Friedman, R., Sedler, M., Myers, P. and Benson, H. (1997), 'Behavioral Medicine, Complementary Medicine and Integrated Care: Economic Implications', in *Primary Care*, ed. J. Randall, and J. Lazar (Philadelphia: W.B. Saunders).

Friedman, R. and Benson, H. (1997), 'Spirituality, Religious Practice and Medical Outcomes', *Mind–Body Medicine*, 2, p. 87.

Friedman, R., Myers, P. and Benson, H. (1998), 'Meditation and the Relaxation Response', in *Encyclopedia of Mental Health*, ed. H.S. Friedman (San Diego: Academic Press).

Friedman, R., Myers, P. and Benson, H. (1999), 'Relaxation Response', in *Illustrated Encyclopedia of Body–Mind Disciplines*, ed. N. Allison (New York: Rosen Publishing Group).

Gawler, I. (1987), *Peace of Mind: How You Can Learn to Meditate and Use the Power of Your Mind* (Cincinnati, OH: Hill of Content Publishing).

Gawler, I. (1996), *Meditation: Pure and Simple* (Cincinnati, OH: Hill of Content Publishing).

Gellhorn, E. (1970), 'The Emotions and the Ergotropic and Trophotropic Systems', *Psycholische Forschung*, 34, pp. 48–94.

Gellhorn, E. and Kiely, W.F. (1972), 'Mystical States of Consciousness: Neurophysiological and Clinical Aspects', *Journal of Nervous and Mental Disease*, 154 (6), pp. 399–405.

Gentry, W.D., Benson, H. and De Wolff, C.J. (eds 1986), *Behavioral Medicine: Work, Stress and Health*, NATO Advanced Science Institutes Series D: Behavioral and Social Sciences, No. 19 (Dordrecht: Martinus Nijhoff).

Ghista, D.N., Nandagopal, D., Ramamurthi, B., Dasa, M.A. and Srinivasam T.M. (1976), 'Physiological Characterization of the 'Meditative State' during Practice (the Ananda Marga System of Meditation) and its Therapeutic Value', *Medical and Biological Engineering*, 13, pp. 209–14.

Girodo, M. (1974), 'Yoga Meditation and Flooding in the Treatment of Anxiety Neurosis', *Journal of Behavior Therapy and Experimental Psychiatry*, 5, pp. 157–60.

Glueck, B.C. and Stroebel, C. (1975), 'Biofeedback and Meditation in the Treatment of Psychiatric Illness', *Comprehensive Psychiatry*, 16, pp. 303–21.

Goleman, B.L., Doitor, P. J. and Murray, E.J. (1979), 'Effects of Zen Meditation on Anxiety Reduction and Perceptual Functioning', *Journal of Consulting and Clinical Psychology*, 47, pp. 551–6.

Goleman, D.J. (ed. 1997), *Healing Emotions: Conversations with the Dalai Lama on Mindfulness, Emotions, and Health* (Boston: Shambhala Publications).

Goleman, D.J. (1971), 'Meditation as Meta-Therapy: Hypotheses Toward a Proposed Fifth State of Consciousness', *Journal of Transpersonal Psychology*, 3, pp. 1–25.

Goleman, D.J. (1996), *The Meditative Mind* (London: Thorsons).

Goleman, D.J. and Gurin, J. (ed. 1993), *Mind, Body Medicine: How to Use Your Mind for Better Health* (Yonkers, NY: Consumer Reports Books).

Goleman, D.J. and Schwarz, G.E. (1976), 'Meditation as an Intervention in Stress Reactivity', *Journal of Consulting and Clinical Psychology*, 44, pp. 456–66.

Goodale, I.L., Domar, A.D. and Benson, H. (1990), 'Alleviation of Premenstrual Syndrome Symptoms with the Relaxation Response', *Obstetrics and Gynecology*, 75, pp. 649–55.

Gordon, J.S. (1996), *Manifesto for a New Medicine: Your Guide to Healing Partnerships and the Wise Use of Alternative Therapies* (Reading, MA: Addison-Wesley).

Govinda, L.A. (1972), 'The Ecstasy of Breaking Through in the Experience of Meditation', in *The Highest State of Consciousness*, ed. J. White (Garden City, NY: Doubleday).

Greenwood, M.M. and Benson, H. (1977), 'The Efficacy of Progressive Relaxation in Systematic Desensitization and a Proposal for an Alternative Competitive Response — The Relaxation Response', *Behavior Research and Therapy*, 15 (4), pp. 337–43.

Griffith, F. (1985 [1974]), 'Meditation Research: Its Personal and Social Implications', in *Frontiers of Consciousness*, ed. J. White (New York: Julian Press).

Gross, S. (1994), 'Surviving Cancer: Mind & Body', *New Orleans Magazine*, 29 (1), pp. 62–7.

Guidano, V.F. and Liotti, G. (1983), *Cognitive Processes and Emotional Disorders: A Structural Approach to Psychotherapy* (New York: The Guilford Press).

Gussner, R.E. (1987), 'Joining Asian-Based Meditation Groups: A Report on Some Survey Frequencies, Mean Scores and Weighted Points', Unpublished Paper (University of Vermont).

Gussner, R.E. and Berkowitz, S.D. (1988), 'Scholars, Sects and Sanghas, I: Recruitment to Asian-Based Meditation Groups in North America', *Sociological Analysis*, 49 (2), pp. 136–70.

Hafner, R.J. (1982), 'Psychological Treatment of Essential Hypertension: A Controlled Comparison of Meditation and Meditation Plus Biofeedback', *Biofeedback and Self-Regulation*, 7, pp. 305–16.

Halgren, E., Walter, R.D., Cherlow, D.G. and Crandall, P. H. (1978), 'Mental Phenomena Evoked by Electrical Stimulation of the Human Hippocampal Formation and Amygdala', *Brain*, 101 (1), pp. 83–117.

Hassed, C. (1996), 'Meditation in General Practice', *Australian Family Physician*, 25 (8), pp. 1257–60.

Haynes, C.T., Herbert, J.R., Reber, W. and Orme-Johnson, D.W. (1977), 'The Psychophysiology of Advanced Participants in the Transcendental Meditation Programme: Correlations of EEG Coherence, Creativity, H-Reflex Recovery, and Experience of Transcendental Consciousness', in *Scientific Research on the Transcendental Meditation Program: Collected Papers*, ed. D.W. Orme-Johnson, and J.T. Farrow, Second edition (Weggis, Switzerland: Maharishi European Research University Press).

Hayward, J. and Varela, F.J. (ed. 1992), *Gentle Bridges: Conversations with the Dalai Lama on the Sciences of Mind* (Boston: Shambhala Publications).

Heiss, W.D., Herholz, K., Pawlik, G., Wagner, R. and Weinhard, K. (1986), 'Positron Emission Tomography in Neuropsychology', in *Methods in Neuropsychology*, ed. M.A. Jeeves, and G. Baumgartner (Oxford: Pergamon Press).

Hellman, C.J.C., Budd, M., Borysenko, J., McClelland, D.C. and Benson, H. (1990), 'A Study of the Effectiveness of Two Group Behavioral Medicine Interventions for Patients with Psychosomatic Complaints', *Behavioral Medicine*, **16**, pp. 165–73.

Herbert, R. and Lehmann, D. (1977), 'Theta Bursts: An EEG Pattern in Normal Subjects Practicing the Transcendental Meditation Technique', *Electroencephalography and Clinical Neurophysiology*, **42**, pp. 397–405.

Herod, E.L. (1995), 'Psychophysical Pain Control During Tooth Extraction', *General Dentistry*, **43** (3), pp. 267–9.

Herron, R., Schneider, R.H., Mandarino, J.V., Alexander, C.N. and Walton, K.G. (1996), 'Cost-effective Hypertension Management: Comparison of Drug Therapies with an Alternative Program', *American Journal of Managed Care*, **2** (4), pp. 427–37.

Herzog, H., Lele, V.R., Kuwert, T., Langen, K.-J., Kops, E.R. and Feinendegen, L.E. (1990–91), 'Changed Pattern of Regional Glucose Metabolism during Yoga Meditative Relaxation', *Neuropsychobiology*, **23**, pp. 182–7.

Hess, W.R. (1925), *On the Relations Between Psychic and Vegetative Functions* (Zurich: Schwabe).

Hirai, T. (1974), *Psychophysiology of Zen* (Tokyo: Igaku Shoin).

Hirai, T. (1975), *Zen: Meditation Therapy* (Tokyo: Goma Shobo).

Hjelle, L.A. (1974), 'Transcendental Meditation and Psychological Health', *Perceptual & Motor Skills*, **39**, pp. 623–8.

Hoffman, J.W., Benson, H., Arns, P. A., Stainbrook, G.L., Landsberg, L., Young, J.B. and Gill, A. (1982), 'Reduced Sympathetic Nervous System Responsivity Associated with the Relaxation Response', *Science*, **215** (4529), pp. 190–2.

Holmes, D.S. (1984), 'Meditation and Somatic Arousal Reduction: A Review of the Experimental Evidence', *American Psychologist*, **39**, pp. 1–10.

Holmes, D.S. (1987), 'The Influence of Meditation Versus Rest on Physiological Arousal: A Second Examination', in *The Psychology of Meditation*, ed. M.A. West (Oxford: Clarendon Press).

Holmes, D.S., Solomon, S., Cappo, B.M. and Greenberg, J.L. (1983), 'Effects of Transcendental Meditation Versus Resting on Physiological and Subjective Arousal', *Journal of Personality and Social Psychology*, **44** (6), pp. 1245–52.

Honsberger, R.W. and Wilson, A.F. (1973), 'Transcendental Meditation in Treating Asthma', *Respiratory Therapy: Journal of Inhalation Technology*, **3**, pp. 79–81.

Hood (Jr), R.W. and Morris, R.J. (1981), 'Sensory Isolation and the Differential Elicitation of Religious Imagery in Intrisic and Extrinsic Persons', *Journal for the Scientific Study of Religion*, **20**, pp. 261–73.

Ikegami, R. (1973), 'Psychological Study of Zen Posture', in *Psychological Studies on Zen*, ed. Y. Akishinge (Tokyo: Zen Institute of Komazawa University).

Istratov, E.N., Liubimov, N.N. and Orlova, T.V. (1996), 'Dinamicheskie osobennosti modifitsirovannogo sostoianiia soznaniia pri transtsendental'noi meditatsii (Dynamic Features of the Modified State of Consciousness during Transcendental Meditation) (Russian)', *Biulleten Eksperimentalnoi Biologii i Meditsiny*, **121** (2), pp. 128–30.

Jacobs, G.D. and Lubar, J.F. (1989), 'Spectral Analyses of the Central Nervous System Effects of the Relaxation Response Elicited by Autogenic Training', *Behavioral Medicine*, **15**, pp. 125–32.

Jacobs, G.D., Benson, H. and Friedman, R. (1993), 'Home-based Central Nervous System Assessment of a Multifactor Behavioral Intervention for Chronic Sleep-Onset Insomnia', *Behavior Therapy*, **24**, pp. 159–74.

Jacobs, G.D., Rosenberg, P. A., Friedman, R., Matheson, J., Guerry, P. M., Domar, A.D. and Benson, H. (1993), 'Multifactor Behavioral Treatment of Chronic Sleep-onset Insomnia using Stimulus Control and the Relaxation Response: A Preliminary Study', *Behavior Modification*, **17**, pp. 498–509.

Jacobs, G.D., Benson, H. and Friedman, R. (1996), 'Topographic EEG Mapping of the Relaxation Response', *Biofeedback and Self-Regulation*, **21** (2), pp. 121–9.

Janby, J. (1977), 'Immediate Effects of the Transcendental Meditation Technique: Increased Skin Resistance during the First Meditation after Instruction', in *Scientific Research on the Transcendental Meditation Program: Collected Papers*, ed. D.W. Orme-Johnson, and J.T. Farrow, Second edition (Weggis, Switzerland: Maharishi European Research University Press).

Jevning, R., Wilson, A.F. and VanderLaan, E.F. (1978), 'Plasma Prolactin and Growth Hormone during Meditation', *Psychosomatic Medicine*, **40**, pp. 329–33.

Jevning, R., Wilson, A.F., Smith, W.R. and Morton, M.E. (1978), 'Redistribution of Blood Flow in Acute Hypometabolic Behavior', *American Journal of Physiology*, **235**, pp. R89–92.

Jevning, R., Wallace, R. and Beidebach, M. (1992), 'The Physiology of Meditation: A Review. A Wakeful Hypometabolic Integrated Response', *Neuroscience and Biobehavioural Reviews*, **16**, pp. 415–24.

Jevning, R., Anand, R., Biedebach, M. and Fernando, G. (1996), 'Effects on Regional Cerebral Blood Flow of Transcendental Meditation', *Physiology & Behavior*, **59** (3), pp. 399–402.

Johnson, S.S. and White, G. (1971), 'Self-Observation as an Agent of Behavioral Change', *Behavior Therapy*, **2**, pp. 488–97.

Jones, D.G. (1980), *Our Fragile Brains: A Christian Perspective on Brain Research* (Downers Grove, IL: Inter-Varsity Press).

Joshi, B. (1984), 'Neurology in Ancient India — Some Evidences', *Indian Journal of History of Science*, **19** (4), pp. 366–96.

Jung, C.G. (1943), *Collected Works*, Vol. 11: *The Psychology of Eastern Meditation* (Princeton, NJ: Princeton University Press).

Kabat-Zinn, J. (1990), *Full Catastrophe Living: Using the Wisdom of Your Body and Mind to Face Stress, Pain, and Illness* (New York: Delacorte Press).

Kabat-Zinn, J. (1982), 'An Out-patient Program in Behavioral Medicine for Chronic Pain Patients Based on the Practice of Mindfulness Meditation: Theoretical Considerations and Preliminary Results', *General Hospital Psychiatry*, **4**, pp. 33–47.

Kabat-Zinn, J., Lipworth, L. and Burney, R. (1985), 'The Clinical Use of Mindfulness Meditation for the Self-regulation of Chronic Pain', *Journal of Behavioral Medicine*, **8**, pp. 163–90.

Kamen, R. (1978), 'Biofeedback and Meditation Effects Muscle Tension and Locus of Control', *Perceptual & Motor Skills*, **46**, pp. 955–8.

Kanas, N. and Horowitz, M.J. (1977), 'Reactions of Transcendental Meditators and Non-Meditators to Stress Films: A Comparative Study', *Archives of General Psychiatry*, **34** (12), pp. 1431–6.

Kanellakos, D. and Lukas, J. (eds 1974), *The Psychobiology of Transcendental Meditation* (Menlo Park, CA: Benjamin Publishing Co.).

Kaplan, K.H., Goldenberg, D.L. and Galvin-Nadeu, M. (1993), 'The Impact of a Meditation-Based Stress Reduction Program on Fibromyalgia', *General Hospital Pyschiatry*, **15**, pp. 284–9.

Kaplan, S. (1978), 'An Appraisal of a Psychological Approach to Meditation', *Zygon*, **13** (1), pp. 83–101.

Kasamatsu, A., Okuma, T., Takenaka, S., Koga, S. and Ikeda, K. (1957), 'The EEG of "Zen" and "Yoga" Practitioners', *Electroencephalography and Clinical Neurophysiology*, **9**, pp. 51–2.

Kasamatsu, A. and Hirai, T. (1966), 'An Electroencephalographic Study on the Zen Meditation (Zazen)', *Folia Psychiat. Neurologica Japonica*, **20**, pp. 315–36.

Kasamatsu, A. and Hirai, T. (1969a), 'An Electroencephalographic Study on the Zen Meditation (Zazen)', *Psychologia*, **12**, pp. 205–25.

Kasamatsu, A. and Hirai, T. (1969b), 'An Electroencephalographic Study on the Zen Meditation (Zazen)', in *Altered States of Consciousness*, ed. C. Tart (Garden City, NY: Andin Books).

Kase, L.M. (1997), *American Health for Women*, **16** (7), pp. 72–6.

Kass, J.D., Friedman, R., Leserman, J., Zuttermeister, P. C. and Benson, H. (1991), 'Health Outcome and a New Index of Spiritual Experience', *Journal for the Scientific Study of Religion*, **30**, pp. 203–11.

Keefe, T. (1975), 'Meditation and the Psychotherapist', *American Journal of Orthopsychiatry*, **45**, pp. 484–48.

Keegan, L. and Cerrato, P. L. (1996), 'Nurses are Embracing Holistic Healting', *RN*, **59** (4), pp. 59–60.

Kiefer, D. (1972), 'Meditation and Biofeedback', in *The Highest State of Consciousness*, ed. J. White (Garden City, NY: Doubleday & Company).

Kiefer, D. (1985), 'EEG Alpha Feedback and Subjective States of Consciousness: A Subject's Introspective Overview', in *Frontiers of Consciousness*, ed. J. White (New York: Julian Press).

Kiely, W. (1974), 'Critique of Mystical States: A Reply', *Journal of Nervous and Mental Disease*, **159**, pp. 196–7.

Kinsman, R.A. and Staudenmayer, H. (1978), 'Baseline Levels in Muscle Relaxation Training', *Biofeedback and Self-Regulation*, **3**, pp. 97–104.

Kirsch, I. and Henry, D. (1979), 'Self-Desensitization and Meditation in the Reduction of Public Speaking Anxiety', *Journal of Consulting and Clinical Psychology*, **47**, pp. 536–41.

Kjaer, T.W., Lou, H.C., Nowak, M., Wildschiodtz, G. and Friberg, L. (1997), 'Brain Activation during Normal Consciousness', The Brain and Self Workshop: Toward A Science of Consciousness, *Consciousness Research Abstracts: A Service of the Journal of Consciousness Studies*, 21–24 August, Elsinore, Denmark, pp. 55–6 (Thorverton: Imprint Academic).

Klajner, F., Hartman, L.M. and Sobell, M.B. (1984), 'Treatment of Substance Abuse by Relaxation Training: A Review of the Literature', *Addictive Behaviors*, **9**, pp. 41–55.

Klemons, I.M. (1977), 'Changes in Inflammation in Persons Practicing the Transcendental Meditation Technique', in *Scientific Research on the Transcendental Meditation Program: Collected Papers*, ed. D.W. Orme-Johnson, and J.T. Farrow, Second edition (Weggis, Switzerland: Maharishi European Research University Press).

Kohr, R.L. (1978), 'Changes in Subjective Meditation Experience during a Short-term Project', *Journal of Altered States of Consciousness*, **3** (3), pp. 221–34.

Kong sprul Blo gros mtha' yas', 'Jam mgon (1813–1899) (1971), *Gdams Ngag Mdzod: A Treasury of Instructions and Techniques for Spiritual Realization* (Delhi: N. Lungtok and N. Gyaltsan).

Kornfield, J. (1979), 'Intensive Insight Meditation: A Phenomenological Study', *Journal of Transpersonal Psychology*, **11**, pp. 41–58.

Kornfield, J. (1989), 'Even the Best Meditators Have Old Wounds to Heal', *Yoga Journal*, **88** (46).

Kosslyn, S.M. (1988), 'Aspects of a Cognitive Neuroscience of Mental Imagery', *Science*, **240**, pp. 1621–6.

Kosslyn, S.M. (1994), *Image and the Brain: The Resolution of the Imagery Debate* (Cambridge, MA: The MIT Press).

Kosslyn, S.M. (1995), 'Mental Imagery', in *An Invitation to Cognitive Science: Visual Cognition*, ed. S.M. Kosslyn, and D. Osherson, Volume 2 (Cambridge: The MIT Press).

Kosslyn, S.M. and Koenig, O. (1992), *Wet Mind: The New Cognitive Neuroscience* (New York: Free Press).

Kretschmer, W. (1962), 'Meditative Techniques in Psychotherapy', *Psychologia*, **5**, pp. 76–83.

Kripalvanandji, S. (1977), *Science of Meditation* (Kayavarohan, India: Sri Kayavarohan Tirth Seva Samaj).

Kutz, I., Caudill, M. and Benson, H. (1983), 'The Role of Relaxation in Behavioral Therapies of Chronic Pain', in *Pain Management*, ed. J.M. Stein, and C.A. Warfield (Boston: Little Brown).

Kutz, I., Borysenko, J.Z. and Benson, H. (1985), 'Meditation and Psychotherapy: A Rationale for the Integration of Dynamic Psychotherapy, the Relaxation Response and Mindfulness Meditation', *American Journal of Psychiatry*, **142**, pp. 1–8.

Kutz, I., Lessermen, J., Dorrington, C., Morrison, C.H., Borysenko, J. and Benson, H. (1985), 'Meditation as an Adjunct to Psychotherapy: An Outcome Study', *Psychotherapy Psychosomatics*, **43**, pp. 209–18.

Laborde, K. (1997), 'A Mantra for All Seasons: Thinking about Meditation', *New Orleans Magazine*, **31** (10), pp. 69–70.

Lakoff, G. and Johnson, M. (1999), *Philosophy in the Flesh: The Embodied Mind and Its Challenge to Western Thought* (New York: Basic Books).

Lancaster, B.L. (1993), 'Self or No-Self? Converging Perspectives from Neuropsychology and Mysticism', *Zygon*, **28** (4), pp. 507–26.

Lang, R., Dehob, K., Meurer, K. and Kauff, W. (1979), 'Sympathetic Activity and Transcendental Meditation', *Journal of Neural Transmission*, **44**, pp. 117–35.

Laughlin (Jr.), C.D., McManus, J. and d'Aquili, E.G. (1993), 'Mature Contemplation', *Zygon*, **28** (2), pp. 133–76.

Laurie, G. (1977), 'An Investigation into the Changes in Skin Resistance during the Transcendental Meditation Technique', in *Scientific Research on the Transcendental Meditation Program: Collected Papers*, ed. D.W. Orme-Johnson, and J.T. Farrow, Second edition (Weggis, Switzerland: Maharishi European Research University Press).

Lavallee, M.R. and Persinger, M.A. (1992), 'Left Ear (Right Temporal Lobe) Suppressions during Dichotic Listening, Ego-Alien Intrusion Experiences and Spiritualistic Beliefs in Normal Women', *Perceptual & Motor Skills*, **75** (2), pp. 547–51.

Lazar, S.W., Bush, G., Fricchione, G., Gollub, R.L., Khalsa, G. and Benson, H. (1999), 'Functional Brain Mapping of the Relaxation Response using 3T fMRI', *Society for Neuroscience Abstracts*, **11** (7), pp. 1581–5.

Lazar, Z., Farwell, L. and Farrow, J.T. (1977), 'Effects of Transcendental Meditation Program on Anxiety, Drug Abuse, Cigarette Smoking and Alcohol Consumption', in *Scientific Research on the Transcendental Meditation Program: Collected Papers*, ed. D.W. Orme-Johnson, and J.T. Farrow, Second edition (Weggis, Switzerland: Maharishi European Research University Press).

Lazarus, A. (1976), 'Psychiatric Problems Precipitated by Transcendental Meditation', *Psychological Reports*, **39**, pp. 601–2.

Lee, M.S., Bae, B.H., Ryu, H., Sohn, J.H., Kim, S.Y. and Chung, H.T. (1997), 'Changes in Alpha Wave and State Anxiety during ChunDoSunBup Qi-training in Trainees with Open Eyes', *American Journal of Chinese Medicine*, **25** (3–4), pp. 289–99.

Lehmann, J.W. and Benson, H. (1982), 'Nonpharmacologic Therapy of Blood Pressure', *General Hospital Psychiatry*, **4**, pp. 27–32.

Lehmann, J.W. and Benson, H. (1983), 'The Behavioral Treatment of Hypertension', in *Hypertension: Physiopathology and Treatment*, ed. J. Genest, O. Kuchel, P. Hamet, and M. Cantin (New York: McGraw-Hill).

Leserman, J., Stuart, E.M., Mamish, M.E. and Benson, H. (1989), 'The Efficacy of the Relaxation Response in Preparing for Cardiac Surgery', *Behavioral Medicine*, **5**, pp. 111–7.

Leserman, J., Stuart, E.M., Mamish, M.E., Deckro, J.P., Beckam, R.J., Friedman, R. and Benson, H. (1989), 'Nonpharmacologic Intervention for Hypertension: Long-term Follow-up', *Journal of Cardiopulmonary Rehabilitation*, **9**, pp. 316–24.

Lesh, T.V. (1970), 'Zen Meditation and the Development of Empathy in Counselors', *Journal of Humanistic Psychology*, **10**, pp. 39–74.

Levander, V.L., Benson, H., Wheeler, R.C. and Wallace, R.K. (1972), 'Increased Forearm Blood Flow During a Wakeful Hypometabolic State', *Federation Proceedings*, **31**, p. 405.

Linden, W. (1971), 'Practicing of Meditation by School Children and Their Levels of Fields Dependence–Independence, Test Anxiety, and Reading Achievement', *Journal of Consulting and Clinical Psychology*, **41**, pp. 139–43.

Lintel, A.G. (1980), 'Physiological Anxiety Responses in Transcendental Meditators and Non-Meditators', *Perceptual & Motor Skills*, **50**, pp. 295–300.

Ludwig, A.M. (1966), 'Altered States of Consciousness', *Archives of General Psychiatry*, **15**, pp. 225–34.

Lukins, R., Davan, I.G. and Drummond, P. D. (1997), 'A Cognitive Behavioural Approach to Preventing Anxiety during Magnetic Resonance Imaging', *Journal of Behavior Therapy & Experimental Psychiatry*, **28** (2), pp. 97–104.

Lukoff, D., Lu, F.G. and Turner, R. (1995), 'A Randomized Controlled Trial of Stress Reduction for Hypertension in Older African Americans', *Hypertension*, **26** (5), pp. 820–7.

MacLean, C.R., Walton, K.G., Wenneberg, S.R., Levitsky, D.K., Mandarino, J.P., Waxiri, R., Hillis, S.L. and Schneider, R.H. (1997), 'Effects of the Transcendental Meditation Program on Adaptive Mechanisms: Changes in Hormone Levels and Responses to Stress after 4 Months of Practice', *Psychoneuroendocrinology*, **22** (4), pp. 277–95.

Main, J. (1979), *Meditation, The Christian Experience* (Montreal: Benedictine Community of Montreal).

Makarec, K. and Persinger, M.A. (1985), 'Temporal Lobe Signs: Electroencephalographic Validity and Enhanced Scores in Special Populations', *Perceptual & Motor Skills*, **60** (3), pp. 831–42.

Mandle, C.L., Domar, A.D., Harrington, D.P., Leserman, J., Bozadjian, E., Friedman, R. and Benson, H. (1990), 'The Relaxation Response in Femoral Arteriography', *Radiology*, **174**, pp. 737–9.

Markand, O.N. (1990), 'Alpha Rhythms', *Journal of Clinical Neurophysiology*, **7**, pp. 163–89.

Marlatt, C.A. and Pagano, R.R. (1984), 'Effects of Meditation and Relaxation Training upon Alcohol Use in Male Social Drinkers', in *Meditation: Classic and Contemporary Perspectives*, ed. J. Shapiro, Deane H. and R.N. Walsh (New York: Aldine Publishing Co.).

Marzetta, B.R., Benson, H. and Wallace, R.K. (1972), 'Combatting Drug Dependency in Young People: A New Approach', *Counterpoint*, **4**, pp. 13–36.

Mason, L.I., Alexander, C.N., Travis, F.T., Marsh, G., Orme-Johnson, D.W., Gackenbach, J., Mason, D.C., Rainforth, M. and Walton, K.G. (1997), 'Electrophysiological Correlates of Higher States of Consciousness during Sleep in Long-term Practitioners of Transcendental Meditation Program', *Sleep*, **20a** (2), pp. 102–10.

Maupin, E.W. (1965), 'Individual Differences in Response to a Zen Meditation Exercise', *Journal of Consulting Pyschology*, **29**, pp. 139–45.

McCuaig, L. (1974), 'Salivary Electrolytes, Protein, and PH during Transcendental Meditation', *Experimentia*, **30**, pp. 998–9.

McIntyre, M.E. and Silverman, F.H. (1974), 'Transcendental Meditation and Stuttering: A Preliminary Report', *Perceptual & Motor Skills*, **39**, p. 294.

McNamara, P.J. (2000), Personal Communication.

Michaels, R.R., Huber, M.J. and McCann, D.S. (1976), 'Evaluation of Transcendental Meditation as a Method of Reducing Stress', *Science*, **192**, pp. 1242–4.

Michaels, R.R., Parra, J., McCann, D.S. and Vander, A.J. (1979), 'Renin, Cortisol, and Aldosterone during Transcendental Meditation', *Psychosomatic Medicine*, **41** (1), pp. 50–4.

Michon, A.L. and Persinger, M.A. (1997), 'Experimental Simulation of the Effects of Increased Geomagnetic Activity upon Nocturnal Seizures in Epileptic Rats', *Neuroscience Letters*, **224** (1), pp. 53–6.

Miller, J.J., Fletcher, K. and Kabat-Zinn, J. (1995), '3 Year Follow-up and Clinical Implications of a Mindfulness Meditation-Based Stress Reduction Intervention in the Treatment of Anxiety Disorders', *General Hospital Psychiatry*, **17**, pp. 192–200.

Mills, G. and Campbell, K. (1974), 'A Critique of Gellhorn and Kiely's Mystical States of Consciousness', *Journal of Nervous and Mental Disease*, **159**, pp. 191–5.

'Mind and Life I', (1991). *Chö Yang: The Voice of Tibetan Religion and Culture (Year of Tibet Edition)*, ed. P. Yeshi, and J. Russell (Dharamsala, India: Library of Tibetan Works and Archives).

Miskiman, D.E. (1977a), 'Long-term Effects of the Transcendental Meditation Program in the Treatment of Insomnia', in *Scientific Research on the Transcendental Meditation Program: Collected Papers*, ed. D.W. Orme-Johnson, and J.T. Farrow, Second edition (Weggis, Switzerland: Maharishi European Research University Press).

Miskiman, D.E. (1977b), 'The Treatment of Insomnia by Transcendental Meditation Program', in *Scientific Research on the Transcendental Meditation Program: Collected Papers*, ed. D.W. Orme-Johnson, and J.T. Farrow, Second edition (Weggis, Switzerland: Maharishi European Research University Press).

Morgan, W. (1995), 'Anxiety and Panic in Recreational Scuba Divers', *Sports Medicine*, **20** (6), pp. 398–421.

Morrell, E.M. (1986), 'Meditation and Somatic Arousal', *American Psychologist*, **41** (6), pp. 712–3.

Morris, K. (1998), 'Meditating on Yogic Science', *The Lancet*, **351** (9108), p. 1038.

Morse, D.R., Martin, J.S. and Furst, M.L. (1977), 'A Physiological and Subjective Evaluation of Meditation, Hypnosis, and Relaxation', *Psychosomatic Medicine*, **39**, pp. 304–24.

Morse, D.R., Martin, J.S., Furst, M.L. and Dubin, L. (1979), 'A Physiological and Subjective Evaluation of Neutral and Emotionally-Charged Words for Meditation (Parts I–III)', *Journal of the American Society of Psychosomatic Dentristry and Medicine*, **26**, pp. 31–8, 56–62, 106–12.

Munro, C. and Persinger, M.A. (1992), 'Relative Right Temporal-Lobe Theta Activity Correlates with Vingiano's Hemispheric Quotient and the 'Sensed Presence'', *Perceptual & Motor Skills*, **75** (3 Pt. 1), pp. 899–903.

Muskatel, N. and Woolfolk, R.L. (1984), 'Effect of Meditation Training on Aspects of Coronary-prone Behavior', *Perceptual & Motor Skills*, **58**, pp. 515–8.

Myers, P., Friedman, R. and Benson, H. (2000), 'Meditation and the Relaxation Response', in *Encyclopedia of Psychology*, ed. A.E. Kazdin (New York: Oxford University Press).

Nagata, K., Fukushima, K., Nunomura, J. and et al. (1990), 'Functional Anatomy of Human Central Auditory System: Cerebral Blood Flow Responses to Verbal and Non-verbal Auditory Stimulation', cited in Austin (1998b).

Natsoulas, T. (1997), 'Consciousness and Self-Awareness', *Journal of Mind and Behavior*, **18**, pp. 53–74.

'Naturally Healthy: Transcendental Meditation May Help Lower Blood Pressure', (1996). *Industry Week*, **245** (18), p. 94.

Newberg, A.B., Personal communication (1999), 10 June.

Newberg, A.B. and d'Aquili, E.G. (1994), 'The Near Death Experience as Archetype: A Model for 'Prepared' Neurocognitive Processes', *Anthropology of Consciousness*, **5**, pp. 1–15.

Newberg, A.B., Alavi, A., Baime, M., Mozley, P. D. and d'Aquili, E.G. (1997), 'The Measurement of Cerebral Blood Flow During the Complex Cognitive Task of Meditation Using HMPAO-SPECT Imaging', Unpublished abstract.

Noble, K.D. (1987), 'Psychological Health and the Experience of Transcendence', *The Counseling Psychologist*, **15**, pp. 601–14.

Odanjnyk, W.V. (1988), 'Gathering the Light: A Jungian Exploration of Meditation', *Quadrant*, **21** (1), pp. 35–51.

Oken, B.S. and Salinsky, M. (1992), 'Alertness and Attention: Basic Science and Electrophysiological Correlates', *Journal of Clinical Neurophysiology*, **9**, pp. 480–94.

Orme-Johnson, D.W. (1973), 'Autonomic Stability and Transcendental Meditation', *Psychosomatic Medicine*, **16**, pp. 203–9.

Orme-Johnson, D.W. (1995), 'Evidence that Transcendental Meditation does not Produce Cognitive Kindling: A Comment', *Perceptual & Motor Skills*, **81** (2), p. 642.

Orme-Johnson, D.W., Kiehlbauch, J. and Moore, R. (1977), 'Personality and Autonomic Changes in Prisoners Practising the Transcendental Meditation Technique', in *Scientific Research on the Transcendental Meditation Program: Collected Papers*, ed. D.W. Orme-Johnson, and J.T. Farrow, Second edition (Weggis, Switzerland: Maharishi European Research University Press).

Orme-Johnson, D.W. and Herron, R.E. (1997), 'An Innovative Approach to Reducing Medical Care Utilization and Expenditures', *American Journal of Managed Care*, **3**, pp. 135–44.

Orne, M. (1962), 'On the Social Psychology and the Psychological Experiment: With Particular Reference to Demand Characteristics and their Implications', *American Psychologist*, **17**, pp. 776–83.

Ornstein, R. (1971), 'The Techniques of Meditation and Their Implications for Modern Psychology', in *On the Psychology of Meditation*, C. Naranjo, and R.E. Ornstein, by (New York: Viking Press).

Otis, L. (1974), 'The Facts on Transcendental Meditation: If Well Integrated, but Anxious, Try TM', *Psychology Today*, **7**, pp. 45–6.

Otis, L. (1984), 'Adverse Effects of Transcendental Meditation', in *Meditation: Classic and Contemporary Perspectives*, ed. J. Shapiro, Deane H. and R.N. Walsh (Hawthorne, NY: Aldine Publishing Co.).

Pagano, R.R. (1981), 'Recent Research in the Physiology of Meditation', in *Advances in Physiological Sciences*, ed. G. Adam, I. Meszaros, and E. Banyai, Volume 17 (Budapest: Pergamon).

Pagano, R.R., Rose, R.M., Stivers, R.M. and Warrenburg, S. (1976), 'Sleep During Transcendental Meditation', *Science*, **191** (4224), pp. 308–10.

Pagano, R.R. and Warrenberg, S. (1983), 'Meditation: In Search of a Unique Effect', in *Consciousness and Self-Regulation*, ed. R. Davidson, G. Schwartz, and D. Shapiro (New York: Plenum).

Parker, J.C., Gilbert, G.S. and Thoreson, R.W. (1978), 'Reduction of Autonomic Arousal in Alcoholics: A Comparison of Relaxation and Meditation Techniques', *Journal of Consulting and Clinical Psychology*, **46**, pp. 879–85.

Parry, S.J. and Jones, R.G. (1986), 'Beyond Illusion in the Psychotherapeutic Enterprise', in *Beyond Therapy: The Impact of Eastern Religions on Psychological Theory and Practice*, ed. G. Claxton (London: Wisdom Publications).

Pasachoff, J.M., Strassburg, M.A. and Benson, H. (1982), 'Body Temperature Changes during the Practice of gTum-mo Yoga', *Nature*, **298** (5872), p. 402.

Patel, C.H. (1973), 'Yoga and Biofeedback in the Management of Hypertension', *Lancet*, **2**, pp. 1053–5.

Patel, C.H. (1975), '12 Month Follow-up of Yoga and Biofeedback in the Management of Hypertension', *Lancet*, **1**, pp. 62–5.

Patel, C.H. (1984), 'Yogic Therapy', in *Principles and Practice of Stress Management*, ed. R.L. Woolfolk and P. M. Lehrer (New York: Guilford Press).

Paty, J., Brenot, P., Tignol, J. and Bourgeois, M. (1978), 'Activités Évoqueés Cérébrales (Variation Contingente Negative et Potentials Évoques) et États de Conscience Modifies (Relaxation Sophronique, Méditation Trancendentale)', *Annales Médico-Psychologiques*, **136** (1), pp. 143–69.

Paul, G. and Trimble, R. (1970), 'Recorded vs. 'Live' Relaxation Training and Hypnotic Suggestion: Comparative Effectiveness for Reducing Physiological Activity and Inhibiting Stress Response', *Behavior Therapy*, **1**, pp. 285–302.

Pelletier, K.R. (1977), 'Effects of Transcendental Meditation Program on Perceptual Style: Increased Field Independence', in *Scientific Research on the Transcendental Meditation Program: Collected Papers*, ed. D.W. Orme-Johnson, and J.T. Farrow, Second edition (Weggis, Switzerland: Maharishi European Research University Press).

Peng, C.K., Mietus, J.E., Liu, Y., Khalsa, G., Douglas, P. S., Benson, H. and Goldberger, A.I. (1999), 'Exaggerated Heart Rate Oscillations during Two Meditation Techniques', *International Journal of Cardiology*, **70**, pp. 101–7.

Persinger, M.A. (1980), *TM and Cult Mania* (North Quincy, MA: Christopher Publishing House).

Persinger, M.A. (1983), 'Religious and Mystical Experiences as Artifacts of Temporal Lobe Function: A General Hypothesis', *Perceptual & Motor Skills*, **57** (3 Pt. 2), pp. 1255–62.

Persinger, M.A. (1984a), 'People Who Report Religious Experiences May also Display Enhanced Temporal-Lobe Signs', *Perceptual & Motor Skills*, **58** (3), pp. 963–75.

Persinger, M.A. (1984b), 'Propensity to Report Paranormal Experiences is Correlated with Temporal Lobe Signs', *Perceptual & Motor Skills*, **59** (2), pp. 583–6.

Persinger, M.A. (1984c), 'Striking EEG Profiles from Single Episodes of Glossolalia and Transcendental Meditation', *Perceptual & Motor Skills*, **58** (1), pp. 127–33.

Persinger, M.A. (1987), *Neuropsychological Basis of God Beliefs* (New York: Praeger).

Persinger, M.A. (1988), 'Temporal Lobe Signs and Personality Characteristics', *Perceptual & Motor Skills*, **66** (1), pp. 49–50.

Persinger, M.A. (1989a), 'Geophysical Variables and Behavior: LV. Predicting the Details or Visitor Experiences and the Personality of Experients: the Temporal Lobe Factor', *Perceptual & Motor Skills*, **68** (1), pp. 55–65.

Persinger, M.A. (1989b), 'Geophysical Variables and Behavior: LIV. Zeitoun (Egypt) Apparitions of the Virgin Mary as Tectonic Strain-Induced Luminosities (Review)', *Perceptual & Motor Skills*, **68** (1), pp. 123–8.

Persinger, M.A. (1992a), 'Enhanced Incidence of 'The Sensed Presence' in People who have Learned to Meditate: Support for the Right Hemispheric Intrusion Hypothesis', *Perceptual & Motor Skills*, **75** (3 Pt. 2), pp. 1308–10.

Persinger, M.A. (1992b), 'Neuropsychological Profiles of Adults who Report 'Sudden Remembering' of Early Childhood Memories: Implications for Claims of Sex Abuse and Alien Visitation/Abduction Experiences (Review)', *Perceptual & Motor Skills*, **75** (1), pp. 259–66.

Persinger, M.A. (1992c), 'Right Hemisphericity, Low Self-Esteem, and Unusual Experiences: A Response to Vingiano (Comment)', *Perceptual & Motor Skills*, **75** (2), pp. 568–70.

Persinger, M.A. (1993a), 'Transcendental Meditation and General Meditation are Associated with Enhanced Complex Partial Epileptic-like Signs: Evidence for 'Cognitive' Kindling?' *Perceptual & Motor Skills*, **76** (1), pp. 80–2.

Persinger, M.A. (1993b), 'Vectorial Cerebral Hemisphericity as Differential Sources for the Sensed Presence, Mystical Experiences and Religious Conversions (Review)', *Perceptual & Motor Skills*, **76** (3 Pt. 1), pp. 915–30.

Persinger, M.A. (1995a), 'Complex Partial Epileptic-Like Signs Contribute Differential Sources of Variance to Low Self-Esteem and Imaginings', *Perceptual & Motor Skills*, **80** (2), pp. 427–31.

Persinger, M.A. (1995b), 'Out-Of-Body-Like Experiences are more Probable in People with Elevated Complex Partial Epileptic-Like Signs During Periods of Enhanced Geomagnetic Activity: A Nonlinear Effect', *Perceptual & Motor Skills*, **80** (2), pp. 563–9.

Persinger, M.A. (1996), 'Feelings of Past Lives as Expected Perturbations within the Neurocognitive Processes that Generate the Sense of Self: Contributions from Limbic Lability and Vectorial Hemisphericity', *Perceptual & Motor Skills*, **83** (3 Pt. 2), pp. 1107–21.

Persinger, M.A. (1997), ''I Would Kill in God's Name:' Role of Sex, Weekly Church Attendance, Report of a Religious Experience, and Limbic Lability', *Perceptual & Motor Skills*, **85** (1), pp. 128–30.

Persinger, M.A. and Valliant, P. M. (1985), 'Temporal Lobe Signs and Reports of Subjective Paranormal Experiences in a Normal Population: A Replication', *Perceptual & Motor Skills*, **60** (3), pp. 903–9.

Persinger, M.A. and Makarec, K. (1987), 'Temporal Lobe Epileptic Signs and Correlative Behaviors Displayed by Normal Populations', *Journal of General Psychology*, **11** (2), pp. 179–95.

Persinger, M.A., Makarec, K. and Bradley, J.C. (1988), 'Characteristics of Limbic Seizures Evoked by Peripheral Injections of Lithium and Pilocarpine', *Pysiology and Behavior*, **44** (1), pp. 27–37.

Persinger, M.A. and Richards, P. (1991), 'Tobacyk's Sex Differences in the Experiences of Ego-Alien Intrusions', *Perceptual & Motor Skills*, **73** (3 Pt. 2), pp. 1151–6.

Persinger, M.A. and Richards, P. M. (1994), 'Quantitative Electroencephalographic Validation of Left and Right Temporal Lobe Signs and Indicators in Normal People', *Perceptual & Mortor Skills*, **79** (3 Pt. 2), pp. 1571–8.

Peters, R.K., Benson, H. and Peters, J.M. (1977), 'Daily Relaxation Response Breaks in a Working Population: 2. Blood Pressure', *American Journal of Public Health*, **67**, pp. 954–9.

Peters, R.K., Benson, H. and Porter, D. (1977), 'Daily Relaxation Response Breaks in a Working Population: 1. Health, Performance and Well-Being', *American Journal of Public Health*, **67**, pp. 946–53.

Petersen, S.E., Fox, P. T., Posner, M.I., Mintum, M. and Raichle, M.E. (1988), 'Positron Emission Tomographic Studies of the Cortical Anatomy of Single-word Processing', *Nature*, **331** (6157), pp. 585–9.

Piggins, D. and Morgan, C. (1977), 'Note upon Steady Visual Fixation and Repeated Auditory Stimulation during Meditation in the Laboratory', *Perceptual & Motor Skills*, **44**, pp. 357–8.

Pirot, M. (1977), 'The Effects of the Transcendental Meditation Technique upon Auditory Discrimination', in *Scientific Research on the Transcendental Meditation Program: Collected Papers*, ed. D.W. Orme-Johnson, and J.T. Farrow, Second edition (Weggis, Switzerland: Maharishi European Research University Press).

Poulet, R. (1996), 'Entspannungstechniken in der Rehabilitation (Relaxation Techniques in Rehabilitation) (German)', *Zeitschrift Fur Gastroenterologie*, **34** (Supplement 2), pp. 80–4.

Puryear, H. and Cayce, C. (1976), 'Anxiety Reduction associated with Meditation: Home Study', *Perceptual & Motor Skills*, **43**, pp. 527–31.

Quirk, M.E., Letendre, A.J., Ciottone, R.A. and Lingley, J.F. (1989), 'Evaluation of Three Psychologic Interventions to Reduce Anxiety during MR Imaging', *Radiology*, **173** (3), pp. 759–62.

Ramamurthi, B. (1995), 'The Fourth State of Consciousness: The Thuriya Avastha (Review)', *Psychiatry & Clinical Neurosciences*, **49** (2), pp. 107–10.

Ramaswami, S. and Sheikh, A.A. (1996), 'Meditation East West', in *Healing East West: Ancient Wisdom and Modern Psychology*, ed. A.A. Sheikh, and K.S. Sheikh (New York, NY: John Wiley & Sons).

Raskin, M. and Bali, L.R. (1976), 'Muscle Biofeedback and Transcendental Meditation: A Controlled Evaluation of Efficacy in the Treatment of Chronic Anxiety', *Archives of General Psychiatry*, **37**, pp. 93–7.

Rimol, A.G.P. (1977), 'The Transcendental Meditation Technique and its Effects on Sensory-motor Performance', in *Scientific Research on the Transcendental Meditation Program: Collected Papers*, ed. D.W. Orme-Johnson, and J.T. Farrow, Second edition (Weggis, Switzerland: Maharishi European Research University Press).

Roach, M. (1998), 'Ancient Altered States', *Discover*, **19** (6), pp. 52–8.

Robbins, T. (1969), 'Eastern Mysticism and the Resocialization of Drug Users: The Meher Baba Cult', *Journal for the Scientific Study of Religion*, **8**, pp. 308–17.

Ross, J. and Persinger, M.A. (1987), 'Positive Correlations between Temporal Lobe Signs and Hypnosis Induction Profiles: A Replication', *Perceptual & Motor Skills*, **64** (3 Pt. 1), pp. 828–30.

Roth, B. and Creaser, T. (1997), 'Mindfulness Meditation-based Stress Reduction: Experience with a Bilingual Inner-city Program', *Nurse Practitioner*, **22** (3), pp. 150–7.

Russel, E.W. (1986), 'Consciousness and the Unconscious: Eastern Meditative and Western Psychotherapeutic Approaches', *Journal of Transpersonal Psycholog*, **18**, pp. 51–72.

Sakairi, Y. (1992), 'Effects of Transcendental Meditation in Reducing Anxiety of Japanese Businessmen', in *Perspectives on Relaxation and Meditation*, ed. M. Blows, and S. Srinivasan (Melbourne: Spectrum Publishers).

Schneider, R.H., Staggers, F., Alexander, C.N., Sheppard, W., Rainforth, M., Kondwani, K., Smith, S. and King, C.G. (1995), 'A Randomized Controlled Trial of Stress Reduction for Hypertension in Older African Americans', *Hypertension*, **26**, pp. 820–7.

Schuman, M. (1980), 'The Psychophysiological Model of Meditation and Altered States of Consciousness: A Critical Review', in *The Psychobiology of Consciousness*, ed. J.M. Davidson, and R.J. Davidson (New York: Plenum).

Schwartz, G.E., Davidson, R.J. and Goleman, D. (1978), 'Patterning of Cognitive and Somatic Processes in the Self-Regulation of Anxiety; Effects of Meditation Versus Exercise', *Psychosomatic Medicine*, **40** (4), pp. 321–8.

Schwartz, G.E., Davidson, R.J. and Goleman, D.J. (1984), 'Patterning of Cognitive and Somatic Processes in the Self-Regulation of Anxiety: Effects of Meditation versus Exercise', in *Meditation: Classic and Contemporary Perspectives*, ed. J. Shapiro, Deane H. and R.N. Walsh (Hawthorne, NY: Aldine Publishing Co.).

Scopen, A. and Freeman, B. (1992), 'Meditation: The Forgotten Western Tradition', *Counselling and Values*, **36**, pp. 123–34.

Seeman, W., Nidich, S. and Banta, T. (1972), 'Influence of Transcendental Meditation on a Measure of Self-actualization', *Journal of Counseling Psychology*, **19**, pp. 184–7.

Shafii, M. (1973a), 'Adaptive and Therapeutic Aspects of Meditation', *International Journal of Psychoanalytic Psychotherapy*, **2**, pp. 364–82.

Shafii, M. (1973b), 'Silence in the Service of the Ego: Psychoanlaytic Study of Meditation', *International Journal of Psychoanalysis*, **54**, pp. 431–43.

Shafii, M., Lavely, R.A. and Jaffe, R. (1974), 'Meditation and Marijuana', *American Journal of Psychiatry*, **131** (1), pp. 60–3.

Shafii, M., Lavely, R.A. and Jaffe, R. (1975), 'Meditation and the Prevention of Alcohol Abuse', *American Journal of Psychiatry*, **132** (9), pp. 942–5.

Shapiro, D.H. (1980), *Meditation: Self-Regulation Strategy and Altered State of Consciousness* (New York: Aldine).

Shapiro, D.H. (1983), 'Meditation As an Altered State of Consciousness: Contributions of Western Behavioral Science', *Journal of Transpersonal Psychology*, **15** (1, 61–81).

Shapiro, D.H. (1992), 'A Preliminary Study of Long-term Meditators: Goals, Effects, Religious Orientation, Cognition', *The Journal of Transpersonal Psychology*, **24** (1), pp. 23–39.

Shapiro, D.H. and Walsh, R.N. (eds 1984), *Meditation: Classic and Contemporary Perspectives* (Hawthorne, NY: Aldine Publishing Co.).

Shapiro, D.H. and Zifferblatt, S. (1976), 'Zen Meditation and Behavioral Self-control: Similarities, Differences, and Clinical Applications', *American Psychologist*, **31** (7), pp. 519–32.

Shapiro, D.H. and Giber, D. (1978), 'Meditation and Psychotherapeutic Effects', *Archives of General Psychiatry*, **35** (3), pp. 294–302.

Short, L. (1995), 'Mysticism, Meditation, and the Non-Linguistic', *Journal of the American Academy of Religion*, **63**, pp. 659–75.

Sifford, D. (1988), 'A Psychiatrist Probes Effects of Transcendental Meditation', *Philadelphia Inquirer*, 19 June, p. F01.

Silverman, J. (1968), 'A Paradigm for the Study of Altered States of Consciousness', *British Journal of Psychiatry*, **114**, pp. 1201–18.

Simon, D.B. (1999), *Returning to Wholeness: Embracing Body, Mind, and Spirit in the Face of Cancer* (New York: Wiley).

Simon, D.B. and Oparil, S. (1977), 'The Transcendental Meditation Program and Essential Hypertension', in *Scientific Research on the Transcendental Meditation Program: Collected Papers*, ed. D.W. Orme-Johnson, and J.T. Farrow, Second edition (Weggis, Switzerland: Maharishi European Research University Press).

Singer, P. (1993 [1979]), *Practical Ethics*, Second edition (Cambridge: Cambridge University Press).

Smith, J.C. (1975), 'Meditation and Psychotherapy: A Review of the Literature', *Psychological Bulletin*, **82**, pp. 558–64.

Smith, J.C. (1976), 'Psychotherapeutic Effects of Transcendental Meditation with Controls for Expectation of Relief and Daily Sitting', *Journal of Consulting and Clinical Psychology*, **44**, pp. 630–7.

Smith, J.C. (1978), 'Personality Correlates of Continuation and Outcome in Meditation and Erect Sitting Control Treatments', *Journal of Consulting and Clinical Psychology*, **46**, pp. 272–9.

Smith, M. (2000), Personal communication, 30 January.

Smythies, J. (1997), 'The Functional Neuroanatomy of Awareness: With a Focus on the Role of Various Anatomical Systems in the Control of Intermodal Attention', *Consciousness and Cognition*, **6**, pp. 455–81.

Solberg, E.E., Halvorsen, R., Sundgot-Borgen, J., Ingjer, F. and Holen, A. (1995), 'Meditation: A Modulator of the Immune Response to Physical Stress? A Brief Report', *British Journal of Sports Medicine*, **29** (4), pp. 255–7.

Solberg, E.E., Berglund, K.A., Engen, O., Ekeberg, O. and Loeb, M. (1996), 'The Effect of Meditation on Shooting Performance', *British Journal of Sports Medicine*, **30** (4), pp. 342–6.

A Sourcebook in Indian Philosophy (1957), ed. S. Radhakrishnan, and C.A. Moore (Princeton: Princeton University Press).

Spanos, N.P., Steggles, S. and Radtke-Bodorick, H.L. (1979), 'Non-analytic Tending, Hypnotic Susceptibility, and Psychological Well Being in Trained Meditators and Nonmeditators', *Journal of Abnormal Psychology*, **88**, pp. 85–7.

Sperber, D. (1996), *Explaining Culture: A Naturalistic Approach* (Cambridge, MA: Blackwell Publishers).

Stainbrook, G.L., Hoffman, H.W. and Benson, H. (1983), 'Behavioral Therapies of Hypertension: Psychotherapy, Biofeedback, and Relaxation/Meditation', *International Review of Applied Psychology*, **32**, pp. 119–35.

Stigsby, B., Rodenberg, J.C. and Moth, H.B. (1981), 'Electroencephalographic Findings during Mantra Meditation (Transcendental Meditation). A Controlled, Quantitative Study of Experienced Meditators', *Electroencephalography & Clinical Neurophysiology*, **51** (4), pp. 434–42.

Stone, B. and Chang, Y. (1997), 'Cultivating Qi: More and More Westerners are Discovering Qigong, an Ancient Amalgam of Dance and Meditation with a Range of Physical Benefits', *Newsweek*, **130** (4), pp. 71–2.

Stuart, E., Friedman, R. and Benson, H. (1993), 'Promoting Nonpharmacologic Interventions to Treat Elevated Blood Pressure', in *Behavioral Science Learning Modules* (Geneva: Division of Mental Health, World Health Organization).

Stuart, E.M., Caudill, M., Leserman, J., Dorrington, C., Friedman, R. and Benson, H. (1987), 'Non-pharmacologic Treatment of Hypertension: A Multiple Risk-factor Approach', *Journal of Cardiovascular Nursing*, **1**, pp. 1–14.

Sugi, Y. and Akutsu, K. (1968), 'Studies on Respiration and Energy-Metabolism during Sitting in Zazen', *Research Journal of Physical Education*, **12**, pp. 190–206.

Sun, F.L., Li, D.M. and Li, G.Y. (1986), 'Influence of Different Combination of Mental Activity and Respiratory Cycle on Heart Rate Variability (Chinese)', *Chung Kuo Chung Hsi'i Chieh Ho Tsa Chih [Chinese Journal of Integrated Traditional and Western Medicine]*, **16** (3), pp. 153–5.

Taimni, I.K. (1961), *The Science of Yoga* (Wheaton, IL: Quest Books).

Taneli, B. and Krahne, W. (1987), 'EEG Changes of Transcendental Meditation Practitioners', *Advances in Biological Psychiatry*, **16**, pp. 41–71.

Tart, C.T. (1971), 'A Psychologist's Experience with Transcendental Meditation', *Journal of Transpersonal Psychology*, **3**, pp. 135–40.

Tart, C.T. (1975), *States of Consciousness* (New York: Dutton).

Tart, C.T. (1990), 'Adapting Eastern Spiritual Teachings to Western Culture: A Discussion with Shinzen Young', *Journal of Transpersonal Psychology*, **22** (2), pp. 140–65.

Taylor, C.B. and Farquher, J.W. (1977), 'Relaxation Therapy and High Blood Pressure', *Archives of General Psychiatry*, **34**, pp. 339–42.

Taylor, E. (1995), 'Yoga and Meditation', *Alternative Therapies*, **1** (4), pp. 77–8.

Tebecis, A.K. (1975), 'A Controlled Study of the EEG During Transcendental Meditation: Comparison with Hypnosis', *Folia Psychiatrica et Neurologica Japonica*, **29** (4), pp. 305–13.

Thompson, M.B. and Coppens, N.M. (1994), 'The Effects of Guided Imagery on Anxiety Levels and Movement of Clients Undergoing Magnetic Resonance Imaging', *Holistic Nursing Practice*, **8** (2), pp. 59–69.

Tianuru, M. and Gitre, L. (1996), 'Get the Stress Out!: How One Woman Overcame the Pressures in Her Life — A Holistic Path That You, Too, Can Take', *Essence*, **26** (11), p. 26.

Tiller, S.G. and Persinger, M.A. (1994), 'Elevated Incidence of a Sensed Presence and Sexual Arousal during Partial Sensory Deprivation and Sensitivity to Hypnosis: Implications for Hemisphericity and Gender Differences', *Perceptual & Motor Skills*, **79** (3 Pt. 2), pp. 1527–31.

Tjoa, A. (1977), 'Some Evidence that the Transcendental Meditation Program Increases Intelligence and Reduces Neuroticism as Measured by Psychological Tests', in *Scientific Research on the Transcendental Meditation Program*, ed. D.W. Orme-Johnson, and J.T. Farrow, Second edition (Weggis, Switzerland: Maharishi European Research University Press).

'Transcendental Meditation seems to Lower Blood Pressure', (1996). *American Journal of Managed Care*, **2** (4), pp. 427–37.

'Transcending Hypertension (Transcendental Meditation Seems to Lower Blood Pressure: taken from American Journal of Managed Care, April 1996) (Health Beat)', (1996). *Harvard Health Letter*, **21** (9), p. 8.

Travis, F.T. and Wallace, R.K. (1997), 'Autonomic Patterns during Respiratory Suspensions: Possible Markers of Transcendental Consciousness', *Psychophysiology*, **34** (1), pp. 39–46.

Travis, F.T. and Wallace, R.K. (1999), 'Autonomic and EEG Patterns During Eyes-Closed Rest and Transcendental Meditation (TM) Practice: The Basis for a Neural Model of TM Practice', *Consciousness and Cognition*, **8**, pp. 302–18.

Travis, F.T. and Pearson, C. (2000), 'Pure Consciousness: Distinct Phenomenological and Physiological Correlates of 'Consciousness Itself'', *International Journal of Neuroscience*, **100**, pp. 77–89.

Tulpule, T. (1971), 'Yogic Exercises in the Management of Ischemic Heart Disease', *Indian Heart Journal*, **23**, pp. 259–64.

United States Congress [Senate Committee on Appropriations, Subcommittee on Departments of Labor, Health and Human Services, Education, and Related Agencies] (1999), *Mind/Body Medicine: Hearing Before a Subcommittee of the Committee on Appropriations, United States Senate, One Hundred Fifth Congress, Second Session, Special Hearing* (Washington, D.C.: U.S. Government Printing Office).

Upadhyaya, J. (ed. 1986), *Vimalaprabhk of Kalki r Puarka on r Laghuklacakratantrarja by r Mañjuryaas*, Volume 1. Bibliotheca Indo-Tibetica Series, No. XI (Saranath, Varanasi: Central Institute of Higher Tibetan Studies).

van der Lans, J. (1985), 'Frame of Reference as a Prerequisite for the Induction of Religious Experience through Meditation: An Experimental Study', in *Advances in the Psychology of Religion*, ed. L.B. Brown (Oxford: Pergamon Press).

Van Nuys, D. (1973), 'Meditation, Attention, and Hypnotic Susceptibility: A Correlational Study', *International Journal of Clinical Experimental Hypnosis*, **21**, pp. 59–69.

Varela, F.J. (1996), 'Neurophenomenology: A Methodological Remedy for the Hard Problem', *Journal of Consciousness Studies*, **3**, pp. 330–50.

Vassallo, J. (1984), 'Psychological Perspectives on Buddhism: Implications for Counselling', *Counselling and Values*, **28**, pp. 179–91.

Venkatesh, S., Raju, T.R., Shivani, Y., Tompkins, G. and Meti, B.L. (1997), 'A Study of Structure of Phenomenology of Consciousness in Meditative and Non-Meditative States', *Indian Jounral of Physiology & Pharmacology*, **41** (2), pp. 149–53.

von Kirchenheim, C. and Persinger, M.A. (1991), 'Time Distortion — A Comparison of Hypnotic Induction and Progressive Relaation Procedures: A Brief Communication', *International Journal of Clinical & Experimental Hypnosis*, **39** (2), pp. 63–6.

Wallace, R.K. (1970), 'Physiological Effects of Transcendental Meditation', *Science*, **167**, pp. 1751–4.

Wallace, R.K. (1971), *Dissertation Abstracts International*, **31**, pp. 4303–13*The Physiological Effects of Transcendental Meditation: A Proposed Fourth State of Consciousness*.

Wallace, R.K. (1974), 'Neurophysiology of Englightenment: Scientific Research on Transcendental Meditation', 26th International Congress of Physiological Sciences (New Delhi: Maharishi International University).

Wallace, R.K., Benson, H. and Wilson, A. (1971), 'A Wakeful Hypometabolic State', *American Journal of Physiology*, **221**, pp. 795–9.

Wallace, R.K. and Benson, H. (1972), 'The Physiology of Meditation', *Scientific American*, **226**, pp. 84–90.

Wallace, R.K., Dillbeck, M., Jacobe, E. and Harrington, B. (1982), 'The Effects of the Transcendental Meditation and TM-Sidhi Program on Aging', *International Journal of Neuroscience*, **16** (1), pp. 53–8.

Walley, M. (1986), 'Applications of Buddhism in Mental Health Care', in *Beyond Therapy: The Impact of Eastern Religions on Psychological Theory and Practice*, ed. G. Claxton (London: Wisdom Publications).

Walrath, L.C. and Hamilton, D.W. (1975), 'Autonomic Correlates of Meditation and Hypnosis', *American Journal of Clinical Hypnosis*, **17**, pp. 190–7.

Walter, D.O. and Rhodes, J.M. (1966), 'Comprehensive Spectral Analysis of Human EEG Generators in Posterior Cerebral Regions', *Electroencephalography and Clinical Neurophysiology*, **20**, p. 224.

Warrenburg, S., Pagano, R.R. and Woods, M. (1980), 'A Comparison of Somatic Relaxation and EEG Activity in Classical Progressive Relaxation and Transcendental Meditation', *Journal of Behavioral Medicine*, **3** (1), pp. 73–93.

Watkins, A. (ed. 1997), *Mind–Body Medicine: A Clinician's Guide to Psychoneuroimmunology* (New York: Churchill Livingstone).

Watts, F.N. (1979), 'Psychological Theory and the Religious Mind: Meditation and Perception', *Theoria to Theory*, **13**, pp. 115–25.

Welwood, J. (1980), 'Reflections of Psychotherapy, Focusing, and Meditation', *Journal of Transpersonal Psychology*, **12** (2), pp. 127–41.

Welwood, J. (1983), 'On Psychotherapy and Meditation', in *Awakening the Heart: East–West Approaches to Psychotherapy and the Healing Relationship*, ed. J. Welwood (Boulder: Shambala).

Wenneberg, S.R., Schneider, R.H., Walton, K.G., Maclean, C.R., Levitsky, D.K., Salerno, J.W., Wallace, R.K., Mandarino, J.V., Rainforth, M.V. and Waziri, R. (1997), 'A Controlled Study of the Effects of the Transcendental Meditation Program on Cardiovascular Reactivity and Ambulatory Blood Pressure', *International Journal of Neuroscience*, **89** (1–2), pp. 15–28.

Wescott, M. (1974), 'Hemisphere Asymmetry of the EEG during the Altered States of Consciousness', *Perceptual & Motor Skills*, **45**, pp. 17–20.

West, M.A. (1979), 'Physiological Effects of Meditation: A Longitudinal Study', *British Journal of Social and Clinical Psychology*, **18**, pp. 219–26.

West, M.A. (1980a), 'Meditation and the EEG', *Psychological Medicine*, **10**, pp. 369–75.

West, M.A. (1980b), 'Meditation, Personality, and Arousal', *Personality and Individual Differences*, **1**, pp. 135–42.

West, M.A. (1987), 'Traditional and Psychological Perspectives on Meditation', in *The Psychology of Meditation*, ed. M.A. West (Oxford: Clarendon Press).

Wilkins, W. (1971), 'Desensitization: Social and Cognitive Factors Underlying the Effectiveness of Wolpe's Procedure', *Psychology Bulletin*, **76** (5), pp. 311–17.

Williams, P. and West, M.A. (1975), 'EEG Responses to Photic Stimulation in Persons Experienced at Meditation', *Electroencephalography & Clinical Neurophysiology*, **39** (5), pp. 519–22.

Williams Jr., R.B., Benson, H. and Follick, M.J. (1985), 'Disease as a Reflection of the Psyche (Letter to the Editor)', *New England Journal of Medicine*, **313**, pp. 1356–7.

Wilson, A.F. (1975), 'Transcendental Meditation of Asthma', *Respiration*, **32**, pp. 74–80.

Wolman, T. (1985), 'Can East and West Meet in Psychoanalysis?' *American Journal of Psychiatry*, **142**, pp. 1227–28.

Woolfolk, R.L. (1975), 'Psychophysiological Correlates of Meditation', *Archives of General Psychiatry*, **32**, pp. 1326–33.

Wright, S. (1997), 'Holistic Health. Journey to the Centre', *Nursing Times*, **93** (17), pp. 28–30.

Wulff, D.M. (1992), *Psychology of Religion: Classic and Contemporary Views* (New York: John Wiley and Sons).

Wulff, D.M. (1997), *Psychology of Religion: Classic and Contemporary Views*, Second edition (New York: John Wiley & Sons).

Younger, J., Adriance, W. and Berger, R. (1973), 'Sleep During Transcendental Meditation (Abstract)', in *Sleep Research*, M.H. Chase, W.C.Stern, and P. L.Walter, eds, Vol.2 (Los Angeles: Brain Information Service/Brain Research Institute, UCLA).

Younger, J., Adriance, W. and Berger, R. (1975), 'Sleep During Transcendental Meditation', *Perceptual & Motor Skills*, **40** (3), pp. 953–54.

Zamarra, J.W., Schneider, R.H., Besseghini, I., Robinson, D.K. and Salerno, J.W. (1996), 'Usefulness of the Transcendental Meditation Program in the Treatment of Patients with Coronary Artery Disease', *American Journal of Cardiology*, **77**, pp. 867–70.

Arthur J. Deikman

A Functional Approach to Mysticism

Because mysticism is associated with religion it has long been regarded as inimical to science, an enemy of the search for objective truth, not to be credited as a discipline through which knowledge of reality can be gained. At least, that seems to be the official attitude that pervades scientific publications and scientific meetings, even at the present time when quantum theory has made consciousness a legitimate subject for research.

In point of fact, informal inquiry reveals that many scientists have had experiences they would describe as transcendent, as going beyond familiar sensory dimensions and providing a taste of the unified reality of which mystics speak. They don't talk about it in public but will do so in private. The greatest scientist of them all, Isaac Newton, was so haunted by that sense of the transcendent that he devoted the latter part of his life to alchemical studies, expressing his yearning in a particularly poignant lament:

> I don't know what I may seem to the world, but as to myself, I seem to have been only like a boy playing on the sea-shore and diverting myself in now and then finding a smoother pebble or a prettier shell than ordinary, whilst the great ocean of truth lay all undiscovered before me (Newton, 1992, p.494).

Albert Einstein, another prodigious pioneer of science, echoes Newton in his belief in the reality of the mystical:

> The most beautiful and profound emotion we can experience is the sensation of the mystical. It is the source of all true science. He to whom this emotion is a stranger, who can no longer wonder and stand rapt in awe, is as good as dead. To know that what is impenetrable to us really exists, manifesting itself as the highest wisdom and the most radiant beauty, which our dull faculties can comprehend only in their primitive forms — this knowledge, this feeling, is at the center of true religion (Einstein, 1991, p. 191).

Not only is mystical experience an occurrence in the lives of most people, including scientists, but the mystical literature, which spans thousands of years and widely disparate cultures, exhibits a remarkable consistency in its description of mystical experience and its instructions for obtaining access to mystical knowledge. William James commented:

Journal of Consciousness Studies, **7**, No. 11–12, 2000, pp. 75–91

There is about mystical utterances an eternal unanimity which ought to make a critic stop and think (James, 1929, p. 410).

In this paper, I will present a way of understanding the mystical experience based on the role of intention in determining consciousness. This approach may enable us to understand a variety of mystical techniques and teachings without becoming entangled in obscure doctrines or religious-sounding terminology.

Meditation and Deautomatization

Before beginning medical school I had a mystical experience while camping on a lake in the Adirondacks. There were other people living in tent cabins along the lake but, essentially, I was alone. I used the isolation to grapple with personal questions and doubts that had emerged from the college years, especially 'What did I really want? Why was I dissatisfied?' I reflected that music and poetry had powerful appeal for me because they seemed to contain something important and satisfying. I decided that there existed a source of what the arts conveyed to me and what I needed was to draw closer to that source.

Having reached that conclusion, I began a routine of sitting each day for a half hour on a boulder perched on the water's edge. With eyes closed, I would try to reach out to that unknown something that I so intensely wanted to find. I didn't know where to look — there was just the wish, the desire, and that push to contact the source.

After a week or so, my perception of my surroundings changed. I began to see the details of what was around me; the stones and leaves appeared more intricately patterned, the colours brighter. Then, I began to sense an invisible emanation coming from the sky, the trees, the surrounding natural world. It was as if I could see it, but I really couldn't. I could feel it, but not with my usual senses. What was emanating to me was intrinsically positive, important, satisfying — something I knew I wanted without question. It was also clear to me that other people did not perceive it. I made a note to myself not to romanticize it; what I perceived was not a guarantee of bliss — I still experienced loneliness at my lakeside camp. Yet, at the same time, the perception was felt to be of paramount value.

The experience continued through the rest of the summer, but the summer came to an end. I returned to begin medical school and the perception became weaker and gradually faded away. Later, when the opportunity to do research arose, I began to read the mystical literature to try and understand what had taken place years earlier. Struck by the unanimity that had so impressed James and others, I concluded that the mystics were describing a real phenomenon, that their instructions must have validity, and that it might be possible to understand mysticism by employing reason, experiment, and knowledge of developmental and cognitive psychology.

I chose to begin by investigating meditation; in particular, the concentrative meditation described in the Yoga of Pantanjali. To do this, I rounded up friends and acquaintances, sat them down opposite a blue vase, and instructed them as follows:

The purpose of the sessions is to learn about concentration. Your aim is to concentrate on the blue vase [located on a table in front of the subjects]. By concentration I do not mean analyzing the different parts of the vase, or thinking a series of thoughts about the vase, or associating ideas to the vase; but rather, trying to see the vase as it exits in itself without any connection to other things. Exclude all other thoughts or feelings or sounds or body sensations. Do not let them distract you, but keep them out so that you can concentrate all your attention, all your awareness on the vase itself. Let the perception of the vase fill your entire mind (Deikman, 1963).

Each subject did this for half an hour, after which I questioned them about their experiences. Most participated in about forty sessions spread out over a few months, but striking changes in perception were reported very soon in the experiment. The vase was seen as becoming more vivid, more rich — 'luminous' was one description. It seemed to acquire a life of its own, to become animated. There was a lessening of the sense of being separate from the vase: 'I really began to feel . . . almost as though the blue and I were perhaps merging or that the vase and I were.' Synaesthetic phenomena were also reported: 'When the vase changes shape, I feel this in my body'; 'I began to feel this light going back and forth.'[1]

Although this was not a controlled scientific study, the reports of the subjects were consistent with those in the mystical literature. As I thought about the changes that had been reported, it occurred to me that they represented a reversal of the normal developmental process whereby infants and children learn to perceive, grasp and categorize objects. This learning progresses and as it does it becomes automatic; they no longer have to pay such close attention to the nature of objects. Instead, more and more attention is freed and put in the service of thought, of abstractions. The meditation activity that my subjects performed was the reverse of the developmental process: the percept (the vase) was invested with attention while thought was inhibited. As a consequence, sensuousness, merging of boundaries and sensory modalities became prominent. A *deautomatization* had occurred, permitting a different experience of the vase than would ordinarily be the case.

Since perceptual automatization is a hierarchical developmental process it would be expected that deautomatization would result in a shift toward a cognitive and perceptual experience that could be characterized as more 'primitive'. There is evidence supporting this. In a statement based on studies of eidetic imagery in children, as well as on broader studies of perceptual development, Heinz Werner concluded:

The image . . . gradually changed in functional character. It becomes essentially subject to the exigencies of abstract thought. Once the image changes in function and becomes an instrument of reflective thought, its structure will also change. It is only through such structural change that the image can serve as an instrument in abstract mental activity. This is why, of necessity. the sensuousness, fullness of detail, the color and the vivacity of the image must fade (Werner, 1957, p.152).

David Shapiro offered experimental evidence supporting this conclusion by studying the response of children of different ages to Rorschach images. He found

---

[1] For a detailed description of the experiment and an analysis of the data, see Tart (1990), pp. 241–65.

that with increasing age the children paid less and less attention to sensual aspects of the Rorschach cards, such as texture and colour, and progressively more attention to meaning, and to formal qualities such as shape and size (Shapiro, 1960).

Complementing Shapiro's findings were those of Daniel Brown who studied the Rorshach response of meditators of different levels of attainment and different meditative techniques. He found that in the case of advanced meditators, prominence was given to 'the pure perceptual features of the inkblots'. As one subject put it, '. . . the meditation has wiped out all the interpretive stuff on top of the raw perception' (Brown and Engler, 1986). These findings are consistent with the a reversal of the developmental shift from the sensory to the abstract — a deautomatization (Deikman, 1966).

Although the concept of deautomatization seems to explain some of the basic cognitive effects of meditation, it has been difficult to test the hypothesis neurophysiologically. Initially, it appeared to be supported by EEG studies of experienced Zen meditators. Kasamatsu and Hirai found an absence of habituation to a click stimulus (measured by alpha blocking) as compared to controls (Kasamatsu & Hirai, 1969). This, too, suggested that a sensory deautomatization had taken place. However, studies of Yogi adepts, as well as Zen practitioners, showed a great variability of EEG response due to the need to control for a variety of variables, such as the type of meditation being practised, whether the eyes were open or closed, the level of advancement of the meditation subjects, their state of arousal at the time, and the meaningfulness of the stimulus (Austin, 1998). However, the data do suggest that a shift toward increased sensory sensitivity takes place when concentrative meditation is practised with an external focus, as in my initial 'blue vase' experiments.

Bimodal Consciousness

The concept of deautomatization fits the meditation data very well and it encouraged me to continue to explore the cognitive basis of mystical activity. To do so, I sought first-hand experience in the spiritual traditions by participating in Zen Buddhism and, later, in Sufism. I soon realized that deautomatization was not the only process at work in mystical schools. Meditation — whether of the Yogic form I had used for the experiments, or the 'mindfulness' meditation of Buddhism — featured a *shift in intention* away from controlling and acquiring and toward acceptance and observation. The emphasis is on taking in instead of acting upon. Indeed this shift of intention is essential and more fundamentally important than the results of formal meditation. A student can meditate for years focused on breathing sensations but if she is inwardly trying to grasp enlightenment, to possess it, that acquisitive aim will lock her into the same form of consciousness with which she had begun. That is why mystics say that 'the secret protects itself'. No cheating is possible because it is the interior orientation that is critical. Psychologically speaking, there must be a shift from the grasping hand to one that is open. As I will now discuss, there are good reasons why this is so.

Consider that our cognitive development from infancy on is aimed toward success in manipulating objects. The pioneering work of Spitz (1925), Piaget (1954), and Gesell (1940) suggested that the infant must learn to perceive incoming stimuli, to make sense of then and to assign them meaning. These early researchers thought the infant started from scratch to create order out of a chaotic and confusing stimulus array. We know now that it is not that bad, some preformed perceptual and cognitive structures are present at birth (Kellman & Arterberry, 1998). For example, newborn infants will mimic the mother's facial movements: if the mother sticks out her tongue or opens her mouth, the infant will do likewise. This has been shown not to be a reflex but a genuine imitative capacity. Some edge perception is present at birth. However, there is still a very big difference between the discrimination of which an infant is capable and that of an adult. If one object is placed upon another, the infant will not recognize that they are separate objects unless one is moved relative to the other. The infant has a long way to go in its critical task of identifying and manipulating objects (Lomas, 1999). For this task upon which biologic survival ultimately depends, the infant must differentiate between objects, between self and others, and between self and objects. It turns out it has a head start in doing so:

> ... research indicates a very early and surprisingly sophisticated understanding of objects. This includes the ability to extrapolate trajectories of objects and the assumption that solid objects cannot pass through each other. A priori, we might not have thought it likely that these conceptions of the world would appear at such an early stage of development (Gopnik and Meltzoff, 1997).

Indeed, we are born ready to perceive the world as a collection of objects, of which we are one. The very concepts by which we think are influenced by this object learning, but we are not usually aware of the assumptions that underlie our reason. The concepts of space, time and causality fundamental to our thinking are actually the space, time and causality that pertain to the world of objects. That there are logics of reality beyond the instrumental or objective modes is indicated by the discoveries of modern physics, particularly the particle/wave duality of light, the evidence for nonlocality, and other paradoxes that have been proved true but that we cannot understand. To experience how object thinking limits our conceptions, try to visualize the universe coming to the end of its extent. You will find you can't do this. Now try and visualize it not coming to an end. You will find you can't do that, either. The problem is that objects come to an end, but the universe is not an object. Similarly, I think that is also why we cannot 'understand' quantum mechanics. We cannot relate it to the behaviour of the objects that we used to develop rational thought (Deikman, 1982). Thus, Feynman's famous quote:

> I think it safe to say that no one understands quantum mechanics. Do not keep saying to yourself, if you can possibly avoid it, 'But how can it be like that?' because you will go 'down the drain' into a blind alley from which nobody has yet escaped. Nobody knows how it can be like that (Pagels, 1990).

These considerations suggest that there are different modes of consciousness to serve our basic intentions — they are functional. To act on the world requires a sharp discrimination between self and others and between self and objects. Likewise, an acute sense of linear time is needed so that planning and anticipation can be done effectively. In contrast, to take in, to receive from the world calls for a different mode of consciousness, one in which boundaries are more diffuse, the Now is dominant, and thought gives way to sensation. These shifts often take place in normal life but we seldom realize what they are. When we manoeuvre a car in heavy traffic our consciousness is different that when, at the end of the day we sink into a hot tub and relax. The difference can be summarized as follows:

Instrumental Consciousness

[Example: Driving in heavy traffic]

Intent:	To act on the environment
Self:	Object-like, localized, separate from others Sharp boundaries Self-centered awareness
World:	Emphasis on objects, distinctions, and linear causality
Consciousness:	Focal attention Sharp perceptual boundaries Logical thought, reasoning Formal dominates sensual Past/future
Communication:	Language

This is the mode of consciousness we employ when planning a business strategy, or manoeuvering strategically at a social event. It's the one you are probably involved in as you read this article, checking for errors in logic, endeavouring to grasp my meaning, perhaps (if you are an author) waiting to see if I will reference something you've written. It's a good mode for that purpose.

Useful and necessary as this self may be, when it dominates consciousness it creates problems for the individual and for society. It underlies the exploitation of others, it supports violence and war, all of which depend on separateness, on disconnection. Disregard for the natural environment is another consequence. From the point of view of instrumental consciousness, 'When you see one redwood, you've seen them all.' Furthermore, because it forms a barrier to experiencing the connectedness of reality, instrumental dominance leads to meaninglessness, alienation, fear of aging and death.

When our intention shifts to receiving, to allowing, to a taking in of the environment, our consciousness changes also. Imagine slipping into a tub at the end of an exhausting day. As you enter the steaming water you can feel your muscles letting go. Your thoughts lose coherence and sensory impressions combine with drifting images. Instead of an emphasis on objects, distinctions and logical planning, as in your ordinary state, in the tub you seem to merge with the environment and what thoughts do arise are tangential and tend not to be logically connected. Rather than being occupied with thinking, in the tub you are occupied with sensations. Thus, instead of focused attention, sharp boundaries, and linear Time streaming from Past to Future, you experience blurred boundaries and tangential fantasies. What dominates awareness is Now, rather than Time. This receptive mode of consciousness can be summarized as follows:

Receptive Consciousness

[Example: Soaking in a hot tub]

Intent:	To receive the environment
Self:	Undifferentiated, nonlocalized, not distinct from environment Blurring or merging of boundaries World-centered awareness
World:	Emphasis on process, merging, and simultaneity
Consciousness:	Diffuse attention Blurred boundaries Alogical thought, intuition, fantasy Sensual dominates formal Now
Communication:	Music/art/poetry/dance

This discussion has necessarily been abstract. The reasoning and description may be logically convincing but it is limited in its impact. I would like you, the reader, to experience at first hand the effect of shifting intention on consciousness. 'He who tastes, knows.' So please follow these instructions:

Select a partner and sit or stand facing each other about an arm's distance away. (A human partner is best, but a flower can be used, or even a tree.) Begin by gazing at your partner's face with the intent of analysing it as if you were going to make a model of it. Note the proportions, study the planes of the head and the relationships of the eyes to the nose and mouth. Then, after doing that for a while, shift your intention to one of receiving, of taking in your partner's face, being open to it, allowing it to be whatever it becomes.

You will notice a different experience of your partner when you shift your intention in that way. Most people report that the receptive intent yields an experience that is 'richer', 'deeper', 'mysterious', meaningful. The instrumental experience is easier to describe, it lends itself to measurement, comparisons, analysis. The receptive experience is more difficult to talk about because our language is adapted to the instrumental mode. Each mode reveals different aspects of your partner's reality.

It is not only intention that is an important determinant of consciousness, the extent of self-awareness or self-consciousness is also a factor. To experience this, try the same procedure again, but this time start by looking at your partner's face while maintaining a clear sense of your self. After registering that experience, allow the your sense of self to subside, diminish, disappear. Notice the change in your experience of your partner. Once again, the experience is likely to be different in the two conditions. I think you will find that as the sense of self diminishes and drops out, the experience becomes 'deeper'. Your partner acquires a dimension of what might be called 'presence'.

The self of instrumental consciousness has distinct characteristics related to that mode. Instrumental consciousness features separation. The emphasis is on boundaries, differences, form and distinctions. Consequently, the self is experienced as a discrete object, basically isolated, whose survival if the dominant concern. I will call it the survival self. That self is described below:

The Survival Self

Characteristics:	Aim of self-preservation Self-focused Self as object distinct from environment
Positive Effects:	Able to defend, acquire Able to achieve material goals
Negative Effects:	Basis for traditional vices Dissatisfaction Access to conceptual meaning only Fear of death
Importance:	Needed for individual survival

In contrast, experience of self when receptivity is high and the survival self subdued, or secondary, can be quite different. This consciousness is not occupied with the personal self but with the larger reality that contains it. In this mode there is a qualitative change in the experience of self such that the term 'spiritual' is appropriate, depending on how far its development has proceeded. The characteristics and effects of the spiritual self are summarized below:

The Spiritual Self

Characteristics:	Aim of service, attunement Other-centered Self identified with larger life process, resonant with environment
Positive Effects:	Satisfaction Basis for traditional virtues Experienced meaning Equanimity
Negative Effects:	Tendency to passivity Ineffective in defending, acquiring
Importance:	May be needed for survival of the human species

It should be noted that these 'selves' are not separate entities. What we consider to be our self is really that with which we have learned to identify. Most of the time we use 'self' to refer to the wishes and emotions localized in the physical body we inhabit. However, if we undergo psychotherapy or practise meditation, we may begin to identify with the activity of observing these same contents; we step back and separate, psychologically, from the passions and concepts that we have considered to be ourselves, but now are the objects of our observation. We may carry the process further and identify with pure awareness — awareness apart from contents — as the most fundamental 'I', suggesting a profound change in our concept of who and what we are (Deikman, 1996; Forman, 1999).

Both instrumental and receptive consciousness are needed. Problems arise when one excludes or crowds out the other. For most of us, instrumental dominance is extreme, but we do not realize this since our culture is strongly materialistic and our science is based on instrumental consciousness. That mode presents us with only a partial view of reality. To meet our needs for connection and meaning a shift is required. It is as if you came to a stream and wanted to drink. If you persisted in trying to grab the water — your usual approach — you would obtain nothing. If you wanted to drink you would have to cup your hands. The requirement has nothing to do with piety; it has to do with the nature of water.

The activity of mystical schools is to help a person 'forget the self', to diminish the extent to which survival needs dominate consciousness, to learn to cup the hands. It is a difficult task. So it is not surprising that a careful study of mystical practice reveals that in addition to meditation, so widely popular and publicized, there is a central emphasis on two other less glamorous activities: renunciation and service.

Renunciation and Service

Renunciation and service are usually discussed in the context of morality, virtue, and saintliness. But we need not approach this as a moral issue, but as a straightforward matter of cognitive psychology. As I have described, our survival as biological organisms takes priority in development. This survival requires the development of a self that can acquire supplies, defend them against others, and take from others what might be needed or desired. This is the self-as-object, the survival self. It pervades our everyday experience. Our society keeps it activated with threats of danger, promises of pleasure, prestige and ease, and encouraging competition for wealth and power. This situation is not just a matter of runaway capitalism. After all, Buddha preached to a society existing two thousand years before our own time. The Buddhist sutras and the scriptures of Vedanta were addressed to people living well before the advent of advertising and the stock market. The fact is that self-centered consciousness has always been with us as a matter of biological necessity. The problem facing spiritual teachers was that they had to start with people who, no matter how self-consciously 'spiritual', were devoted to the survival self. The teacher had to bring about a transition to a consciousness that was primarily other-centred, rather than self-centred. Only then could they taste of a consciousness that features a sense of the connectedness of everything, a unity, a reconciliation of the polar opposites that comprise our usual perspective. This cannot occur in the instrumental mode. Thomas Merton commented on this incompatibility in his book, *Zen and the Birds of Appetite*. He describes meat-eating birds (the survival self) looking for carrion:

> Zen enriches no one. There is no body to be found. The birds may come and circle for a while in the place where it is thought to be. But they soon go elsewhere. When they are gone, the 'nothing,' the 'no-body' that was there, suddenly appears. That is Zen. It was there all the time but the scavengers missed it, because it was not their kind of prey (Merton, 1968, p. ix).

Profound connection is what the word 'spiritual' properly refers to. The spiritual is not a matter of visions of angels, or of being carried away by ecstatic emotion. The mystics are clear about that. At its most basic, *the spiritual is the experience of the connectedness that underlies reality.* The depth of that experience depends on the capacity of the individual to set aside considerations of self, thereby gaining access to connection. Although people differ in the extent and frequency with which they gain that access, the genuine experience abolishes competitive comparisons. 'I am more spiritual than he' is no longer meaningful because the 'I' and the 'he' are now experienced as part of a greater whole, not separate. Comparison requires separation.

Evidence for Connection

What evidence do we have that reality is in some way connected so as to be a unified whole rather than a collection of independently existing parts? It is common to cite quantum mechanics in support of this proposition. Quantum theory, whose predictions have been repeatedly confirmed, have led many physicists to the conclusion that reality is an interconnected whole, capable of instantaneous response at a distance. In one well-known experiment involving the emission of paired photons, a change in the polarization of one photon is accompanied by a simultaneous change in the polarization of the other — no matter how far apart they are. This change is not the result of a signal passing from the first to the second (that would exceed the speed of light). Rather, there is an instantaneous correlation of events that implies a unity of which both protons are a part. The results of this experiment are often cited to support mystics' assertions. These findings may indeed be based in the same reality of which mystics speak, but they may not. Furthermore, physicists are not in agreement as to the interpretation of this and other experiments. Just as some physicists believe that the act of measurement 'collapses' the probability wave function to produce an event, others dispute the metaphor of 'collapse' and the putative role of human consciousness in that process. The fact is, the theory of physics is in continuous development and evolution. Jeremy Bernstein has warned:

> The science of the present will look as antiquated to our successors as much of the nineteenth-century science looks to us now. To hitch a religious philosophy to a contemporary science is a sure route to obsolescence (Bernstein, 1978/1979).

Although the conclusions of particle physicists and the poetic utterances of mystics do invite risky comparisons, we need not rely on drawing parallels between them. Instead, we can focus on two other sources that testify to the interconnectedness and unified nature of reality: (1) the consensus of the mystical literature and (2) the reports of persons for whom service (helping others) is a major focus of their lives.

The compelling consensus of mystics is that the perception of oneself as an object — fundamentally isolated within our own consciousness — is an illusion, a misconception that is the source of human destructiveness and suffering. It might be argued that this consensus is due to social contagion, ideas spreading through direct contact from: one mystic to another, across cultural and geographic boundaries. Against such a proposition is the fact that Buddhism, Taoism, the Upanishads and the 'wisdom' books of the Old Testament all arose in different cultures at about the same time, around 500BC. Something seemed to be happening during that time that resulted in a direct experience of a reality not easily comprehended and hard to imitate. Conceptual transmission by itself could not do this, especially as the mystical experience is ineffable. Techniques such as meditation could be passed along via trade routes but there must be a common reality that is thereby revealed. Something had to be there to be discovered.

Further evidence against merely social contagion is the fact that mystics from theistic religions assert a reality that is in conflict with the dogma of their church. Sometimes the conflict is open, as in the case of Hallaj, the Sufi mystic who proclaimed 'I am God' and was dismembered for his blasphemy. Christian mystics tend to be more indirect in their metaphors. They may not assert the position of Hallaj that each person is fundamentally identical with the Godhead instead of being separate, however they describe something similar that is not really compatible with Christian dogma. Here is a representative statement by St John of the Cross:

> That inward vision is so simple, so general and so spiritual that it has not entered into the understanding enwrapped or clad in any form or image subject to sense; it follows that sense and imagination (as it has not entered through them nor has taken their form or color) cannot account for it or imagine, so as to say anything concerning it, although the soul be clearly aware that it is experiencing and partaking of that rare and delectable wisdom (St John, 1953, p. 457).

The usual theological concepts have no place in such an experience. Theistic teaching is of God the Father, of Heaven and Hell, but Christian mystics like St John of the Cross are quite explicit in stating that the experience of the reality of God, the Ultimate, cannot be expressed in terms of the things of this world. The problem for theologians is that the concept of reward and punishment, handed out by an omnipotent, omniscient God, is a derivative of the family experience, of child and parent — definitely a conception of this world. The difference between mystics' experience and theological dogma is the reason why mystics have been a perpetual problem for traditional religion. This conflict attests to the fundamental nature of the mystics' experience. It feels ultimate, beyond the domain of the sensory and the rational, more real.

As I noted earlier, there is the additional fact that non-mystics also report experiences consistent with mystics' reports, although these moments when connection is vivid and boundaries dissolve are usually brief and of less depth. As Austin has pointed out, there is a difference between the connectedness and no-self that a lover may feel in the transports of sexual union, and the radical shift in world perspective that takes place in the much more rare event of kensho or enlightenment (Austin, 1998). Nevertheless, both experiences are along the same dimension of connection, as opposed to separation.

If connection is real, and if to experience that dimension of reality requires an appropriate mode of consciousness, then we are now in position to understand why mystical schools in addition to prescribing meditation, stress the critical role of renunciation and service.

Since survival self aims dictate the nature of our experience, we can understand that meditation offers some relief from that tyranny by (1) shifting intention from acting to allowing, (2) from identification with emotions to identification with the observer, and (3) shifting from instrumental thinking to receptive experience. Furthermore, renunciation is not to be equated with self-denial, self-mortification, or asceticism. As one Zen master put it, 'Renunciation is not giving up the things of this world; it is accepting that they go away' (Suzuki, 1968). 'Accepting that they go away' is an orientation that opens the grasping hand and facilitates the shift away from the acquisitive aims that activate survival self consciousness. Without that letting go, renunciation could be utilized as just another way to fulfill survival self aims, something that one teacher has labelled 'spiritual materialism' (Trungpa, 1973). Mystics are acutely aware of the problem. Rabia, a Sufi mystic, prayed dramatically for relief from self-centred aims:

> Oh Lord:
> If I worship you from fear of hell, cast me into hell,
> If I worship you from desire for paradise, deny me Paradise
> (Shah, 1968, pp. 219–20).

The Service Experience

Service is probably the most effective activity for providing access to the connectedness of reality. However, like renunciation, 'service' is loaded with moral and religious associations. It is thought to mean sacrifice, the handing over of time and money and the reward of being a 'good' person entitled to a heavenly homesite. The functional dynamics of service are not appreciated. Consider the problem of motivation. If one does a good deed in the expectation that it will be noted in the Book of Heavenly Record, what is taking place is a commercial transaction. The survival self is still running the show. To illustrate this point, imagine a business man who becomes dissatisfied with material possessions. He then reads about the bliss of enlightenment wants that. So he joins a spiritual group and faxes a notice of his new intention to the computer control centre in his brain. An underling reads the fax and rushes to the boss. 'This guy says he's no longer interested in money; he wants enlightenment. What program should we install?' The boss glances quickly at the fax. 'It's the same program: Acquisition.'

It is very hard to find a way of being active that is not self-centred, that is not ultimately selfish. The cynic argues: 'Doing good gives you pleasure, makes you feel good, so it is just another pleasure-seeking activity and, therefore, basically selfish.' The argument can be hard to counter, but there is a way out of the quandary: *serving-the-task*. A carpenter may finish the underside of a chair even though he will receive no more money for doing so and his customers don't care. He does it because it feels *called for*. His motivation is not in the service of the survival self, but a response to a sense of wholeness or of need. True service, the kind that opens the doors of perception, is of this type.

Serving-the-task requires a balance of instrumental and receptive modes for optimum effectiveness. Instrumental consciousness is needed to act, but receptive consciousness allows access to subtle information derived from the unified, connected aspects of the world. This helps sense the way a particular action would fit the situation in its less obvious aspects. The experience of 'being in the zone' reported by athletes, or the 'good hour' experienced by psychotherapists, is probably based on an optimum balance of the two modes.[2]

Persons performing service in a major way are very aware of the difference between self-consciously 'doing good' versus serving-the-task, doing what is called for. The former can lead to burn-out, or self-inflation, whereas the latter energizes and connects. The difference between the two types was summarized for me by a physician who established a medical clinic in Tibet:

> There's three kinds of people — I don't know if I can say it right — there's the one who's walking on the beach and he sees a beer can on the beach and he looks around and makes sure everybody's watching and picks up the beer can and throws it away. . . . The second kind of person is walking on the beach, sees the beer can thrown on the beach, but there's nobody around but he still picks it up and throws it in the garbage can because he knows God is watching. Then there's the third kind of person who's walking along the beach, sees the beer can, throws it in the garbage and doesn't care who is watching just because that's what needs to be done. I guess it's that third kind of motivation that's not ego-directed that one seeks. It's hard to get there . . .

Recently, I interviewed twenty-four service providers almost all of whom gave evidence that people who serve-the-task experience a sense of connection to something larger than themselves. Their reports are very consistent. Here is a representative statement from a man who founded an organization providing care for AIDS sufferers. He spoke of the development of capacity to serve-the-task, and the change in the experience of the self that accompanies it:

> . . . a self-conscious highly moralized 'doing-good' is *very* far from the place that I recognize as valuable. . . . When I'm more self-consciously helping it's usually because I'm in a survival mode. . . . What's going through my mind is fundamentally different. . . . [In true service] I'm not serving myself, there is not that aspect to it, or wanting to get brownie points for Heaven. . . . 'Doing what needs to be done' is the

---

[2] See also Csikszentmihaly (1957).

way I used to say it to the Shanti volunteers. . . . There's an extension of self that occurs . . . an extension of my self to include the other person. What's in his best interest is in *my* best interests . . . an evolution goes on from doing things *to* the patient or the person you serve, to doing things *with* the person you serve, to doing things *as* the person you serve. There's an extension of myself to include the other person. . . . You're serving something greater and deeper than the person in front of you, knowing that person will benefit as a consequence if you can get to this place.

He concluded:

[When serving-the-task] we've allowed our personalities, our egos, to move from the driver's seat to the backseat. And what's sitting in front is your highest self and my highest self. And *that's* what's connected . . . we allowed our higher selves to emerge . . . who I was serving was a lot more than just the human being in front of me.

Another service provider, a management consultant to non-profit organizations, also commented on the experience of connection:

I feel that connection is real. I think it's not just the two people connecting. I think it's the two people connecting to whatever this is . . . there's a feeling of a larger connectedness than just between two people.

Almost the same words are used by a physician who founded an organization that provides support for cancer patients. She said she knows when something is really service:

It's a sense of connection that you have to something beyond the moment when you do that. . . . It's like seeing both of you as part of a much larger process that has no beginning and no end.

The experience of connection can be very helpful to the service provider. A man who heads a hospice describes his experience:

I see in the midst of this that I am caring for myself in taking care of this other person, that I don't have such a feeling of separation in this world. When I'm standing at arm's length from this person, trying to keep their separate existence, I feel continually isolated and fragmented in a way. Whereas when I let it in, include it in my life, I don't have that feeling of fragmentation or separation so much anymore.

The testimony for connection among people who serve-the-task is striking and compelling. If we grant the possibility that the experience of connection reflects what is real, the importance of service in the mystical tradition makes perfect sense. When a server can lessen the dominance of the survival self — her 'ego needs' — she can then experience a different organization of consciousness, one that is responsive to connectedness. Through that connectedness she experiences a different, larger sense of self. What stands in the way of our accepting such testimony is the invisible nature of that connection; It is not perceptible by vision or touch. The closest some servers can come to describing the quality of the experience is to speak of 'energy':

Some kind of current goes through the space you're in . . . you can really feel this flow happening. Whether it's energy or current or what it is, but I definitely know when it's happening . . .

The connection is at an energetic level . . . it's like food for the emotional or nervous system that really is a tangible energy exchange.

I felt very connected to the men I was sitting next to, and in fact there was almost a literal electric charge that was passing back and forth between us . . .

The nature of the connection cannot be specified, at least so far. But the testimony of the mystical literature, referred to earlier, says that the connection is real — not an illusion.

Mystical Knowledge

I do not know if energy is an accurate metaphor for the connectedness to which these people gain access, but their consensus suggests that they are experiencing something real as a consequence of the change in their motivation, in their guiding intention, a change that lessens the power of the survival self to determine consciousness. The functional understanding of mysticism that I have proposed makes this effect of serving-the-task understandable and unites these service experiences with the classical mystical literature.

This balanced interplay between modes may be what Yeats was referring to when he described Michelangelo's creative activity:

Like a spider moving upon the water,
His mind moves upon silence (Yeats, 1951, pp. 327–8).

We are now in a position to appreciate the straightforward nature of mystical knowledge. This knowledge does not require living in a monastery, wearing foreign clothing, sitting cross-legged in meditation, burning incense or chanting sutras. Exotic practices are not essential, they may even be barriers if they lead practitioners to imagine they are 'advanced', or being 'spiritual' , thus reinforcing survival self consciousness. What is required is a shift from a consciousness focused on the disconnected aspect of reality to a mode of consciousness responsive to its connected aspects. Although we may be intellectually persuaded that a unified world exists, the difficulty is to experience that world, not just to believe it. That experience is the goal of mysticism.

Far from being esoteric, mystics propose the most modern, and at the same time the most ancient instruction for effective functioning and a fulfilled life: 'know thyself'. But the Self of which mystics speak is often capitalized to indicate it is different from, and superordinate to, the self of which we are usually conscious. Mystics teach a way of attaining that knowledge of Self. The procedures of meditation, renunciation and service that mystics employ are not really mysterious, just radically different from our usual object-oriented, instrumental approach.

Thousands of books of philosophy line the shelves of our libraries without one book providing a satisfactory answer to the fundamental question 'What is the meaning of life?' No verbal answer has ever sufficed — thus the thousands of books. The problem is that the mode of consciousness that asks the question is not the mode of consciousness that can hear the answer. When Job questions the meaning of his life his comforters offer logic and words — to no avail. Job finally is satisfied only by seeing (experiencing) Jehovah, not just hearing about Him.

Judging by the reports those who serve-the-task, service can provide a non-verbal answer also. I say this because for people who serve in that way, the question of the meaning of life no longer arises. That non-verbal experience is what mysticism is about. With this in mind, we can now understand why the basic instruction of the mystical traditions is to 'forget the self'. To forget the self is not a matter of morality, goodness, or sainthood, but a matter of access to the connected aspects of the world and to a different, more extended experience of the self. 'Forgetting the self' is not easy, but mystics have developed ways of facilitating that process. The various techniques and activities of the mystical traditions may appear exotic, but they can be understood as a way of going beyond the limitations of instrumental, self-centred, consciousness.

Such a development is more important now than ever before. When we consider the problems that confront us — sociological, environmental, and technological — we can see that ameliorating and solving these problems will require a shift in which connected, other-centred consciousness becomes more dominant. Because of this, the further progress and survival of the human race may depend on that very shift in consciousness to which the mystical traditions are devoted. For this reason alone, as well as for achieving a more profound understanding of reality, the mystical traditions deserve our study and close attention.

References

Austin, James H. (1998), *Zen and the Brain: Toward an Understanding of Meditation and Consciousness* (Cambridge, MA: MIT Press).

Bernstein, Jeremy (1978/1979), 'A cosmic flow', *American Scholar*, Winter, pp. 6–8.

Brown, Daniel and Engler, Jack (1986), 'The stages of mindfulness meditation: a validation study'. in *Transformations of Consciousness: Conventional and Contemplative Perspectives on Development*, Ken Wilber, Jack Engler and Daniel Brown (Boston, MA: Shambala).

Csikszentmihaly, Mihaly (1997), *Finding Flow: The Psychology of Engagement with Everyday Life* (New York: Basic Books).

Deikman, Arthur J. (1963), 'Experimental meditation', *Journal of Nervous and Mental Disease*, **136**, pp. 329–43.

Deikman, Arthur J. (1966), 'Deautomatization and the mystic experience', *Psychiatry*, **29**, pp. 324–38.

Deikman, Arthur J. (1982), *The Observing Self* (Boston, MA: Beacon Press).

Deikman, Arthur J. (1996), '"I" equals awareness', *Journal of Consciousness Studies*, **3** (4), pp. 350–6.

Einstein, Albert (1991), in *The Enlightened Mind*, ed. Stephen Mitchell (New York: Harper Collins).

Forman, Robert (1999), *Mysticism, Mind, Consciousness* (Albany: SUNY Press).

Gesell, Arnold (1940), *The First Year of Life: A Guide to the Study of the Pre-school Child* (New York: Harper and Row).

Gopnik, Alison and Meltzoff, Andrew (1997), *Words, Thoughts, and Theories* (Cambridge, MA: MIT Press).

Gill, Merton and Brenman, Margaret (1959), *Hypnosis and Related States: Psychoanalytic Studies in Regression* (New York: International Universities Press).

Hartmann, Heinz (1958), *Ego Psychology and the Problem of Adaptation* (New York: International Universities Press).

James, William (1929), *The Varieties of Religious Experience* (New York: The Modern Library).

Kasamatsu, Akira and Hirai, Tomia (1969), 'An electroencephalographic study of Zen meditation (zazen)', *Psychologia*, **12**, pp. 205–25. Cited in *Meditation: Classical and Contemporary Perspectives*, Deane H. Shapiro and Roger Walsh (New York: Aldine, 1984), p. 480.

Kellman, Philip J. and Arterberry, Martha E. (1998), *The Cradle of Knowledge: The Development of Perception in Infants* (Cambridge, MA: MIT Press).

Lomas, Dennis (1999), 'Review of Kellman and Arteberry, *The Cradle of Knowledge*', *Journal of Consciousness Studies*, **6** (5), pp. 88–9.

Merton, Thomas (1968), *Zen and the Birds of Appetite* (New York: New Directions).

Newton, Isaac (1992), cited in *The Oxford Dictionary of Quotations* (Oxford: Oxford University Press).

Piaget, Jean (1954), *The Construction of Reality in the Child* (New York: Basic Books).

Shah, Idries (1968), *The Way of the Sufi* (London: Jonathan Cape).

Shapiro, David. (1960), 'A perceptual understanding of color response', in *Rorschach Psychology*, ed. M. Richers-Ovsiankina (New York: Wiley).

Spitz, Renée (1925), *The First Year of Life* (New York: International Universities Press).

St John of the Cross (1953), *The Complete Works of St. John of the Cross*, Vol.1. (Westminster: Newman Press).

Suzuki, Shunryu (1968), Lecture, July. Zen Mountain Center, *Wind Bell*, **7**, p. 28.

Tart, Charles (1990), *Altered States of Consciousness* (3rd Edition; San Francisco, CA: Harper).

Trungpa, Chogyam (1973), *Cutting Through Spiritual Materialism* (Berkeley, CA: Shambala).

Werner, Heinz (1957), *Comparative Psychology of Mental Development* (New York: International Universities Press).

Yeats, William Butler (1951), *The Collected Poems of W.B. Yeats* (New York: Macmillan).

Stanley Krippner

The Epistemology and Technologies of Shamanic States of Consciousness

Shamanism can be described as a group of techniques by which its practitioners enter the 'spirit world', purportedly obtaining information that is used to help and to heal members of their social group. The shamans' epistemology, or ways of knowing, depended on deliberately altering their conscious state and/or heightening their perception to contact spiritual entities in 'upper worlds', 'lower worlds' and 'middle earth' (i.e., ordinary reality). For the shaman, the totality of inner and outer reality was fundamentally an immense signal system, and shamanic states of consciousness were the first steps toward deciphering this signal system. Homo sapiens sapiens was probably unique among early humans in the ability to symbolize, mythologize and, eventually, to shamanize. This species' eventual domination may have been due to its ability to take sensorimotor activity and use it as a bridge to produce narratives that facilitated human survival. Shamanic technologies, essential for the production and performance of myths and other narratives, interacted with shamanic epistemology, reinforcing its basic assumptions about reality.

> The brain is a machine assembled not to understand itself, but to survive.
>
> (E.O. Wilson, 1998)

Although the term 'shaman' is of uncertain derivation, it is often traced to the language of the Tungus reindeer herders of Siberia where the word *šaman* translates into 'one who is excited, moved, or raised' (Casanowicz, 1924; Lewis, 1990, pp. 10–12). An alternative translation for the Tungus word is 'inner heat', and an alternative etymology is the Sanskrit word *saman* or 'song' (Hoppal, 1987). Each of these terms applies to the activities of shamans, past and present, who enter what is often described as 'an ecstatic state' in order to engage in spiritual practices that benefit their community (pp. 91–2). The adaptive character of shamanism is confirmed by its ubiquitous appearance around the world, not only in hunter-gatherer and fishing societies, but in centralized societies as well.

Journal of Consciousness Studies, **7**, No. 11–12, 2000, pp. 93–118

Much of the behaviour of other animals is instinctive, and their experience modifies these complex, inborn patterns of behaviour. However, drives and biological propensities, not innate behaviour patterns, characterize humans. Non-human animals, especially gorillas and chimpanzees, probably compare environmental stimuli to the memory images from past interactions. Humans fall on this continuum as well, and the satisfaction of their vital needs was once highly dependent on their ability to use these images to produce the tools and procedures appropriate for drive satisfaction. Eventually, these procedures included a variety of social interactions including speech and ritual behaviour (Guryev, 1990, p. 124; V. Turner, 1968).

Ritual afforded an opportunity to express the community's conceptions of reality in a social setting. Ritual, a step-by-step social performance, is the key to the structure of a group's mythology, or worldview. In shamanic societies especially, ritual is a stylized technology, one whose symbols and metaphors may well trigger healing, relieve suffering, and provide a link between the ordinary world and those realms purportedly traversed by the shaman (Krippner, 1993; E. Turner, 1992, p. 14; V. Turner, 1968).

The *Veladas* of María Sabina

Shamanic rituals were essential to the career of the Mazatec Indian María Sabina, who lived in the state of Oaxaca, Mexico. Born about 1894, María Sabina led a life of severe hardship. Her father died when she was quite young, and her first husband abused her terribly. After his death, she married again but her second husband died when she was in her 40s. Since childhood, María Sabina had been interested in herbs and worked for a period of time as a *curandera* or herbalist. Later, she felt that she had been called to become a *sabía* (i.e., 'one who knows') and ingested psilocybin mushrooms as a way of 'knowing' the condition and treatment of her clients. During my interviews with her in 1980, doña María told me that Jesus Christ and other spiritual entities came to her and her client during the *veladas* (evening mushroom ceremonies), bringing information about her client's problem and its resolution.

As a *sabía* or shamanic healer, María Sabina manifested considerable control during the *veladas*, chanting liturgies containing an overlay of Roman Catholic imagery which cloaked the odes used by the Indian priests who had been overthrown by the Spaniards in the 1520s. The Spanish Inquisition outlawed the *veladas*, but the Mazatecs took them underground for four centuries. One night, María Sabina dreamed that it was her mission to share this sacred knowledge with the world. Soon after this dream, on June 29, 1955, a group of U.S. investigators headed by R. Gordon Wasson arrived. Eventually, doña María and the psilocybin mushrooms were featured in *Life* magazine, and the field of ethnomycology was born (Estrada, 1981; Wasson, 1981). Doña María's reported dream is unique for several reasons: it ran counter to the attempt of male elders to keep their practices secret, and its egalitarian and universal motive violated the political power of her society's male hierarchy. She paid dearly for this action; her grocery store was burned to the ground and her son was murdered.

María Sabina's worldview is expressed in her chants; in one, she apparently alludes to her shamanic journeys:

> I am a woman who flies.
> I am the sacred eagle woman, [the mushroom] says;
> I am the Lord eagle woman;
> I am the lady who swims;
> Because I can swim in the immense,
> Because I can swim in all forms.
> I am the shooting star woman,
> I am the shooting star woman beneath the water,
> I am the lady doll,
> I am the sacred clown,
> Because I can swim,
> Because I can fly (Estrada, 1981, abridged, pp. 93–4, 96).

Doña María's feelings of unity with nature and with the spirit world is revealed by another set of chants; the lyrics also portray her active role in attaining knowledge:

> I have the heart of the Virgin,
> I have the heart of Christ,
> I have the heart of the Father,
> I have the heart of the Old One,
> It's that I have the same soul,
> The same heart as the saint, as the saintess;
> I am a spirit woman,
> A woman of good words, good breath, good saliva,
> I am the little woman of the great expanse of the waters,
> I am the little woman of the expanse of the divine sea.
> I am a woman who looks into the insides of things,
> A woman who investigates, Holy Father,
> I am a woman born, I am a child born,
> I am a woman fallen into the world (pp. 107, 129–30).

In other words, María Sabina employed an investigatory way of knowing; she 'looks into the insides of things'. She, and other shamans, learn from 'the spirits', 'the waters', and 'the divine sea'. Tradition and holy writ might provide source material for the shaman, but it is his or her 'heart' and 'soul' that are the final arbiters of knowledge.

Shamanism as a Biologically Derived Specialization

Winkelman (1997) proposes that María Sabina and other shamans represent a 'biologically derived' human specialization, and that these potentials are actualized through social adaptations. This proposition could be used to explain the worldwide appearance of shamans as well as the fundamental role of altered conscious states and/or heightened perception in shamanic healing and divination practices. An example of divination has been given by Lerche (2000). In his quest for the lost tribes of the Peruvian Chachapoya (or 'cloud people'), he consulted a shaman who drew on the power of ritual objects. The shaman had a vision that some of the tombs remained unharmed and, soon after the consultation, Lerche detected a mummy bundle in a tomb high on a cliff (p. 68).

These potentials can be described as 'neurognostic' because they involve neural networks that provide the biological substrate for ways of knowing (Laughlin *et al.*, 1990), i.e., epistemology. I would add that these neurognostic potentials are not the exclusive domain of shamans; primordial humans performed healing and divinatory functions themselves before specialization established a hierarchy. Evidence for this position can be found in fairly egalitarian tribal societies such as the !Kung of southwestern Africa where about half the males and a sizable number of females shamanize, producing the 'boiling energy' (i.e., sweat) used in their healing rituals (Katz, 1982).

Neurognostic potentials provide the basis for those forms of perception, cognition, and affect that are structured by the organism's neurological systems. They are probably reflected in what Jungians call 'archetypes', which can be conceptualized as the predispositions that provide organizing principles for the basic modes of consciousness and elementary behaviour patterns, including the intuitive capacity to initiate, control, and mediate everyday behaviour.

Stevens (1982) suggests that 'from the viewpoint of modern neurology, Jung's work stands as a brilliant vindication of . . . the value of intuitive knowledge' (pp. 273–4). When ritualized shamanic performance is described as 'archetypal', the activity reflects biologically based modes of consciousness, a replacement of the ordinary waking state through discharge patterns that produce interhemispheric synchronization and coherence, limbic-cortex integration, and integral discharges that synthesize cognition, affect, and behaviour (Winkelman, 1992). Shweder (1979) found that Zinacanteco shamans in Mexico possess cognitive capacities that distinguish them from non-shamans such as having available a number of constructive categories, imposing these forms onto ambiguous situations; these integrative capacities may have facilitated the development of shamanic epistemologies over the millennia.

A variety of procedures, agents, and other technologies are available to evoke limbic system slow wave discharges that synchronize the frontal cortex (Mandell, 1980). In addition, shamans can be characterized as 'fantasy-prone' (Wilson & Barber, 1983), endowed with capacities, genetic to some degree, that facilitate their use of imaginative processes. Fantasy-proneness exists on a continuum; most humans engage in fantasy, imagination, and play (especially 'pretending' and 'role-playing') periodically, but shamans draw upon this trait for their specialization.

Many of the early shamans may not have been dependent on transient consciousness alteration but manifested a heightened perceptual style that was part of their everyday state of consciousness. Berman (2000) suggests that 'heightened awareness' may be a more accurate description of shamanic consciousness than 'altered state' because their intense experience of the natural world is described by them in such terms as 'things often seem to blaze' (p. 30). Paradoxically, shamans are characterized both by an acute perception of their environment and by imaginative fantasy. These traits (the ability to construct categories, the potential for pretending and role-playing, and the capacity to experience the natural world vividly) gave shamans an edge over peers who had simply embraced life as it presented itself, without the filters of myth or ritual (Berman, 2000, p. 81).

All of these traits may be related to the evolution of the human brain, namely the development of specialized subsystems that are activated during shifts in consciousness. The hallmark of cortical evolution is not the ever-increasing sophistication of specialized cortical circuitry but an increasing representational flexibility that allows environmental factors to shape the human brain's structure and function (Gazzaniga, 1994; Quartz & Sejnowski, 1997). Pinker (1997) suggests that the 'mind' is made up of many modules, each honed by aeons of evolution, and shamans may have learned to integrate these modules (Winkelman, 2000, p. 7). If so, shamanic technologies represent the initial institutionalized practices for this integration, both through shifts in consciousness and community bonding rituals (Winkelman, 1997). These practices became codified in the form of myth, ritual, and ceremony, providing for social solidarity and specialization.

McClenon (1997) hypothesizes that the benefits of shamanic states of consciousness elicited an evolutionary increase in genes that would expedite this condition. However, all cultural changes in the past 90,000 to 100,000 years of *homo sapiens sapiens* (i.e., modern humans) have been environmental, not genetic (DeMause, 1998). Therefore, this essay takes the position that once *homo sapiens sapiens* arrived on the scene, and once shamanism developed as a societal specialization, the contributions of shamanism to the evolution of human consciousness took on socio-cultural roots that built upon humanity's biological (i.e., neurognostic) groundings.

The initiation and direction of thought and behaviour owes as much to social construction as it does to biology (Rychlak, 1997, p. 143). Furthermore, all human societies contain inventive people but some of them provide more unusual materials and more favorable conditions for utilizing new technologies than do others in the same environment (Diamond, 1997, p. 408). It is likely that spiritual activities originally involved the entire clan, but changing social and economic conditions brought about shamanic specialization and, later, a priesthood (Anisimov, 1963) and social inequality (Berman, 2000, p. 82).

Shamanic Technologies

The oral traditions that preserved the myths that structured a culture's identity and worldview may not have been originated by shamans, but eventually were passed down by them (Wiercinski, 1989). For example, María Sabina and her fellow shamans preserved, in their chants and rituals, Mazatec mythologies for more than four centuries, preserving their cultural identity in the face of Spanish oppression. To facilitate this societal function, many shamans developed techniques to assist the elicitation and movement of 'inner' heat, to enable their shamanic journeys, and to facilitate their contact with the 'upper' and 'lower' worlds. This technology allowed them to encounter spirits, ancestors, animal totems, and other resources that had found their way into mythological songs and stories.

Epistemology is concerned with the nature, characteristics and processes of knowledge, and in this essay I am suggesting that shamanic epistemology drew upon perceptual, cognitive, affective and somatic ways of knowing that assisted early humans to find their way through an often unpredictable, sometimes hostile, series of environmental challenges. Not only did early humans have to become aware of potentially dangerous environmental objects and activities, they needed to have explanatory stories (enacted as mythic rituals) at their disposal to navigate through the contingencies of daily encounters and challenges. The acute perceptual abilities of shamans, in combination with their intuition and imagination, met their societies' needs.

Eliade (1972/1951) writes of the 'technologies of the sacred', and, for me, shamanism is most accurately defined as a collection of these technologies. Shamanism comprises a group of techniques by which practitioners deliberately alter or heighten their conscious awareness to enter the so-called 'spirit world', accessing material that they use to help and to heal members of the social group that has acknowledged their shamanic status.[1] In psychological terms, shamans are socially designated practitioners who claim to self-regulate their psychological functions to obtain information unavailable to other members of their social group. Shamans were probably humanity's original specialists, combining the roles of healers, storytellers, weather forecasters, performing artists, ritualists, and magicians. A chief or chieftainess directed the tribe's political, civic, and military life, and the shamans were in charge of a tribe's spiritual life, but occasionally these two roles converged in a single, remarkable individual.

Mythological worldviews arise from epistemologies which, in turn, are fueled by the motives, needs, and traditions of a group in a specific time and place. Examples would be pre-classical worldviews that conceptualized people as an integral part of nature; knowledge was mediated through tribal shamans and their activities. For the ancient Greeks and other classical groups, knowledge was obtained through rationally constructed metaphysical systems; in Asia and other parts of the world, these systems were less individualistic and more communal. In medieval European societies, knowledge was scholastic and could be found in the correct interpretation of sacred scriptures. The modern approach to knowledge involves a proper application of the empirical scientific method, taking as axiomatic that there can only be one possible answer to any question — a position shared by the metaphysical and scholastic epistemologies that were based on very different assumptions (Krippner, 1995). Although I disagree with the anti-epistemological slant of many so-called 'postmodernists', I am pleased that

---

[1] In this essay, the term 'consciousness' is used to describe an organism's pattern of perceiving, thinking, and feeling at a given point in time. 'Awareness' is used to denote 'conscious awareness', hence is a more limited and specific term than 'consciousness'. Some writers (e.g., Goldman, 2000, p. 3) use the terms 'conscious' and 'aware' interchangeably, but there are values in making a differentiation, especially when discussing epistemology and consciousness.

postmodernism points to the need for honouring multiple narratives, and becoming aware of the process by which narratives are constructed (see Berman, 2000, p. 323).

Tribal people did not necessarily insist that their mythic worldview was applicable to their neighbours; even when locked in battle, there often was a regard and respect for their opponents' courage. In postmodern writing, there is also a respect for diversity, empathy for other human beings, and concern for other life forms; all are reminiscent of shamanic worldviews. Postmodernists hold that there can be many viable worldviews, depending on who is asking the question and the methodology used in answering it (Krippner, 1995). Therefore, the case can be made that postmodernists have returned full circle to certain premodern shamanic perspectives, regaining valuable aspects of an epistemology that was denigrated as a result of colonization and conquest.

Shamanic eclecticism and syncretization was apparent in my interviews with María Sabina, who put her epistemology into concrete terms. At the time of our interviews, doña María had retired from active shamanizing, but she told me, 'When someone came to me for help, we would eat the mushrooms together. Jesus Christ is in the mushrooms and he revealed to us the solution to the problem.' Wasson (1981) observed that the mythical origin of doña María's *veladas* dates back to the time when Piltzintecuhtli, the 'Noble Infant', received the sacred plants as a gift from Quetzalcoatl. Doña María's references to Jesus represent a synthesis of the Christian and the pre-Conquest religions (p. 17).

Categories of Spiritual Practitioners

Winkelman (1992) studied the records of religious and magical practices in forty-seven different societies, past and present, finding documentary evidence from these societies identifying several categories of spiritual practitioners. These practitioners claimed to have access to spiritual entities (e.g., deities, ghosts, spirits). They directed a society's spiritual activities (e.g., prayer, sacred ceremonies), employing special powers (e.g., casting spells, bestowing blessings, exorcising demons) that allowed them to influence the course of human affairs in ways not possible by other members of their social group.

Winkelman found remarkable similarities among these clusters of practitioners, especially regarding the manner in which their roles changed as societies became more complex. For example, he found shamans in those groups with no formal social classes; their presence was typical of hunting and gathering tribes and fishing societies. The Creek, Crow, and Kiman were among the Native American tribes that awarded considerable prestige to the shamans in their midst. Each society had a different word to describe what are now called 'shamans', and the specific duties expected of these practitioners differed from group to group.

Once a society became sedentary, centralized, and began to practice agriculture, social stratification took place; in addition to the division of labour, political and economic divisions occurred. Priests or priestesses emerged, taking control of a society's religious rituals while the shaman's political power and social status were reduced. According to Winkelman, the term 'shaman/healer' (or 'shamanic healer') is a more accurate description of this practitioner because healing became his or her major function.

The role of the shamanic healer became specialized and formal; official initiation ceremonies and training procedures became more common. Political development beyond the level of the local community was observed in almost all the societies in which priests were present. The Jivaros in South America and the Ibo tribe in western Africa are among the few groups in which priests were assigned a healing function; priests also served healing purposes in Japanese Buddhist and Kurd Dervish groups. However, the shamanic healer typically engaged in more self-regulatory activities and the accessing of changed states of consciousness than did priests and priestesses.

Political integration became even more complex when separate judicial, military, and legislative institutions appeared. Along with this complexity, the malevolent practitioner (i.e., sorcerer or witch) appeared. Originally, shamans cast hexes and spells on tribal enemies; these functions were taken over by the sorcerer and, for a price, were often directed against members of one's own social group. Potions and charms became the province of witches and their associates. The shamanic healer's scope of action was now reduced not only by priests, but by sorcerers and/or witches as well. There were sorcerers among the Aztecs. There were witches among the Navahos. In my visit to Oaxaca to interview María Sabina, I found a society replete not only with *sabias* (shamanic healers) such as doña María, but sorcerers (*brujos*) as well as the local Roman Catholic priest.

Further political complexities and continued dependence on agriculture became associated with the development of another practitioner, the diviner or medium, such as those found among the Eurasian Kazakhs. At one time the shaman's repertoire had included divination and talking with spirits; later, mediums and diviners began to specialize in this feat, often 'incorporating' the spirits and allowing them to speak and act through their voices and bodies. At this point, the shaman's role was dispersed to the extent that the only remaining functions were specialized healing capacities as the performing of healing songs and dances, dispensing herbal medicines, and diagnosis, bone-setting, midwifery and surgery. Winkelman refers to these practitioners as 'healers' (or 'shamanistic healers'). Like shamanic healers, shamanistic healers held the healing of one's spirit in high regard, but became more involved in individual work than in community work. Furthermore, changing one's state of consciousness and journeying to the spirit world no longer was a core element of their work, as was the case with shamans and shamanic healers.

This classification system was found to be quite accurate when cross-societal comparisons were made (Winkelman, 1997). With only two exceptions, shamans never were found in tribal groups that displayed an administrative political organization beyond the local level. No shamans were found in sedentary societies where the nomadic way of life was absent. When Winkelman traced the development of these four categories (i.e., the 'shaman complex', priests, diviners, malevolent practitioners), he did not assign the terms 'higher' and 'lower' to the states of consciousness utilized while engaging in their practices.

The shaman's ways of knowing depended on accessing information from spiritual entities in 'upper worlds', 'lower worlds' and in 'middle earth' (i.e., ordinary reality). In contrast, the priest's epistemology was dependent on a body of revealed knowledge, often preserved in the form of sacred scripture. Diviners used their own bodies as vehicles for information that was transmitted through them, while malevolent practitioners also depended upon traditional knowledge, either written or passed down verbally. It was not unusual for this material to resemble a 'cook-book' that spelled out the technology which was to be used to inflict various hexes and spells. In contrast, shamanic ways of knowing were dynamic and active. Shamanism demanded both flexibility and strength on the part of the practitioner who would bargain, negotiate, or plead with spiritual entities for the knowledge that would save his or her community from a plague or restore a lost soul to its owner.

Shamanic States of Consciousness

The word 'consciousness' is used in various ways, but I define it as the pattern of an organism's perceptual, cognitive, and affective activities and/or experiences at any given moment in time. An alteration of consciousness is a significant shift or deviation in an organism's customary pattern as experienced by that organism and/or observed by others. Some of these shifts have been considered 'states' of consciousness because they are marked by behaviours and experiences that typically cluster together; each society has its own conception of what constitutes an 'ordinary' state of consciousness and what may be considered 'changed' or 'altered' states of consciousness. Winkelman (1992) notes that in each of the forty-seven societies he studied at least one type of practitioner demonstrated a shift in consciousness associated with his or her apprenticeship and role-training. Wade (1996) adds that 'Virtually all shamanic experiences occur in an altered state, which cannot be regarded as a naturally-occurring developmental stage' (p. 277).

Bourgignon (1976) studied 488 societies (57% of those represented in an ethnographic atlas), reporting that 437 of them (89%) had one or more institutionalized, culturally patterned changed state of consciousness, some of which were only experienced by the society's spiritual practitioners. What can we make of the other 11%? Berman (2000) proposes that 'such beliefs and practices, even if wired into the brain in terms of capacity, get triggered only in certain cultural contexts' (p. 29). This emphasis on context is apparent in Peters and Price-Williams' (1980) comparison of forty-two societies from four different cultural areas. They determined three commonalties among changed states of consciousness entered by shamans: voluntary control of entrance and duration of the altered state; ability to communicate with others during the altered state; memory of the experience at the conclusion of the altered state. Shamans in eighteen of the cultures studied by Peters and Price-Williams (1980) engaged in spirit 'incorporation', ten in out-of-body experience or journeying, eleven in both, and three in some different altered state. However, there are shamanic groups, such as the Navaho *hataali*, who deny entering altered states. The *hataali* rely on knowledge, not trance phenomena or magical effects. Their chant work is 'a restrained and dignified procedure', and they represent, for the client, 'a stable dependable leader who is a helper and guide until the work is ended' (Sandner, 1979, p. 258). To me, this seems more like a case of heightened perception than an altered state.

Those shamans who enter altered states employ various technologies. These include ingesting mind-altering plants (e.g. María Sabina), chanting (again, doña María), concentrating, dancing, drumming, jumping, fasting, running, visualizing, participating in sexual activity, refraining from sexual activity, engaging in lucid dreaming, and going without sleep. Rarely is one procedure used in isolation. For example, mind-altering plants are often ingested in the evening; sleep deprivation, restricted night-time vision, and accompanying music often enhance the experience's profundity. Song and dance were important elements in ritual, and probably preceded it. Naturally occurring altered states, such as dreaming and daydreaming, may also be utilized (Harner, 1988; Rogers, 1982). Whitley (1998) suggests that one of the functions of rock and cave image-making may have been to record the images elicited in shamanic states of consciousness.

The Ojibway Indians shocked Jesuits priests on their arrival in North America with their behaviour during their traditional healing procedures. It was customary for Ojibway *wabeno* (shamans) to heal by means of drumming, rattling, chanting, dancing erotically (while naked), and handling live coals. The *wabeno* then rubbed their heated hands over the client while chanting the songs previously learned in their vision quests (Grim, 1983, pp. 144–5). Among the Dieguenos and Luisenos Indians of southern California, potential shamans were selected as early as nine years of age on the basis of their dreams. It was important that a prospective shaman in these tribes also have visionary experiences that result from ingesting such mind-altering plants as datura or jimson weed during their ceremonials. During these altered states, the novice received a guardian spirit in the form of an animal totem as well as healing songs and other knowledge about cures and dream interpretation (Rogers, 1982, p. 21).

Symbolic manipulation is apparent in shamanic rituals, and altered states often help to access these symbols. Symbols are more than ritual markers that denote the beginning, middle, or end of the process; they serve as keys that unlock the door to a full participation in the ritual, taking participants into another order of reality where spirits come to life and healing dramas unfold (V. Turner, 1968). The drum often symbolizes the 'World Tree' the shaman needs to climb so as to reach the 'upper world' (or descend to the 'lower world') during the altered state. What they find in these realms differs from society to society; in some, the 'upper world' is the home of ancestors, but for others, they reside in the 'lower world'.

The ritualistic blowing of smoke in four directions symbolizes an appeal to spirits in the 'four quarters' of the universe. Directionality is apparent in the elaborate Navaho sand paintings that the shamans destroy after they have served their purpose. Symbolism is also evident in the reports from those vision quests of the

Plains Indians that helped future warriors contact their guardian spirits. Dobkin de Rios (1984) describes these quests as attempts at 'personal ecstatic learning' in the service of eliciting biochemical changes in the body that would enhance the altered state. Hence, tribal shamans played an important role in preparing, instructing, and guiding their initiates, as well as interpreting their visions (p. 57).

The Evolving Mind

As the study of the origin, nature, and limits of knowledge, epistemology is closely associated with Western concepts of consciousness (Winkelman, 2000, p. 177). For many years, Durkheim's (1912/1995) theories were especially influential. Taking Australian totemism as the prototype for all early spiritual experience, Durkheim focused on the feelings of security gained by life in a secure group. He conjectured that early tribes projected these feelings on to whatever object they were close to at the time they experienced them. In this way, plants, animals, rocks, and other objects were imbued with 'power', the capacity to instill strong feelings and to assist the person who befriended, ate, or wore them. According to Durkheim, ritual behaviour preceded language, which only became necessary when communication with imaginary beings was mandatory.[2]

More recently, neuropsychology has impacted explanations of these phenomena. A perspective that is especially useful in understanding shamanic epistemologies has been proposed by Newton (1996) who attempts to unravel certain entrenched philosophical puzzles concerning both consciousness and representational thought. Taking exception to purely linguistic theories of cognition, Newton takes a parsimonious 'postmodern' position on humanity's attempts to represent reality. For Newton, humanity's variegated experiences with reality demonstrate the vast range of specific sensorimotor images and sensations that constitute its direct, ongoing understanding of the environment. For Newton, thinking makes use of the same neurological (i.e., neurognostic) structures involved in sensorimotor activity, structures that take the form of analogue models of reality; the resulting images ground humankind's concepts, constructs, and intentions.

To support this thesis Newton cites behavioural data, findings from neuroscience, and evolutionary evidence, that language was a tool for communication before it became the primary determinant of cognition. Taking issue with both the 'reductionists' who explain sensory phenomena simply as brain properties and the 'new mysterians' who see consciousness as something beyond the reach of physical theory, Newton constructs a sturdy framework that unifies not only body and mind but linguistic and nonlinguistic human activities as well. Donald's (1991) model, compatible with that of Newton, gives mythmaking a key role in human evolution, and describes 'scenario-building' as the primary function of human mental complexity (also see Alexander, 1979). When mythic worldviews

---

[2] Durkheim's work has been unjustly ignored by many contemporary writers. His suggestion that language is associated with 'displaced reference' (i.e., to communicate what is imagined or imaginary) is worthy of consideration when discussing shamanic states of consciousness.

were performed ritually, participants were confronted with representations of objects and events in addition to those items themselves.

Corballis (1991) posits a hypothetical 'generative assembling device' in the human brain, and gives it credit for constructing these cognitive representations from 'small vocabularies of primitive units' (p. 219). Jerison (1990) describes language as a 'sensory-perceptual development' and states that its role in communication first evolved as a side effect to its role in reality construction; thus, 'we need language more to tell stories than to direct actions. In the telling we create mental images in our listeners that might normally be produced only by the memory of events as recorded and integrated by the sensory and perceptual systems of the brain' (pp. 15–16). This capacity required an enormous amount of neural tissue, and the convolutions of the human brain were associated with the development of language and related capacities for mental imagery (p. 16).

Some of these mental images are termed 'images of achievement' by Vandervert (1996) because they reflect a learned imaging process in the cerebral-motor cortex. This process extends into the extrapolated anticipatory future by means of fast time computations of the cerebellum, and these images continually predict the outcomes of the next steps of human action or achievement. These images are often symbolic in nature, allowing for a condensation of considerable information and meaning.

Since the time of Goethe, many scholars have proposed that the epistemology of primordial people began with their sensorimotor experiences (Flaherty, 1992, p. 168). According to these scholars, mythmaking, a basic propensity of humankind, has its referents in bodily functions as well as in observable nature. Sansonese (1994) notes, 'The more ancient the myth, the more often do parts of the human body play an explicit role in the myth' (p. 7), for example, Adam's Rib and the Egyptian myth of Set and Isis. It will be recalled that one of the possible derivations for the term 'shaman' is 'one who is excited, moved, or raised' while another is 'inner heat'; both refer to bodily processes and the appreciation of the sensory world. In addition, they both are examples of politicized talents (along with fire mastery, symbolic death, and entering 'trance') that privatize shamanism and restrict its membership.

In his account of the evolution of the human mind, Mithen (1996) describes the emergence of general intelligence as well as of four specialized 'cognitive domains', namely technical intelligence, social intelligence, natural history intelligence, and language. It is likely that these 'domains' share information in what Baars (1997) refers to as a 'global workspace'. Consistent with Newton's (1996) emphasis on language as a tool for communication (and contrary to Durkheim's position), Mithen (1996) holds that language was originally social. Once the capacity for language was present it was highly adaptive, eventually providing early humans with the ability to reflect on their own and other people's mental states (p. 140). In this way, it began to interact with social intelligence and, still later, early humans were able to talk about tool-making (technical intelligence) as well as hunting and plant gathering (natural history intelligence). Such capacities were advantageous because they could construct more accurate, hence more adaptable, models and descriptions of external events (Povinelli, 1993, p. 507).

Once these intelligences became linked across their respective domains, the resulting 'linkage' enabled the production of symbolic artifacts and images as a means of communication. It also led to the essentially human tendency to attribute personality and social relationships to plants and animals, a result of the integration of social intelligence and natural history intelligence. Artifacts indicating human body decoration (e.g., pieces of ochre) date back 80,000 years or more (Gore, 1997, p. 98); other artifacts demonstrating the capacity for visual decoration (e.g., beads, pendants) date back 40,000 years (Mithen, 1996, p. 155) to the time after the Cro-Magnon people emerged. A human-shaped ivory statuette from Hohlenstein-Stadel in southern Germany is the earliest existing statuette and has been dated at 30,000 to 33,000 years (Mithen, 1996, pp. 162). The origins of shamanism are often traced back at least 30,000 years (Eliade, 1972/1951, pp. 503).

In western Europe, the Upper Paleolithic era began some 35,000 years ago, and is best known for its remarkable efflorescence of image-making (Clottes & Lewis-Williams, 1998/1996). For example, the paintings in the Lascaux caves of southern France date back 17,000 years. The prone figure depicted on one of the walls is often regarded as a shaman experiencing an altered state of consciousness (e.g., Eliade, 1972/1951, p. 504), but Berman (2000) asks, if shamanism was so important in Paleolithic times why do such figures occur so rarely? (p. 25). No matter what these images represent, it is possible that symbolic image-making had been accomplished earlier but was executed on materials that did not survive.

During my visit to Lascaux in 1997, our group was allowed only thirty-five minutes to tour the cave and appreciate its images; even so, it would take the cave's atmosphere several hours to recuperate from our intrusion. We were overwhelmed by the raw power of the colourful wild horses, antlered reindeer, and massive bison we encountered. Negative space, a technique not used again in Europe until the 16th century, was utilized to create perspective. The cave's surface brings a three-dimensionality to the paintings — a naturally-formed hole provides the eye for one animal, and a bulging rock becomes the shoulder of a bison.

There are a plethora of geometric forms thought by some to be signatures of the artists; if so, this convention was not revived until the Renaissance. Some animals have been cleverly painted so that they share body parts, while other figures are superimposed on each other and distinguished by colour shading (Societe Prehistorique Francaise, 1990; Vanaria, 1997). And, for some observers, the most exceptional feature of the drawings is their narrative form; they appear to tell a story (Delluc et al., 1990, p. 57). I agree with Tattersall's (1998) comment that upon leaving Lascaux one is overawed by the magnificence of what these remote ancestors wrought many millennia ago. However, Hughes (2000) notes that the rock paintings in the sacred cave sites scattered across northwestern Australia, 'are as impressive as anything in the caves of Lascaux or Altamira, and tens of thousands of years older. As far as we know, The Australian Aborigines stood at the very dawn of human image-making' (pp. 110–11).

In the European caves, 'a small nodule becomes an animal's eye; sometimes a natural swell of the rock face was taken to delineate the chest or shoulder of an animal; sometimes the edge of a shelf became the back of an animal. To these natural features, the artists added lines, thereby transforming the given into the created. Frequently these images appear to be coming out of the rock wall. At Rouffignac, for instance, a horse's head is painted on the side of a protruding flint nodule. The rest of the horse is apparently behind the rock face' (Clottes & Lewis-Williams, 1998/1996, p. 16). To some, these features suggest a search for spirit animals that could become 'allies' if they could be drawn by shamans through a permeable 'membrane' that separated the ordinary and the non-ordinary worlds (*ibid.*). In the Niaux cave, for example, the shadows cast across the rock can represent, to the expectant eye, the outline of a bison; then only a few deft strokes were needed to add the rest of the body. If the light is moved, the animal disappears back through the 'membrane'. The person has thus mastered the spirit animal; he or she can make it come and go at will (p. 17). Once more, Berman (2000) cautions that there are other explanations for the profusion of animal images, one of them a simple desire to execute a naturalistic portrayal. Sometimes, grazing deer are simply grazing deer (p. 31).

Symbolic or not, Winkelman (2000) points out that neuropsychology provides a basis for these rock art motifs; hardwired neurologically structured perceptual constants are the structural basis of these motifs, reflecting perceptions obtained through shamanic states of consciousness. The animal images reflect 'the importance of neurognostic perspectives in understanding shamanism' (p. 6). Clottes and Lewis-Williams (1998/1996) take a somewhat extreme position, stating that 'all shamanic activity and experience necessarily take place within a particular kind of universe, or cosmos. [But] the ways in which this shamanic cosmos is conceived are generated by the human nervous system rather than by intellectual speculation or detached observation of the environment' (p. 19). For me, neurognostic potentials and social construction operate in tandem, and the ensuing dance produces a phenomena that needs to be examined from the vantage point of both perspectives.

Commenting on the paintings themselves, Mithen (1996) deduces, 'There is nothing gradual about the evolution of the capacity for art: the very first pieces that we find can be compared in quality with those produced by the great artists of the Renaissance. . . . All that was needed was a connection between these cognitive processes which had evolved for other tasks to create the wonderful paintings in Chauvet Cave' which date back some 30,000 years (pp. 162–3). Also predating Lascaux was the extraction of decorative red and black pigment from Bomvu Ridge in South Africa, some 40,000 years ago (Boshier & Costello, 1975).

The magnificent distinctiveness of these works is noteworthy in view of Ludwig's (1992) proposition that 'the visionary or magic function of these media . . . was more important than esthetics' (p. 459). 'The shaman artist . . . employed carved masks, music and art for the purposes of healing, negotiation with unseen spirits, exerting magical influences on creatures, and depicting his [or her] adventures in the spirit world' (*ibid.*). Again, neurognostic structures can be hypothesized to have formed the basis for these creative products; Clottes (in Gore, 2000) asserts 'People can no longer say art evolved from crude beginnings' (p. 108).

The sepia, black, and red ochre Chauvet, Altamira, and Lascaux paintings might be symbolic. However, Berman (2000) offers an alternative: the experience of these early humans was direct and immediate (p. 81). This epistemology runs through many postmodern writings; for example, Globus (1995) remarks, 'We do not know reality, according to postmodernism, by means of any representations of reality. We know reality directly and immediately; there is nothing that gets between us and the reality we always and already find ourselves in' (p. 127).

Modernity, in contrast, relies on representations of reality — mental and neural representations that mediate between humanity and the world. In other words, modern epistemologies assume that an investigator can provide a near-identical match between words and the phenomena they attempt to describe. Postmodern epistemologies assume that this type of representation is impossible, and that symbolism, metaphor, and allegory provide better descriptions of one's immediate outer and inner experience and that several descriptions, some of them paradoxical, frequently are used to 'deconstruct' a phenomenon in an attempt to creatively fathom it.

Shamanic Epistemology

For the shaman, everything provided knowledge about everything else, and the whole of being was 'fundamentally an immense signal system' (Kalweit, 1992, p. 77). Shamanic states of consciousness were the first steps toward deciphering (or deconstructing) the signal system, and this was made possible once humanity's symbolic capacity matured. At that point 'language shifted from a social to a general-purpose function, consciousness from a means to predict other individuals' behaviour to managing a mental database of information relating to all domains of behaviour. A cognitive fluidity arose within the mind, reflecting new connections rather than new processing power' (Mithen, 1996, p. 209). To this discussion of signal systems, I would add that role-playing, as well as language, be considered a likely contender as the mechanism for cognitive fluidity. Pretending and role-playing enable people to represent the internal state of others, a skill that enables cognitive cross-referencing to take place.

Clottes and Lewis-Williams (1998) have proposed three stages of shamanic consciousness. In Stage One, people move from alert consciousness to a 'light' alteration, beginning to experience geometric forms, meandering lines, and other 'phosphenes' or 'form constants', so named because they are wired into the nervous system. For example, the Tukano of South America use undulating lines of dots to represent the Milky Way, the goal of shamanic journeying.

In Stage Two, people begin to attribute complex meanings to these 'constants', and in Stage Three, these constants are combined with images of people, animals, and mythical beings. Experients began to interact with these images, often feeling themselves to be transformed into animals, either completely or partially (e.g., the celebrated Les Trois Freres animal/human); shamanic journeys are generally felt to be more feasible in this form (p. 19). Various chambers of Upper Paleolithic caves seem to have been restricted to advanced practitioners; some caves have spacious chambers embellished with large, imposing images while elsewhere there are often small, sparsely decorated diverticules into which only a few people could congregate (p. 20).

From an epistemological perspective, the shaman could gain knowledge from his or her journeys into other realms of existence, and communicate the results to members of the community (Flaherty, 1992, p. 185). Shamans provided information from a database consisting of their dreams, visions, intuitions, as well as their keen observations of the natural and social world. Sansonese (1994) suggests that there was 'a degree of genetic predisposition for falling into trance' and that this ability made a significant contribution to social evolution (p. 30). For example, there was a succession of Indo-European shamans whose traditions included parent-to-child transmissions of shamanic lore that, in turn, institutionalized extended-family shamanic groups (*ibid.*).

The ability to manipulate symbols was essential in the interpretation of dreams and visions as well as in the creation of myths. For Sansonese (1994), 'a myth is an esoteric description of a heightened proprioception' (p. 36). 'Myth describes a systematic exploration of the human body by privileged members of archaic cultures. Myth springs from an age of universal narcissism, rooted, one must suppose, in the elemental struggle for survival' (p. 37). Explanations were needed for birth, death, illness, procreation, and other bodily phenomena, as well as for cyclones, forest fires, floods, sunsets, eclipses, and the changes of seasons.

There were many contenders for survival millennia ago. However, Mithen (1996) proposes that *homo sapiens*, who date from about 250,000 years ago (Jerison, 1990, p. 10), had an evolutionary advantage over other early humans. *Homo sapiens sapiens* were able to use symbolism in image-making and story-telling, both of which were adaptive because they helped to make sense of one's body, one's peers, and one's environment.

Neanderthals were powerfully built, large-brained people who seemed to display an equivalent sophistication to modern humans in their manufacture of stone tools, and had the vocal mechanisms needed for rudimentary speech. But Neanderthals lived in inclement climates (Mithen, 1996, p. 125), were prone to degenerate diseases (p. 126), and lacked the technology to sew garments and — most curiously — the ability to produce elegant pictorial images. There are a few pieces of pierced bone attributed to Neanderthals, but even these artifacts are in doubt (p. 135). There is no conclusive evidence that ritual was a part of Neanderthal burials, or that human-made objects were placed within the graves (p. 136). In any event, the Neanderthals disappeared less than 30,000 years ago (Tattersall, 1998). In the meantime, with specialized intelligences that could effectively communicate with each other, *homo sapiens sapiens* were probably unique among early humans in their ability to symbolize, mythologize, and, eventually, to shamanize.

Taussig (1987) describes the 'inscription of a mythology in the Indian body' where 'power is invested' (p. 27), while Sansonese (1994) remarks, 'Something is being described in myth, something about the human body, something essential to its workings but also truly technical and beyond mere fetish' (p. 38). He also notes that 'the development of myth parallels the esoteric impulse in storytelling' (p. 38). The domination of *homo sapiens sapiens* may have been due to their ability to take sensory and motor activity, using it as a bridge to produce stories that assured their survival (Boaz, 1997; Cavalli-Sforza & Cavalli-Sforza, 1995; Fagan, 1990; Kingdon, 1993; Ruhlen, 1994; Stringer & McKie, 1996).

The way people come to report the feeling states that arise within their own bodies is incompletely understood (Lubinski & Thompson, 1993). Nevertheless, these private events have been a prime source for the creation of myths by the shaman and the community (Devereux, 1997). Lubinski and Thompson (1993) have underscored the role of pharmacological agents in bringing internal feeling states into awareness, citing animal research to buttress their argument. Merkur's (1998) description of 'psychedelic ecstasies' includes categories in which internal dialogues reflect feeling states invoked by LSD-type drugs, while Nesse and Berridge (1997) have identified the associated neural mechanisms, noting their evolutionary origins.

To the impact of external pharmacological agents, one might add the contribution of the body's own biochemistry, especially during rapid eye movement (REM) sleep, often characterized by dreaming. Ullman (1987) claims that REM sleep reflects a genetic imperative that often orients the dreamer's 'felt connections to others' in the interest of species survival; research with other organisms suggests that REM sleep or a precursor is the earliest form of mammalian sleep (Siegel, 1997).

Hobson (1988), operating from a different paradigm, adds that dreaming is a 'behavioural state' that reflects an evolutionary specialization (pp. 112–13). He continues, 'in dreams, problems are not only posed but sometimes even solved' (p. 16) and somatic stimuli are one source of the images that the brain converts into dream narratives (p. 46). I would suggest that shamans were especially adroit in using dream and psychedelic imagery to address and find solutions to the conundrums periodically faced by members of their community and the group as a whole.

Shamanism and 'Higher' States

Wilber (1981) notes that shamans were the first practitioners to systematically access 'higher' states of consciousness. He categorizes these 'higher' states as the 'subtle' (those leading to enhanced mental imagery both with form, e.g., angels, spirits; and without form, e.g., 'white light', 'music of the spheres'); the 'causal' (those states in which there are no longer any forms in one's awareness, e.g., 'pure awareness', 'the void'); and the 'absolute' (the state in which consciousness has experienced its 'true nature' and in which a 'ground of being' is experienced). According to Wilber the shamans' focus has been on 'subtle' states because their technology was directed toward assisting other people with the images obtained in their shamanic journeys.

Wilber (1981) has taken the position that consciousness not only unfolds during the life-span of an individual, but during the evolution of humanity in general, with some individuals representing the 'farthest reaches' of that development (p. 142). In his hierarchy of 'higher' states of consciousness, shamans are placed at the 'subtle' level because their technology, described as 'crude' (p. 142), was directed toward assisting others with the images and knowledge that was produced in shamanic journeys. Wilber grants that an occasional shaman broke into the 'causal' realm, but insists that it was not until the emergence of the meditative and contemplative traditions that 'causal' and 'absolute' states could be systematically attained. This evolution of consciousness, according to Wilber, was not part of a biological process but due to the development of such elements of spiritual practice as 'rigorous systems of ethics', 'emotional transformation', the 'training of attention and concentration', and the 'cultivation of wisdom'.

However, Eliade (1972/1951) found comparative examples of the oldest types of Christian and Hindu mystical experience in Alaskan Eskimo shamanism. Walsh (1990) found 'rigorous systems of ethics' in those North American shamanic traditions emphasizing compassion. He discovered 'emotional transformation' among Australian aboriginal shamanic initiation programs, and 'training of attention and concentration' among Eskimo initiates who were subjected to a 30-day period of isolation where they were directed to 'think only of the Great Spirit'. Furthermore, Walsh found 'cultivation of wisdom' in Ainu, Cuna, and Zuñi shamanic traditions where entire mythologies, pharmacopoeia, and song cycles had to be memorized and understood. After surveying the cross-cultural research, Coan (1987) warns, 'It would be a mistake to assume that shamanism represents just one stage either in the evolution of human society or in the evolution of human consciousness' (p. 62).

Brown and Engler (1986) administered the Rorschach Inkblot Test to practitioners of 'mindfulness meditation', discovering that their responses illustrated their stages of meditative development, reflecting 'the perceptual changes that occur with intense meditation' (p. 193). One Rorschach was unique in that the 'advanced master' integrated all 10 inkblots into a single associative theme (p.191). However, Klopfer and Boyer (1961) had obtained a similar protocol from an Apache shaman. This shaman used the inkblots to teach the examiner about his lived worldview and his ecstatic flights through the universe. Brown and Engler (1986) suggested that this may be a response that, regardless of the spiritual tradition, points 'a way for others to "see" reality more clearly in such a way that it alleviates their suffering' (p. 214).

Moreover, a careful reading of Wilber (1981) suggests a limited familiarity with the literature on shamanism. He refers to Eliade's (1972/1951) *Shamanism: Archaic Techniques of Ecstasy* as 'the definitive study of the subject' (p. 70). Yet, it takes nothing away from the importance of this pioneering work to suggest that Eliade 'did not address the subject matter in the appropriate cultural context' (Ripinsky-Naxon, 1993, p. 11). For example, Eliade displayed 'personal bias' in using the term 'degenerate' to describe the use of mind-altering substances by shamans, failing to 'recognize the critical role of hallucinogens' in many forms of shamanism (p. 103).

In addition, Wilber (1981) makes such sweeping generalizations that it is hard to believe that he recognizes the varieties of shamanic experience. He calls the bird 'the classic symbolism of shamanism' (p. 70), although in some shamanic societies, the deer or the bear is the central totem (e.g., Ripinsky-Naxon, 1993). Wilber claims that the 'true' shamanic experience involves 'a severe crisis' (pp. 73–4) although there are accounts of shamanic callings that do not involve physical, emotional, or spiritual catastrophes (e.g., Krippner & Welch, 1992). Indeed, the shamanic 'crisis' could well be a political strategy that limits the number of contenders for the shamanic role in those societies that demand it.

Wilber describes shamanism as a 'religion', albeit one that is 'extremely crude, very unrefined, and not highly evolved' (p. 75), placing it at the fifth level of an eight-level spectrum (p. 253). But most writers on shamanism focus on its technologies, its worldviews, and its ways of knowing rather than on its resemblance to institutionalized religions (Harner, 1980; Krippner & Welch, 1992). Indeed, there are Buddhist shamans, Islamic shamans, Christian shamans, and neo-pagan shamans. At most, shamanic practices have led to religious syncreticism (Ripinsky-Naxon, 1993, p. 207), e.g., Tibetan Buddhism and Taoism reflect earlier shamanic practices. By writing about 'the true shaman' (p. 76) rather than of shamans and shamanic experiences (Heinze, 1991; Walsh, 1990), Wilber focuses on a hypothetical figure that has been socially constructed over the ages. He could have served his purposes better by spreading his net more widely, catching and evaluating an assortment of practitioners and social groups who have manifested so-called 'subtle' states over the millennia.

Wilber probably would consider María Sabina's *veladas* typical 'subtle' state imagery, but what could María Sabina have chanted that would have been more meaningful to her clients and more descriptive of her work?

> These are my children,
> These are my babies,
> These are my offshoots,
> My buds,
> I am only asking, examining,
> About His business as well,
> I begin in the depth of the water,
> I begin where the primordial sounds forth,
> Where the sacred sounds forth.
> I am a little woman who goes through the water,
> I am a little woman who goes through the stream,
> I bring my light,
> Ah, Jesus Christ,
> Medicinal herbs and sacred herbs of Christ,
> I'm going to thunder,
> I'm going to play music,
> I'm going to shout,
> I'm going to whistle,

It's a matter of tenderness, a matter of clarity,
There is no resentment,
There is no rancor,
There is no argument,
There is no anger,
It is life and well-being.

(Estrada, 1981, abridged, pp. 136, 150-151, 165, 175)

In these brief excerpts from María Sabina's *veladas*, we find a woman who goes into the primordial waters of oceanic consciousness. However, she does not stay there because her orientation is toward service, toward healing, toward her community, and toward the children and babies to whom she strives to bring life and well-being.

Obviously, there is no way of knowing if María Sabina had reached the 'causal' or 'absolute' realm of Wilber's hierarchy. If so, what knowledge would she have obtained that would have been more useful to her in her mission than the symbolic images and metaphors that emanated in her *veladas*? Nor is Coan (1987) impressed by Wilber's 'sharp dichotomy' (p. 143); the shaman can use many dimensions of consciousness at different times for different purposes. No shamanic performance is ever exactly the same!

These *veladas* demonstrate María Sabina's shamanic ways of knowing by means of the 'sacred herbs' that facilitate her journey through the 'heart' and through the 'water', bringing her 'light' and 'tenderness' in the service of 'life and well-being'. Here we have an example of the shamanic images 'that are directed at reestablishing and maintaining a balanced relationship between nature and the community and at caring for the spiritual and physical welfare of its members' (Ripinsky-Naxon, 1993, p. 207). The *veladas* also provide examples of ritual as social performance (V. Turner, 1968) and of symbols that seem to 'trigger' healing (E. Turner, 1992). From a postmodern perspective, it is merely an intellectual exercise to arrange such manifestations of consciousness on a scale of 'lower' to 'higher' without considering the demands of a local situation at a particular moment in time.

Discussion

Western science is characterized by a search for satisfactory explanations of 'reality'. This search is achieved by statements of general principles; these can be tested experimentally or through repeated observations (Goldstein & Goldstein, 1978). Shamanic epistemology also attempts to explain 'reality', employs repeated observations, and makes statements about general principles. However, credence is given to revelation and inspiration from the 'spirit world', from plant and animal 'allies', and from 'journeys' associated with changed states of consciousness. A provocative example is the complex brew *ayahuasca,* which goes by many other names, depending on the part of the Amazon where it is used. Shamans have imbibed *ayahuasca* for hundreds of years, but its origin remains a mystery to Western investigators. Some tribes attribute this knowledge to spiritual beings from subaquatic realms, others to the intervention of giant serpents (Luna & White, 2000).

Narby (1998) comments, 'Here are people without electron microscopes who choose, among 80,000 Amazonian plant species, the leaves of a bush containing a . . . brain hormone, which they combine with a vine containing substances that inactivate an enzyme of the digestive tract, which would otherwise block the effect. And they do this to modify their consciousness. It is as if they knew about the molecular properties of plants and the art of combining them, and when one asks them how they knew these things, they say their knowledge comes directly from [the] plants' (p. 11). For three decades, I worked with an intertribal medicine man and shamanic healer, Rolling Thunder. When I asked him how he was able to identify the curative power of plants he had never used previously, he told me, 'I ask the plant what it is good for. Some plants are only meant to be beautiful. Other plants are meant for food. Still others are to be used as medicine. Once a healing plant has spoken to me, I ask its permission to take it with me and add it to my medicine pouch.' Rolling Thunder's epistemology was remarkably similar to that of the Amazonian shamans who work with *ayahuasca*.

In a world beset by quandaries and crises, survival no longer depends upon the process of natural selection or chance mutations, but rather on intentional deliberations and conscientious decision-making. Western modernity has failed to build a universal human culture upon a foundation of abstract rational thought. Humanity can not repeat the past, but postmodernity would do well to reconsider the personal, metaphorical language that the Royal Society of London deliberately scuttled in its attempt to produce a universal language of objective and unequivocal symbols (Mahoney & Albert, 1997, p. 23). The failure of this project ignored one of the points permeating this essay: language makes use of the same structures as those involved in sensorimotor activity; these structures take the form of analogue models of reality, and the resulting images ground humankind's concepts, constructs, and intentions.

Vandervert's model (1996) provides a 'neuro-epistemological' framework for this proposition; he writes that 'the neuro-algorithmic organization of the phylogenetic brain is that which evolved originally as the algorithms for perception, learning-memory, cognition, and emotion-motivation involved in the struggle for survival' (p. 82). These representations are reflected in shamanic technologies which, first and foremost, were devoted to finding game animals, locating and using medicinal plants, determining the best time to plant and harvest crops, and other matters of daily survival. Shamanic technologies also had spiritual uses, but contemporary Westerners often emphasize the transcendental side of shamanism to the neglect of its practical aspects.

Vandervert (1997) proposes that 'image-schemas' (see Mandler, 1988) are not tantamount to the organism's storehouse of images, but the space-time representations that co-exist with perceptual processes, both of which precede mental imagery. These space-time simulation structures are genetic in origin and are responsible for the state-estimating functions that are connected to the cerebrum's mapping systems. The resulting image-schemas are whetted by experience as well as by developmental processes.

Vandervert's proposal that image-schemas represent 'foundational meanings' (p. 111) is reminiscent of Jung's description of 'archetypes', the structural predispositions that allegedly provide the organizing principles for consciousness and behaviour. These image-schemas collectively represent what Vandervert considers to be a 'calculus' of archetypal processing. Such image-schematic processing, although a process of natural selection, had the immanent potential to lead to emergent future state estimates (i.e., nonlinear simulations) that extended beyond purely naturally selected states. This combination of image-schematic elements extended beyond the selective mechanism that evoked them. In this way, image-schematic simulations imparted a freedom beyond natural selection that provided a world of potentially new paths for human intention.

The nervous system evolved in ways that enabled it to foresee many future events, and rapid simulation was the basic approach to survival-conducive prediction (Fox, 1988, pp. 160–1). The nervous system's ability to produce such simulation structures as image-schemas permitted anticipatory, feedforward processing (see Pribram, 1991, chap. 6). For Vandervert, image-schemas represent the foundational structures needed 'for modeling/mapping functions conducive for survival'. Without this ability to make estimates of future conditions, vertebrate organisms could not have survived to reproduce (pp. 114–55). According to Vandervert, these processes originated in the cerebellum but eventually involved 'the entire mapping machinery of the brain' (p. 118); the auditory-vocal sharing of image-schematics eventually led to language (p. 120).

I would propose that the image-schemas of those men and women who a community held to be shamanic practitioners were especially adept when prediction was demanded. Game needed to be located, weather patterns needed to be forecast, enemy movements needed to be anticipated, and flight paths needed to be discovered. These tasks required feedforward processing, and the shamanic fine-tuning of image-schemas through heightened perception and/or changed states of consciousness may have assisted this assignment. Such neurognostic frameworks are needed to coalesce human neurophysiology with human epistemology, and to explore what Chalmers (1996) refers to as 'the hard problem': how consciousness arises from physical systems. 'While evolution can be very useful in explaining why particular physical systems have evolved, it is irrelevant to the explanation of the bridging principles in virtue of which some of these systems are conscious' (p. 121).

One final example from the life of María Sabina demonstrates these image-schemas. When she was called to shamanize, doña María received the image of an open book that grew until it reached the size of a person. She was told that 'This is the Book of Wisdom. It is the Book of Language. Everything that is written in it is for you. The Book is yours, take it so that you can work'. In accepting this call, doña María became a "woman of language" and what Rothenberg (1981) calls a 'great oral poet' (p. 10).

Now may be the time to reconsider the ways of knowing exemplified by doña María, and their sources in imagination, intuition, visions, dreams, the senses, and the body.[3] Perhaps these ways of knowing can enter into tandem with intellect and reason to construct cooperative and collaborative lifestyles for the pluralistic world in which we live, a world which shamanic epistemology would appreciate and enjoy.[4]

References

Alexander, R.D. (1979), *Darwinism and Human Affairs* (Seattle: University of Washington Press).

Anisimov, A.F. (1963), 'The shaman's tent of the Evenks and the origin of the shamanistic rite', trans. E. Dunn & S. Dunn, in *Studies in Siberian Shamanism*, ed. H.N. Michael (Toronto: Arctic Institute of North America, University of Toronto).

Baars, B.J. (1997), *In the Theater of Consciousness: The Workspace of the Mind* (New York: Oxford University Press).

Berman, M. (2000), *Wandering God: A Study In Nomadic Spirituality* (Albany, NY: State University of New York Press).

Boaz, N.T. (1997), *Eco Homo: How the Human Being Emerged From the Cataclysmic History of the Earth* (New York: Basic Books).

Boshier, A. & Costello, D. (1975), *Witchdoctor* (Johannesburg: Museum of Man and Science).

Bourgignon, E. (1976), *Possession* (San Francisco, CA: Chandler & Sharp).

Brown, D.P. & Engler, J. (1986), 'The stages of mindfulness meditation: A validation study. Parts I & II', in *Transformations of consciousness*, K. Wilber, J. Engler & D.P. Brown (Boston, MA: Shambhala/New Science Library).

Casanowicz, I.M. (1924), *Shamanism of the Natives of Siberia* (Washington, DC: Annual Report to the Smithsonian Institution).

Cavalli-Sforza, L.L. & Cavalli-Sforza, F. (1995), *The Great Human Diasporas: The History of Diversity and Evolution*, trans. S. Thorne (New York: Addison-Wesley).

Chalmers, D.J. (1996), *The Conscious Mind: In Search of a Fundamental Theory* (New York: Oxford University Press).

Clottes, J. & Lewis-Williams, D. (1998), *The Shamans of Prehistory: Trance and Magic in the Painted Caves*, trans. S. Hawkes (New York: Harry N. Abrams; original work published 1996).

Coan, R.W. (1987), *Human Consciousness and Its Evolution: A Multidimensional View* (New York: Greenwood Press).

Corballis, M.C. (1991), *The Lopsided Ape: Evolution of the Generative Mind* (New York: Oxford University Press).

Delluc, B., Delluc, G. & Delvert, R. (1990), *Discovering Lascaux* (Lucon: Sud Ouest).

deMause, L. (1998), 'The history of child abuse', *Journal of Psychohistory*, **25**, pp. 216–36.

deRios, M.D. (1984), *Hallucinogens: Cross-cultural Perspectives* (Albuquerque, NM: University of New Mexico Press).

Devereux, P. (1997), *The Long Trip: A Prehistory of Psychedelia* (New York: Penguin/Arkana).

Diamond, J. (1997), *Guns, Germs, and Steel: The Fates of Human Societies* (New York: Norton).

---

[3] Reports reminiscent of shamanic epistemology and technologies appear from time to time in first-person reports regarding technical and creative accomplishments. Robert Louis Stevenson wrote that ideas for some of his short stories came from the 'little people' who influenced his dreams; Giuseppe Tartini dreamed that a devil composed a piece of violin music for him which he later transcribed; Sriniwasa Ramanujan noted that the Hindu goddess Namakkal provided him with original mathematical insights while he dreamed; Herman Hilprecht attributed an archeological discovery to a Babylonian priest who visited him in a dream; Francisco Candido Xavier's prodigious literary output was supposedly made possible by discarnate 'spirits' who dictated his poetry, plays, and best-selling novels; Johannes Brahms confided that his best symphonic work was divinely inspired (e.g., Krippner & Dillard, 1998).

[4] This study was supported by the Saybrook Graduate School and Research Center Chair for the Study of Consciousness in honour of Dr. Stanley Krippner.

Donald, M. (1991), *Origins of the Modern Mind: Three Stages In the Evolution of Culture and Cognition* (Cambridge, MA: Harvard University Press).

Durkheim, E. (1995), *The Elementary Forms of Religious Life*, trans. K.E. Fields (New York: Free Press; original work published 1912).

Eliade, M. (1972), *Shamanism: Archaic Techniques of Ecstasy*, trans. W.R. Trask (Princeton, NJ: Princeton University Press; original work published 1951).

Estrada, A. (ed. 1981), *María Sabina: Her Life and Chants* (Santa Barbara, CA: Ross-Erickson).

Fagan, B.M. (1990), *The Journey From Eden: The Peopling of Our World* (London: Thames & Hudson).

Flaherty, G. (1992), *Shamanism and the Eighteenth Century* (Princeton, NJ: Princeton University Press).

Fox, R. (1988), *Energy and the Evolution of Life* (New York: Freeman).

Gazzaniga, M.S. (1994), *Nature's Mind* (New York: Basic Books).

Globus, G. (1995), *The Postmodern Brain* (Philadelphia, PA: John Benjamins).

Goldman, A.I. (2000), 'Can science know when you're conscious? Epistemological foundations of consciousness research', *Journal of Consciousness Studies*, **7**, pp. 3–22.

Goldstein, M. & Goldstein, I.E. (1978), *How We Know: An Exploration of the Scientific Process* (New York: Plenum Press).

Gore, R. (1997), The dawn of humans. *National Geographic*, September, pp. 92–9.

Gore, R. (2000), People like us. *National Geographic*, January, pp. 90–117.

Grim, J.A. (1983), *The Shaman: Patterns of Siberian and Ojibway Healing* (Norman, OK: University of Oklahoma Press).

Guryev, D. (1990), *The Riddle of the Origin of Consciousness*, trans. A. Lehto (Moscow: Progress Publishers).

Harner, M. (1980), *The Way of the Shaman* (New York: Harper and Row).

Harner, M. (1988), 'Shamanic counseling' in *Shaman's Path*, ed. G. Doore (Boston, MA: Shambhala).

Heinze, R-I. (1991), *Shamans of the 20th Century* (New York: Irvington).

Hobson, J.A. (1988), *The Dreaming Brain* (New York: Basic Books).

Hoppal, M. (1987), 'Shamanism: An archaic and/or recent belief system', in *Shamanism: An Expanded View of Reality*, ed. S. Nicholson (Wheaton, IL: Quest).

Hughes, R. (2000), 'The real Australia', *TIME*, September 11, pp. 99–100, 102, 104, 106–7, 110–11.

Jerison, H. (1990), 'Paleoneurology and the evolution of mind', in *The Workings of the Brain: Development, Memory, and Perception*, ed. R.R. Llinas (New York: W.H. Freeman).

Kalweit, H. (1992), *Shamans, Healers, and Medicine Men* (Boston, MA: Shambhala; original work published 1987).

Katz, R. (1982), *Boiling Energy: Community Healing Among the Kalahari Kung* (Cambridge, MA: Harvard University Press).

Kingdon, J. (1993), *Self-made Man: Human Evolution from Eden to Extinction* (New York: John Wiley & Sons).

Klopfer, B. & Boyer, L.B. (1961), 'Notes on the personality structure of a North American Indian shaman: Rorschach interpretation', *Projective Techniques and Personality Assessment*, **25**, pp. 170–8.

Krippner, S. (1993), 'Cross-cultural perspectives on hypnotic-like procedures used by native healing practitioners', in *Handbook of Clinical Hypnosis*, ed. J.W. Rhue, S.J. Lynn & I. Kirsch (Washington, DC: American Psychological Association).

Krippner, S. (1995), 'Psychical research in the postmodern world', *Journal of the American Society for Psychical Research*, **89**, pp. 1–18.

Krippner, S. & Dillard, J. (1988), *Dreamworking* (Buffalo, NY: Bearly).

Krippner, S. & Welch, P. (1992), *Spiritual Dimensions of Healing: From Tribal Shamanism to Contemporary Health Care* (New York: Irvington).

Laughlin, C., McManus, J. & d'Aquili, E. (1990), *Brain, Symbol, and Experience: Toward a Neurophenomenology of Consciousness* (Boston, MA: Shambhala).

Lerche, P. (2000), Quest for the lost tombs of the Peruvian cloud people. *National Geographic*, September, pp. 64–81.

Lewis, I. (1990), 'Shamanism: Ethnopsychiatry', *Self and Society*, **18**, pp. 10–21.

Lubinski, D. & Thompson, T. (1993), 'Species and individual differences in communication based on private states', *Behavior and Brain Sciences*, **16**, pp. 627–80.

Ludwig, A.M. (1992), 'Culture and creativity', *American Journal of Psychotherapy*, **46**, pp. 454–69.
Luna, L.E. & White, S.F. (2000), 'Introduction' in *Ayahuasca Reader: Encounters with the Amazon's Sacred Vine* (Santa Fe, NM: Synergetic Press).
Mahoney, M. & Albert, C.J. (1997), 'Worlds of words', *Constructivism in the Human Sciences*, **1** (3/4), pp. 22–6.
Mandell, A. (1980), 'Toward a psychobiology of transcendence: God in the brain', in *The Psychobiology of Consciousness*, ed. J.M. Davidson & R.J. Davidson (New York: Plenum).
Mandler, H. (1988), 'How to build a baby: On the development of an accessible representational system', *Cognitive Development*, **8**, pp. 141–9.
McClenon, J. (1997), 'Shamanic healing, human evolution, and the origin of religion', *Journal for the Scientific Study of Religion*, **36**, pp. 345–54.
Merkur, D. (1998), *The Ecstatic Imagination: Psychedelic Experiences and the Psychoanalysis of Self-Actualization* (Albany, NY: State University of New York Press).
Mithen, S. (1996), *The Prehistory of the Mind* (New York: Thames and Hudson).
Narby, J. (1998), *The Cosmic Serpent: DNA and the Origins of Knowledge* (New York: Jeremy P. Tarcher/Putnam).
Nesse, R.N. & Berridge, K.C. (1997), 'Psychoactive drug use in evolutionary perspective', *Science*, **278**, pp. 63–6.
Newton, N. (1996), *Foundations of Understanding* (Philadelphia, PA: John Benjamins).
Peters, L.G. & Price-Williams, D. (1980), 'Towards an experiential analysis of shamanism', *American Ethnologist*, **7**, pp. 397–418.
Pinker, S. (1997), *How the Mind Works* (New York: W.W. Norton).
Povinelli, D.J. (1993), 'Reconstructing the evolution of mind', *American Psychologist*, **48**, pp. 493–509.
Pribram, K.H. (1991), *Brain and Perception* (Hillsdale, NJ: Lawrence Erlbaum).
Quartz, S.R. & Sejnowski, T.J. (1997), 'The neural basis of cognitive development: A constructivist manifesto', *Behavioral and Brain Sciences*, **20**, pp. 537–96.
Ripinsky-Naxon, M. (1993), *The Nature of Shamanism* (Albany, NY: State University of New York Press).
Rogers, S.L. (1982), *The Shaman: His Symbols and His Healing Power* (Springfield, IL: Charles Thomas).
Rothenberg, J. (1981), 'Preface', in Estrada (1981).
Ruhlen, M. (1994), *The Origin of Language: Tracing the Evolution of the Mother Tongue* (New York: John Wiley & Sons).
Rychlak, J.F. (1997), *In Defense of Human Consciousness* (Washington, DC: American Psychological Association).
Sandner, D. (1979), *Navaho Symbols of Healing* (New York: Harcourt Brace Jovanovich).
Sansonese, J.N. (1994), *The Body of Myth: Mythology, Shamanic Trance, and the Sacred Geography of the Body* (Rochester, VT: Inner Traditions International).
Shweder, R.A. (1979), 'Aspects of cognition in Zinacanteco shamans: Experimental results', in *Reader in Comparative Religion: An Anthropological Approach* , ed. W.A. Lessa & E.Z. Vogt (4th ed.; New York: Harper & Row).
Siegel, J.M. (1997), 'Monotremes and the evolution of REM sleep', *Sleep Research Society Bulletin*, **4**, pp. 31–2.
Societe Prehistorique Francaise (1990), *La vie prehistorique* [Prehistoric life] (Dijon: Fantan).
Stevens, A. (1982), *Archetypes* (New York: William Morrow).
Stringer, C. & McKie, R. (1996), *African Exodus: The Origins of Modern Humanity* (New York: Henry Holt).
Tattersall, I. (1998), *Becoming Human: Evolution and Human Uniqueness* (New York: Harcourt Brace).
Taussig, M. (1987), *Shamanism, Colonialism, and the Wild Man: A Study In Terror and Healing* (Chicago, IL: University of Chicago Press).
Turner, E., with Blodgett, W., Kahuna, S. & Benura, F. (1992), *Experiencing Ritual: A New Interpretation of African Healing* (Philadelphia, PA: University of Pennsylvania Press).
Turner, V. (1968), *The Drums of Affliction: A Study of Religious Processes Among the Ndembu of Zambia* (Oxford: Clarendon Press).
Ullman, M. (1987), 'Dreams and society', in *The Variety of Dream Experience*, ed. M. Ullman & C. Limmer (New York: Continuum).

Vanaria, T. (1997), 'Creation theory', *Ambassador*, March, pp. 20–25, 40.

Vandervert, L.R. (1996), 'From *idiots-savants* to Albert Einstein: A brain-algorithmic explanation of savant and everyday performance', *New Ideas in Psychology*, **14**, pp. 81–92.

Vandervert, L.R. (1997), 'The evolution of Mandler's conceptual primitives (image-schemas) as neural mechanisms for space-time simulation structures', *New Ideas in Psychology*, **15**, pp. 105–23.

Wade, J. (1996), *Changes of Mind: A Holonomic Theory of the Evolution of Consciousness* (Albany, NY: State University of New York Press).

Walsh, R. (1990), *The Spirit of Shamanism* (Los Angeles, CA: Jeremy P. Tarcher).

Wasson, R.G. (1981), 'A retrospective essay', in Estrada (1981).

Whitley, D.S. (1998), 'Cognitive neuroscience, shamanism and the rock art of native California', *Anthropology of Consciousness*, **9**, pp. 22–37.

Wiercinski, A. (1989), 'On the origin of shamanism', in *Shamanism: Past and Present*, ed. M. Hoppal & O.J. von Sadovskzy (Los Angeles, CA: International Society for Trans-Oceanic Research).

Wilber, K. (1981), *Up from Eden: A Transpersonal View of Human Evolution* (Garden City, NY: Doubleday).

Wilson, E.O. (1998), *Consilience: The Unity of Knowledge* (New York: A.A. Knopf).

Wilson, S.C., & Barber, T.X. (1983), 'The fantasy-prone personality: Implications for understanding imagery, hypnosis, and parapsychological phenomena', in *Imagery: Current Theory, Research, and Application*, ed. A.A. Sheikh (New York: John Wiley & Sons).

Winkelman, M. (1992), *Shamans, Priests and Witches: A Cross-Cultural Study of Magico-Religious Practitioners* (Tempe, AZ: Anthropological Research Papers, Arizona State University).

Winkelman, M. (1997), 'Altered states of consciousness and religious behavior', in *Anthropology of Religion: A Handbook of Method and Theory*, ed. S. Glazier (Westport, CT: Greenwood).

Winkelman, M. (2000), *Shamanism: The Neural Ecology of Consciousness and Healing* (Westport, CT: Bergin & Garvey).

Phillip H. Wiebe

Critical Reflections on Christic Visions[1]

This paper discusses Christic visions as a significant kind of religious experience requiring explanation. It is based upon research published in 'Visions of Jesus: Direct Encounters for the New Testament to Today' (1997), in which I draw on information obtained from 30 living visionaries, using 21 categories to classify their experiences, including 15 phenomenological ones.

Proposed explanations can be plausibly classified as falling into three broad categories: supernaturalistic, mentalistic and neurophysiological. I argue that no single explanation in any of these broad classes can adequately account for the detailed phenomena reported by visionaries. I demonstrate the ineffectiveness of mentalistic explanations, including several made popular by well-known psychologists, and argue that they cannot be improved without adverting to neurophysiological concepts.

I argue that one of the most advanced neurophysiological explanations developed by recent psychiatric researchers cannot account for a particular kind of experience frequently reported in vision experiences. I also show that well-known supernaturalistic explanations for Christic visions do not provide adequate explanations, and identify some of the features of such visions that continue to tempt percipients toward supernaturalism.

I: Introduction

Visions form a significant sub-category of religious experience, given their capacity to influence people with respect to religious practices and beliefs about ultimate reality. Drawing her examples primarily from Buddhism, Christianity, Hinduism and Islam, Caroline Franks Davis (1989, chap. 1) identifies six broad categories of religious experiences in her study of its evidential strength, viz., visionary, quasi-sensory, revelatory, interpretive, regenerative, and numinous experiences. As the descriptions to follow will show, the phenomena I shall refer to here as visions of Christ could be placed into the visionary or quasi-sensory

---

[1] Presented at the University of Vermont at a symposium titled 'Cognitive Science and the Study of Religious Experiences', June 4–7, 1998.

Journal of Consciousness Studies, **7**, No. 11–12, 2000, pp. 119–141

categories. But, however they are categorized, they have significance for the Christian religion. Depending on how broadly 'vision' is defined, one could plausibly say that this religion owes its existence largely to such experiences. The *New Testament* includes accounts of experiences in which Jesus Christ was thought to have been encountered just after his death. These phenomena, also known as appearances and apparitions, have been reported throughout the history of the Christian Church, and continue to be reported.

In this paper I will critically reflect on some of the salient elements of Christic[2] visions, and comment on various explanations that have been proposed for them and similar experiences. The information I will offer derives primarily from my interviews of thirty living visionaries who reported having one or more Christic visions. The visionaries reported that they were awake (except in one case), that their eyes were open, and that the figure that appeared to them was Jesus Christ. These visions do not appear to have been deliberately induced by such techniques as ingestion of hallucinogens, fasting, or depriving oneself of oxygen, and they were not part of a near-death experience. Most of the visions approximate to what Augustine of Hippo (1982, vol. 12, sec. 6, chap. 15) called corporeal visions, since visionaries seem to have used their eyes to acquire the sensory images they reported. Augustine was first to give a sustained discussion of apparitions and visions in Christian theological history, categorizing them as corporeal (or bodily), imaginative, or intellectual. Only corporeal visions were said to involve the external senses. Imaginative visions, as the name suggests, involved only what has been called 'the imaginative faculty'. Christic visions have been widely interpreted as imaginative in character.

II: Description

Although Christic visions might seem well-defined, detailed descriptions obtained from the thirty visionaries I interviewed shows this is not the case. I use the term 'vision' loosely in order to identify the phenomena under scrutiny, because it comes closest to conforming with common usage. The terminology that is used must be tentative, for questions can be raised about the appropriateness of grouping certain kinds of experiences together with a view to explaining them. For example, we could debate the plausibility of grouping experiences involving intersubjectively observable effects along with perceptual experiences having no such effects. We could also question whether Christic visions should be treated separately from other experiences that are described as Christic, e.g., the moving crucifixes studied by William Christian (1992); experiences in which people have a sense of presence but do not see, hear, or touch a Christic figure; dreams that feature the person of Christ and are taken to be revelatory;[3] Christian conversion experiences; and so on. The use of the same term to describe experiences having significant differences *suggests* that they are sufficiently alike to be

---

[2] The *Oxford English Dictionary* describes this word as obsolete, but an adjectival form of 'Christ' or 'Jesus' is needed, so I have adopted this term.

[3] Some of these phenomena are reported and discussed by G. Scott Sparrow (1995).

explained in much the same way. Even describing visions as *Christic* raises significant questions including: why visionaries choose this way of describing the visions; what criteria they follow, if any, in identifying the figure as Christ; how significant for visionaries is conformity to the traditional appearance and expectations of the appearance of Christ in making the identification; and whether variations in appearance provide a plausible basis for classifying the visions into different categories. These remarks indicate that the rich dialectic found elsewhere in exact or scientific studies is present in the study of visions.

Relying upon reports of experiences that those who have them provide — and in this kind of experience we have no other choice — presents the usual problems associated with human subjects. These include mistaken memories, exaggeration, the possible imposition of order on experiences that might be somewhat disordered, possible fraud, and so on. These problems are capable in principle of being overcome, however, as studies in NDEs during the last three decades have demonstrated. Raymond Moody (1977) says that the first reports of NDEs he gave were met with scepticism and criticism, but this is not the situation at present. Thousands of similar reports show that the NDE is much like his first reports. Carol Zaleski (1987) has effectively argued that reports of recent experiences render credible the claims of similar visions from historical accounts. The cases on which I will critically reflect here are small in number, comparatively speaking, so my conclusions will be tentative.

Variations in demographic characteristics, such as age, marital status, ethnicity, and religious backgrounds of visionaries, are to be expected.[4] But more significant are the rich variations in the characteristics of the experiences themselves, as well as the events preceding and following them. These factors have a bearing on how Christic visions are to be explained. Christic visions include some experiences that resemble dreams ('dreaming while awake'), others that resemble ordinary waking experience, and still others that fall between these two. In order to appreciate some of the important differences, I have placed them on a rough continuum and recognize six types on this continuum. Wade Savage (1975) remarks that a continuity hypothesis asserting, roughly, that sensations, perceptions, hallucinations, dreams, fantasies, thoughts, etc., differ not in kind but in degree, has been part of traditional scientific and philosophic wisdom for a long time.[5] I will describe a representative cases from each of the six types, beginning with a trance or dreamlike experience.[6]

Joy Kinsey's vision occurred in Oakland, California in 1957 after receiving prayer in her church. As a minister placed his hands on her head in a gesture of blessing, she lost consciousness and the vision began. In it she encountered Christ who conversed with her about her life. As the vision neared its conclusion she was

---

[4] See Wiebe (1997), Appendix I, for details.

[5] James Gibson (1996, p. 317) also suggests as much. Medical researcher Ernest Hartmann (1975, p. 72) and psychiatrist John Strauss (1969) concur. Other examples of this approach to perception can be found in Roland Fischer (1975) and in Launay and Slade (1981), which purports to measure the disposition to experience hallucinatory perception.

[6] These cases are described in more detail in Wiebe (1997), chap. 2.

instructed to drink a goblet filled with wine. After doing so she awakened, found that three hours had elapsed, and discovered that the people around her were in a state of consternation because of the strong aroma of sweet wine that came from her and filled the small church. She says that she felt so drunk she was unable to stand on her own and needed two people to help her to walk. Although Joy's vision occurred while her eyes were closed, and so fell outside the strict boundary I had imposed on my investigation, I included it because of the surprising event — her 'drunken' condition — that accompanied it. Because causal connections between relevant events are so hard to identify, I describe it as a concomitant rather than speculate on what might have caused it. Such concomitants obviously give visionaries a sense or perhaps provide the basis from which they infer that something external to themselves has been encountered.

The second type of experience I encountered was one in which the whole visual domain that the visionary knew himself or herself to be in inexplicably changed. The experience of Jim Link from Keswick, Ontario, in 1962 is representative. He said that as he sat down to watch television one evening, as was his habit, the screen became invisible and the sound inaudible. Jim wondered if he had gone blind, so he looked in the direction of the window beside him, but he could see neither the window nor the walls of his living room. He said he felt as though he was enveloped in a curtain, but he could not see one. Then a figure in regal robes appeared, and beckoned to Jim. This figure wore a hood that prevented its face from being seen, but was still identified by Jim as Christ. This experience convinced Jim that Christ was real. Although Jim had the sense that his whole perceptual domain had been altered, he had no sense of having lost consciousness or having left his body.

The third type consists of private experiences that take place in a public setting, but involve no alteration of the whole perceptual domain. Helen Bezanson, now of Black Creek, British Columbia, said her experience in 1955 began in a church service with a tactile sensation of someone touching her hand. Her eyes were closed in prayer at the time, so she opened them to see if someone had touched her, but no one was even near enough to do so. She closed them again, and again felt the same touch. When she opened them a second time she saw a figure standing on a pedestal some nine feet away whom she immediately identified as Christ. He was surrounded by radiance, not simply in a halo around his head but in the shape of an oval around his entire body. Helen looked around the room at the other people who were present, to see if any of them gave any indication that they saw the same thing, but none did. She was able to look away and back again several times. The vision finally disappeared, but not before communicating the sense to Helen that she was accepted and loved.

Barry Dyck's experience is also an example of a private one, but since he was alone we do not know what another person might have reported had someone been present. I count this is a fourth type of experience. Barry says that Christ appeared to him in 1974 in the middle of the night at the end of his hospital bed. Barry was in traction, with strict instructions not to move, after having broken three neck vertebrae in a skiing accident on Mount Baker in Washington state.

Barry sat up and grasped the hands of the figure he took to be Christ, and begged to die because his pain was excruciating. In wordless communication Barry was informed that this would not be permitted. The vision disappeared and he fell asleep. He says that when he awakened the next morning his pain and swelling were gone. He convinced the attending doctor to release him from hospital, and within a week resumed his regimen of exercise and running. He was expected to have a recovery period lasting for the better part of a year. This experience was lifelike in a number of ways — although it also differed — not least of which was the alleged effect (healing) the experience had on the observable order. Private experiences that create effects that are publicly observable are deemed to have a reality that is withheld from experiences not having such effects.

A fifth type of Christic vision has often been reported in the history of Christian experience, although only one visionary I interviewed mentioned having experienced something similar. In this type of Christic vision visionaries seem to see some period of the life of Jesus, usually his life as a child or his crucifixion. A remarkable recent account of such an experience has been given by Karen Feaver, legislative assistant to Congressman Frank Wolf, who alleges that as a preacher in China recently told a crowd unfamiliar with Christianity about the suffering of Christ a vision of him suffering on a cross appeared to all present.[7] This type of experience is lifelike because of its collective character, but its seeming 're-creation' of a past event renders it highly peculiar.

The sixth category of such visions consists of experiences said to have been witnessed by groups of people, but involving no 're-creation' of events from earlier history. Reverend Kenneth Logie of Oakland, California says that on two occasions in the 1950s a figure identified as Christ was collectively seen in the services in his church. Fifty people were present on the first occasion, and about two hundred on the second. The second incident was also alleged to have been photographed. I have discussed details of the second incident elsewhere (Wiebe, 1997, pp. 77f). Such collective experiences, especially if they were photographed, are sufficiently like ordinary perception to evoke the belief among visionaries that they have encountered some form of reality external to themselves. The world of ordinary objects, of course, is asserted to be real because they are collectively experienced. Because of unusual features or effects of this type of visionary experience, visionaries often consider this reality to transcend or differ from the known natural order.

The six categories just sketched do not do complete justice to all the phenomenological variations reported by the visionaries I interviewed. For example, some visionaries said their experiences combined tactile and visual perceptions (they 'saw' what they 'touched') in ways that were so realistic that they felt sure they had encountered a form of reality external to themselves. Also, one visionary said that her ordinary perceptions of a Christic figure were followed by an out-of-the-body experience. Another said that the larger-than-life Christic figure was projected onto the wall in front of her, but she could see it with her eyes open or shut. In yet another incident one person saw the Christic figure that

[7] Reported in *Christianity Today*, May 16, 1994.

another felt but did not see. And so on. I cannot explore the phenomenological elements in more detail here.

III: Analysis of Vision Experiences

Christic visions offer us many elements on which we might critically reflect. I shall draw attention first to 21 factors that have a bearing on the degree to which these experiences deviate from or conform to ordinary experience.[8] No single experience was without an aberrant element, but neither did any experience exhibit all of them.

A. Normal or altered visual space:

This refers to whether the vision seemed to the visionary to occur in the locale in which he or she was situated, or whether the locale seemed altered, as in the second experience described above.

B. Volitional elements:

(a) Whether an attempt was made to generate visions directly by an 'act of the will'.

(b) Whether an attempt was made to generate visions by indirect causal mechanisms, e.g., fasting, oxygen or sleep or sensory deprivation, etc.

C. Perceptual elements:

(a) Kinaesthetic perception, e.g., one visionary reported that the vision was preceded by being pinned to the floor by some invisible force for two fifteen minutes periods.

(b) Visual perception:
   (1) Whether the figure appeared to be three-dimensional.
   (2) Whether the figure appeared solid rather than transparent.
   (3) Whether the visionary object appeared to be about the right size for a human form.
   (4) Whether the figure appeared to move due to a power within itself rather than as a result of being acted upon by another object, e.g., one visionary said that she saw a 'living statue'.
   (5) Whether the visionary could look away from the visionary figure and then look back again and see the same object.
   (6) Whether radiance accompanied the figure.
   (7) Whether the appearance was full or incomplete, e.g., some visionaries reported that only the upper torso or face appeared.
   (8) Whether the figure obscured other objects or was obscured by them, e.g., one visionary said Christ appeared in a chair diagonally opposite to her

---

[8] Some of these are reported in Wiebe (1997), Appendix II.

in a restaurant, and obscured the back of the chair just as an ordinary person would.

(9) Whether the vision occurred in colour.

(10) Whether the eyes of the visionary were open. This was a condition for being considered for this study, but one visionary was unsure about whether or not his eyes were open.

(c) Haptic experience:

(1) Whether touch was tried and was found to be possible.

(2) Whether the haptic and visual senses meshed well with one another, e.g., visionaries who touched what they saw said that they felt with their hands what their eyes saw.

(d) Auditory perceptions:

(1) Whether auditory perceptions derived from the object that appeared in visual space, rather that from within the visionary's own head.

(2) Whether auditory perceptions meshed well with other perceptual elements, e.g., whether the lips of the figure moved simultaneously with the words that were heard.

D. Effects to the spatio-temporal-causal order:

(a) Whether causal effects or concomitants occurred.

(b) Whether the experience was collective when several potential visionaries were present.

(c) Whether there was no causal anomaly, i.e., the space–time–causal domain was not disordered. One visionary reported that Christ appeared to her as she knelt by her bed, but he seemed to occupy the same space as the bed.

Theorists who hold that visions have an endogenous source will eventually need to identify the relevant neural mechanisms implicated in various experiences. For example, if both tactile and visual sensations that mesh well are involved, an adequate explanation will need to show how brain functions that integrate these two sensory modalities are involved. Detailed attention to the kind of phenomenological elements I have identified will be required among those who are inclined to the position that an explanation for visions is likely to be found in the neurophysiological processes that constitute or undergird human experience. Descriptions of visions in devotional literature seldom focus attention on such phenomenological elements, but instead try to identify the way in which a person's world view, belief system, attitudes, and practices are involved. To examine detailed phenomenological elements is to signal an interest in looking at experiences scientifically.

My examination of these visionary experiences indicates that, given their complex phenomenological variations, neither adequate descriptions nor classifications, let alone plausible explanations, have yet been developed. Moreover, the variety of religious backgrounds and degrees of apparent commitment to Christianity raise questions about the extent to which Christic visions reflect rather than cause religious commitment. Several people of Jewish background, several people of virtually no religious background, and quite a number of people with nominal attachment to a Christian church at the time the visions occurred were among those I interviewed. Most were people who regard themselves as quite ordinary, and none were in religious orders that cultivate visionary experiences, although a few were quite religious.

Part of the common 'wisdom' about visionary experiences is that they strongly reflect prior beliefs of those who have them.[9] The Christic visions described in the hagiographies of the Christian faith often describe individuals living lives of many deprivations, much fasting, penance, and prayer, and extended periods of contemplation of the sufferings of Christ. That such 'saints' experience Christic visions does not seem all that surprising — their religious activities seem to play a significant causal role in such visions. I submit, however, that we do not presently know the frequency of Christic visions, and neither do we know the backgrounds of those who report these experiences. I think we need to be open about the extent to which the content of Christic visions is shaped by expectations of what such experiences would be like. I surmise that the common 'wisdom' about them just described might derive from concentrating too much on the experiences of Christian 'saints'.

I grant that all the visionaries I interviewed lived in a culture influenced by Christian teaching, but I think it is too simplistic to assert that this was the obvious reason their visions were Christic, rather than of something or someone else. Neither the people who have Christic visions nor the detailed character of their experiences are well enough known to offer any plausible generalisations at the present time, in my opinion.

Christic visions are generally accompanied by significant emotions, including a number related to a sense of psychological well-being. The emotion of feeling loved, cared for, or comforted was mentioned by 43% (12) of the visionaries, the sense of being forgiven and accepted by 14% (4), and the sense of being challenged to regard Christ as real by 11% (3). Several said that gratitude, awe, or an understanding of the importance of love was evoked in them, and several mentioned that they had the sense of being confronted by absolute power. Of course a number of visionaries said that several emotions or feelings among the ones mentioned had been evoked. Perhaps having experiences that evoke emotions of these kinds would be sufficient to render them religious, but the experiences were also religious because of the Christic figure thought to have been encountered or represented.

One of the thought-provoking features of Christic visions is the firm and generally instantaneous belief that Christ has been seen or encountered. One would

---

[9]   Steven Katz, 'Language, Epistemology, and Mysticism', in his *Mysticism and Philosophical Analysis* (1978), discusses this issue at some length with reference to mystical experience in general. Visions are often classed with other religious experiences as mystical, and no harm need come from doing so, but generalizations about mystical states do not always apply. Much more careful study needs to be done, in my opinion, before offering generalizations about subclasses of mystical experience.

think that visionaries would evince more doubt about the identity of the being that they supposedly saw, given the fact that no definitive account of how Christ appeared in real life. Some visionaries regarded this aspect of their experience as self-disclosing, as though someone appeared to them and somehow made his identity known to them without using normal criteria for identification. One might think that Christic visions would immediately result in intense religious devotion among those who have them. Some visionaries reported that this was not the case, however. This is just one more case where common beliefs were not borne out by observations.

Much more could be said about these curious phenomena. The comments I advance here must be considered tentative, since the sample on which I am reflecting here is not very large.

IV: Explanations and Causes

Numerous explanations have been offered for visionary experiences. Few have been offered explicitly for Christic visions, apart from those found in theological discussions. The Christian Church has generally endorsed supernatural realities, such as the resurrected body of Christ and angels, and have appealed to these to account for Christic visions. The leading view has been that visions of Christ are produced by angels who mediate images of the resurrected body of Christ to visionaries. *The Catholic Encyclopedia* (1912; entry on 'Vision') summarizes a long tradition by saying that in a vision, 'either a figure really present externally strikes the retina and there determines the physical phenomenon of the vision; or an agent superior to man directly modifies the visual organ and produces in the composite a sensation equivalent to that which an external object would produce'. It favours the action of angels in the case of Christic visions, rather than the resurrected Christ himself, basing this on theological dogma that Christ does not leave his heavenly abode and allow his body to be seen directly.

Defenders of supernaturalistic causes seldom speculate on why Christic visions exhibit the variation they do. For example, they do not explain why Christ or the images mediated by angels would occasionally be transparent, sometimes are seen in the form of only a face or a torso, occasionally exhibit radiance, sometimes exhibit no movement, occasionally are seen in an altered environment, etc. These lacunae indicate that supernaturalistic causes are not intended to do more than sketch an explanation. In that respect they differ little from causal explanations belonging to the broad domain of mentalism or folk psychology. Explanations appealing to the causal power of supernatural agencies are widely questioned, of course, by those who look to existing sciences for explanations. But they have not disappeared entirely in Western culture.

Functional explanations have been offered for visionary experiences, although not specifically for Christic visions, as far I know. Victor and Edith Turner (1982) suggest, for instance, that Marian visions could be explained by their capacity to render plausible some elements of the Catholic faith, which is under attack. But functional explanations are seldom satisfying on their own, and are often supplemented with attempts to identify further causes of the phenomena.[10] This fact suggests that functional explanations are not at all adequate. This can be illustrated by reference to the Turners' explanation for visions of Mary. We might grant that Marian visions have the function that the Turners ascribe to them, for instance, but still want to know why they happen to one person rather than another, why they happen on one occasion rather than another, and why they take one form on one occasion but another on a different occasion. Their suggested explanation does not address these important matters, showing that functional explanations do not exhaust the demands of explanation. These remarks do not show that functional explanations have no value at all, but they do show that their value is seriously limited.

Many explanations appealing to psychological states of visionaries have been proposed. For example, Gardner Murphy (1945) once maintained that visions are brought on by the wishes of visionaries to have such experiences, and in doing so he typifies a significant number of simple theories that postulate mental states as causes. In popular discussions people refer to hopes to have them, to expectations or beliefs that they are about to experience visions, and to other cognitive and broadly mental states as supposed causes. These attempts are seldom supplemented with empirical evidence designed to show that wishes, hopes, or expectations were present prior to the onset of visions. Moreover, since many of these mental states are capable of occurring in degrees, such as wishing to have an experience, little is said about the degree to which a mental state must occur before a vision occurs, what level it must drop to in order to make the vision disappear, and, most importantly of all, what it is about such mental states that is particularly conducive to producing visions. The detailed causal mechanism, in short, is not identified. The demand that mentalistic theories more completely describe this mechanism, moreover, is one that they cannot meet. The value of mentalistic explanations has been exhausted, and any more complete account would have to identify features of the visionaries' neurophysiological or perhaps neuropsychological structures.

The incompleteness of mentalistic explanations can be seen in Michael Carroll's study of visions of the Virgin Mary, as reported by fifty visionaries. He suggests that these occur as a result of repressed sexual impulses, observing that 80% of the visionaries apparently lacked regular sexual partners (Carroll, 1986, pp. 141f). If sexual repression were found to be common to visionaries in general[11] and plausibly assigned a causal role in the occurrence of visions, we would still want to know what it is about sexual repression that causes visions to occur. Jung's theory about the role of the collective unconscious in the experience of hallucinations is also sketchy (Jung, 1919).

---

[10] Lisa Blackman (1996) describes Foucault's approach to hallucinations (from *Madness and Civilization*) as one that sees them as a tool for shaping the concept of personhood and consequently serving to control populations (p. 322). This is also a functionalist view.

[11] Two-thirds of the visionaries I interviewed were married at the time of the visions, which casts doubt on the suggested correlation between sexual repression and having a vision. Of course, the amount of sexual activity of people, especially those belonging to celibate religious orders, is notoriously difficult to determine.

Julian Jaynes (1976) identifies stress as triggering visions, or *hallucinations*, to use his preferred term. His approach is more empirical than many others that appeal to mental states or processes, for he defines stress operationally (p. 91). Jaynes considers the threshold for hallucinations in normal people to be very high, so they hardly ever occur. But in psychosis-prone people, the threshold is somewhat lower, probably caused 'by the buildup in the blood of breakdown products of stress-produced adrenalin which the individual is, for genetical reasons, unable to pass through the kidneys as fast as a normal person' (p. 93). Jaynes discusses a few apparitions from classical literature to show how his theory would interpret them. He understands St. Paul's conversion experience as one in which a hallucinated voice was interpreted as the voice of Christ (p. 96). But Jaynes does not address the alleged intersubjectively observable effects of this conversion experience, viz., the light that all were reported to have seen or the voice all were said to have heard. Jaynes raises a interesting methodological problem, for he seems willing enough to acknowledge that St. Paul had an extraordinary auditory experience, based upon the accounts in *Acts*, but he glosses over the intersubjectively observable effect(s) also alleged in the accounts to have been part of the experience. These intersubjectively observable effects would cast doubt on the adequacy of his theory, and suggest that the cause was exogenous. Jaynes does not justify his decision to accept that portion of the accounts in *Acts* that accords with his theory, and to gloss over another portion that conflicts with it. Such uneven treatment of evidence is common in theorizing, of course, but some justification is required.

V: Psychiatric Models of Explanation

A widely embraced view among psychiatric researchers for the emergence of hallucinatory experiences in waking consciousness is expressed in the *perceptual release theory*. It asserts that information obtained through sensory perception is stored, altered, and then 'released into consciousness' at a later time and experienced as an hallucination. Louis West says that this mechanism was advanced as the basis for both dreams and hallucinations more than a century ago by such prominent figures as Jean Esquirol (West, 1975, p. 287) and Hughlings Jackson (West, 1962, p. 277). It was also endorsed by Sigmund Freud (*The Interpretation of Dreams*, lect. VII, pt. B).

Researchers in the twentieth century have attempted to identify the neural structures that are implicated in the experience of hallucinations. Frank Fish, for example, emphasized the role of overactive reticular systems in causing hallucinations, based upon his observations of schizophrenics (Fish, 1961, p. 832). Ernest Hartmann speculates that defects in the norepinephrine systems involved in neurotransmission could account for some forms of hallucination, and believes that the chemical substructure of such functions as reality-testing might be found in the ascending norepinephrine systems that extend to the cerebral cortex (Hartmann, 1975, p. 76). Many kinds of hallucinatory phenomena have been documented, especially associated with psychological disorders, and many theories to explain their occurrence have been proposed.[12]

Magnetic resonance imaging (MRI) and computerized tomography (CT) have recently been used to detect neurophysiological anomalies associated with hallucinations of various kinds, including visual and auditory (verbal or musical).[13] For example, P. Paquier et al. (1992) recently reported a case of a 52 year old, hearing-impaired woman, who experienced musical perceptions in her left ear. The tunes she would occasionally hear were familiar, and were not influenced by attempts to communicate with her verbally. MRI and CT findings showed a right subarachnoid hemorrhage, but no evidence of brainstem lesions, suggesting that these musical hallucinations resulted from the hemorrhage. Pharmacological studies also show that biochemical phenomena are implicated in the onset and disappearance of hallucinations. Jeremy Couper (1994) reports that a hearing-impaired woman began to experience musical hallucinations in the ear with which she heard best, after having a stroke and an epileptic seizure. After she was given two doses of an anticonvulsant, the hallucinations stopped. Other therapeutic techniques have reduced hallucinations. Ralph Hoffman and his research associates report that when transcranial magnetic stimulation (TMS) was applied to speech perception areas of the cerebral cortexes of three schizophrenics who heard 'voices', these hallucinations either disappeared for a time or were significantly reduced (Hoffman et al., 1999).

Recent technology is also deepening our understanding of visual hallucinations. Karen Shedlack and her research associates obtained MRI scans of five geriatric patients experiencing visual hallucinations, and compared them with scans of 12 healthy patients who did not. They conclude that 'structural abnormalities in the area of the primary visual pathway may predispose some older individuals, particularly those with poor peripheral visual acuity, to develop the symptoms of visual hallucination' (Shedlack et al., 1994, p. 283). Nancy Benegas and her research associates report that a 51 year old woman complained of 'seeing a picture within a picture' in her lower left visual field (Benegas et al., 1996). This picture was completely different from what she saw in her larger visual field, and she knew it was hallucinatory. The inset picture consisted of a red background filled with several people milling about, and occasionally lasted for several hours. An MRI revealed a right parietooccipital infarction that the researchers consider to have contributed to this visual anomaly. After six months or so the 'picture' disappeared. N. Adachi and associates report that a Japanese woman became blind because of operations for cataracts and glaucoma, and experienced visual hallucinations often the face of Kabuki actor or an imaginary animal for 22 years before undergoing tests (Adachi et al., 1994). The disorder of experiencing visual hallucinations associated with acquired blindness is known as the Charles Bonnet syndrome.[14] At 86 years of age this woman was examined using a CT scan and

---

[12] See Brasic (1998) for a brief review.

[13] Anthony David (1999) has recently reviewed recent successes in capturing neural activity in auditory hallucinations using various tomographic and imagining technologies.

[14] Named after Charles Bonnet, who first reported it in1769 (Needham & Taylor, 1992, p. 245).

MRI, which showed that her temporal lobes were moderately atrophied, and that associated blood flows were asymmetrical. The researchers suggest that 'cortical and/or subcortical dysfunction of the temporal lobes is the likely cause of visual hallucinations in the Charles Bonnet syndrome' (Needham & Taylor, 1992, p. 99). Laurent Cohen and his research associates also report a case of a thirty year old man who began to experience visual hallucinations of a specific face after a right temporal hemorrhage (Cohen et al., 1992). The face was that of a familiar friend, and was in colour and of normal size. It coincided with the time he had made an appointment to see that friend, which was unexpectedly cancelled earlier in the day. These researchers suggest that the hallucination was epileptic, and that the neurons underlying the representation of the man's friend were at a 'higher level of activity', and were consequently 'preferentially selected in the course of the epileptic discharge'.

The regions of the brain involved in experiencing hallucinations naturally include those cortical areas associated with a particular kind of hallucination, whether auditory or visual, but other areas of the brain are also involved. D.A. Silbersweig and research associates (Silbersweig et al., 1995) studied five schizophrenic patients who hallucinated when they were not medicated, and found activity in subcortical nuclei (thalamic, and striatal), in limbic structures (especially the hippocampus), and in paralimbic regions (parahippocampal, cingulate gyri, and orbitofrontal cortex). Medications have long been known to generate visual hallucinations. James Bourgeois and his research associates (Bourgeois et al., 1998) report that when serotonin inhibitors fluoxetine and sertraline were given to a man suffering from dysthymic disorder, he had visual hallucinations, but when nefazodone therapy was substituted, the hallucinations disappeared. By many ingenious and some serendipitous discoveries, the neurological features associated with hallucinatory experience are being mapped.

The concept of hallucination is complex, and under critical scrutiny.[15] K.W.M. Fulford recently offered the following classification, in an effort to bring some order into the numerous phenomena said to be hallucinatory: (a) normal illusions, such as the bent appearance of a stick in water, (b) disruptions of perceptions caused by some physical cause, e.g., 'seeing stars' from a blow to the head, (c) physical symptoms, such as double vision, (d) distortion of perceptions caused by psychological factors, e.g., the depressive who perceives an innocent remark as critical, (e) type-I pseudo-hallucinations, i.e., perceptions without a stimulus which are experienced as real, yet are located as originating inside one's head rather that in outside space, e.g., a voice located as coming from inside one's left inner ear, (f) type-II pseudo-hallucinations, i.e., perceptions located as originating in outside space, yet not experienced as real, for example, the alcoholic with *delirium tremens* who sees snakes, yet knows they are not there, (g) normal hallucinations, i.e., brief hallucinatory perceptions in the absence of a stimulus,

---

[15] See Aleman and de Haan (1998) and Liester (1998) for illustrations of on-going discussions. They discuss the issue of pathological and non-pathological experiences. H. Walter and research associates have used CT technology to compare the hallucinations of normal people with those of psychotic patients (Walter et al., 1990).

experienced as outside and as real at the time, as when a tired doctor, nearly asleep, hears a telephone ring, only to be assured by the hospital switchboard that she 'must have imagined it', and (h) normal imagery, i.e., images so vivid so as to be experienced in outside space and differing from other hallucinations inasmuch as one can change them by effort of will, (i) hysterical hallucinations and (j) visions.[16] Negative hallucinations, i.e., failing to see things that are present, are also being investigated (e.g. by Spanos *et al.*, 1989). This list clearly indicates that the concept is far from simple, and the claim that a single explanation could account for all of them seems doubtful. The fact that the term 'hallucination' is used by researchers to refer to such a variety of experiences casts uncertainty upon the relevance of all of their investigations to the Christic visions under scrutiny in this article. Some of the Christic visions I investigated, for example, involved several sensory modalities at once, such as vision and audition.[17] However, the Charles Bonnet syndrome apparently involves hallucinatory experience in only the visual modality (Fong & Wing, 1997, p. 769), suggesting that findings concerning this kind of experience for understanding Christic visions must be treated with caution. Anthony David and Geraldo Busatto say that if hallucinations were to be rigidly defined as a percept in the absence of an external stimulus, where that percept is unbidden, outside of conscious control, and registered as though in external space, most of the experiences of psychiatric patients normally deemed hallucinatory would be excluded (David & Busatto, 1998, p. 336).

VI: The Information Processing Theory

The ideas central to the *perceptual release theory* have found their way into a more complex theories, known as the *information processing theory*. This theory attempts to do justice to a variety of hallucinatory experiences by consider various sources of perceptual aberrations. Needham and Taylor argue that the *perceptual release theory* on its own, widely associated with L.J. West, cannot account for all hallucinatory experiences, for West's approach stresses the role that sensory deprivation has in causing the release of stored perceptions into conscious life (Needham and Taylor, 1992, p. 247). They noted that visual hallucinations were not well correlated with increasing blindness, and consequently suggest that the mechanism involved is similar to the phantom-limb experience, where amputees experience a missing limb as still being present.[18]

---

[16] Fulford (1991), pp. 230–1. Fulford adds the qualifier 'having "supernatural external stimuli?"' to the category of visions, indicating his own uncertainty about their place.

[17] John Hendrickson and Adityanjee (1996) report on a case of schizophrenic who experienced auditory hallucinations of a voice telling him to jump off buildings or stab himself or his mother, visual hallucinations of 'little people' who were only an inch tall, gustatory hallucinations of sweet tastes, and tactile hallucinations of some substance like grease trickling down his face. They do not indicate the extent to which these occurred simultaneously, or meshed well with each other when they did occur together.

[18] They follow R. Melzack, who postulates the existence of a neural network for the 'body-self' that generates sensory 'phantoms' (Needham & Taylor, p. 247): cf. Melzack (1989; 1990). Geoffrey Schultz *et al.* (1996), including Melzack, suggest that this neural network provides a basis for hypothesizing a 'top-down' causal mechanism.

Mardi Horowitz's *information processing theory* identifies four broad determinants in explaining how and why hallucinations occur, each of which is capable of being enhanced by neurophysiological findings. The first fact that must be recognized about hallucinations is that they are a form of image representation (Horowitz, 1975, p. 168). All of the major sensory systems produce image subsystems that are capable of being activated by electrical, mechanical, or chemical stimulation, e.g., by stimulating the neural tract between the eyes and the cortex. Sub-cortical stimulation might not only reactivate particular memories, but might also stimulate a sudden increase in image thinking. For example, Wilder Penfield stimulated the temporal lobe of patients so that vivid scenario-like imagery was created. Images can be generated by psychological stimuli as well, as when Freud's 'commanded' patients to have and report visual pictures when he released his hand from their foreheads (Horowitz, 1975, p. 172; cf. Freud, 1952, lect. 2).

The second determinant in image formation is the capacity of the image-forming systems to obtain information from both internal and external origins. Horowitz says that upon entering a hallucinatory state, a percipient blends information coming from internal and external origins. When the images that derive from the fantasy or from memory become intrusive, the percipient may attempt to 'stabilize a sense of reality through the use of checking maneuvers, including changes in perception (looking "harder," closing one's eyes, looking away) and in thought (trying to suppress the image, trying to think of something else, evaluating the probability of such events being real)' (Horowitz, 1975, p. 175). In the most advanced stage of hallucination the percipient reacts to the intense images as if they were real.

According to Horowitz, a sustained level of external sensory input is normally required to inhibit the emergence of percepts and memory traces from within the brain itself. When external input falls below a certain threshold, but cortical arousal remains constant, previously recorded perceptions are released into awareness and are experienced there as hallucinations. L.J. West notes, for instance, that when a mystic reduces sensory input by deliberately withdrawing from the outside world, this allows visions to emerge into awareness (West, 1962, p. 289). West identifies two prerequisites for released perceptions to become conscious with hallucinatory vividness: 'First there must be a sufficient general level of arousal for awareness to occur. Second, the particular perception-bearing circuits must reverberate sufficiently to command awareness' (West, 1975, p. 301). If the representational system is relatively inactive, the stored perceptions released into consciousness will be experienced only as fantasies or illusions; if it is active, these perceptions will be experienced as dreams or hallucinations (ibid.). West's second prerequisite means that the neural mechanisms responsible for perceptual experiences of particular kinds must be sufficiently active to attract the attention of the percipient. While the brain is always active, those systems associated with perception in particular must also be active.

Research on hallucinators with perceptual deficiencies seems to corroborate the claim that the relative absence of external stimuli allows hallucinatory perception to become more prominent. German Berrios (1991) reports that musical hallucinations are often related to deafness, and seemingly are associated with pathology of the right hemisphere. These perceptual anomalies often occur with aging, as various perceptual powers deteriorate. K. Podoll and research associates report on a 83 year old woman who suffered from progressive deafness, and then for twenty years permanently heard various melodies played on instruments (Podoll *et al.*, 1991). These included melodies she knew, as well as some that were unfamiliar. Stephen and Richard Rojcewicz (1997) argue that the prevalence of auditory hallucinations featuring *human* voices among those who suffer from schizophrenia arises from the impoverishment of their relations with other people. Anthony David and his research associates report on an interesting case where the brain responses of a male schizophrenic to verbal stimulation were measured when he experienced auditory hallucinations (David *et al.*, 1996). Using MRI technology, they found that the response of his temporal cortex to speech was markedly reduced when he experienced auditory hallucinations. Even the presence of medication did not affect this measured result. This case suggests that the impact of external stimuli is reduced when internal stimulation, in the form of auditory hallucinations, is high.

Visual hallucinations are also considered to be implicated in instances where people are visually impaired, and thus deprived of normal visual stimulation. Samson Fong and Yun Kwok Wing report that a 41 year old man with visual impairment developed complex and vivid visual hallucinations, the content of which was significantly shaped by his Chinese background.[19] They consider the lack of normal visual stimulation to be a factor in the onset and persistence of the hallucinations. Ronald Siegel and Murray Jarvik say that when the level of cortical arousal is high, information is given to the visionary that appears to be projected onto a sensory field outside the body, especially if other sensory inputs are reduced, for example, by being in dim light or having one's eyes closed. Images are retrieved from memory and are then altered to conform to cultural determinants.[20] Siegel and Jarvik suggest that their account of projected sensory outputs might explain the archetypes that Carl Jung said were part of humanity's collective unconscious, since their account refers to common CNS mechanisms.

The third determinant, according to the *information processing theory*, is the susceptibility of the information processing system to becoming impaired. Horowitz says that when visual sensation takes place, the visionary assesses the image to determine whether it is real or has been seen before, evaluates the object that is imaged as dangerous, gratifying, etc., and also establishes the spatial characteristics of the image (Horowitz, 1975, p. 184). Experiments show that visionaries who have never experienced a certain image will be more likely to label the experience hallucinatory than those who have already experienced it (Heilbrun

---

[19] Fong & Wing (1997), pp. 769f. His hallucinations began with flickering lights, and shortly afterward he saw Buddha in different colours, miniature ghosts, a human skeleton, and a paper-man fighting with swords. He saw the images vividly and in external space, but believed they were not of real objects.

[20] Siegel & Jarvik (1975) pp. 136f. cf. Weinstein (1962) for observations about differences in the content of hallucinations among different ethnic groups.

and Brun, 1984, p. 508). Moreover, the brevity and the ambiguity of an image experience can also contribute to its being considered hallucinatory. Heilbrun and Brun note that everyone occasionally experiences the kind of disorder that could increase the risk of hallucination. It is common, for instance, to have a deficiency in the mechanism that assigns meaning to ambiguous stimuli, or to experience disorder if one is forced to use a weak sensory modality, e.g., when the hearing-impaired find that their only source of vital information is auditory (Heilbrun and Brun, 1984, p. 508).

The fourth determinant contributing to the emergence of intrusive images is the impairment of cognitive functions (Horowitz, 1975, p. 188). Horowitz notes that clinical evidence supports the claim that shocking visual perceptions can be repeated in waking life long after the initial experience is over. For example, combat veterans often relive their terrifying experiences, and drivers report visual images of headlights after night driving. These episodes often enter awareness without intention, and resist conscious efforts to prevent their recurrence. C.J. Brabbins (1992) has reported on three cases of visual hallucinations among elderly women who did not appear to suffer from the Charles Bonnet Syndrome, but experienced cognitive impairment. In their experiences they exhibited clear consciousness, and vivid and detailed visual perceptions of faces of people, without any accompanying auditory hallucination. Jerome Schneck (1990) also reports that visual hallucinations can occur without the Charles Bonnet Syndrome among people who experience grief.

Horowitz considers the four determinants related to image formation and interpretation to be varied enough to explain many hallucinatory experiences, and rejects the adequacy of a single model or a succinct explanation. Ronald Siegel echoes the value of approaching hallucinations schematically, and with an appeal to various possible mechanisms when he says that they 'arise from common structures in the brain and the nervous system, common biological experiences, and common reactions of the brain to stimulation or deprivation' (Siegel, 1992, p. 11). He notes that they can be experienced by anyone, not just those suffering from psychological disorders.

The *information processing theory* is a complex one, for it uses concepts deriving from various theoretical frameworks. Neurophysiological concepts are interwoven with folk psychological concepts having varying degrees of specificity. Some of the folk concepts appear to be explicable in behavioural terms, e.g., the concept of checking maneuvers described in the second element of the theory. Other folk concepts appear to be used as they are commonly understood, e.g., the concepts of fantasy, thought, representation, percept, visual picture, image intensity, stored perception, weak thought-image, gratifying object, kinesthetic image, and conscious effort. Still others appear to be operationally definable, or are approaching such definition in the hands of cognitive scientists, e.g., the concepts of memory, dream, sensory input, perceptual release, consciousness, attention, sensory system, sensory deprivation, sensory awareness, cognitive impairment, conflict, and emotional state.

The nature of theorizing at the present time is such that different theoretical frameworks are intimately involved in attempting to understand the mechanisms involved in hallucinatory experiences of all kinds, including visions. The relationships between concepts deriving from different domains of discourse are unclear, rendering imprecise the nature of the explanation provided by this theory.[21] It seems capable of accounting for some of the features of visions, e.g., partial objects, such as faces or torsos, rather than full figures; movement of the visionary object in the visionary's visual space; the meshing together of haptic, auditory and visual elements; spatial anomalies, such as finding that the Christic figure was superimposed on the space filled by an object of furniture; finding that the whole domain in which the visionary object is located has been altered; and so on. Several phenomena seem to be poorly handled by the theory in question, however.

Consider the curious phenomenon of repeatedly experiencing a tactile or visual perception, for example. Helen Bezanson reported that she felt a tactile sensation on her hand, then opened her eyes and observed that this could not have come from a person standing nearby, then closed her eyes and felt the same tactile sensation again. According to the *information processing theory*, a tactile percept (or its neurophysiological equivalent) stored somewhere in her brain was released into her conscious experience, apparently because her representation system was 'switched on' at a time when the influence of the external image formation system had decreased in intensity, perhaps because her eyes were shut. When she opened her eyes, the external system increased in intensity and the internal source disappeared, for so she no longer felt the tactile sensation. After she closed her eyes again, the external system again decreased in intensity, the internal source was intensified, and the 'same' tactile percept, phenomenologically speaking, was experienced. It is something of a marvel, however, that the 'same' hallucination would be experienced to coincide with the closing of her eyes. One would think most visionaries would have a vast repertoire of percepts 'waiting' to be released into consciousness as soon as the neuropsychological conditions sketched in the theory were satisfied. But let us give the theory the benefit of any doubt in the case of Helen's tactile hallucination.

Now consider the visual perceptions that followed. Helen found that a specific aberrant perception occurred each time she looked at a particular place in the room, that it did not follow her eyes as she looked around the room, and that it featured the same figure each time, as well as the pedestal that was not part of the room's appointments. The first peculiarity to note here is that the tactile hallucinations that were featured moments ago suddenly stopped. We might wonder why one comparatively simple kind of hallucination stopped, and highly complex visual ones began. Helen described the Christic figure as looking directly at her, and as making motions with his hands that Helen interpreted as indicating that he was accepting her. If a significant triggering mechanism for the tactile

---

[21] The combination of various levels of theoretical discourse, combined with the gradual definition of mentalistic concepts using behavioral and other operational criteria, suggests that functional materialists are closer to identifying the future of folk psychology than eliminative materialists.

hallucinations was having her eyes closed, since that might have decreased the source of external images, one wonders why she would have visual hallucinations now that her eyes were open. The supposed levels of cortical arousal must have changed quickly so that having her eyes open no longer prevented a hallucination from occurring.

Having the same visual hallucination as she looked at a particular point in the room is also remarkable, for the mechanism that seems to be relevant is a neurophysiological and/or neuropsychological condition correlated with having her head positioned in a particular way and having her eyes focused on a particular point. When she turned away the hallucination was gone, but when she turned back again the hallucination was in the same place. Again we might expect that a vast array of different visual percepts would be available for release into consciousness. Her seeing the same hallucination in the same spot in her visual space, associated with a specific place in the room, is also remarkable. These cases in which a visionary object is superimposed on the place one knows oneself to be in seem to be more difficult to explain than cases in which the whole perceptual domain is changed, as in Jim Link's vision. We can assume that Helen was familiar with images of Christ, with pedestals, with smiling, with the radiance that sometimes surrounds objects, e.g., coals of fire, with hand motions conveying acceptance, with emotions such as feeling accepted and loved, etc. So it is reasonable to suppose that percepts corresponding to each of these were part of her stored memories. But it is also remarkable that the complex produced by each of these elements would be combined and then released into her consciousness in what seems to have been an orderly way.

Helen did not evince evidence suggesting that the event exhibited the sort of disorderliness often found in dreams, but it is possible that any disorder that did occur had been forgotten or unconsciously edited out between the time the vision occurred and the time she related it to me. All in all, the *information processing theory* does not provide a very convincing account of why she would have two different kinds of hallucinations and why they would be repeated several times to coincide with specific behaviours. An obdurate defender of the theory could of course promise that in the future these features will all be explained in an expanded or refined version of theory. Meanwhile, we have Helen's interpretation of this incident as one in which a transcendent form of reality had been encountered.

The *information processing theory* seems to be readily capable of explaining contrary observations. This could be seen as a defect or an advantage, depending on one's methodological point of view. If the Christic figure that appears to visionaries is greatly in keeping with the expectation of a visionary, the proponent of the theory can simply point to this expectation, a concept perhaps definable operationally, as well as to memories of pictures purporting to represent Christ that the visionary might have seen. However, if the figure that appears is vastly different than the expectation of a visionary, the theory can draw attention to the manner in which previous perceptions become distorted, or are altered as they are released into consciousness. In the heyday of logical positivism excessive adaptability was taken as a defect of a theory, especially by methodologists influenced by Karl Popper. Defenders of other methodological positions, such as inductivism, conventionalism, and Imre Lakatos's account of research programs, have not considered such flexibility to be grounds for objection.

About twenty per cent of the Christic visions I investigated were reported as having occurred simultaneously to visionaries or as leaving causal traces in the ordinary spatio-temporal world. These are very intriguing visionary phenomena, for they do not appear to be explicable by reference to the visionaries' perceptual histories and to mechanisms internal to visionaries. They also *appear* to challenge the hegemony of the naturalistic project of placing all human experience within a conceptual framework that is ultimately dependent upon the forms of reality studied by physicists. Some discussions of naturalism take for granted that physical entities and processes are well enough known to rule out the compatibility of naturalism with parapsychological phenomena, while other discussions are open to their compatibility, e.g., Carl Jung's account of synchronicity (Jung, 1971). Jung's position is endorsed by Stanislav Grof, who says that academic psychology and psychiatry have dismissed what he calls *spirituality* as 'a product of superstition, primitive magical thinking, and outright pathology' (Grof, 1993, p. 204). But he notes that modern consciousness research is changing attitudes toward this important domain of experience.

VII: Concluding Remarks

Christic visions raise difficult questions about the relationship between naturalism and religious belief systems. The traditional Christian explanation for Christic visions used the conceptual resources available in that tradition, including the resurrected Christ and the mediating actions of angels, evidently understood literally. These claims reflect the substantial ontological commitments of early Christianity. Ontological issues have been important for most of its history as well. Only in the last century or so have Christian theologians backed away from discussing these matters. Wolfhart Pannenberg traces this reluctance to the repudiation of metaphysics among philosophers as diverse as the logical positivists, Friedrich Nietzsche, and Martin Heidegger (Pannenberg, 1990, pp. 3f). According to Pannenberg, the metaphysical claims found in the sacred writings and traditions of the Church are now proclaimed as elements of the original teachings (the *kerygma*) without further elaboration, or are demythologized. Western culture is loath to accord authority to any religion to speak on questions of ontology; science is increasingly viewed as having the sole authority to rule on such questions.

Mircea Eliade has given a classic description of the ways in which the sacred perspective on the universe has been replaced with a profane one, remarking that the sacred interpretation gives people the sense that they are confronted by 'the manifestation of something of a wholly different order, a reality that does not belong to our world' (Eliade, 1959, p. 11). The elimination of persons in favour of sense impressions, or, more recently, brain states, and the attempt to understand flora and fauna as only complex atomic structures, can be seen as part of the profaning of the universe — a research programme, to use the language of Lakatos, that ranks with the most ambitious undertaken in the history of human thought. But the desacralization of human experience is not complete, and among the experiences that stand in its way are Christic visions.[22] These visions elude adequate naturalistic explanation at present, in my opinion, and continue to provide a profound sense that a reality that does not belong to our world has been manifested. But fuller understanding of them awaits further study.

References

Adachi, N, Nagayama, M. Animi, K. Arima, K. *et al.* (1994), 'Asymmetrical blood flow in the temporal lobe in the Charles Bonnet syndrome: Serial neuroimaging study', *Behavioural Neurology*, **7**, pp. 97–9.

Aleman, Andre and de Haan, Edward H.F. (1998), 'On redefining hallucination', *American Journal of Orthopsychiatry*, **68**, pp. 656–9.

Augustine of Hippo (1982), *The Literal Meaning of Genesis*, trans. J.H. Taylor (New York: Newman Press).

Benegas, Nancy M., Liu, G.T., Volpe, N.J. and Galetta, S.L. (1996), '"Picture within a picture" visual hallucinations', *Neurology*, **47**, pp. 1347–8.

Bentall, R.P. & Slade, P.D. (1985), 'Reliability of a scale measuring disposition toward hallucination: A brief report', *Personality and Individual Differences*, **6**, pp. 527–9.

Bourgeois, James A., DeJuan, Thomas, Johansen, Thomas and Walker, David M. (1998), 'Visual hallucinations associated with fluoxetine and sertraline', *Journal of Clinical Psychopharmacology*, **18**, pp. 482–3.

Berrios, German E. (1991), 'Musical hallucinations: A statistical analysis of 46 cases', *Psychopathology*, **24**, pp. 356–60.

Blackman, Lisa (1996), 'Using an archaeology to contest the voice of reason: A history of the present psychological "Regime of Truth"', in *Problems of Theoretical Psychology* (Proceedings of the Sixth Biennial Conference of The International Society for Theoretical Psychology), ed. Charles W. Tolman *et al.* (North York, ON: Captus Press).

Brabbins, C.J. (1992), 'Dementia presenting with complex visual hallucinations', *International Journal of Geriatric Psychiatry*, **7**, pp. 455–7.

Brasic, James R. (1998), 'Hallucinations', *Perceptual and Motor Skills*, **86**, pp. 851–77.

Carroll, Michael P. (1983), 'Visions of the Virgin Mary: The effect of family structures on Marian apparitions', *Journal for the Scientific Study of Religion*, **22**, pp. 205–21.

Carroll, Michael P. (1986), *The Cult of the Virgin Mary: Psychological Origins* (Princeton: Princeton University Press).

Catholic Encyclopedia, The (1912), 15 vols, ed. Charles Herbermann *et al.* (New York: Robert Appleton).

Christian, William A. Jr. (1992), *Moving Crucifixes in Modern Spain* (Princeton, NJ: Princeton University Press).

Cohen, Laurent, Verstichel, Patrick and Pierrot-Deseilligny, Charles (1992), 'Hallucinatory vision of a familiar face following right temporal hemorrhage', *Neurology*, **42**, p. 2052.

Couper, Jeremy (1994), 'Unilateral musical hallucinations and all that jazz', *Australian and New Zealand Journal of Psychiatry*, **28**, pp. 516–19.

David, Anthony S. (1999), 'Auditory hallucinations: Phenomenology, neuropsychology and neuroimaging update', *Acta Psychiatrica Scandinavica Supplementum*, **99**, pp. 95–104.

---

[22] The idea of the soul capable of existing apart from the body is another. Carol Zaleski, author of several recent books examining ancient visions in the light of recent near-death experiences, says that talk of the soul cannot be eliminated without impoverishing our understanding of what it means to be fully human. Although she is reluctant to embrace ontological dualism, she does not object to speaking about leaving one's body in a near-death experience, provided this way of speaking is treated symbolically, along lines suggested by Paul Tillich and Paul Ricouer (Zaleski, 1996, pp. 58f).

David, Anthony, and Busatto, Geraldo (1998), 'The hallucination: a disorder of brain and mind', in *Disorders of Brain and Mind*, ed. Maria A. Ron and Anthony S. David (Cambridge: Cambridge University Press).

David, Anthony S., Woodruff, P.W.R. *et al.* (1996), 'Auditory hallucinations inhibit exogenous activation of auditory association cortex', *Neuroreport: An International Journal for the Rapid Communication of Research in Neuroscience*, **7**, pp. 932–6.

Davis, Caroline Franks (1989), *The Evidential Force of Religious Experience* (Oxford: Clarendon Press).

Eliade, Mircea (1959), *The Sacred and the Profane: The Nature of Religion*, trans. Willard R. Trask (New York: Harcourt, Brace & World).

Fischer, Ronald (1975), 'Cartography of inner space', in Siegel and West (1975).

Fish, Frank J. (1961), 'A neurophysiological theory of schizophrenia', *Journal of Mental Science*, **107**, pp. 828–39.

Fong, Samson Yat Yuk, and Wing, Yun Kwok (1997), 'Charles Bonnet syndrome with major depression in a Chinese middle-aged man', *Australian and New Zealand Journal of Psychiatry*, **31**, pp. 769–71.

Foucault, M. (1971), *Madness and Civilization: A History of Insanity in the Age of Reason* (London: Routledge).

Freud, Sigmund (1952), *The Origin and Development of Psycho-Analysis* (Chicago, IL: Encyclopaedia Britannica, Inc.).

Fulford, K.W.M. (1991), *Moral Theory and Medical Practice* (New York: Cambridge University Press).

Gibson, James J. (1966), *The Senses Considered as Perceptual Systems* (Westcott, CT: Greenwood Press).

Grof, Stanislav (1993), *The Holotropic Mind: The Three Levels of Human Consciousness and How They Shape our Lives* (San Francisco, CA: Harper).

Hartmann, Ernest (1975), 'Dreams and other hallucinations: An approach to the underlying mechanism', in Siegel and West (1975).

Heilbrun, A.B. & Blum, N.A. (1984), 'Cognitive vulnerability to auditory hallucination: Impaired perception of meaning', *British Journal of Psychiatry*, **144**, pp. 508–12.

Hendrickson, John, and Adityanjee (1996), 'Lilliputian hallucinations in schizophrenia: Case report and review of literature', *Psychopathology*, **29**, pp. 35–8.

Hoffman, Ralph E., Boutros, E., Nashaat, N. *et al.* (1999), 'Transcranial magnetic stimulation of left temporoparietal cortex in three patients reporting hallucinated "voices"', *Biological Psychiatry*, **46**, pp. 130–2.

Horowitz, M.J. (1975), 'Hallucinations: an information-processing approach', in Siegel and West (1975).

Jaynes, Julian (1976), *The Origins of Consciousness in the Breakdown of the Bicameral Mind* (Toronto: University of Toronto Press).

Jung, Carl G. (1971), 'On synchronicity', in *The Portable Jung*, ed. Joseph Campbell, trans. R.F.C. Hull (New York: Viking Press).

Jung, Carl G. (1919), 'The psychological foundations of belief in spirits', *Proceedings of the Society for Psychical Research*, **31**. Reprinted in *Contributions to Analytical Psychology*, trans. H.G. and C.F. Baynes (New York: Harcourt, Brace and Co., 1928).

Katz, Steven T. (1978), *Mysticism and Philosophical Analysis* (Oxford: Oxford University Press).

Launay, G. and Slade, P. (1981) 'The measurement of hallucinatory predisposition in male and female prisoners', *Personality and Individual Differences*, **2** pp. 221–34.

Liester, Mitchell B. (1998), 'Toward a new definition of hallucination', *American Journal of Orthopsychiatry*, **68**, pp. 305–12.

Melzack, R. (1989), 'Phantom limbs, the self and the brain', *Canadian Psychology*, **30**, pp. 1–30.

Melzack, R. (1990), 'Phantom limbs and the concept of neuromatrix', *Trends in Neurosciences*, **13**, pp. 88–92.

Moody, Raymond (1977), *Reflections on Life After Life* (New York: Bantam Books).

Murphy, Gardner (1945), 'An outline of survival evidence', *Journal of the American Society for Psychical Research*, **39**, pp. 2–34.

Needham, Walter E. and Taylor, R.E. (1992), 'Benign visual hallucinations, or "phantom vision" in visually impaired and blind persons', *Journal of Visual Impairment and Blindness*, **86**, pp. 245–8.

Pannenberg, Wolfgang (1990), *Metaphysics and the Idea of God*, trans. Philip Clayton (Grand Rapids, MI: Wm. B. Eerdmans).

Paquier, P., Van Vugt, Bal, P., Cras, P. *et al.* (1992), 'Transient musical hallucinations of central origin', *Journal of Neurology, Neurosurgery and Psychiatry*, **55**, pp. 1069–73.

Podoll, K., Thilmann, A.F. and Noth, J. (1991), 'Musikalishe Halluzinationen bei Schwerhoerigkeit im Alter', *Nervenarzt*, **62**, pp. 451–3.

Rojcewicz, Stephen, J. and Richard (1997), 'The "human" voices in hallucinations', *The Journal of Phenomenological Psychology*, **28**, pp. 1–41.

Savage, C. Wade (1975), 'The continuity of perceptual and cognitive experiences', in Siegel and West (1975).

Schneck, Jerome M. (1990), 'Visual hallucinations as grief reaction without the Charles Bonnet syndrome', *New York State Journal of Medicine*, **90**, pp. 216–17.

Schultz, Geoffrey, Needham, Walter, Taylor, Robert, Shindell, Steve and Melzack, Ronald (1996), 'Properties of complex hallucinations associated with deficits in vision', *Perception*, **25**, pp. 715–26.

Shedlack, Karen J., McDonald, William M. Laskowitz, Daniel T. and Krishnan, K. Ranga Rama (1994), 'Geniculocalcarine hyperintensities on brain magnetic resonance imaging associated with visual hallucinations in the elderly', *Psychiatry Research*, **54**, pp. 283–93.

Siegel, Ronald K. (1992), *Fire in the Brain: Clinical Tales of Hallucination* (New York: Dutton / Penguin Books USA).

Siegel, Ronald K. and M.E. Jarvik, M.E. (1975), 'Drug-induced hallucinations in animals and man', in Siegel and West (1975).

Siegel, R.K. and West, L.J. (ed. 1975), *Hallucinations: Behavior, experience and theory* (New York: Wiley).

Silbersweig, D.A., Stern, E. Frith, C. *et al.* (1995), 'A functional neuroanatomy of hallucinations in schizophrenia', *Nature*, **378**, pp. 176–9.

Spanos, Nicholas P., Flynn, Deborah M. and Gabora, Natalie J. (1989), 'Suggested negative visual hallucinations in hypnotic subjects: When no means yes', *British Journal of Experimental and Clinical Hypnosis*, **6**, pp. 63–7.

Sparrow, G. Scott (1995), *I am With You Always: True Stories of Encounters with Jesus* (New York: Bantam Books).

Strauss, John S. (1969), 'Hallucinations and delusions as points on continua functions', *Archives of General Psychiatry*, **21**, pp. 581–6.

Turner, Victor and Turner, Edith (1982), 'Postindustrial Marian pilgrimage', in *Mother Worship*, ed. J.J. Preston (Chapel Hill, NC: University of North Carolina).

Walter, H., Podreka, I, Steiner, M., Suess, E. *et al.* (1990), 'A contribution to classification of hallucinations', *Psychopathology*, **23**, pp. 97–105.

Weinstein, Edwin A. (1962), 'Social aspects of hallucinations', in *Hallucinations*, ed. L.J. West (New York: Grune and Stratton).

West, Louis J. (1962), 'A general theory of hallucinations and dreams', in *Hallucinations*, ed. L.J. West (New York: Grune & Stratton).

West, Louis J. (1975), 'A clinical and theoretical overview of hallucinatory phenomena', in Siegel and West (1975).

Wiebe, Phillip H. (1997), *Visions of Jesus: Direct Encounters from the New Testament to Today* (New York: Oxford University Press).

Zaleski, Carol (1987), *Otherworld Journeys* (New York: Oxford University Press).

Zaleski, Carol (1996), *The Life of the World to Come* (New York: Oxford University Press).

Maps and Analyses

Ken Wilber

Waves, Streams, States and Self

Further Considerations for an Integral Theory of Consciousness

Although far from unanimous, there seems to be a general consensus that neither mind nor brain can be reduced without remainder to the other. This essay argues that indeed both mind and brain need to be included in a nonreductionistic way in any genuinely integral theory of consciousness. In order to facilitate such integration, this essay presents the results of an extensive cross-cultural literature search on the 'mind' side of the equation, suggesting that the mental phenomena that need to be considered in any integral theory include developmental levels or waves of consciousness, developmental lines or streams of consciousness, states of consciousness, and the self (or self-system). A 'master template' of these various phenomena, culled from over one-hundred psychological systems East and West, is presented. It is suggested that this master template represents a general summary of the 'mind' side of the brain–mind integration. The essay concludes with reflections on the 'hard problem', or how the mind-side can be integrated with the brain-side to result a more integral theory of consciousness.

Introduction

The amount of theory and research now being devoted to the study of consciousness is rather amazing, given its history of neglect in the previous decades. As encouraging and salutary as this research is, I believe that certain important items are still missing from the general discussion of the role and nature of consciousness. In this essay, I would therefore like to outline what I believe is a more integral model of consciousness, not to condemn the other approaches but to suggest ways in which their important contributions can be even further enriched by a consideration of these neglected areas.

This is a follow-up to a previous essay published in this journal (Wilber, 1997b). Since this is also a summary of evidence and arguments developed elsewhere, I will rarely quote other authorities in this presentation; works of mine that

Journal of Consciousness Studies, **7**, No. 11–12, 2000, pp. 145–76

I reference in this article do so extensively, and interested readers can follow up with those references.[1]

Much of today's research into consciousness focuses on those aspects that have some sort of obvious anchoring in the physical brain, including the fields of neurophysiology, biological psychiatry, and neuroscience. While there seems to be an uneasy consensus that consciousness (or the mind) cannot be fully reduced to physical systems (or the brain), there is as yet no widespread agreement as to their exact relation ('the hard problem'). *This article attempts to provide a compendium of those aspects from the 'mind' side of the equation that need to be brought to the integrative table.*

Integral Psychology (Wilber, 2000b) compared and contrasted over one hundred developmental psychologists — West and East, ancient and modern — and from this comparison a 'master template' was created of the full range of human consciousness, using each system to fill in any gaps left by the others. This master template, although a simple heuristic device and not a reading of the 'way things are', suggests a 'full-spectrum catalogue' of the types and modes of consciousness available to men and women. This catalogue might therefore prove useful as we seek a 'brain-mind' theory that does justice to both sides of the equation — the brain and the mind.

After outlining this 'full-spectrum' catalogue of mind, this essay will suggest a tentative model for fitting mind with brain, culture, and social systems. It will, in other words, summarize one version of a more comprehensive or integral theory of consciousness, which combines the full-spectrum mind catalogue (or master template) with current neuroscience, brain research, and cultural and social factors, all of which seem to play a crucial role in consciousness.

To begin with the full-spectrum catalogue of mind states: The conclusion of the cross-cultural comparison presented in *Integral Psychology* is that there are at least five main components of human psychology that need to be included in any comprehensive theory: developmental *levels* of consciousness, developmental *lines* of consciousness, normal and altered *states* of consciousness, the *self* or self-system, and what will be called the four *quadrants* (which include culture and worldviews, neurophysiology and cognitive science, and social systems). To take them in order.

Levels or Waves

Apparently not all components of the psyche show development. However, there is considerable evidence that some aspects of cognition, morals, psychosexuality, needs, object relations, motor skills, and language acquisition proceed in developmental stages, much as an acorn unfolds into an oak through a series of process phases (Alexander and Langer, 1990; Loevinger, 1976; Wilber, 2000b). These

---

[1] The journal's editors were divided over this approach. All felt that failing to include the original references in this article — several thousand of them — was reader-unfriendly and should be discouraged, but others acknowledged that the added length would be prohibitive. I have compromised and added a few representative references in each of the fields.

stages or levels of development are not the rigid, linear, rungs-in-a-ladder phenomenon portrayed by their critics, but rather appear to be fluid, flowing, overlapping waves (Beck & Cowan, 1996).

All three terms — structures, levels, and waves — have been used in the literature to describe these developmental milestones. 'Structure' indicates that each stage has a holistic pattern that blends all of its elements into a structured whole. 'Level' means that these patterns tend to unfold in a relational sequence, with each senior wave transcending but including its juniors (just as cells transcend but include molecules, which transcend but include atoms, which transcend but include quarks). And 'wave' indicates that these levels nonetheless are fluid and flowing affairs; the senior dimensions do not sit on top of the junior dimensions like rungs in a ladder, but rather embrace and enfold them (just as cells embrace molecules which embrace atoms). These developmental stages seem to be more like concentric spheres of increasing embrace, inclusion, and holistic capacity.

When it comes to consciousness itself, evidence suggests that there are indeed various levels or waves of consciousness unfolding, which appear to span an entire spectrum from subconscious to self-conscious to superconscious (Murphy, 1992; Wilber, 2000b; Wilber et al., 1986; Wade, 1996). This overall spectrum of consciousness is well-known to the world's major wisdom traditions, where one version of it appears as the Great Chain of Being, which is said to range from matter to body to mind to soul to spirit (Smith, 1976). The Great Chain is perhaps a misnomer. It is not a linear chain but a series of enfolded spheres: it is said that spirit transcends but includes soul, which transcends but includes mind, which transcends but includes body, which transcends but includes matter. Accordingly, this is more accurately called 'the Great Nest of Being'. Some modern thinkers accept the existence of matter, body, and mind, but reject soul and spirit. They therefore prefer to think of the levels of consciousness as proceeding from, e.g., preconventional to conventional to postconventional. The essential points can be made using any of these levels, but because we will also be discussing spiritual or 'superconscious' states, let us for the moment simply assume that the overall spectrum of consciousness does indeed range from prepersonal to personal to transpersonal (Murphy, 1992; Walsh, 1999).

Based on various types of cross-cultural evidence, many scholars have suggested that we can further divide this overall spectrum of consciousness into seven colors or bands or waves (as with the seven chakras); others suggest around twelve (as with Aurobindo and Plotinus); some suggest even more (as in many of the well-known contemplative texts. See Wilber, 2000b, for over one hundred models of the levels of consciousness, taken from premodern, modern, and postmodern sources). In many ways this seems somewhat like a rainbow: we can legitimately divide and subdivide the colours of a rainbow in any number of ways. I often use nine or ten basic levels or waves of consciousness (which are variations on the simple matter, body, mind, soul, spirit), since evidence suggests that these basic waves appear to be largely universal or generally similar in deep features wherever they appear. (e.g., The human mind, wherever it appears, has a capacity to form images, symbols, and concepts. The contents of those images and symbols vary from culture to culture, but the capacity itself appears to be universal [Arieti, 1967; Beck & Cowan, 1996; Berry *et al.*, 1992; Gardiner *et al.*, 1998; Shaffer, 1994; Sroufe *et al.*, 1992].) This general stance is well stated by Berry *et al.* (1992), summarizing the existing research: 'Cross-cultural Psychology is a comprehensive overview of cross-cultural studies in a number of substantive areas — psychological development, social behaviour, personality, cognition, and perception — and covers theory and applications to acculturation, ethnic and minority groups, work, communication, health, and national development. Cast within an ecological and cultural framework, it views the development and display of human behaviour as the outcome of both ecological and sociopolitical influences, and it adopts a "universalistic" position with respect to the range of similarities and differences in human behaviour across cultures: basic psychological processes are assumed to be species-wide, shared human characteristics, but culture plays variations on these underlying similarities' (which will be investigated below as the 'four quadrants').[2]

Nonetheless, all of these various codifications of the developmental levels appear to be simply different snapshots taken from various angles, using different cameras, of the great rainbow of consciousness, and they all seem useful in their own ways. They are simple categorizations provided by humans; but each of them, if carefully backed by evidence, can provide intriguing clues to this mystery of consciousness.

That these levels, nests, or waves are arranged along a great rainbow or spectrum does not mean that a person actually moves through these waves in a merely linear or sequential fashion, clunking along from body, then to mind, then to soul, then to spirit. Those are simply some of the basic levels of consciousness that are potentially available. But an individual possesses many different capacities, intelligences, and functions, each of which can unfold through the developmental levels at a different rate — which brings us to the notion of various independent modules in the human psyche, which can also be referred to as lines or streams.

Lines or Streams

Evidence suggests that through the developmental levels or *waves* of consciousness, move various developmental lines or *streams* (such as cognition, morals, affects, needs, sexuality, motivation, and self-identity [Gardner, 1983; Loevinger, 1976; Wilber, 1997a; 2000b]). It further appears that, in any given person, some of these lines can be highly developed, some poorly (or even pathologically)

---

[2] Research (summarized by, e.g., the references in this paragraph) suggests that some of these psychological structures are universal, some are culture-specific, and some are individual. All three are important; but clearly not all structures are universal. However, since this paper presents a cross-paradigmatic model, the structures mostly focused on are those for which there is suggestive evidence that they are generally universal and cross-cultural wherever they appear (i.e., they do not necessarily appear in all cultures, but when they do, they show a similar pattern). These basic levels or basic structures are matter, sensation, perception, impulse, image, symbol, concept, rule, formal, vision-logic, psychic, subtle, causal, and nondual, which can be grouped into nine or ten functional units as: sensorimotor, emotional-sexual, rep-mind, rule/role mind, formal-reflexive, vision-logic, psychic, subtle, causal, nondual (Wilber, 2000b).

developed, and some not developed at all. Overall development, in short, is a very uneven affair!

The reason seems to be that the numerous developmental lines are to some degree *independent modules*, and these modules can and do develop in relatively independent ways (but not totally independently). Each of these modules probably evolved in response to a series of specific tasks (e.g., cognition of the external world, needs and desires in different environments, linguistic communication, sexual release mechanisms, and so on). There is an enormous amount of theory and research on modularity (both pro and con), although it is generally accepted in the psychological literature.[3]

According to this body of developmental research, a person can be at a relatively high level of development in some lines (such as cognition), medium in others (such as morals), and low in still others (such as spirituality). Thus, *there is nothing linear about overall development*. It is a wildly individual and idiosyncratic affair (even though many of the developmental lines themselves unfold sequentially).

But what about spirituality itself? Does it unfold in stages? Before addressing that issue, let's examine states of consciousness.

States of Consciousness

Several states of consciousness are quite familiar. For example, waking, dreaming, and deep sleep. Those are some of the 'normal' or 'ordinary' states. Some of the 'altered' or 'nonordinary' states appear to include peak experiences, religious experiences, drug states, holotropic states, and meditative or contemplative states (Goleman, 1988; Grof, 1998; Tart, 1972). Evidence strongly suggests that a person at virtually any *stage* or level of development can have an altered *state* or peak experience — including a spiritual experience (Wilber, 1983; 2000b). Thus, the idea that spiritual experiences are available only at the higher stages of development seems to be incorrect. States themselves rarely show development, and their occurrence is often random; yet they seem to be some of the most profound experiences human beings ever encounter. Clearly, those important aspects of spirituality that involve altered states do not follow any sort of linear, sequential, or stage-like unfolding.

What types of higher states are there? Considerable cross-cultural comparisons (Adi Da, 1979; Forman, 1990; 1998a; Murphy, 1992; Smart, 1984; Smith, 1976; Walsh, 1999; Wilber, 2000b), taken as a whole, suggest that there are at least four higher or transpersonal states of consciousness, which might be called *psychic*, *subtle*, *causal* and *nondual*. (As we will see in a moment, when these temporary

---

[3] There is moderate to strong evidence for the existence of the following developmental lines: cognition, morals, affects, motivation/needs, ideas of the good, psychosexuality, kinesthetic intelligence, self-identity (ego), role-taking, logico-mathematical competence, linguistic competence, socio-emotional capacity, worldviews, values, several lines that might be called 'spiritual' (care, openness, concern, religious faith, meditative stages), musical skill, altruism, communicative competence, creativity, modes of space and time perception, death-fear, gender identity, and empathy. Much of this evidence is summarized in Wilber (1997a; 2000b).

states become permanent traits, these transitory states are converted into permanent structures of consciousness, and I will call those permanent structures, levels, or waves by the same four names.)

Briefly, it appears that the psychic state is a type of *nature mysticism* (where individuals report an phenomenological experience of being one with the entire natural-sensory world; e.g., Thoreau, Whitman. It is called 'psychic', not because paranormal events occur — although evidence suggests that they sometimes do — but because it seems to be increasingly understood that what appeared to be a merely physical world is actually a psychophysical world, with conscious, psychic, or noetic capacities being an intrinsic part of the universe, and this seems to result in a phenomenological experience of oneness with the natural world [Fox, 1990]). The subtle state is a type of *deity mysticism* (where individuals report an experience of being one with the *source* or *ground* of the sensory-natural world; e.g. St. Teresa of Avila, Hildegard of Bingen). The causal state is a type of *formless mysticism* (where individuals experience cessation, or immersion in unmanifest, formless consciousness; e.g., pseudo-Dionysus, *The Cloud of Unknowing*, Patanjali; see Forman, 1990). And the nondual is a type of *integral mysticism* (which is experienced as the union of the manifest and the unmanifest, or the union of Form and Emptiness; e.g., Lady Tsogyal, Sri Ramana Maharshi, Hui Neng, [e.g., Forman, 1998b]).

As suggested elsewhere (Wilber, 2000b), these apparently are all variations on the natural states of waking, dreaming, and deep sleep — which seems to be why a person at virtually any stage of development can experience any of these nonordinary states (because everybody, even an infant, wakes, dreams, and sleeps). However, in order for these *temporary* states to become *permanent* traits or structures, they must enter the stream of development (see below). Of course, for most people, the dream and deep sleep states are experienced as being less real than the waking state; but with prolonged meditative practice, it is said that these states can be entered with full awareness and an expansion of consciousness, whereupon they yield their higher secrets (Deutsche, 1969; Gyatso, 1986; Walsh, 1999).

In many of the wisdom traditions, the three great normal *states* (of waking, dreaming, and deep sleep) are said to correspond to the three great *bodies* or *realms* of being (gross, subtle, and causal). In both Vedanta and Vajrayana, for example, the bodies are said to be the energy support of the corresponding mind or state of consciousness (i.e., every mental mode has a bodily mode, thus preserving a bodymind union at all levels). The gross body is the body in which we experience the waking state; the subtle body is the body in which we experience the dream state (and also certain meditative states, such as savikalpa samadhi, and the bardo state, or the dream-like state which is said to exist in between rebirths); and the causal body is the body in which we experience the deep dreamless state (and nirvikalpa samadhi and the formless state [Deutsche, 1969; Gyatso, 1986]).

The point is that, according to these traditions, each state of consciousness has a corresponding body which is 'made' of various types of gross, subtle, and very subtle energy (or 'wind'), and these bodies or energies 'support' the corresponding mind or consciousness states. In a sense, we can speak of the gross bodymind, the subtle bodymind, and the causal bodymind (using 'mind' in the very broadest sense as 'consciousness').[4] The important point, which I will provisionally accept for this 'master template', is simply that *each state of consciousness is supported by a corresponding body*, so that consciousness is never merely disembodied.[5]

The Relation of Structures and States

One way of looking at the evidence thus far is to say, merely as heuristic device, that *states* of consciousness (with their correlative bodies or realms) contain various *structures* of consciousness. For example, the waking state can contain the preoperational structure, the concrete operational structure, the formal operational structure, and so on. In Vedanta, these structures or levels of consciousness are known as the *koshas* (or sheaths). The subtle body, experienced in the dream state (and the bardo realm, savikalpa samadhi, etc.), is said to support three major koshas or consciousness structures — the *pranamayakosha* (élan vital), the *manomayakosha* (conventional mind), and the *vijnanamayakosha* (higher and illumined mind). The reason that both Vedanta and Vajrayana maintain this is that, for example, each night when you dream (when you are in the subtle body), you have access to these three structures (you can experience sexual élan vital, mental images and symbols, and higher or archetypal material — i.e., the dream state can *contain* all three of those structures), but you do not experience the gross body, the sensorimotor realm, or the gross physical world — those are not directly present. In the dream you are phenomenologically existing in a subtle body experiencing the various consciousness structures supported by that subtle body and contained in that state.

In short, any given broad *state* of consciousness (such as waking or dreaming) can contain several different *structures* (or levels) of consciousness. These structures, levels, or waves, as earlier suggested, span the entire spectrum, and also include many of those structure-stages that have been so extensively studied by western developmental psychologists, such as the structure-stages of moral, cognitive, and ego development (e.g., Cook-Greuter, 1990; Gilligan *et al.*, 1990; Graves, 1970; Kegan, 1983; Kohlberg, 1981; Loevinger, 1976; Piaget, 1977;

[4] In my own system, the 'body/energy' component is the Upper-Right quadrant, and the 'mind/consciousness' component is the Upper-Left quadrant. For a discussion of body/realms — e.g., gross body (Nirmanakaya), subtle body (Sambhogakaya), causal body (Dharmakaya) — as the energetic support or 'body' of each of the consciousness levels and states, see Wilber, 1995, note 1 for chap. 14.

[5] Even though it is said by, e.g., the Tibetan tradition, that subtle consciousness/energy or the subtle mind/body can detach from the gross mind/body, as in the chonyid bardo realm following death; and the causal mind/body can detach from both the subtle and gross mind/body, as in the chikhai bardo or the clear-light emptiness post-death experience (Gyatso, 1986). This conception allows consciousness to extend beyond the physical body but never to be merely disembodied (since there are subtle and causal bodies); and it presents a body/mind (or matter/consciousness) nonduality at every level. Whether or not these higher, subtle energies and their corresponding states actually exist in any fashion that can be satisfactorily verified is open to question, but I have provisionally included them in the 'master template' simply because the cross-cultural evidence for them is suggestive, and until more definitive studies can be done I believe it would be premature to reject them.

Wade, 1996). When, for example, Spiral Dynamics (a psychological model developed by Don Beck and Christopher Cowan [1996], based on the research of Clare Graves) speaks of the red meme, the blue meme, the orange meme, and so on, those are structures (levels) of consciousness.

Why do all these distinctions seem to be important? One reason is that recognizing the difference between states of consciousness and structures of consciousness allows us to understand how a person at any stage or structure of development can nevertheless have a profound peak experience of higher and transpersonal states — for the simple reason that everybody wakes, dreams, and sleeps (and thus they have access to these higher states and realms of subtle and causal consciousness, no matter how 'low' their general stage or level of development might be). However, the ways in which individuals *experience* and *interpret* these higher states and realms will depend largely on the level (or structure) of their own development (see below).

Phenomenal States

Finally, and following this simple heuristic, within the major structures of consciousness there appear to be various *phenomenal states* (joy, happiness, sadness, desire, and so on). In short, one way of conceptualizing these events is to say that within broad states of consciousness there are structures of consciousness, within which there are phenomenal states (Combs, 1995; Wilber 2000b).

Notice that neither states of consciousness nor structures of consciousness are directly experienced by individuals.[6] Rather, individuals directly experience specific phenomenal states. Structures of consciousness, on the other hand, are *deduced* from watching the behaviour of numerous subjects. The *rules* and *patterns* that are followed by various types of cognitive, linguistic, moral (etc.) behaviours are then abstracted. These rules, patterns, or structures appear to be very real, but they are not directly perceived by the subject (just as the rules of grammar are rarely perceived in an explicit form by native language speakers, even though they are following them). This is why structures of consciousness are almost never spotted by phenomenology, which inspects the present ongoing stream of consciousness and thus only finds phenomenal states. This appears to be a significant limitation of phenomenology. That is, phenomenology usually focuses on phenomenal states and thus fails to spot the existence structures of consciousness. Thus, if you introspect the phenomenal states of body and mind, you will never see something that announces itself as a 'stage-4 moral thought' (Kohlberg); nor will you find something called 'the conformist stage' (Loevinger); nor will you spot 'the relativistic stage' (Graves). The only way you spot those *intersubjective structures* is to watch populations of subjects interact, and then look for regularities in behaviour that suggest they are following

---

[6] States of consciousness are in one sense experienced by subjects — the dream state, for example — but usually what is actually experienced is some specific, if different or altered, phenomenal state. The individual then compares many similar phenomenal states and concludes they all belong to a broad state of consciousness (such as dreaming, or intoxication, or some such). Thus, both broad states and basic structures tend to be missed by phenomenology's adherence to phenomenal states. See note 7.

intersubjective patterns, rules, or structures. This suggests that phenomenology is a useful, if limited, aspect of a more integral methodology.[7]

Developmental Aspects of Spirituality

It appears that all *structures* of consciousness generally unfold in a developmental or stage-like sequence, and, as virtually all developmentalists agree, *true stages cannot be skipped* (Combs, 1995; Cook-Greuter, 1990; Gilligan *et al.*, 1990;

---

[7] On the limitations of phenomenology, see Wilber, 1995, note 28 for chap. 4, and Wilber, 2000b, note 21 for chap. 14.

First-person phenomenological investigations of consciousness can easily spot *phenomenal states* and even first-person *phenomenal stages*. For example, in the 'highest yoga' school of Tibetan Buddhism (anuttaratantra yoga), there are ten major stages of meditation, each marked by a very specific phenomenological experience: during meditation, a person first experiences a mirage-like appearance, then smoke-like, then fireflies, then flickering lamp, then a steady lamp (all of these stages are said to result from the progressive transcendence of the gross bodymind); then the individual begins to experience the subtle realms: an expanse like a clear autumn moonlight, then clear autumn sunlight, which takes one to the causal or unmanifest realm, which is an experience like 'the thick blackness of an autumn night', and then the breakthrough to the nondual (Gyatso, 1986). Those specific experiences appear to be genuine stages in this particular meditative line (they are all said to be necessary and none can be skipped), and any individual, sitting in meditation, could indeed see or spot these stages by him- or herself, because they present themselves as successively perceived phenomenal states. This is why I maintain that the phenomenological method can register phenomenal states and phenomenal stages in the 'I' (or Upper-Left quadrant). And this is why the world's contemplative literature is full of these types of states and stages.

But that phenomenological method cannot easily spot *subjective structures* (i.e., psychological structures in the Upper-Left quadrant, such as those discovered by Graves, 1970; Piaget, 1977; Loevinger, 1976; etc.), nor can it spot *intersubjective structures* and *intersubjective stages* (or those in the Lower-Left quadrant, e.g., Gebser's worldviews, Habermas' stages of communicative competence, interpersonal moral stages, Foucault's interpretative-analytic side of the structures of power, etc.). As suggested in the main text, no amount of introspection by individuals will disclose social structures of oppressive power (e.g. Foucault), moral stages (e.g., Carol Gilligan), linguistic structures (e.g., Chomsky), stages of ego development (e.g., Jane Loevinger), stages of values (e.g., Clare Graves), and so on — all of those are inherently invisible to mere phenomenology. This is why phenomenological approaches tend to be strong in the 'I' components but weak in the 'we' components. (Cultural phenomenologists, such as some ethnomethodologists, are strong in the 'we' or intersubjective components, but not in stages or structures of intersubjectivity. When those stage-structures are presented, phenomenology shades into neostructuralism; both of those approaches thus appear to be useful aspects of a more integral approach.)

The general inadequacy of phenomenology for spotting intersubjective structure-stages seems to be the major reason that the world's contemplative literature is virtually silent on these important intersubjective aspects of consciousness. This also appears to be why research into nonordinary states of consciousness, such as Grof's holotropic model of the mind (Grof, 1985; 1998), produces incomplete cartographies (both psychedelic research and holotropic breathwork are very good for spotting experiential, phenomenal, first-person states, but fare less well in spotting intersubjective and interobjective patterns; hence the lopsidedness of such cartographies and their inadequacy in dealing with many important aspects of consciousness in the world [Wilber 1995; 1997a]).

This is might also be why many contemporary meditation theorists are hostile to structure-stage conceptions — their phenomenological methodology does not spot them, so they assume they are imposed on consciousness for suspect reasons by categorizing theorists.

In short, it appears that phenomenological methods tend to excel in spotting (in the UL) individual phenomenal states and phenomenal stages, but not individual structures; and while they excel in spotting different cultural and intersubjective patterns, they miss the intersubjective structures and stages (of the LL; not to mention the Right-Hand patterns, which are not discussed in this note). A more integral approach would likely result from a combination of I, we, and it dimensions, using research methodologies that are 'all-quadrant, all-level' (see below).

Kegan, 1983; Loevinger, 1976; Wade, 1996). For example, in the cognitive line, there is sensorimotor, preoperational, concrete operational, formal operational, vision-logic, and so on. Researchers are unanimous that none of those stages can be skipped, because each incorporates its predecessor in its own makeup (in the same way that cells contain molecules which contain atoms, and you cannot go from atoms to cells and skip molecules). No true stages in any developmental line can be skipped, nor can higher stages in that line be 'peak experienced'. A person at preoperational cannot have a peak experience of formal operational. A person at Kohlberg's moral-stage 1 cannot have a peak experience of moral-stage 5. A person at Graves's animistic stage cannot have a peak experience of the integrated stage, and so on. Not only are those stages in some ways learned behaviours, they are incorporative, cumulative, and enveloping, all of which preclude skipping.

But the three great *states* (of waking, dreaming, sleeping) represent *general realms* of being and knowing that can be accessed at virtually any stage in virtually any line — for the simple reason that individuals wake, dream, and sleep, even in the prenatal period (Wilber, 1997a; 2000b). Thus, gross, subtle, and causal *states* of consciousness are available at virtually any structure/stage of development.

However, the ways in which these altered states will (and can) be *experienced* depends predominantly on the *structures* (stages) of consciousness that have developed in the individual (Wilber, 1983; 2000b). As we will see, individuals at, for example, the magic, mythic, and rational stages can all have a peak experience of a subtle realm, but how that subtle realm is experienced and interpreted depends in large measure on the structures of consciousness that are available to unpack the experience.

(Technical point: the lower reaches of the subtle I call the 'psychic'; and the union of causal emptiness with all form I call 'nondual'. This gives us the four major transpersonal states that I mentioned [psychic, subtle, causal, and nondual]; but they are all variations on the normal states available to virtually all individuals, which is why they are generally available at almost any stage of development. See *Integral Psychology* [Wilber, 2000b] for a full discussion of this theme.)

Evidence suggests that, under conditions generally of prolonged contemplative practice, a person can convert these *temporary* states into *permanent* traits or structures, which means that they have access to these great realms on a more-or-less *continuous* and *conscious* basis (Shankara, 1970; Aurobindo, 1990; Walsh, 1999). In the case of the subtle realm, for example, this means that a person will generally begin to lucid dream (which is analogous to savikalpa samadhi — or stable meditation on subtle forms) (LaBerge, 1985); and with reference to the causal, when a person stably reaches that wave, he or she will remain tacitly conscious even during deep dreamless sleep (a condition known as permanent turiya, constant consciousness, subject permanence, or unbroken witnessing, which is analogous to nirvikalpa samadhi, or stable meditation as the formless) (Alexander and Langer, 1990). Pushing through even that level, the causal form-less finds union with the entire world of form, a realization known as nondual (sahaja, turiyatita, bhava) (Adi Da, 1977, 1979; Alexander and Langer, 1990; Wilber, 1999a).

In each of those cases, those great realms (psychic, subtle, causal, nondual) are no longer experienced merely as *states*, but have instead become permanently available patterns or structures of consciousness — which is why, when they become a permanent competence, I then call them the psychic level (or structure or wave), the subtle level, the causal level, and the nondual. The use of those four terms to cover *both* structures and states has led some critics to assume that I was confusing structures and states, but this is not the case.[8]

The important question then becomes: do those four *states*, as they become permanent *structures*, show stage-like unfolding? Are they then actually *levels* of consciousness? In many ways, the answer appears to be 'yes' (again, not as rigid rungs but as fluid and flowing waves). For example, a person who reaches *stable* (permanent) causal witnessing will automatically experience lucid dreaming (because stable causal witnessing means that one witnesses *everything* that arises, which includes the subtle and dream states), but not vice versa (i.e., somebody who reaches stable subtle awareness does not necessarily reach pure causal witnessing) — in other words, this is a stage sequence (i.e., the causal is a higher level than the subtle — e.g., the anandamayakosha is a higher level than the vijnanamayakosha, or the overmind is a higher level than the intuitive mind, and so on — exactly as maintained by the great wisdom traditions [Smith, 1976; Walsh 1999]).

This is why Aurobindo says, of these higher, transpersonal levels/structures: 'The spiritual evolution obeys the logic of a successive unfolding; it can take a new decisive main step only when the previous main step has been sufficiently conquered: even if certain minor stages can be swallowed up or leaped over by a rapid and brusque ascension, the consciousness has to turn back to assure itself

[8] Nonetheless, using the same terms to cover both the transpersonal structures and the transpersonal states was perhaps an unhappy choice; in my defence, I would say that three decades ago, there were only so many terms to go around, and we used them as parsimoniously as possible. In Vedanta, as previously mentioned, the subtle body/realm or *sukshma-sharira* (experienced in, e.g., the dream state, the chonyid bardo state, and savikalpa samadhi) includes or supports three *structures* or levels — the pranamayakosha or emotional-sexual level, the manomayakosha or mental level, and the vijnanamayakosha or higher-mental/soul level — and I have, from the beginning, used the world 'subtle' to refer to both the *overall* subtle state/realm (the prana-, mano-, and vijnana-mayakosha) *and* the highest structure in it (the vijnanamayakosha); the context usually indicates which is meant. In Vedanta, the causal state/realm has just one structure, the anandamayakosha, so there is less semantic problem.

There is a substantial amount of agreement in the traditions (e.g., contemplative Christianity, Kabbalah, Vajrayana, Sufism, Vedanta) about these transpersonal realms, structures, and states — but the terminology used by different scholars to translate them is indeed a semantic nightmare. So let me just say that I use four major terms (psychic, subtle, causal, and nondual) to refer to the various transpersonal occasions, including transpersonal *states* (e.g., subtle, causal, and nondual states of consciousness, experienced in, e.g., dream state, savikalpa samadhi, deep sleep, nirvikalpa samadhi, jnana samadhi, sahaja, etc.); *realms*, bodies, or spheres of being (e.g., gross body/realm, subtle body/realm, causal body/realm); and *structures*, waves, or levels of consciousness (e.g., psychic level or illumined mind, subtle level or intuitive mind, causal level or overmind, and nondual or supermind, to use Aurobindo's terminology for the corresponding levels). For those concerned with these intricacies, the context will usually indicate which is meant. See Wilber (2000b) for a further discussion of these technical issues.

that the ground passed over is securely annexed to the new condition; a greater or concentrated speed [which is indeed possible] does not eliminate the steps themselves or the necessity of their successive surmounting' (Aurobindo, *The Life Divine*, II, 26 [1990]). His overall writing makes it clear that he does not mean that in a rigid ladder fashion, but more as was suggested: a series of subtler and subtler waves of consciousness unfolding, with much fluid and flowing overlap, and the possibility of nonlinear altered states always available. But for those states to become structures, 'they obey the logic of a successive unfolding', as all true stages do. The world's contemplative literature, taken as a whole, is quite clear on these points, and in this regard we justifiably speak of these transpersonal structures as showing some stage-like and level-like characteristics.[9]

Again, that is *not* the entire story of spirituality. In a moment I will suggest that spirituality is commonly given at least four different definitions (the highest levels of any of the lines, a separate line, an altered state, a particular attitude), and a comprehensive or integral theory of spirituality ought charitably to include all four of them. Thus, the developmental aspects we just discussed do not cover the entire story of spirituality, although they appear to be an important part of it.

To give a specific example: If we focus on the cognitive line of development, we would have these general levels or waves in the overall spectrum of cognition: sensorimotor, preoperational, concrete operational, formal operational, vision-logic, psychic, subtle, causal, and nondual. Those nine general *levels* or *structures* Aurobindo respectively called sensory/vital, lower mind, concrete mind, logical mind, higher mind, illumined mind, intuitive mind, overmind, and supermind, stretching along a single rainbow from the densest to the finest to the ground of them all.

The respective *worldviews* of those nine general structures of consciousness might be described as: archaic, magic, mythic, rational, aperspectival, psychic (yogic), subtle (saintly), causal (sagely), and nondual (siddha) (Adi Da, 1977; Gebser, 1985; Wilber 1996a; 1996b; 1997a; 2000b).

Those are *levels* of consciousness or *structures* (stages), during whose *permanent* unfolding, no stages can be readily skipped; but at virtually any of those stages, a person can have a peak experience of psychic, subtle, casual, or nondual *states*. Overall or *integral development* is thus a continuous process of converting temporary states into permanent traits or structures, and in that integral development, no structures or levels can be bypassed, or the development is not, by definition, integral.

Uneven Development

This does not prevent all sorts of spirals, regressions, temporary leaps forward via peak experiences, and so on. Notice, for example, that somebody at the psychic *level* can peak experience the causal *state*, but cannot stably access that realm because their *permanent* development has not yet reached the causal as a stage (or

---

[9] For a definitive cross-cultural study of meditative stages, see Daniel P. Brown, 'The Stages of Meditation in Cross-Cultural Perspective', chap.8 in Wilber *et al.* (1986). For charts comparing a dozen meditative systems containing stages, see Wilber (2000b).

a permanent acquisition or structure). In order for that to happen, they must traverse the subtle realm (converting it into an objective stage) before they can *stably* maintain the witnessing position of the causal (turiya), because the permanent witness is, by definition, continuously aware of all that arises, and that means that if the subtle arises, it is witnessed — which means the subtle has become a permanently available pattern or structure in consciousness. Thus, stages in integral development, as elsewhere, cannot be skipped. (They do not have to be perfected or mastered to the nth degree, but they do have to be established as a general competence. Somebody who cannot witness the subtle state cannot, by definition, be the causal witness — hence, the stage-like nature of these higher structures as they become *permanent* acquisitions.) See appendix A.

Still, what usually happens is that because these three great realms and states (waking/gross, dream/subtle, and formless/causal) are constantly available to human beings, and because as states they can be practised to some degree independently of each other (and might even develop independently to some degree [Wilber, 2000b]), many individuals can and do evidence a great deal of competence in some of these states/realms (such as meditative formlessness in the causal realm), yet are poorly or even pathologically developed in others (such as the frontal or gross personality, interpersonal development, psychosexual development, moral development, and so on). The 'stone Buddha' phenomenon — where a person can stay in extraordinary states of formless absorption for extended periods — and yet be poorly developed, or even pathologically developed, in other lines and realms, is an extremely common phenomenon, and it happens largely because integral development has not been engaged, let alone completed. Likewise, many spiritual teachers show a good deal of proficiency in subtle states, but little in causal or gross, with quite unbalanced results — for them and their followers. In short, what usually happens is that development is partial or fractured, and this fractured development is taken as the paradigm of natural and normal spiritual development, and then students and teachers alike are asked to repeat the fracture as evidence of their spiritual progress.

The fact that these three great realms/states can be engaged separately; the fact that many contemporary writers equate spirituality predominantly with altered and nonordinary states (which is often called without irony the fourth wave of transpersonal theory); the fact that lines in general can develop unevenly (so that a person can be at a high level of development in some lines and low or pathological in others) — and that this happens more often than not — have all conspired to obscure those important aspects of spiritual development that do indeed show some stage-like phenomena. My point is that *all* of these aspects of spirituality (four of which I mentioned and will elucidate below) need to be acknowledged and included in any comprehensive theory of spirituality — and in any genuinely integral spiritual practice.[10]

---

[10] For integral spiritual practice, see Wilber (1999a) and Murphy and Leonard (1995).

A final point about the word 'integral' and about Jean Gebser's structures. Although I am a long-time fan of Gebser, I believe his work is now hindering the field of consciousness studies. First, Gebser does not have a clear understanding of the quadrants, so he tends to conflate different phenomenological languages, different validity claims, and different evidential data. Second, his

A Grid of Religious Experiences

If we combine the idea of *levels* of development with *states* of consciousness, and we realize that a person at virtually any level or stage of development can have a peak experience or an altered state, the result a useful grid of many of the various types of spiritual and nonordinary experiences.

For example, let us use Jean Gebser's (1985) terms for some of the lower-to-intermediate levels of consciousness: archaic, magic, mythic, rational, and aperspectival (there are higher, transpersonal structures, as we have seen, but these will do for now). To those five levels, let us add the four states of psychic, subtle, causal, and nondual. The point is that a person at any of those five structures can peak experience any of those four states, and that gives us a grid of twenty types of spiritual, transpersonal, or nonordinary experiences (Wilber, 1983; 2000b).

As suggested earlier, the reason this grid occurs is that the way in which individuals *interpret* an altered state depends in part upon their general level of development. For example, individuals at the mythic level might peak experience a psychic state, but they generally interpret that psychic peak experience in the terms of their mythic structure. Likewise, there is a magic experience of a subtle state, a mythic experience of a subtle state, a rational experience of a subtle state; and so on with causal and nondual.[11] Putting these altogether gives us a

---

'archaic structure' is, in my opinion, charged with the retro-Romantic (and pre/trans) fallacy. Third, and most troublesome, his 'integral structure' actually contains *at least* five structures (namely, vision-logic, psychic, subtle, causal, and nondual; or, to use Aurobindo's terms, higher mind, illumined mind, intuitive mind, overmind, and supermind — all of which are collapsed into 'the' integral structure by Gebser. Although there is evidence that he realized this later in life, he did not live to adequately correct it). Even according to more conventional maps, such as Spiral Dynamics, what Gebser calls 'integral' actually contains green, yellow, turquoise, and coral structures. In short, I believe Gebser's investigation of 'the' integral structure was pioneering but is now outdated.

Nonetheless, I continue to refer to the entire vision-logic realms (and second-tier thinking) as 'integral', simply because it has become a very common usage. But clearly, the truly integral 'level' is the nondual, which is not actually a level or state but the ever-present ground of all levels and all states (see, e.g., the last chapter of Wilber, 1997a).

Lastly, there is the issue of levels of consciousness and levels (planes, realms, axes, spheres) of reality; for a discussion of this theme, particularly in reference to postmodern, post-metaphysical epistemologies, I refer the reader to a series of long endnotes in Wilber, 2000b), beginning with note 3 for chap. 1.

[11] Any of the widely accepted developmental lines can be used to create and research these types of grids. For example, in the cognitive line we have preoperational (preop), concrete operational (conop), formal operational (formop), and postformal (which has various levels, up to and including the transpersonal waves, but this simple division will work for this example). An individual at preop can temporarily experience a psychic, subtle, causal, or nondual state; so can an individual at conop, formop, and postformal. In each case, it appears that the individual interprets those states largely in the categories of the cognitive level at which he or she is presently adapted. For instance, a conop experience of a subtle state tends to be interpreted in very literal-concrete terms (just as mythic symbols at that stage are also taken very literally; e.g., Moses actually did part the Red Sea) and often very ethnocentrically ('only those who believe in my God will be saved'); whereas a person at postformal cognition interprets a subtle-state experience in pluralistic, metaphorical, and aperspectival terms ('I experienced a ground of being that is present in all sentient beings but is expressed differently by each, with no expression being better than another'); and someone directly at the transpersonal waves experiences these realms in their self-transcending immediacy, beyond conceptualization, pluralistic or otherwise.

phenomenological grid of the many types of altered, nonordinary, and religious experiences available to men and women.[12]

The Self

So far we have explored states, waves, and streams. We might look now at the 'self' (or self-system or self-sense), and although there are many ways to view the self, one heuristically useful device is to view the self as that which integrates or balances all of those various aspects (Wilber, 1996c; 1997a; 2000b; Wilber *et al.*, 1986). For the striking thing about the levels, lines, and states is that in themselves they appear to be devoid of an inherent self-sense, and therefore the self can *identify* with any of them (as suggested by ancient theorists from Plotinus to Buddha). That is, one of the primary characteristics of the self seems to be its capacity to *identify* with the basic structures or levels of consciousness, and every time it does so, according to this view, it generates a specific type of self-identity, with specific needs and drives. The self thus appears to be a functional system (which includes such capacities as identification, will, defence, and tension regulation [Wilber *et al.*, 1986]), and it also undergoes its own type of development through a series of stages or waves (as investigated by, e.g., Jane Loevinger, 1976; Robert Kegan, 1983; Susanne Cook-Greuter, 1990; etc.). The main difference between the self-stages and the other stages is that the self has the job of balancing and coordinating all of them.

This balancing act, this drive to integrate the various components of the psyche, appears to be a crucial feature of the self. Psychopathology, for example, cannot easily be understood without it (Blanck and Blanck, 1974; 1979; Kohut, 1971; 1977). The basic structures of consciousness do not themselves get sick or

---

As suggested, any of the more dependable models of developmental lines can be used to research these types of grids, such as the self-stages (including research tools) presented by Jane Loevinger, Susanne Cook-Greuter, or Robert Kegan; the Graves values scale; Gebser's structures; Maslow's needs hierarchy; Bill Torbert's stages of action-inquiry, and so on. This offers a series of fruitful empirical, phenomenological, and structural research strategies for mapping states onto structures.

[12] This simple example uses Gebser's structures, which cover the lower-to-intermediate structures (up to centauric vision-logic). But there are higher, transpersonal structures that need to be added to the grid, and there are also more sophisticated maps of the lower-to-intermediate structures, such as Spiral Dynamics — e.g., there can be a purple, red, blue, orange, green, yellow, and turquoise peak experience of a psychic, subtle, causal, or nondual state. Also, as a person permanently evolves into higher structures, such as the psychic or subtle, they can still peak experience yet higher realms, such as causal and nondual.

If we use a general scheme — of, say, 12 levels and 4 states — that gives us around 48 types of transpersonal peak experiences and nonordinary states, although in actuality some of the squares in that grid do not occur (e.g., once at the psychic level, one no longer has psychic peak experiences, for that is now a permanent acquisition). But by and large, those three dozen or so types of nonordinary and spiritual experiences appear to be very real and can be fruitfully cataloged using this grid. I believe that this approach enriches and advances our understanding of these phenomena, the study of which seems to have stalled. (For more details on this grid, see Wilber, 1983; 2000b.)

There has been a great deal of research and models based primarily on altered and nonordinary states (Grof 1985; 1998; Tart 1972; Fisher, 1971; Wolman & Ullman, 1986; White, 1972, etc.), and a great deal of research and models on various structures of consciousness (Graves, 1970; Loevinger, 1976; Piaget, 1977; Gilligan, 1982; 1990; Fowler, 1981; Selman & Byrne, 1974; etc.), but very few proposals for an 'all-quadrants, all-structures, all-states' model that combines the best of both. The importance of this more integral research agenda will be highlighted in the main text.

'broken'. They either emerge or they don't, and when they do, they are generally well functioning (barring organic brain damage). For example, when concrete operational thinking ('conop') emerges in a child, it emerges more-or-less intact — but what the child does with those structures is something else indeed, and that specifically involves the child's self-sense. For the child can take any of the contents of the conop mind and repress them, alienate them, project them, retroflect them, or deploy any number of other defensive mechanisms (Vaillant, 1993). This a disease, not of conop, but of the self.

(Here is a more extreme example: a psychotic might be, among other things, temporarily plugging into a subtle realm and hence begin dream-like hallucinations. The subtle realm is not malfunctioning, it is working just fine; but the self cannot *integrate* these realms with the gross/frontal structures, and therefore it suffers a severe pathology. The pathology is not in the subtle, it is in the self-system and its failed capacity to integrate.)

Most psychopathology (on the interior domains) seems to involve some sort of failure in the self's capacity of differentiation and integration — a failure that occurs during what can be called a *fulcrum* of self-development (Blanck and Blanck, 1974; 1979; Kegan, 1983; Wilber, 2000b; Wilber *et al.*, 1986).[13] A fulcrum occurs each time the self encounters a new level of consciousness. The self must first *identify* with that new level (embed at that level, be in fusion with that level); it eventually *disidentifies* with (or transcends) that level so as to move to a yet higher wave; then it ideally *integrates* the previous wave with the higher wave.

A miscarriage at any of those points in the particular fulcrum (failed identification, failed differentiation, failed integration) will generate a pathology; and the type of the pathology depends upon *both* the level of consciousness that the fulcrum occurs and the phase within the fulcrum that the miscarriage occurs (Wilber *et al.*, 1986). If we have nine general levels or waves of consciousness (each of which has a corresponding fulcrum that occurs when the self identifies with that level), and each fulcrum has these three basic subphases (fusion, transcendence, integration), then that gives us a typology of around twenty-seven major self pathologies (which range from psychotic to borderline to neurotic to existential to transpersonal). Far from being a mere abstract typology, there are abundant examples of each of these types (Rowan, 1993; Walsh and Vaughan, 1993; Wilber, 2000b; Wilber *et al.*, 1986).[14]

---

[13] Individual psychopathology appears to be an all-quadrant affair (see below), and thus important aspects of its genesis can be found in all four quadrants: there are contributing factors from the Upper-Right quadrant (e.g., brain physiology, neurotransmitter imbalance, poor diet); Lower-Right quadrant (e.g., economic stress, environmental toxins, social oppression); and the Lower-Left quadrant (cultural pathologies, communication snarls). Treatment likewise can involve all four quadrants (including psychopharmacology [UR] where appropriate). I am here focusing only on some of the important factors in the Upper-Left quadrant. For the contributions of all four quadrants to pathology, see Wilber (1995; 1996d; 1997a; 2000b).

[14] To say that the self 'identifies' with a level is not to picture this in an all-or-none fashion. Even with the proximate self-sense (e.g., as investigated by Loevinger), research indicates that individuals tend to give around 50% of their responses from one level and 25% responses from the level above and below it. As suggested in the main text, the self is more a *centre of gravity* than a monolithic entity. This also appears to include the existence of numerous subpersonalities (Rowan, 1990; Wilber 2000b).

Again, none of this is a rigid, linear type of classification. The various waves and fulcrums overlap to a great extent; different pathologies and treatment modalities also overlap considerably; and the scheme itself is a simple generalization. But it does go a long way toward developing a more comprehensive overview of both pathology and treatment, and as such it seems to constitute an important part of any genuinely integral psychology.

The fluid nature of all of these events highlights the fact that the self-system is perhaps best thought of, not as a monolithic entity, but as the *centre of gravity* of the various levels, lines, and states, all orbiting around the integrating tendency of the self-system (Wilber, 1997a; 2000b). When any aspects of the psyche become cut off from this self-organizing activity, they (as it were) reach escape velocity and spin out of orbit, becoming dissociated, fragmented, alienated pockets of the psyche. Therapy, on the interior domains, thus generally involves a recontacting, befriending, reintegrating, and 're-entry' of the dissociated elements back into the orbit of conscious inclusion and embrace.

Four Meanings of 'Spiritual'

If we focus for a moment on states, levels, lines, and self, we will find that they appear to underlie four of the most common definitions of 'spirituality'.

In *Integral Psychology*, I suggest that there are at least four widely used definitions of spirituality, each of which contains an important but partial truth, and all of which need to be included in any balanced account: (1) spirituality involves peak experiences or altered states, which can occur at almost any stage and any age; (2) spirituality involves the highest levels in any of the lines; (3) spirituality is a separate developmental line itself; (4) spirituality is an attitude (such as openness, trust, or love) that the self may or may not have at any stage.[15]

We have already discussed some of the important ingredients of each of those usages. We have particularly examined the idea of spirituality as involving peak experiences or altered states (#1). Here is a quick review of the other three.

Often, when people refer to something as 'spiritual', they explicitly or implicitly mean the highest levels in any of the developmental lines. For example, in the cognitive line, we usually think of transrational awareness as spiritual, but we

---

[15] These are not the only four definitions of spirituality. In *A Sociable God*, nine different definitions are outlined. But these four are some of the most common and, I believe, most significant. In *A Sociable God*, I distinguish between *legitimate* (or translative) spirituality, which seeks to fortify the self at its present level of development, no matter how high or low; and *authentic* (or transformative) spirituality, which seeks to transcend the self altogether (or at least transform it to a higher wave of consciousness). The first three uses of 'spirituality' (given in the main text) are different definitions of authentic spirituality, in that all of them include, at least in part, the idea that real spirituality involves a change in level of consciousness (either temporary, as in #1, or permanent, as in #2 and #3). The fourth usage is a good definition of legitimate spirituality, in that it seeks to promote the health of the self at whatever level it is at, without vertically changing consciousness. As suggested in the main text, all four of these uses of spirituality are valid, in my opinion, and all four of them seem to represent very real and important functions that spirituality can perform. The difficulty appears to be that some religious and spiritual theorists (and movements) latch onto just one narrow aspect of the spiritual impulse in humans and claim it is the only impulse worth acting on, which seems to distort both legitimate an authentic spirituality and often sets the self in a spiral of deception and deceit.

don't often think of mere rationality or logic as spiritual. In other words, the highest levels of cognition are often viewed as spiritual, but the low and medium levels less so. Likewise with affects or emotions: the higher or transpersonal affects, such as love and compassion, are usually deemed spiritual, but the lower affects, such as hate and anger, are not. Likewise with Maslow's needs hierarchy: the lower needs, such as self-protection, are not often thought of as spiritual, but the highest needs, such as self-transcendence, are.

This is a legitimate usage, in my opinion, because it reflects some of the significant developmental aspects of spirituality (namely, the more evolved a person is in any given line, the more that line seems to take on spiritual qualities). This is not the only aspect of spirituality — we have already seen that states are very important, and we will see two other aspects below — but it is a factor that needs to be considered in any comprehensive or integral account of spirituality.

The third common usage sees spirituality as a separate developmental line itself. James Fowler's stages of faith is a well-known and well-respected example (Fowler, 1981). The world's contemplative literature is full of meticulously described stages of contemplative development (again, not as a series of rigid rungs in a ladder but as flowing waves of subtler and subtler meditative experiences, often culminating in causal formlessness, and then the breakthrough into permanent nondual consciousness (Brown & Engler, 1986; Goleman, 1988). In this very common usage, the spiritual line begins in infancy (or even before, in the bardo and prenatal states), and eventually unfolds into wider and deeper spheres of consciousness until the great liberation of enlightenment. This is yet another important view of spirituality that any comprehensive or integral theory might want to take into account.

Viewing spirituality as a relatively independent line also explains the commonly acknowledged fact that somebody might be highly developed in the spiritual line and yet poorly — or even pathologically — developed in other lines, such as interpersonal or psychosexual, often with unfortunate results.[16]

The fourth usage is that spirituality is essentially an attitude or trait that the self may or may not possess at any stage of growth, and this attitude — perhaps loving kindness, inner peace, charity, or goodness — is what most marks spirituality. In this usage, you could have, for example, a spiritual or unspiritual magic wave, a spiritual or unspiritual mythic wave, a spiritual or unspiritual rational wave, and so on, depending on whether the self had integrated that wave in a healthy or

---

[16] This phenomenon (i.e., a person can be highly developed in certain spiritual traits but poorly developed in others, such as psychosexual, emotional, or interpersonal skills) can be believably explained by three of the four definitions (e.g., #1: if spirituality is defined as an altered states, those can certainly occur in a personality that is dysfunctional; #2: if spirituality is the highest levels in any of the lines, a person can be highly developed in some lines and poorly or pathologically in others; #3: if spirituality is a separate line itself, then individuals can be highly advanced in that line and poorly or pathologically developed in others). This uneven mixture (of spiritual and pathological) is not easily explained by definition #4 (i.e., if spirituality is something that either is or is not present at any stage, then the only way to get uneven and mixed development is to revert to one of the other definitions, but that 'developmental ranking' is what this definition claims to avoid). Nor can uneven development be explained by single ladder models of development (according to which, a person failing a lower stage could not advance to a higher).

unhealthy fashion. This, too, is a common and important usage, and any integral account of spirituality would surely want to take it into consideration.[17]

Two general claims: One, those four major definitions are indeed common definitions of 'spirituality'. They are not the only uses, but they are some of the most prevalent. And two, those four common uses arise because of the actual existence of states, levels, lines, and self, respectively. People seem to intuitively or natively grasp the existence of states, levels, lines, and self, and thus when it comes to spirituality, they often translate their spiritual intuitions in terms of those available dimensions, which gives rise to those oft-used definitions.

Those definitions of spirituality are not mutually incompatible. They actually fit together in something of seamless whole, as I try to suggest in *Integral Psychology*. We can already see, for example, that any model that coherently includes states, levels, lines, and self can automatically give a general account of those four aspects of spirituality. But in order to see how this would specifically work, we need one more item: the four quadrants. (The four quadrants are not to be confused with the four uses of spirituality; the number four in this case is coincidental.) But the four quadrants are crucial, I believe, in seeing how the many uses of spirituality can in fact be brought together into a more mutual accord.

Quadrants

Most people find the four quadrants a little difficult to grasp at first, then very simple to use. The quadrants refer to the fact that anything can be looked at from four perspectives, so to speak: we can look at something from the inside or from the outside, and in the singular or the plural. For example, my own consciousness in this moment. I can look at it from the inside, in which case I see all my various feelings, hopes, fears, sensations, and perceptions that I might have in any given moment. This is the first-person or phenomenal view, described in 'I' language. But consciousness can also be looked at in an objective, 'scientific' fashion, in which case I might conclude that my consciousness is the product of objective brain mechanisms and neurophysiological systems. This is the third-person or objective view, described in 'it' language. Those are the inside and the outside views of my own consciousness.

But my consciousness or self does not exist in a vacuum; it exists in a community of other selves. So in addition to a *singular* view of consciousness, we can look at how consciousness exists in the *plural* (as part of a group, a community, a collective). And just as we can look at the inside and the outside of the individual, we can look at the inside and the outside of the collective. We can try to understand any group of people from the inside, in a sympathetic resonance of mutual understanding; or we can try to look at them from the outside, in a detached and objective manner (both views can be useful, as long as we honour each).

---

[17] This discussion earlier suggested a 'grid of religious experiences'. Notice that that grid is simply what we see if we combine factors 1 and 2/3 — that is, if we map the various states of consciousness on the various structure-stages. Thus, even that grid recognizes some of these major uses, suggesting again their widespread importance.

On the inside of the collective, we see all of the various shared worldviews (archaic, magic, mythic, rational, etc.), ethics, customs, values, and intersubjective structures held in common by those in the collective (whether that be family, peers, corporation, organization, tribe, town, nation, globe). The insides of the collective are described in 'we' language and include all of those intersubjective items that you might experience if you were truly a member of that culture. From the outside, we see all of the objective structures and social institutions of the collective, such as the physical buildings, the infrastructures (foraging, horticultural, agrarian, industrial, informational), the techno-economic base, the quantitative aspects of the society (the birth and death rates, the monetary exchanges, the objective data), modes of communication (written words, telegraph, telephone, internet), and so on. Those are all 'its' or patterns of interobjective social systems.

So we have four major perspectives (the inside and the outside of the singular and the plural): I, it, we, and its. Since the objective dimensions (the outside of the individual and the outside of the collective) are both described in third-person it-language, we can reduce the four quadrants to just three: I, we, and it. Or first-person, second-person, and third-person accounts.[18] Or art, morals, and science. Or the beautiful, the good, and the true.

The major point is that each of the levels, lines, and states of consciousness has these four quadrants (or simply the three major dimensions of I, we, and it) (Wilber, 1995, 1996d, 1997a, 2000b).[19] This model therefore explicitly integrates first-, second-, and third-person accounts of consciousness at each of the levels, lines, and states. This gives what I believe is a more comprehensive and integral model of consciousness. This 'all-quadrants, all-levels, all-lines, all-states' model is sometimes referred to simply as 'all-quadrant, all-level', or AQAL for short. I have explored this model at length in several books, such as *Sex, Ecology, Spirituality*; *A Brief History of Everything*; and *Integral Psychology*. If we systematically investigate the implications of this AQAL model, we might also find that it opens up the possibility of a more integral approach to education, politics,

---

[18] Technically, 'we' is first-person plural, and 'you' is second person. But I include first-person plural ('we') and second person ('you/Thou') as *both* being in the Lower-Left quadrant, which I refer to in general as 'we'. The reason I do so is that there is no second-person plural in English (which is why southerners have to say 'you all' and northerners say 'you guys'). In other words, when 'we' is being done with respect, it implicitly includes an I-Thou relationship (I cannot truly understand thee unless WE share a set of common perceptions).

Both the Lower-Left quadrant and the Upper-Left quadrant are postulated to exist 'all the way down'; that is, this is a form of modified panpsychism ('pan-interiors'), which seems to be the only model capable of faithfully rendering this 'master template' (see Appendix B; Wilber, 2000b). This implies that intersubjectivity also goes 'all the way down' and that humans, as 'compound individuals', contain all the pre-human forms of intersubjectivity as well. Thus, in humans, intersubjectivity is not established merely by exchange of linguistic signifiers, which is the commonly accepted notion. Rather, humans contain pre-linguistic intersubjectivity (established by, e.g., emotional or prereflexive co-presence with and to the other); linguistic intersubjectivity (established by the co-presence of interiority whose exteriors are linguistic signifiers but cannot be reduced to those exteriors); and trans-linguistic intersubjectivity (established by the simple presence of Presence, or nondual Spirit). In short, intersubjectivity is established at all levels by an interior resonance of those elements present at each level, a resonance that appears to span the entire spectrum of consciousness, pre-linguistic to linguistic to trans-linguistic. The suggestion that I limit intersubjectivity to the exchange of linguistic signifiers is quite off the mark (see Wilber, 1995).

business, art, feminism, ecology, and so on (see, e.g., Crittenden, 2001; Wilber, 2000c).

It should be emphasized that this article has dealt almost exclusively with only one quadrant, namely, the interior of the individual (which is called the 'Upper-Left quadrant'). But in other works I have dealt extensively with the other quadrants, and my point is certainly that all of the quadrants need to be included in any balanced account of consciousness.

The Religious Grid, Revisited

To see why the four quadrants are important for understanding even individual psychology, we can return to our 'religious grid' as an example. We earlier discussed only the Upper-Left quadrant factors (the interior of the individual), which is fine for the phenomenology of spiritual experiences. But for an integral account, we need also to include the other quadrants.

---

[19] Here is one example of the importance of taking the four quadrants into account when dealing with states and structures. We saw that all individuals have access to the three great realms/states of gross, subtle, and causal, simply because everybody wakes, dreams, and sleeps. Thus, even an infant has access to these three great realms. But the way in which the infant (or anybody) interprets these *states* depends in part upon its *stage*-structure of development (e.g., a subtle state can be experienced by the archaic, magic, mythic, rational, etc. structures, with a different 'flavour' in each case). Moreover — and of crucial importance — all of the states and stages are firmly set in the four quadrants (intentional, behavioural, cultural, and social). Thus, an infant is often plunged into the subtle/dream state, but it will not have the dream thought 'I must go to the grocery store and buy some cereal', for those specific sociocultural items have not yet entered its awareness. The infant definitely has access to a subtle state, but it has not yet developed the specific structures (of language, cognition, and cultural perceptions) that will allow it to have those specific thoughts in the subtle/dream state.

Thus, it appears that the three general states are largely *given*, but the various structure-stages *develop*. And because all of them are set in the four quadrants, even the states (which are given prior to culture) are nonetheless firmly molded by the particular culture in which they unfold (because they are molded, in fact, by all four quadrants — intentional, behavioural, cultural, and social).

This allows us to see how an infant can definitely experience a subtle or causal state, but that state is nevertheless unpacked only by a preconventional, egocentric, preformal structure, not a postconventional, global, worldcentric structure (which has not yet developed). This more integral view allows us to steer a course between those who maintain that infants are directly in touch with a pure spiritual reality, and those who maintain that infants are narcissistic and preconventional. (See *Integral Psychology*, chap. 11, 'Is There a Childhood Spirituality?' [Wilber, 2000b].)

As the infant develops through the various levels/structures/waves of consciousness, with all of their various lines, those structures will increasingly provide the content for much of the subtle states (in addition to any truly archetypal material that might be given as part of the subtle itself; but even the latter will be molded in its existence and expression by the four quadrants). Thus, at some point, the young child might indeed develop the conventional thought, 'I must go to the grocery store', and that thought, molded by all four quadrants, might then invade the dream state. A child in a different culture might dream in French or Chinese; not 'cereal' but 'baguettes', and so on. In this way, the *development* in the structures (levels and lines) profoundly influences the content of the general states, which nonetheless are *given* in their general form.

This also allows us to see how all individuals can have access to the three great realms of being (gross, subtle, and causal), and yet still show stage-like development that colors these realms, for the development in the structures will often give content and form to the states. A four-quadrant analysis of states and structures thus allows us to incorporate the best of the ancient models of consciousness with more modern and postmodern research. For further discussion of these themes, see *Integral Psychology* (Wilber, 2000b) and the websites www.IntegralAge.org, http://surf.to/kenwilber, www.enlightenment.com, and iKosmos.com.

The Upper-Right quadrant (the exterior of the individual): During any spiritual, religious, or nonordinary state of consciousness, what are the neurophysiological and brain-state correlates? These might be investigated by PET scans, EEG patterns, physiological markers, and so on. Conversely, what are the effects of various types of physiological and pharmacological agents on consciousness? An enormous amount of this type of research has already been done, of course, and it continues at an increasing pace. Consciousness is clearly linked in complex ways to objective biological and neurophysiological systems, and continued research on these correlations is surely an important agenda. This type of consciousness research — anchored in the brain side of the brain–mind connection — is now one of the most prevalent in conventional consciousness studies, and I wholeheartedly support it as providing some crucial pieces of the overall puzzle.

Nobody, however, has successfully demonstrated that consciousness can be reduced without remainder to those objective systems; and it is patently obvious that phenomenologically it cannot. Unfortunately, the tendency of the third-person approaches to consciousness is to try to make the Upper-Right quadrant the only quadrant worth considering and thus reduce all consciousness to objective 'its' in the individual body/brain — but those cover only one-fourth of the story, so to speak.

Still, this is an incredibly important part of the story. This quadrant, in fact, is the home of the increasingly dominant schools of psychology and consciousness studies (e.g., cognitive science, evolutionary psychology, systems theory applied to brain states, neuroscience, biological psychiatry, etc.). This quadrant provides the 'brain' side of the equation that needs to be correlated with the 'mind' side (represented by, for example, the master template or full-spectrum cartography of waves, streams, and states summarized in this article).[20] And my further point is that those are just two of the quadrants that need to be brought to the integral table.

The Lower-Left quadrant (the interior of the collective): How do different intersubjective, ethical, linguistic, and cultural contexts mold consciousness and altered states? The postmodernists and constructivists have demonstrated, correctly I believe, the crucial role played by background cultural and intersubjective contexts in fashioning individual consciousness (Wilber, 1995; 1998). But many postmodernists have pushed this insight to absurd extremes, maintaining the

---

[20] Even though the Upper-Right quadrant is today of such importance (as evidenced by the increasing dominance of cognitive science, evolutionary psychology, neuroscience, biological psychiatry, etc.), it is the one about which I have written the least. The reasons for this are simple: (1) this quadrant is investigated by the scientific method, or empiric-analytic inquiry, which is fairly straightforward in its operation and interpretation; (2) there is an enormous amount of work already being done in this quadrant; (3) the data collected in this quadrant, once verified, tends to be stable and trustworthy, requiring only modest amounts of interpretation (unlike the interior quadrants, which are made of interpretations). In short, I have written the least about this quadrant not because it is the least important but because it needs the least attention. In chapter 14 of *Integral Psychology* I give an overview of this quadrant and its investigation by the field of consciousness studies — particularly discussing the mind/body or Left/Right 'hard problem' of consciousness (as summarized in Appendix B), and I cite several dozen books that have begun the crucially important endeavor of mapping Upper Left and Upper Right correlations, a mapping on which any truly integral psychology will depend.

self-contradictory stance that cultural contexts create all states. Instead of trying to reduce consciousness to 'it'-language, they try to reduce all consciousness to 'we'-language. All realities, including those of objective science, are said to be merely cultural constructions. To the contrary, research clearly indicates that there are numerous quasi-universal aspects to many human realities, including many altered states (e.g., all healthy humans show similar brainwave patterns in REM sleep and in deep dreamless sleep). Nonetheless, these patterns are indeed given some of their contents and are significantly molded by the cultural context, which therefore forms an important part of a more integral analysis (Wilber, 1995; 1998; 2000b; 2001). (For the nature of intersubjectivity itself, and the reasons that it cannot be reduced to the exchange of linguistic signifiers, see note 18.)

Lower-Right quadrant (the exterior of the collective): How do various techno-economic modes, institutions, economic circumstances, ecological networks, and social systems affect consciousness and altered states? The profoundly important influence of objective social systems on consciousness has been investigated by a wide variety of approaches, including ecology, geopolitics, ecofeminism, neoMarxism, dynamical systems theory, and chaos and complexity theories (e.g., Capra, 1997; Diamond & Orenstein, 1990; Lenski, 1995). All of them tend to see the world ultimately as a holistic system of interwoven 'its'. This, too, is an important part of an integral model. Unfortunately, many of these theorists (just like specialists in the other quadrants) have attempted to reduce consciousness to just this quadrant — to reduce consciousness to digital bits in a systems network, a strand in the objective Web of Life, or a holistic pattern of flatland its, thus perfectly gutting the I and the we dimensions. Surely a more integral approach would include all of the quadrants — I, we, it, and its — without trying to reduce any of them merely to the others.[21]

Of course, the foregoing analysis applies not only to states but also to levels, lines, and self: all of them need to be situated in the four quadrants (intentional, behavioural, cultural, and social) for a more integral understanding, resulting in an 'all-quadrants, all-levels, all-lines, all-states' panoptic.

A Research Suggestion

I have tried to suggest that many of the levels, lines, and states in the various quadrants are, in principle, capable of being investigated via a type of 'simultracking' (Wilber, 1997b; revised, with an addition by Roger Walsh, for

---

[21] An integral approach also lends itself to a more comprehensive understanding of the various types of unconscious processes. The question regarding any sort of unconscious is: can an event occur that is part of the existence of an individual but does not register in consciousness? The answer appears to be definitely yes; but an integral model can be more precise. Evidence suggests that aspects of virtually any level in any line in any quadrant can in fact be unconscious — and can to some degree be made conscious (directly or indirectly) through various techniques. This making conscious the unconscious is said to be connected with various types of liberation. For the kinds of unconscious processes (and liberation) in each of the four quadrants, see *Sex, Ecology, Spirituality*, second revised edition, note 28 for chap. 4 and note 1 for chap. 14. For the types of the unconscious in the Upper-Left quadrant, see *The Atman Project* (CW2) and *The Eye of Spirit* (CW7). I still believe that the five types of unconscious in the UL (first outlined in *The Atman Project*) are of considerable importance for individual psychology.

inclusion in volume 7 of *Collected Works*). The specific research agenda is spelled out in that essay, but the point is simple enough: in addition to the extensive research that is now being done *separately* on the various levels, lines, and states in the various quadrants, the time is now ripe to (1) begin detailed correlations of these events with each other; and thus (2) move toward a more integral theory, not only of consciousness, but of the Kosmos at large; a theory that (3) would begin to show us the how and why of the *intrinsic* connections between all things in existence.[22] This would truly be a 'theory of everything', at least in outline, even if all of the details remain beyond our grasp.

In short, whether or not one agrees with my particular version of an integral model of consciousness, I believe the evidence is now quite substantial that any comprehensive model would want to at least consider taking into account quadrants, waves, streams, states, and self. This fledging field of integral studies holds great promise, I believe, as an important part of a comprehensive and balanced view of consciousness and Kosmos.

Appendix A: Stages of Spiritual Unfolding?

This essay has suggested that there are at least four different, commonly used definitions of 'spirituality' (i.e., spirituality involves altered states, the highest levels in any of the lines, a separate line itself, a quality of the self at any given level), and that each of them appears to reflect an important phenomenon in consciousness (i.e., states, levels, lines, and self). In recent years there has been an intense, sometimes acrimonious debate about whether or not spirituality involves stages, some claiming that it definitely does, others responding that it definitely does not, with each side often adding ad hominen explanations of the other's motives.

A more integral view of spirituality recognizes that both sides are correct. Some aspects of spirituality clearly show stages, and some aspects do not. In the four aspects listed above, the first and the last do not involve stages. The second and the third do.

We can examine a few of these developmental aspects of spirituality by using Robert Forman's excellent article, 'What does mysticism have to teach us about consciousness?' (Forman, 1998b). Forman begins by highlighting three particularly important and apparently universal types of mystical consciousness, which he calls the 'pure consciousness event' (PCE), which is a state of formless consciousness with no thoughts, objects, or perceptions; the 'dual mystical state'

---

[22] All four of the quadrants have various types of waves, streams, and states (among other items). That is, all four quadrants possess levels of development and lines of development (e.g., grades and clades in biological evolution; technological lines of development through the levels of foraging, horticultural, agrarian, industrial, informational, etc.); and all four quadrants also show various types of states (e.g., brain states, states of material affairs, gaseous states, etc.). Thus, all quadrants have waves, streams, and states (in addition to aggregates, heaps, etc). But in the Left-Hand quadrants, these are all ultimately related to consciousness itself (levels of consciousness, lines of consciousness, and states of consciousness — both individual and collective), whereas in the Right-Hand quadrants, we find that levels, lines, and states primarily involve matter (e.g., physiological brain states, biomaterial grades and clades, technological modes, etc.). The Left-Hand quadrants are the interiors, the Right-Hand quadrants the exteriors, of each and every holon (Wilber 1995, 1996d, 1998). See Appendix B.

(DMS), where formless consciousness is present (usually as a type of witnessing awareness) simultaneously with forms and objects of thought and perception (but the subject–object duality is still in place, hence 'dualistic' mystical state); and the 'unitive mystical state' (UMS), where subject and object are one or nondual.

In my scheme, the PCE is a causal (formless) *state* of consciousness. The DMS generally begins as a *state* of consciousness but can increasingly become a more-or-less permanent *structure* of causal witnessing (i.e., the causal state has become a causal structure). The UMS often begins as a temporary *nondual state* but also increasingly can become a permanent nondual structure or wave. I agree entirely with Forman that those are three very real and quasi-universal mystical events; I am also in substantial agreement with his conclusions about what these events mean for consciousness studies, which is why they are part of the 'full-spectrum cartography' or 'master template' presented in *Integral Psychology*.

Forman points out, correctly I believe, that these events are often temporary (in which case they are what I call *states*), but they can become more-or-less permanent acquisitions (in which case I call them *structures*, even if some of them are 'formless' or 'structureless'; structure or level or wave simply signifies constancy). As Forman says, 'Their discriminating feature is a deep shift in epistemological structure: the experienced relationship between the self and one's perceptual objects changes profoundly. In many people this new structure becomes permanent' (p. 186).

The question then becomes, are these shifts sequential and stage-like? Forman cautiously replies, 'Usually'. 'These long-term shifts in epistemological structure often take the form of two quantum leaps in experience [namely, the shift from PCE to DMS, and then from DMS to UMS]; typically they develop sequentially' (p. 186). Forman then adds 'I say typically because sometimes one may skip or not attain a particular stage. Ken Wilber claims sequence. William Barnard, however, disputes this claim of sequence' (p. 186). After several mutually fruitful discussions on this topic, Forman realizes that my position is actually more complex. As we have seen, there are temporary peak experiences of higher realms available at virtually every stage, and thus, for example, even if one is permanently at the DMS, one can still temporarily peak experience the UMS. This makes it very hard to spot any sort of sequentiality, because structure-stages (which are sequential) and states (which are not) can and do fall all over each other. Thus, for these higher events, I maintain that there are both sequential and non-sequential spiritual phenomena (aspects #1 and #4 are not stage-like, aspects #2 and #3 are), and those who claim only one or the other do not appear to have a very integral model.

My further claim is simply this: in the *permanent* acquisition of these higher competences, certain prerequisites must be met. For example, using Forman's useful categories, in order for the DMS state to be a permanent acquisition, one must have some sort of access to the PCE, because the DMS is a combination of the experience of pure consciousness alongside waking objects and thoughts. Of necessity, there is some sort of stage sequencing, however brief (i.e., one can attain PCE without attaining DMS, but not vice versa). Likewise with the UMS, in which the final barrier between pure causal consciousness and the world of form is transcended (either temporarily as a nondual state, or permanently as a nondual wave). In order for that to happen, consciousness must relinquish all attachments to any particular objects, while the objects are still present (i.e., DMS), or else the hidden attachment will prevent true unity and produce at best a type of pseudo-nonduality. Thus, the DMS must be passed through, however briefly, in order for a permanent acquisition of constant unitive consciousness. That is, one can attain the DMS without attaining UMS, but not vice versa: we have a stage sequence with reference to permanent acquisition.

(For further discussion of these themes, see *Integral Psychology*; also, with reference to the Vedantic/TM model of the seven states of consciousness, which Forman's work is partially inspired by, see chap. 10 of *The Eye of Spirit*, second revised edition, CW7.)

One final comment about the UMS (unitive mystical state) and nature mysticism. These two items are often confused, but they are actually quite distinct. Here, from *Integral Psychology*, is an endnote dealing with this topic (note 14 for chap. 7), using James Mark Baldwin's notion of 'unity consciousness' as a beginning point:

> Baldwin's 'unity consciousness' is a gross-realm unity or nature mysticism (psychic level). It does not recognize archetypal mysticism, subtle consciousness, lucid dreaming, or savikalpa samadhi (all forms of deity or subtle-level mysticism); nor does it recognize formless consciousness (causal), and therefore it does not reach the pure nondual (which is a union of form and emptiness). Union with nature, when it does not recognize the formless state of cessation, is always psychic-level, gross cosmic consciousness, or nature mysticism (not nondual or integral mysticism). Nonetheless, it is a genuine and profound transpersonal experience.
>
> One of the easiest ways to tell if a 'unity experience' is gross realm (nature mysticism), subtle realm (deity mysticism), causal realm (formless mysticism), or genuine nondual consciousness (union of the form in all realms with the pure formless) is to note the nature of consciousness in dreaming and deep sleep. If the writer talks of a unity experience while awake, that is usually gross-realm nature mysticism. If that unity consciousness *continues into the dream state* — so that the writer talks of lucid dreaming, union with interior luminosities as well as gross exterior nature — that is usually subtle-realm deity mysticism. If that consciousness *continues into the deep sleep state* — so that the writer realizes a Self that is *fully present in all three states* of waking, dreaming, and deep sleep — that is usually causal-realm formless mysticism (turiya). If that formless Self is then discovered to be one with the form in all realms — gross to subtle to causal — that is pure nondual consciousness (turiyatita).
>
> Many nature mystics, ecopsychologists, and neopagans take the gross-realm, waking-state unity with nature to be the highest unity available, but that is basically the first of four major samadhis or mystical unions. The 'deep self' of ecopsychology is thus not to be confused with the True Self of Zen, Ati of Dzogchen, Brahman-Atman of Vedanta, etc. These distinctions also help us situate philosophers like Heidegger and Foucault, both of whom talked of mystical-like unions with nature. Those were often profound and authentic experiences of gross-realm unity (Nirmanakaya), but again, those should not be confused with Zen or Vedanta, for the latter push through to causal formlessness (Dharmakaya, nirvikalpa samadhi, jnana samadhi, etc.), and then into pure nondual unity (Svabhavikakaya, turiyatita) with any and all realms, gross to subtle to causal. Many writers confuse

Nirmanakaya with Svabhavikakaya, which ignores the major realms of interior development that lie between the two (e.g., Sambhogakaya and Dharmakaya). (Wilber, 2000b, p. 235.)

Appendix B: The Hard Problem

The 'all-quadrant, all-level' model presented in this article, because it includes the transpersonal and nondual waves also has — or claims to have — an answer to the 'hard problem' of consciousness (the problem of how we can get subjective experience out of an allegedly objective, material, nonexperiential world).

The wisdom traditions generally make a distinction between relative truth and absolute truth (the former referring to relative truths in the conventional, dualistic world, and the latter referring to the realization of the absolute or nondual world, a realization known as satori, moksha, metanoia, liberation, etc.). An integral model would include both and suggest that, from the relative perspective, all existing entities have four quadrants, including an interior and an exterior, and thus 'subjective experience' and 'objective matter/energy' arise correlatively from the very start.[23] From the absolute perspective, an integral model suggests that the final answer to this problem is actually discovered only with satori, or the personal awakening to the nondual itself. The reason that the hard problem remains hard is the same reason that absolute truth cannot be stated in relative words: the nondual can only be known by a change of consciousness, not a change of words or maps or theories.

The hard problem ultimately revolves around the actual relation of subject and object, and that relation is said to yield its final truth only with satori (as maintained by most philosophers of the great nondual traditions, from Plotinus to Lady Tsogyal to Meister Eckhart [Wilber, 1996c, 1997a]). We could say that what is 'seen' in satori is that subject and object are nondual, but those are only words, and when stated thus, the absolute or nondual generates only paradoxes, antinomies, contradictions. According to this view, the nondual 'answer' to the hard problem can only be seen from the nondual state or level of consciousness itself, which generally takes years of contemplative discipline, and therefore is not an 'answer' that can be found in a textbook or journal — and thus it will remain the hard problem for those who do not transform their own consciousness.

On the relative plane, the relative solution to the relation of subject and object is best captured, I believe, by a specific type of panpsychism, which can be found in various forms in Leibniz, Whitehead, Russell, Charles Hartshorne, David Ray Griffin, David Chalmers, etc., although I believe it must be modified from a monological to a quadratic formulation, as suggested in *Integral Psychology* (especially note 15 for chap. 14).

David Chalmers (1997), in a particularly illuminating discussion, reaches several important conclusions:

(1) 'One is forced to the conclusion that no reductive explanation of consciousness can be given' (p. 44). That is, consciousness (or experience or proto-

---

[23] By 'existing entity' I mean 'holon', as described later in the text. See Wilber (1995; 2000b).

experience — or as I technically prefer it, interiority) is an intrinsic, given component of the Kosmos, and it cannot be completely derived from, or reduced to, something else. In my view, this is because every holon has an interior and exterior (in both singular and plural). Thus, only an integral model that includes consciousness as fundamental will likely succeed.

(2) 'Perhaps the best path to such an integrated view is offered by the Russellian picture on which (proto)experiential properties constitute the intrinsic nature of physical reality. Such a picture is most naturally associated with some form of panpsychism. The resulting integration may be panpsychism's greatest theoretical benefit' (p. 42). As I would put it, the general idea is simply is that physics (and natural science) discloses only the objective, exterior, or extrinsic features of holons, whose interior or intrinsic features are subjective and experiential (or proto-experiential). In other words, all holons have a Left- and Right-Hand dimension.

(3) Once that interior/exterior problem is handled (with a modified panpsychism, which suggests that all holons have an interior and exterior), we face a second problem. 'The second is the problem of how fundamental experiential or proto-experiential properties at the microscopic level somehow together *constitute* the sort of complex, unified experience that we possess. (This is a version of what Seager calls the "combination problem".) Such constitution is almost certainly required if our own experiences are not to be epiphenomenal, but it is not at all obvious how it should work: would not these tiny experiences instead add up to a jagged mess? . . . *If* [the combination problem] can be avoided, then I think [this modified panpsychism] is clearly the single most attractive way to make sense of the place of experience in the natural order' (p. 29). Chalmers echoes Thomas Nagel in saying that the combination problem is central to the hard problem. As Chalmers says, 'This leaves the combination problem, which is surely the hardest' (p. 43).

But, as I try to show in *Integral Psychology* (especially note 15 for chap. 14), the combination problem is actually something that has been successfully handled for quite some time by developmental psychology (and Whiteheadian process philosophy). In essence, with each wave of development, the subject of one stage becomes an object of the next (as Robert Kegan would put it), so that each stage is a prehensive unification of all of its predecessors. In Whitehead's famous dictum, 'The many become one and are increased by one'. This process, when viewed from the interior, gives us, in healthy development, a cohesive and unified self-sense (reaching from sensation to perception to impulse to image to symbol... and so on up the waves of the Great Nest, where each wave *transcends and includes* — or moves beyond but embraces — its predecessors, thus gathering together into one the many subunits that precede it; thus each healthy wave successfully solves the combination problem). This same process, when viewed from the exterior, appears as, for example: many atoms become one molecule, many molecules become one cell, many cells become one organism, and so on.

On both the interior and the exterior, the result is not a 'jagged mess' because each unit in those series is actually a *holon* — a whole that is a part of other wholes. As I try to show in SES and BH, both the interiors and the exteriors of the Kosmos are composed of holons (that is, all holons have an interior and exterior, in singular and plural); and thus the 'combination problem' is actually an inherent feature of holons in all domains. All four quadrants are composed of whole/parts or holons, all the way up, all the way down, and because each holon is already a whole/part, each holon is an existing solution to the combination problem. Far from being rare or anomalous, holons are the fundamental ingredients of reality in all domains, and thus the combination problem is not so much a problem as it is an essential feature of the universe.

Assuming that the combination problem can be thus solved, the way is open for a holonic model of the Kosmos ('all-quadrants, all-levels'), a subset of which is an integral theory of consciousness. Of course, what I have presented here and in other writings is only the briefest skeleton of such a model, but I believe that these preliminary speculations are encouraging enough to pursue the project more rigorously.

Finally, let me return to the original point. The hard problem can perhaps best be solved on the relative plane with a holonic or integral model. But that is still just a conceptual tool on the relative plane. You can completely learn or memorize the holonic model, and yet you still experience your consciousness as residing 'in here', on this side of your face, and the world as existing 'out there', dualistically. That dualism is ultimately overcome, not with any model, no matter how 'nondualistic' it calls itself, but only with satori, which is a direct and radical realization (or change in level of consciousness), and that transformation cannot be delivered by any model, but only by prolonged spiritual practice. As the traditions say, you must have the actual experience to see exactly what is revealed, just as you must actually see a sunset to know what is involved (cf. *Eye to Eye*, Wilber, 1996c). But the mystics are rather unanimous: the hard problem is finally (dis)solved only with enlightenment, or the permanent realization of the nondual wave. For a discussion of this theme, see *The Eye of Spirit*, second revised edition (found in CW7), especially chaps. 3 and 11 (particularly note 13), and the revised 'An Integral Theory of Consciousness', also found in CW7.

References

Adi Da (Da Free John) (1977), *The Paradox of Instruction* (Clearlake, CA: Dawn Horse Press).

Adi Da (Da Free John) (1979), *The Enlightenment of the Whole Body* (Clearlake, CA: Dawn Horse Press).

Alexander, C. and Langer, E., eds. (1990), *Higher Stages of Human Development: Perspectives on Adult Growth* (New York: Oxford University Press).

Arieti, S.(1967), *The Intrapsychic Self* (New York: Basic Books).

Aurobindo, Sri (1990 [1939]), *The Life Divine* (Wilmot, WI: Lotus Light Publications).

Baldwin, J.M. (1973), *Dictionary of Philosophy and Psychology: Bibliography of Philosophy, Psychology, and Cognate Subjects* (Peter Smith Publishers).

Baldwin, J.M. (1975), *Genetic Theory of Reality* (Philosophy in America Series) (AMS Press).

Baldwin, J.M. (1990a), *Fragments in Philosophy and Science : Being Collected Essays and Addresses* (AMS Press).

Baldwin, J.M. (1990b), *Development and Evolution: Including Psychophysical Evolution, Evolution by Orthoplasy and Theory of Genetic* (AMS Press).

Beck, D. and Cowan, C. (1996) *Spiral Dynamics : Managing Values, Leadership, and Change* (London: Blackwell).

Berry, J., Poortinga, Y., Segall, M. and Dasen, P. (1992), *Cross-cultural Psychology: Research and Applications* (Cambridge: Cambridge University Press).

Blanck, G. and R. Blanck (1974), *Ego Psychology: Theory and Practice* (New York: Columbia University Press).

Blanck, G. and R. Blanck (1979), *Ego Psychology II: Developmental Psychology* (New York: Columbia University Press).

Blanck, G. and R. Blanck (1986), *Beyond Ego Psychology* (New York: Columbia University Press).

Brown, D. and Engler, J. (1986) 'The stages of mindfulness meditation: A validation study. Part I and II', In *Transformations of Consciousness*, Wilber, K., Engler, J., Brown, D. (Boston and London: Shambhala).

Capra, F. (1997), *The Web of Life : A New Understanding of Living Systems* (New York: Doubleday).

Chalmers, D. (1996), *The Conscious Mind: In Search of a Fundamental Theory* (New York: Oxford University Press).

Chalmers, D. (1997), 'Moving forward on the problem of consciousness', *Journal of Consciousness Studies*, **4** (1), pp. 3–46.

Combs, A. (1995), *The Radiance of Being: Complexity, Chaos, and the Evolution of Consciousness* (St. Paul, MN: Paragon House).

Cook-Greuter, S. (1990) 'Maps for living', *Adult Development* 2.

Cook-Greuter, S. and Miller, M. (ed. 1994), *Transcendence and mature Thought in Adulthood* (Rowman & Littlefield).

Crittenden, J. (2001, forthcoming), *Kindred Visions* (Boston and London, Shambhala).

Diamond, I. and Orenstein, G. (1990), *Reweaving the World: The Emergence of Ecofeminism* (San Francisco: Sierra Club Books).

Deutsche, E. (1969) *Advaita Vedanta* (Honolulu: East-West Center).

Fisher, R. (1971), 'A cartography of the ecstatic and meditative states: The experimental and experiential features of a perception-hallucination continuum', *Science* **174**, pp. 897–904.

Forman, R. (ed. 1990), *The Problem of Pure Consciousness* (New York: Oxford University Press).

Forman, R. (1998a), *Mysticism, Mind, Consciousness* (Albany, NY: SUNY Press).

Forman, R. (1998b), 'What does mysticism have to teach us about consciousness?', *Journal of Consciousness Studies*, **5** (2), pp. 185–201.

Fowler, J. (1981), *Stages of Faith: The Psychology of Human Development and the Quest for Meaning* (San Francisco, CA: Harper).

Fox, W. (1990), *Toward a Transpersonal Ecology* (Boston and London: Shambhala).

Gardiner, H., Mutter, J., and Kosmitzki, C. (1998), *Lives Across Cultures: Cross-Cultural Human Development* (Boston, MA: Allyn and Bacon).

Gardner, H. (1972), *The Quest for Mind* (New York: Vintage).

Gardner, H. (1983), *Frames of Mind* (New York: Basic Books).

Gebser, J. (1985 [1949]), *The Ever-Present Origin* (Athens, OH: Ohio University Press).

Gilligan, C. (1982), *In a Different Voice* (Cambridge, MA: Harvard university Press).

Gilligan, C., Murphy, J. and Tappan, M. (1990), 'Moral development beyond adolescence', in Alexander and Langer (1990).

Goleman, D. (1988), *The Meditative Mind: Varieties Of Meditative Experience* (Los Angeles, CA: Tarcher).

Graves, C. (1970), 'Levels of existence: An open system theory of values', *Journal of Transpersonal Psychology*, **10**, pp. 131–55.

Grof, S. (1985), *Beyond the Brain: Birth, Death and Transcendence in Psychotherapy* (Albany: SUNY Press).

Grof, S. (1998), *The Cosmic Game: Explorations of the Frontiers of Human Consciousness* (Albany: SUNY Press).

Gyatso, K. (1986), *Progressive Stages of Meditation on Emptiness* (Oxford: Longchen Foundation).

Kegan, R. (1983), *The Evolving Self: Problem and Process in Human Development* (Cambridge, MA: Harvard University Press).

Kegan, R. (1994), *In Over Our Heads: The Mental Demands of Modern Life* (Cambridge, MA: Harvard University Press).

Kohlberg, L. (1981) *Essays on Moral Development*, Vol. 1 (San Francisco, CA: Harper).

Kohut, H. (1971), *The Analysis of the Self* (New York: IUP).

Kohut, H. (1977), *The Restoration of the Self* (New York: IUP).

LaBerge, E. (1985), *Lucid Dreaming* (Los Angeles, CA: Tarcher).

Lenski, G. (1995), *Human Societies* (New York: McGraw-Hill).

Loevinger, J. (1976), *Ego Development* (San Francisco, CA: Jossey-Bass).

Lovejoy, A. (1964 [1936]), *The Great Chain of Being* (Cambridge, MA: Harvard University Press).

Murphy, M. (1992), *The Future of the Body* (Los Angeles, CA: Tarcher).

Murphy, M. and Leonard, G. (1995), *The Life We Are Given* (New York: Tarcher/Putnam).

Parsons, T. (1951), *The Social System* (Englewood Cliffs, N.J.: Prentice-Hall).

Parsons, T. (1966), *Societies* (New York: Free Press).

Piaget, J. (1977), *The Essential Piaget*, ed. J. Buchler (New York: Dover).

Rowan, J. (1990), *Subpersonalities* (London: Routledge).

Rowan, J. (1993), *The Transpersonal* (London: Routledge).

Shaffer, D. (1994), *Social and Personality Development* (Pacific Grove, CA: Brooks/Cole).

Selman, R. and Byrne, D. (1974), 'A structural analysis of levels of role-taking in middle childhood', *Child Development*, **45**.

Shankara (1970 [1947]), *Crest-Jewel of Discrimination*, tr. C.Isherwood and Prabhavananda (New York: New American Library).

Smart, N. (1984 [1969]), *The Religious Experience of Mankind* (New York: Scribner's).

Smith, H. (1976 [1993]), *Forgotten Truth: The Common Vision of the World Religions* (San Francisco, CA: Harper).

Sroufe, L., Cooper, R. and DeHart, G. (1992), *Child Development* (New York: McGraw-Hill).

Tart, C. (ed. 1972), *Altered States of Consciousness* (New York: John Wiley 1969; New York: Doubleday, 1972).

Vaillant, G. (1993), *The Wisdom of the Ego* (Cambridge: Harvard University Press).

Wade, J. (1996), *Changes of Mind: A Holonomic Theory of the Evolution of Consciousness* (New York: SUNY Press).

Walsh, R. (1999), *Essential Spirituality: Exercises from the World's Religions to Cultivate Kindness, Love, Joy, Peace, Vision, Wisdom, and Generosity* (New York: John Wiley & Sons).

Walsh, R. and Vaughan, F. (ed. 1993), *Paths Beyond Ego* (Los Angeles, CA: Tarcher).

White, J. (ed. 1972), *The Highest State of Consciousness* (New York: Anchor Books).

Wilber, K. (1983), *Sociable God* (New York: New Press/McGraw-Hill).

Wilber, K. (1993, [1977]), *The Spectrum of Consciousness* (Wheaton, IL: Quest).

Wilber, K. (1995), *Sex, Ecology, Spirituality: The Spirit of Evolution* (Boston and London: Shambhala).

Wilber, K. (1996a [1980]), *The Atman Project*, second edition (Wheaton, IL: Quest).

Wilber, K. (1996b [1981]), *Up From Eden*, second edition (Wheaton, IL: Quest).

Wilber, K. (1996c [1983]), *Eye to Eye*, third edition (Boston and London: Shambhala).

Wilber, K. (1996d), *A Brief History of Everything* (Boston and London: Shambhala).

Wilber, K. (1997a), *The Eye of Spirit: An Integral Vision for a World Gone Slightly Mad* (Boston and London: Shambhala).

Wilber, K. (1997b), 'An Integral Theory of Consciousness', *Journal of Consciousness Studies*, **4**, 1, pp. 71–92

Wilber, K. (1998), *The Marriage of Sense and Soul: Integrating Science and Religion* (New York: Random House).

Wilber, K. (1999a), *One Taste: The Journals of Ken Wilber* (Boston and London: Shambhala).

Wilber, K. (1999b), *The Collected Works of Ken Wilber, Volumes 1-4* (Boston and London: Shambhala).

Wilber, K. (2000a), *The Collected Works of Ken Wilber, Volumes 5-8* (Boston and London: Shambhala).

Wilber, K. (2000b), *Integral Psychology: Consciousness, Spirit, Psychology, Therapy* (Boston and London: Shambhala).

Wilber, K. (2000c), *A Theory of Everything: An Integral Vision for Business, Politics, Science and Spirituality* (Boston and London: Shambhala).

Wilber, K. (2001, forthcoming), *Boomeritis* (Boston and London: Shambhala).

Wilber, K., Engler, J. and Brown, D. (1986), *Transformations of Consciousness* (Boston and London: Shambhala).

Wolman, B. and Ullman, M. (ed. 1986), *Handbook of States of Consciousness* (New York: Van Nostrand Reinhold).

Zimmerman (ed. 1998 [1993]) *Environmental Philosophy*, second edition (Upper Saddle River, NJ: Prentice Hall).

Christian de Quincey

The Promise of Integralism

A Critical Appreciation of Ken Wilber's Integral Psychology[1]

I therefore sought to outline a philosophy of universal integralism. Put differently, I sought a world philosophy — or an *integral* philosophy — that would believably weave together the many pluralistic contexts of science, morals, aesthetics, Eastern as well as Western philosophy, and the world's great wisdom traditions. Not on the level of details — that is finitely impossible; but on the level of *orienting generalizations* . . . a holistic philosophy for a holistic Kosmos, a genuine Theory of Everything.

— Ken Wilber (TOE, p. 38).

Introduction

Why do so many people think Ken Wilber is one of the most important thinkers of our time? Why are so many disturbed by what he writes? In this review of his work, I hope to throw some light on both questions.

First, Wilber's contribution: In a remarkable outpouring of books and articles — his *Collected Works* (Wilber, 1999–2000) already fill eight thick volumes (and he's only 51 years old) — he makes one of the strongest rational cases for opening up the modern worldview to include not only consciousness, but Spirit, too. With a characteristic combination of verve, wit, intelligence, humour, and provocation he takes his readers beyond the narrow confines of mere materialism and objectivity without sacrificing the many undoubted benefits of the rationalist-empiricist tradition, *and* without falling prey to the world-denying tendencies of various forms of idealism.

In short, he provides a postmodern worldview that includes the best of empirical science and rational philosophy, and the best of visionary religion and

---

[1] This critique is presented in the context of Ken Wilber's recently published eight-volume *Collected Works*. However, given its scope, I will focus primarily on his latest books, *Integral Psychology* (2000a) and *A Theory of Everything* (2000b). I will particularly deal with the ideas in *Integral Psychology*, since Wilber's work places development of the psyche/self at the core of his analyses of other disciplines (e.g., politics, art, economics, ecology, spirituality and gender issues). And because of the focus of this journal, within the topics covered in *Integral Psychology*, I will give special attention to Wilber's contribution to consciousness studies and philosophy of mind.

Journal of Consciousness Studies, **7**, No. 11–12, 2000, pp. 177–208

mysticism. More than that: Perhaps other than Kant and Hegel, no-one has presented a comparable comprehensive framework for integrating the 'three cultures' of science, morality and art. He achieves this by the apparently simple device of focusing on what is possibly the greatest central 'orienting generalization' of modernity — the notion of *evolution* — and extending it to a conclusion consistent with its own empirical findings and logic: Beyond the current highest stage of evolution, represented by the human brain and consciousness, lie further stages of biological, psychological, cultural, and social development.

And if human consciousness is the current apex of terrestrial evolution (situated within an incomparably vaster cosmic — or 'Kosmic' — evolution), then we have every reason to believe further stages of evolution await either our own species or whatever will succeed us. Those 'higher' stages, Wilber argues, drawing on the perennial philosophy of the world's great wisdom traditions, move through higher psychic, and even more subtle, levels (correlated with developments in brain tissue and sociocultural dynamics), culminating in the realization of Spirit (1981).

Wilber is not centrally concerned with the next stage (or species) in human evolution at some *future* date. He is most interested in the fact that the world's great wisdom traditions — across all cultures, for millennia — have reported that higher stages of consciousness development were attained by numerous men and women in the past. Those higher states and stages of consciousness, therefore, are not awaiting us in some far-off time to come — they are potentially available to us right now, today.

Nevertheless, according to Wilber and many scholars he cites, there is a trajectory of consciousness evolution for our species as a whole. For example, even though at the time of the Buddha some individuals attained very advanced states of consciousness, their society *on average* was at a lower (probably pre-rational) developmental stage. Thus, today, our species has evolved to a higher average level of consciousness (the rational stage — Piaget's concrete operational, or formal operational). Furthermore, it seems a significant number of people have already developed to the next stage, vision-logic; and a smaller number to even higher stages.

So, although a particular individual could, at any epoch, develop to a higher stage of consciousness, the average level of consciousness for societies and the species as a whole also evolves through identifiable stages (see for example Gebser, 1985; Aurobindo, 1939). Thus, today, at the species level of 'formop', on the threshold of vision-logic, some individuals can be at less-developed stages (e.g., pre-egoic mythic or magic), while others can be at more advanced stages (e.g., transegoic subtle, causal, and even the highest stage of all: nondual).

Wilber's great contribution to modern intellectual debate is to have made a provocative case for not only extending modern science — a model of evolution reaching beyond rational creatures all the way to Spirit — but for *integrating* it with premodern spiritual wisdom to produce a truly postmodern, all-encompassing spectrum of consciousness.

In a word, his central achievement is to have brought together humanity's two great orienting generalizations of 'Evolution' and 'Spirit' — one a relatively recent discovery of science, the other an ancient, and perennial, discovery of religion and mysticism. This is a remarkable accomplishment not only because of the scope of the disciplines Wilber attempts to integrate but also because of the level of detail from each discipline he brings to the discussion.

For readers unfamiliar with his work, the following will give some idea of the wide reach of his intellectual net:

> Wilber's approach is the opposite of eclecticism. He has provided a coherent and consistent vision that seamlessly weaves together truth-claims from such fields as physics and biology; the ecosciences; chaos theory and the systems sciences; medicine, neurophysiology, biochemistry; art, poetry, and aesthetics in general; developmental psychology and a spectrum of psychotherapeutic endeavors, from Freud to Jung to Piaget; the Great Chain theorists from Plato to Plotinus in the West to Shankara and Nagarjuna in the East; the modernists from Descartes and Locke to Kant; the Idealists from Schelling to Hegel; the postmodernists from Foucault and Derrida to Taylor and Habermas; the major hermeneutic tradition, Dilthey to Heidegger to Gadamer; the social systems theorists from Comte to Marx to Parsons and Luhmann; the contemplative and mystical schools of the great meditative traditions, East and West, in the world's major religious traditions. All of this is just a sampling. (Jack Crittenden's forward to Wilber's *Eye of Spirit*, 1997, pp. viii-ix, and *Collected Works* vol. 7, p. 406.)

Such a panoramic and synoptic intellectual viewfinder is so inclusive that Wilber himself has referred to his overall model as *A Theory of Everything* (TOE) (2000b). In this paper I will examine some of the key elements of Wilber's 'integration' — his vast and majestic intellectual edifice — to see if they hold together as he proposes. Has Wilber produced a true Taj Mahal of the intellect or is his structure more like a clever and creative house of cards, standing impressively as each part rests on its neighbours, but vulnerable to collapse when some particular component is picked up for close scrutiny?

Is Wilber, as some commentators suggest, the latest in a long line of great speculative philosophers, following in the footsteps of thinkers such as Plato, Plotinus, Hegel, and Whitehead in the West, and Shankara, Nagarjuna,[2] and Aurobindo in the East?[3] Or is he, rather, the latest 'new, new thing' in contemporary avant-garde intellectual circles, who may shine brilliantly for his followers today, but quickly fade into the pages of history once the next 'new, new thing' comes along? The truth, I suspect, lies somewhere in between. At the very least, Wilber has earned a place of prominence in the field of transpersonal theory — undoubtedly the most influential theoretician in transpersonal psychology today.

---

[2] Strictly speaking, Nagarjuna should not be included in a list of 'speculative' thinkers — his philosophy was aimed at transcending all speculative, conceptual, linguistic, cognitive, and even experiential distinctions. Nevertheless, since Wilber echoes Nagarjuna's nondual stance, he does to some extent stand in that lineage. (I thank Kaisa Puhakka for drawing my attention to the non-speculative nature of Nagarjuna's philosophy.)

[3] See, for example, Michael Murphy's appreciation of Wilber in Rothberg & Kelly (1998).

The Four Phases of Wilber

Like so many others in the field of consciousness studies and transpersonal theory, I was impressed by Ken Wilber's earlier works, such as *The Spectrum of Consciousness* (SoC) (1977), *The Atman Project* (AP) (1980), *Up From Eden* (UE) (1981) and a wonderful anthology, *Quantum Questions* (QQ) (1984), where he drew from the founding greats of quantum theory to show that subatomic physics could no more enlighten us about consciousness and mysticism than the physics of Newton. But it was the publication of *Sex, Ecology, Spirituality* (SES) (1995) that, in my opinion, distinguished Wilber as an intellectual force, and, by his own reckoning, launched him into a new phase in his career as a philosopher/ psychology theorist. In SES, for the first time, Wilber went beyond the levels or 'spectrum' of consciousness that characterized his speculative model up to that point, and introduced his new mandala of the Four Quadrants (see below).

With the appearance of SES, after an interregnum of about five years following the death of his wife, no-one could be in any doubt about Wilber having regained his prodigious productivity. SES was a blockbuster of 800-plus pages (200-plus of which were endnotes). In short succession, he pumped out a series of other books, including *A Brief History of Everything* (BH) (1996) a 'not-too-brief' popularized version of SES aimed at a wider audience, and Wilber's first to crack the *New York Times* bestseller lists; *The Eye of Spirit* (EoS) (1997); *The Marriage of Sense and Soul* (MSS) (1998); and *One Taste* (OT) (1999), a year-long journal of personal experiences and critical observations. And now in 2000, he has published two more: *Integral Psychology* (IP) and *A Theory of Everything* (TOE) (with references to a companion volume he's calling by the unfortunate title *Boomeritis*).

Throughout this prolific career, Wilber has maintained a thematic constancy: the evolution of Spirit and the development of consciousness. Nevertheless, his work has been punctuated by watersheds that mark different phases in his own development: beginning as a self-styled 'Romantic' (typified by SoC), by which he means a belief in the efficacy of regressing to a 'golden age' of consciousness as a way to spiritual development (Phase-1); next, a sharp about-face with an epiphany he expressed as the 'pre/trans fallacy' (AP and UE) that pointedly contradicted the Romantic ideal of 'return', and emphasized the Great Chain of Being as an evolutionary/developmental model (Phase-2); then, a detailed refinement and expansion of the 'spectrum' to include relatively independent psychological developmental lines progressing through the levels of the Great Chain (*Transformations of Consciousness*, revisited and deepened in EoS) (Phase-3); and now, all those levels and lines (streams, waves and spirals) are differentiated and organized within the mandala of the four quadrants (SES, EoS, MSS, IP, and TOE). Phases 1 to 3 could be summarized in the slogan 'all levels'; Phase 4 as 'all-levels, all quadrants'.

Readers of his newer books will find a few new twists — spirals and waves — that soften the charge of linearity often levelled at him. With each new refinement (Wilber has a way of assimilating and accommodating the barbs of his critics), his model grows increasingly complex, mind-numbingly so, as we will see. In fact, the complexity of his latest model incorporating waves and streams and spirals and lines, weaving up and down the 'spectrum' and in and out of the 'quadrants', reminds me a little of the heroic efforts made with Ptolemaic epicycles to save the problematic cosmology of Aristotle. However, unlike with Ptolemy, it just may be the case that Wilber's 'integral epicycles' reflect an accurate accounting of the actual complexity of human psycho-spiritual development. If that is so, then Wilber's increasingly complex models may be, as he himself believes, a significant contribution toward the launch of the Human Consciousness Project (psychology's equivalent of the Human Genome Project in biology).

Science, at the very least, needs to acknowledge the reality of the interior depth of the world — of subjectivity, the domain of experience. As Wilber says, it is beyond ludicrous to believe that only exteriors exist. Such a view is utterly nonsensical. Exteriors can exist only in the presence of interiors. To claim otherwise would be like saying the world consists only of 'ups', and that 'downs' are just figments, or, to use a favourite phrase of eliminative materialists, just 'folk fictions.' Exteriors (objective realities) without interiors (subjective realities) are meaningless. The 'fiction' is to believe that one could exist without the other.

And so we have Wilber's other major orienting generalization: The world, including human beings, consists of exteriors and interiors, the two great domains of his Four Quadrants (see Figure 1).

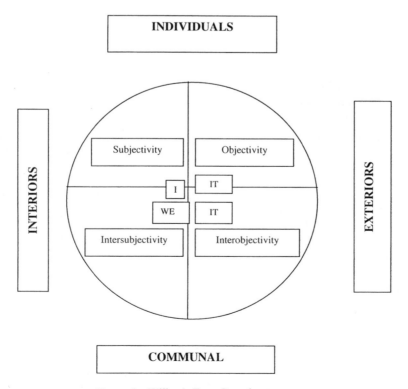

Figure 1 Wilber's Four Quandrants

Why, then, *four* quadrants, not just two domains? You will see from the figure that exteriors and interiors alike come in two forms: individual and communal. So, in the Upper Left (UL) quadrant, we see individual-interiors (the domain of individual subjects). In the Lower Left (LL), we find communal-interiors (the domain of mutual intersubjectivities). In the Upper Right (UR), we see individual-exteriors (the domain of atomistic objects). In the Lower Right (LR) quadrant, we find systems-exteriors (the domain of networks of objects). This is Wilber's map of reality, his ontological mandala.

But that is only part of the map. Remember his other great orienting generalizations: Evolution and Spirit. Each quadrant is co-evolving, from the lowest, simplest forms to the highest, or *deepest*, most complex realities. That means, simply, that individual-interiors (subjects) evolve, communal-interiors (cultures) evolve, individual-exteriors (individual physical objects) evolve, and network-exteriors (objective, physical systems) evolve. Further, nothing evolves in any single quadrant without a concomitant evolution in all the other quadrants.

Which brings us to the central orienting generalization of Wilber's entire cosmology: *Everything that exists consists of holons*. (Wilber got the term 'holon' from Arthur Koestler, 1969.) Very simply, everything is simultaneously a part of something larger than itself (a higher whole), and a whole in its own right made up of its own smaller parts. As well as consisting of a part-whole relation within its own quadrant, every holon, says Wilber, *necessarily* partakes of all four quadrants. Nothing exists merely as an exterior (or interior) reality, and nothing is ever simply an individual (or a system). All systems consist of individual parts, and all individuals are embedded in systems. And, of course, all exteriors have interiors, and vice versa.

To understand how the world is put together and how it works, Wilber says, we need to pursue an 'all quadrant, all-level' approach — meaning we need to take into account not only interiors and exteriors, individuals and systems, but also the fact that each holon evolves within all four quadrants through the various levels identified in the Great Chain of Being, on the one hand, and in evolutionary sciences on the other. This, in a nutshell, is what Wilber unfolds in his *Collected Works*.[4]

Style and Substance

His impressive contribution to transpersonal theory and the integration of East and West psychologies and philosophies is, however, shadowed by questions and concerns about his style, and problems with the substance of some of his ideas. The French have a saying, 'le style c'ést l'homme même' ('the style is the man') — and it seems particularly appropriate when discussing Wilber's work. I'm very sensitive to taking this tack because I want to avoid the *ad hominem* style that

---

[4] In a review of this length it is not easy to do justice to Wilber's *Collected Works*. Thankfully, his thematic constancy throughout gives his overall output a kind of holographic character: Pick up almost any single volume and you can get information about the whole. In this paper, I have focused mostly on *Integral Psychology*. A much longer 'critical appreciation' of Wilber will be available as an online ebook, *Edifice Complex: Taj Mahal or House of Cards?* (from www.iKosmos.com).

others have so often complained of in Wilber. Yet his *style* has generated as much debate as the substance of his ideas, and any comprehensive critique, I feel, must address this, more so in a review that focuses on his first book to deal specifically with psychology (IP). The psychological dimensions of Wilber's work cannot be ignored — particularly because Wilber himself applies his stage-model of psychological development to those he critiques (e.g., Whitehead), and implicitly to himself (he claims that one cannot talk meaningfully or with veracity of higher states or stages of consciousness unless one has achieved constancy at those levels).[5]

Wilber has been criticized, sometimes severely, for his argumentative, polemical, abrasive manner, often triggering a like-minded reaction from his critics (and those he critiques), resulting in what might be called the 'Great Chain of Being Nasty'. Wilber seems to evoke extremes: For the most part, people seem to either love him or hate him (I count myself among the exceptions).

But why the 'contemptuous rhetoric', as philosopher Michael Zimmerman called it? Why this 'most disturbing aspect' of Wilber? Why does he seem driven to master the domain of reason, to construct an impenetrable intellectual edifice — an 'edifice complex'? At first, the emotional edge to the style may seem at odds with the drive toward precision and reason; but, on deeper reflection, I think they may be intimately related. I sometimes get the impression that this immense rational fortress has been erected to withstand any possible intrusion of ambiguity, paradox, or mystery, and is designed to shut out the messiness of intense feeling.[6] Everything, it seems, *must* fit. Hence Wilber's lifelong effort to develop a catch-all TOE, his four-quadrant model, into which *everything* must fit. Nothing that is real can fall outside the four quadrants (and even what is imaginary or phantasmagoric must find its place there, too).

Wilber is, at times, vehemently anti-feeling,[7] and in the grand hierarchy of his system feeling and emotion are clearly not only 'sub-rational', but also epistemologically inferior. His insistent critique of psychological regression (returning to earlier biographical experiences), and regression in general (for example, Romanticism, or what he humorously and derisively calls the 'Regress Express') reveals a fiery determination to invalidate any possible psychotherapeutic intervention that might require one to open up to experiential residues or

---

[5] Some critics in the field of transpersonal psychology have questioned whether Wilber's vitriol and anger, and lack of compassion, are compatible with the kind and level of consciousness required to speak and write from experience about higher, spiritual, states or stages of consciousness (personal communications).

[6] In Wilber's all-encompassing system there is, of course, a place for paradox: at the level of cognition he calls 'vision-logic'. But the point is that by slotting paradox (or mystery) into its proper rational place in the model, the system itself consumes and eliminates paradox. Neat rational categories cannot retain the felt ambiguity and mystery of paradox.

[7] His works are littered with cutting and often disparaging references to 'narcissistic' feelings, to Romantics who long to ride the 'Regress Express' to primitive emotional states, and to Eco-minded 'mushiness' — as though 'standing in nature and egocentrically emoting' (SES, p. 447) is all that feeling-based consciousness could achieve. His critique of feeling seems to completely miss the intrinsically relational and intersubjective quality of feeling-based consciousness (see de Quincey, 2000a). For Wilber, only when we have transcended feeling and developed to the higher consciousness of reason can we adopt the 'perspectival' stance that allows for taking the role of the other, beyond self-centered narcissism.

echoes from some long-buried childhood trauma (perhaps even a prenatal or perinatal incident?).[8]

In *Eye of Spirit*, Wilber gives a wonderfully insightful critique of the various forms of reductionism that attempt to deny the validity claims of any quadrant other than its own. He says, 'ignored truths actually reappear in the system as an internal and massive self-contradiction . . . [the] denied quadrant will in fact sneak into your system' (p. 23). Is the vehemence in Wilber's writing, I wonder, an example of the 'reappearance' of ignored feeling, 'sneaking' back into his system?

In any case, Wilber is very clearly against the ontological significance of feeling. It is certainly true that in *Integral Psychology*, as we will see, he 'categorically rejects' the notion that feeling could play a fundamental ontological role. For Wilber, feelings are a lure for 'regressive' Romantics who hark back to some mythical golden age, or for narcissistic individuals (typified by the Boomer generation) who prefer the easy, ego-inflation and self-absorption of self-indulgent feelings to the hard road of mature rationality and 'transrational' spiritual practice.

In place of the messiness of feeling, Wilber offers us his neat, massive intellectual construction. But what if something doesn't fit? What if the model, the towering edifice, should turn out to be a house of cards and not a Taj Mahal? What if the pre/trans fallacy is itself a fallacy (as Michael Washburn proposes [Rothberg & Kelly, 1998])? What if the criterion of falsifiability fails to function as an adequate demarcation between science and non-science, and therefore the attempt to 'marry' science and religion fails? (Ferrer, 1998a).[9] What if one of the four quadrants

---

[8]   Wilber has been a severe critic of Stan Grof's model of perinatal matrices and the idea that reliving the existential pangs of the birth experience could be a gateway to transpersonal consciousness (Wilber, 1995; Grof, 1985).

[9]   Jorge Ferrer has offered one of the most incisive critiques of Wilber's epistemology based on the 'outmoded' notion of falsifiability. Contemporary philosophy of science, Ferrer argues, has long since demonstrated the unworkability of Popperian falsifiability as a methodology for gaining genuine knowledge. Furthermore, he argues that Wilber's broad empiricism based on the tripartite methodology of (1) injunction, procedure, or practice, (2) direct apprehension of data, and (3) communal confirmation (verification or refutation) of the data by a 'community of the adequate,' even if workable in science, cannot be effectively imported into the domains of religion and spiritual disclosure. Therefore, Wilber's attempt in *The Marriage of Sense and Soul*, in particular, and throughout his work in general, to integrate science and religion cannot succeed, says Ferrer.

Wilber has responded by claiming that Ferrer has misrepresented his (Wilber's) epistemology, claiming that Ferrer has accused him of attempting to import positivistic *sensory empiricism* into religion, ignoring the validity of epistemological pluralism. In his response, Wilber points out that he neither claimed that all empiricism is sensory, nor that he denied epistemological pluralism — in fact, that he explicitly advocates it. Wilber is right on both counts. However, this is not what Ferrer attributes to Wilber, and the essence of his critique has not been adequately addressed by Wilber.

Both Ferrer's critique and Wilber's response can be found in the same issue of *The Journal of Transpersonal Psychology* (1998). Ferrer continues the dialogue in a forthcoming book *Revisioning Transpersonal Theory* (in press), where he takes Wilber to task on a number of other important issues, such as: (1) 'neo-structualism', arguing that Wilber reifies and elevates deep structures of the psyche to unwarranted metaphysical status; (2) 'subtle objectivism', the claim that deep structures are 'pre-given' metaphysically; (3) 'essentialism', the claim that deep structures are more essential than their surface manifestations; (4) 'self-refuting fallacies', where Wilber's pronouncements about higher, postrational, levels of consciousness are undermined and refuted by Wilber's own adherence to neo-structuralism 'unless Wilber claims to be speaking from the highest spiritual structure' — which, by the way, Wilber denies he has ever claimed (TOE, p. 132); (5) '"bad" hermeneutics' — a

is empty? What if there's no explanation for how the two great domains of interior and exterior interrelate? What if subtle energies, so integral to the perennial philosophy and the Great Chain of Being, don't fit into any of the quadrants?[10] What if the Great Chain of Being itself cannot map onto the four quadrants? What then?

In the following sections I will examine what I think are problems with Wilber's model. It is important to keep in mind, however, that I am deliberately focusing here on areas I believe he would do well to pay closer attention to. As a result, it may seem that I'm being unduly negative, looking only at what I take to be some of his shortcomings, while not giving equal space to his accomplishments. Actually, I have already acknowledged his significant contributions (and have more to add); but — to repeat — I think there are problematic details in his work that, if not addressed, could sabotage his impressive achievements. So, in this spirit of collegial critique, I offer the following observations concerning: (1) his approach to intersubjectivity; (2) his approach to the mind–body problem; (3) his critique of panpsychism and Whitehead; followed by comments on the Human Consciousness Project.

Intersubjectivity

One aspect of Wilber's work, particularly in Phase-4, that I emphatically endorse is his repeated emphasis on including intersubjectivity in any comprehensive understanding of consciousness. Not only is it essential, it is *fundamental*. Wilber and I agree on this:

> Failing to see that subjective experiences *arise in the space created by intersubjective structures* is one of the main liabilities of many forms of spiritual and transpersonal psychology (IP, p. 119).

And, I would add, of contemporary philosophy of mind. However, when I examine Wilber's writings I find his discussion of intersubjectivity to be very weak. In fact, as I will explain in a moment, Wilber's 'intersubjectivity' leaves one quarter of his quadrant model empty — a precarious, unstable foundation for the great integral edifice.

In IP, he gives a very clear account of his understanding of intersubjectivity:

> You, as subject, will attempt to understand me as *a subject* — as a person, as a self, as a bearer of intentionality and meaning. *You will talk to me, and interpret what I say* [emphasis added]; and I will do the same with you. We are not subjects staring at subjects; we are subjects trying to understand subjects — we are in the intersubjective circle, the dialogical dance (p. 161).

---

critique of Wilber's interpretation of Buddhist philosopher Nagarjuna; (6) 'doctrinal ranking of traditions' — a critique of Wilber's 'neo-perennialism' that privileges nondual spirituality, and implicit marginalization of 'any mystic or tradition that does not seek attainment of nondual states' (Ferrer, in press).

[10] I explore the issue of subtle energy in the context of Wilber's four quadrants in a forthcoming book, *Edifice Complex*, and conclude that although subtle mind is an essential element of the Great Chain of Being, and therefore of his model, the complementary 'subtle bodies' (again essential to perennial wisdom) cannot be made to fit into any of the four quadrants. This is a major problem because it means that the Great Chain of Being does not map onto the four quadrants — a conflict between the two foundations of Wilber's grand edifice, potentially undermining his entire project.

Then, in the next paragraph: 'the *interior* of a holon can *only* be accessed by inter-pretation'. In *Eye of Spirit*, he makes the same point: 'the *only* way you and I can get at each other's interiors is by dialogue and interpretation (EoS, p. 14). In SES, he is even more emphatic: '. . . interiors must be interpreted. If I want to know what your brain looks like from within, what its actual lived interior is like (in other words, your mind), then I must talk to you. There is absolutely no other way. . . . And as we talk, I will have to interpret what you say' (p. 134). Then, missing the subtle reduction he has just expressed, he goes on to say, in contradiction: 'But you can only study interiors empathically, as a feel from within, and that means interpretations' (p. 134). (Later on, in IP, he wavers: 'the only way you can get at interiors is via introspection and interpretation'; here, Wilber recognizes that interpretation *alone* is insufficient to 'get at' interiors [pp. 172–3]).

He leaves us in no doubt what he means by 'intersubjectivity': It is a subject-to-subject connection mediated by language and interpretation — and '*only* . . . by interpretation'. There is no unmediated, *direct* experience of the other. Wilber's 'interpretative circle', he makes clear, is identical to the 'hermeneutic circle'. But interpretation is a cognitive operation, a manipulation of symbols, or, at best, an extraction of meaning from symbols. In either case, interpretation is always at least one remove from *immediate* experience.

True intersubjectivity, as I understand it, is unmediated. It is *direct* sub-ject-to-subject sharing of presence — where both (or more) subjects either mutu-ally *condition* each other's sense of self, or, more strongly, mutually *co-create* each other's sense of self.

We need to make an important distinction between two basic meanings of intersubjectivity — standard and experiential — with a further sub-distinction of the experiential meaning:

Intersubjectivity-1: This standard meaning derives from Cartesian subjectivity (isolated, independent subjects).[11] Here, individual subjectivity ontologically

---

[11] Subjectivity has two distinct meanings — subjectivity-1: 'experienced interiority', and subjectivity-2: 'private, independent, isolated experience'.
   Subjectivity-1: In the first case, subjectivity means, essentially, a capacity for feeling that is intrinsic, or interior, to the entity under consideration — a what-it-feels-like-from-within. The key notion here is 'experienced interiority' as distinct from vacuous (i.e. without experience) external relations. A sub-ject is constituted by internal relations, and these are *felt* or experienced. Without experience there could be no subjectivity (and vice versa; in fact, the two words are virtually synonymous); and experi-ence is always internal or intrinsic to the subject — that is to say, experience doesn't 'happen to' a sub-ject, it is *constitutive* of the subject.
      Subjectivity has a point of view. It 'takes account of', or feels, its own being. Its being is validated, felt, or known from within itself, not just from without — hence it is *first-person*. It cannot be fully accounted for by external, mechanical relations. A subject lives or endures through time, feeling its own continuity.
   Subjectivity-2: In another, related through restricted, sense, subjectivity means an isolated, independ-ent, self-sufficient locus of experience. Classically, this is the Cartesian ego, wholly private, and inde-pendent of all reality external to it. In the first case, subjectivity-1, experienced interiority is not auto-matically self-contained within its own private domain — it is interior, but not necessarily independent or isolated. The question of whether it is self-contained or interdependent is left open: It is possible for subjectivity-1 to be either interior and *shared*, or interior and *private*. In this second, Cartesian, case, the subject is not only interior, it is self-contained and private. Such independent egos, or subjects — Leibniz called them 'monads' — can communicate only via mediating signals, whereas subjectivity-1

precedes intersubjectivity. Individual, isolated subjects come first, and then through communication of signals arrive at consensual agreement. Here, the 'inter' in intersubjectivity refers to agreement 'between' subjects about so-called objective facts — and the subjects don't even have to interact (their agreement could be validated by a third party, as indeed is often the case in science).

- Intersubjectivity-1 (very weak Cartesian meaning): consensual validation between independent subjects via exchange of signals. *Cartesian intersubjectivity* relies on exchange of physical signals. It is physically *mediated* intersubjectivity — remote and, therefore, very weak.

Intersubjectivity-2a: Here, the sense of individual subjects remains, but now intersubjectivity refers to how the experience or consciousness of participating subjects is influenced and conditioned by their mutual interaction and engagement. The emphasis here is on the 'experienced interiority' of the subjects as they interact, not on their 'objective' agreement about some item of knowledge. Although this is a significant shift of emphasis from the standard meaning of intersubjectivity, nevertheless it is still 'weak' compared with the 'strong' version we will look at below. It is 'weak', not because the participation and engagement involved is weak — indeed it could be intense — but because it refers to changes that happen to the *form* of consciousness of the participating subjects, not to the *fact* of such consciousness. It is a 'weak' meaning of intersubjectivity because it addresses psychological rather than ontological issues; it is 'weak' because it still posits subjectivity as ontologically prior to intersubjectivity. Here, the 'inter' in intersubjectivity refers to the mutual 'structural coupling' of experiencing subjects, where the *already existing* interiorities of the participating subjects are interdependently shaped by their interaction.

- Intersubjectivity-2a (weak-experiential meaning): mutual engagement and participation between independent subjects, which *conditions* their respective experience. It is *psychological intersubjectivity* relying on nonphysical presence, and affects the contents of pre-existing subjects. It is direct *immediate* mutual apprehension between subjects.

Intersubjectivity-2b: This is the most radical meaning, and the one that poses the greatest challenge to philosophy of mind. According to this 'stronger' meaning, intersubjectivity is truly a process of co-creativity, where *relationship* is ontologically primary. All individuated subjects co-emerge, or co-arise, out of a holistic 'field' of relationships. In this sense, the being of any one subject is thoroughly dependent on the being of all other subjects, with which it is in relationship. Here, intersubjectivity precedes subjectivity (in the second, Cartesian, sense [see footnote 11], but subjectivity in the first sense, of experienced interiority, is implicit throughout). The *fact*, not just the form, of subjectivity (second, Cartesian sense) is a consequence of intersubjectivity. Here, the 'inter' in intersubjectivity refers

---

can communicate by participating in shared presence. With subjectivity-1, interiority or feeling can be 'intersubjective' and precede individual subjects; in subjectivity-2, interiority is *always* private, and intersubjectivity, if it occurs, is always secondary.

to an 'interpenetrating' co-creation of loci of subjectivity — a thoroughly holistic and organismic mutuality.

- Intersubjectivity-2b (strong-experiential meaning): mutual co-arising and engagement of interdependent subjects, or 'intersubjects' that *creates* their respective experience. It is *ontological intersubjectivity* relying on co-creative nonphysical presence, and brings distinct subjects into being out of a prior matrix of relationships.

The basic difference to note here is between (1) *intersubjective agreement* where my language about the world conforms to yours through exchange of conceptual and linguistic tokens, and (2a) *intersubjective participation* or (2b) *intersubjective co-creativity* where my experience of myself shows up qualitatively differently when I engage with you as a reciprocating center of experience. On this understanding, then, what I call 'true intersubjectivity' is unmediated communication or co-creative sharing of presence — it is direct *subject-to- subject* or 'I-to-I' communion. For shorthand, I sometimes refer to it as 'I–I.'[12]

Wilber's 'intersubjectivity' is not wrong; it's just very weak. It's what standard linguistic philosophy, social theory, and philosophy of science refer to as 'intersubjectivity' (and is really objectivity or interobjectivity [Velmans, 1993]). Yes, two or more subjects come together or share information via language, and therefore come to know something about each other. And, in *this* sense, there is a subject-to-subject communication. But, as I point out and as Wilber emphasizes, such communication is mediated via exchanges of linguistic tokens, which are *exteriors*. In this kind of 'intersubjectivity' *alone* there is no direct *interior-to-interior* connection or sharing. And unmediated *interior-to-interior* connection or sharing is *inter*-subjectivity of a different order.[13]

Wilber does emphasize that a central function of the Lower Left 'intersubjective' cultural quadrant is *meaning* — and he would unhesitatingly agree that meaning cannot be reduced to physical scratches on paper or digital blips on a screen (in fact, he sides with first-person subjectivists in criticizing philosophers such as Daniel Dennett and other cognitivists and eliminativists for reducing semantics to syntax). But the point is, according to Wilber's model, for meaning to be *communicated* or shared, it can do so 'only' by dialogue and interpretation, by 'talk' — that is, by exchange of linguistic tokens, physical signals. No room here for silent engaged presence (de Quincey, 1998). No room for shared feeling. No room for telepathic communion. No room, in other words, for true intersubjectivity where

---

[12] In SES (p. 306), Wilber notes that Ramana Maharshi often refers to 'I-I,' indicating the relationship between the personal I and the divine I. Thus, 'I-I' is the all-pervasive divine Self, the ever-present witness that embraces all individual Is. I find it interesting that Jamaican Rastafarians, also, acknowledge this and speak of 'I and I' — indicating the intersubjective relationship between the creator Jah and individual Is, and between Rastafarians themselves participating in the Jah's glory. I've always appreciated that perspective.

[13] Actually there is direct interior-to-interior engagement even when contact is made via language — in fact, that's the *only* way people can share meaning and understand each other. But the point is that the actual sharing of meaning is not accomplished by linguistic exchanges, but by the accompanying *interior-to-interior participatory presence* — by true intersubjectivity. As we know from evidence for telepathy, shared meaning doesn't even require language (or any exchange of physical signals).

one subject is actually shaped or changed by literally participating in, and incorporating, something of the being of another subject (weak intersubjectivity-2a), and certainly no room for one or more subjects dynamically, mutually creating each other's 'node' or nexus of subjectivity within the (universal) matrix of the ground of being of intersubjective relationships.

Wilber is clearly aware that LR exchanges *by themselves* cannot account for intersubjectivity (LL phenomena) — yet almost all his references to intersubjectivity are couched in terms of communities engaged in linguistic exchange.[14] As anyone familiar with his work would suspect: Wilber knows better. He knows that LL signifiers cannot be reduced to exchanges of LR signifieds. But he does not talk, or write, that way most of the time. My proposal for including actual intersubjectivity (that is, non-physically-mediated meaning) does not preclude physical correlates of such shared meaning (e.g., changes in brain states or marks on paper or dots on screen or spoken words). Like Wilber, I agree that every interior has (*must have*) a corresponding exterior. My concern, my objection, is that when he confines intersubjectivity to *only* dialogue or talk and interpretation he leaves no room for intersubjective interiority. I'm puzzled why Wilber doesn't see this, and shift his emphasis from language to presence (or *interiority*) when talking about intersubjectivity.

Wilber's ambiguous position on intersubjectivity is well summarized in SES. In a long footnote, he says: 'the linguistic signifiers (or the material components of a sign, the written symbol or the physical air vibrations of the spoken word) are all Right-Hand components, whereas the signifieds (the interior meanings that a person associates with a word) are all Left-Hand occasions . . .' (fn. #24, pp. 545–6). As we'd expect, Wilber is here emphasizing that 'interior meanings' are not reducible to exterior linguistic signs or tokens. But, on the next page, he slides away from this important distinction and talks of 'the distinction between *linguistically generated* intersubjectivity (Left) and self-referentially closed systems (Right)' (emphasis added) (p. 546). In one linguistic swoop, he contradicts his earlier distinction by collapsing (Left) intersubjectivity to 'linguistic generation,' which just a few sentences earlier he identified as 'Right'.

Wilber is here citing Habermas, and he does so approvingly. Now, admittedly, he may mean by 'linguistic' the combination of both (exterior) signifiers and (internal) signifieds, and therefore that he does mean to include interiors when talking of 'linguistically generated intersubjectivity'. I don't doubt that he does. However, my concern is that by almost always coupling intersubjectivity to linguistic exchanges, Wilber leaves readers with the impression that only via language can intersubjectivity occur. (As we've seen, this is actually what he does say — that what makes the difference in intersubjectivity is words.)

My point is that it is really the other way around: It is not the case that only via language can intersubjectivity occur, but that actually only via intersubjectivity can language carry and exchange meaning. In other words, intersubjectivity is not

[14] See, for example, *Integral Psychology*, pp. 73, 77, 114, 119, 122, 145, 161, 183, 186, 192, 254, 255, 278, 283, 284, 286, 288.

'linguistically generated,' it precedes language, and is its ground of being, its context of meaning.

To add to the ambiguity, Wilber later on does talk the language of presence — the foundational experience of intersubjectivity:

> ... consciousness is an inseparable mixture of experience and mental-cultural molding. ... Every experience is a context; every experience, even simple sensory experience, is always already situated, is always already a context, is always already a holon. ... As Whitehead would have it, every holon is already a prehensive unification of its entire actual universe: nothing is every simply present.
>
> ... but contexts touch immediately. It does not require 'mystical pure consciousness' to be in immediate contact with the data of experience. When any point in the mediated chain is known (or experienced), that knowing or prehending is an immediate event in itself, an immediate 'touching.' The touching is not a touching of something merely present but rather is itself pure Presence (or prehension) (SES, p. 600).

Here, Wilber has clearly expressed the profound intersubjectivity intrinsic to Whitehead's ontology (which, ironically, elsewhere Wilber denies).

But there's another, more serious, problem: If the defence of Wilber's position on intersubjectivity is based on the fact that as a whole his philosophy is 'nondual' then, actually, the defence evaporates. For in that case, the notion that all beings are immediately co-present in Spirit — that intersubjectivity arises from direct and immediate contact of all interiors with Spirit — applies to *all four quadrants* (for, ultimately, in Wilber's scheme, even all exteriors are Spirit). There would be nothing special about LL. In what way would LL intersubjectivity differ from intersubjectivity in any of the other quadrants? Wilber's answer: through cultural exchanges of meaning via linguistic tokens. And so we're back to the original problem. Thus, it seems, by taking the 'One Taste' perspective (where *everything* is intersubjective), Wilber is forced to single out a particular type of 'intersubjectivity', i.e. exchange of linguistic tokens.

Bottom line: This is not an incidental or 'nit-picking' critique. Basically, to spell it out: *One quarter of Wilber's four quadrants is left void or vacant.* His LL is not what he claims it to be, i.e., the locus of intersubjectivity.

Given Wilber's central project: to include interiority of the Kosmos at all levels (and not as modernity has done, attempt to reduce all aspects of reality to merely atomistic or functional-fitting systems exteriors), I have no doubt that he intends to have true intersubjectivity in the LL quadrant. And I'm sure he believes this is what he has done. But by describing and explaining LL intersubjectivity in terms and ideas derived from sociolinguists, such as Herbert Mead and Jürgen Habermas, he has unwittingly inherited their covert (and not always so covert) materialism and linguistic behaviourism. Rather, had he drawn more on the work of Martin Buber (1970), and even A.N. Whitehead (1979) to characterize his LL version of intersubjectivity, he would have, or at least could have, avoided this unfortunate, limiting — and highly significant — instance of subtle reductionism. Wilber has been quick, and at times unmerciful, in pointing out this kind of reductionism practised by many systems and eco-theorists.

It is precisely the lacuna of true intersubjectivity in consciousness studies and philosophy of mind that prompted me to present a paper at the Tucson III 'Toward a Science of Consciousness' conference, in 1998, calling for comprehensive first-, *second-*, and third-person perspectives in investigating consciousness. It seemed to me to be such a glaring oversight that I wondered if I was somehow blind or mistaken: Had no-one in philosophy of mind really seriously considered the second-person perspective? So, as part of a reality check, I sent an early draft of my paper to a number of theorists in consciousness studies, and Wilber was among them. He wrote back affirming my perception, pointing out that except for his own work (meaning his LL quadrant), few contemporary consciousness theorists besides me were taking intersubjectivity seriously. I was pleased to see Wilber subsequently emphasize what I was calling for: a comprehensive 1st, 2nd, and 3rd person approach to consciousness studies (which he now calls the '1-2-3 of consciousness studies' [Wilber, 2000c]).[15]

In the four quadrants model, Wilber is weakest in his treatment of LL intersubjectivity and second-person perspective, and — not incidentally, I think — he wants to downplay the ontological and epistemological significance of feeling, so central to a more comprehensive and deep understanding of intersubjectivity. As noted earlier, the root of the problem is his 'categorical rejection' of the ontological significance of feeling.

In other words, it is the *felt relational* component of Wilber's theoretical psycho-philosophical work that is most conspicuously missing. This criticism in one form or another, with varying degrees of emotionality, has been levelled at Wilber from many quarters (e.g., feminists, eco-systems theorists, spiritual practitioners) for whom relation is primary.

In the 'I–We–It' stakes, Wilber is strongest on the I and It. His writings lack a sense of felt bodily meaning and relationship. And this has tended to alienate him from those for whom 'We' is primary. Wilber has a tendency to reduce 'We' to the terms of 'I–It' — *even while proclaiming the very opposite.*[16]

---

[15] I do note, however, that when talking of intersubjectivity and the '1-2-3 of consciousness studies', Wilber makes no reference to my paper on intersubjectivity which points out how contemporary philosophy of mind, in particular, and consciousness studies, in general, have overlooked the second-person perspective. (A shorter version of this paper appeared in *IONS Review* [de Quincey, 1998].) Wilber uses phrases very similar to what I wrote in my intersubjectivity paper (e.g., that in intersubjective dialogue participants needn't 'agree with each other,' and that what is needed now is a 'comprehensive theory' of consciousness that includes 1st, 2nd, and 3rd person perspectives).

I do not wish to imply that Wilber consciously borrowed my ideas — I'm sure he receives and reads a great deal of material, and cannot keep track of what are his own original ideas and those he picks up from his voracious reading. But I do want to state for the record that the call for a comprehensive 1, 2, 3 of consciousness studies was first presented in my Tucson paper in 1998, and that Wilber had read it a year or so before publication of his call for 'The 1-2-3 of Consciousness Studies' in *Integral Psychology* (Wilber, 2000c).

A condensed version of my Tucson 'Intersubjectivity' paper was published by MIT Press (Hameroff *et al.*, 1999).

[16] Even though I point out what I take to be a deficiency in Wilber's treatment of intersubjectivity, I hope he sees me as an ally in the project to put the second-person perspective on the radar screen in consciousness studies and philosophy of mind. I think there is room in his four quadrants for true intersubjectivity, and I'm just trying to clarify what it is. I've been passionate about this issue for many years, and have tried to draw attention to it in my own work.

The Mind–Body Problem

Readers of *JCS* will probably be most interested in Wilber's contribution to the mind–body issue, particularly because the 'hard problem' has been a major theme in the journal since its inception. I will argue that Wilber's model doesn't even begin to offer a solution to this perennial 'world knot' as Schopenhauer called it, and furthermore that this omission seriously undermines the rational integrity of his four quadrant system. Instead of explaining how the interior and exterior domains relate and interact, Wilber asks us to be content with promissory integralism.

What does he actually offer as a solution to the mind-body problem? He is quite explicit:

> [T]he ultimate mind/body problem — the relation of interior-subjective to exterior-objective — is solved only in nondual awakening, which transcends and includes the quadrants. My claim, then, is that an 'all-level, all-quadrant' view substantially handles the mind/body problem in all its major forms (SES/CW 6, pp. 453–4).

So, how does he 'handle' it? In IP, following Vedanta, he identifies three bodies, each with its correlated mind:

> the gross body of the waking state (which supports the material mind); the subtle body of the dreaming state (which supports the emotional, mental, and higher mental levels); and the causal body of deep sleep (which supports the spiritual mind) (p. 13).

But we have to be careful here about terminology. Let's look, first, at what he means by 'mind'. On the one hand, he uses 'mind' to mean a particular level of the Great Chain of Being (which, in one of its simpler expressions, evolves from matter, to body, to mind, to soul, to spirit). Here, mind is clearly distinguished from spirit. Yet, in IP he talks of mind in a broader, differentiated, ontological sense that includes 'material mind' of the waking state (then, presumably, the redundant, tautological notion of 'mental mind' of dreams), and, finally, the higher 'spiritual mind' of deep sleep. But now his use of 'mind' in this sense conflicts with how he uses it in the Great Chain. In the first case, 'mind' is just one level of reality; in the second, it spans the spectrum from 'material mind' to 'mental mind' to 'spiritual mind'. Presumably, what he calls 'mind' in the Great Chain, is equivalent to 'mental mind' in his states-of-consciousness spectrum? But this is all very confusing. Whereas the notion of 'mental mind'[17] is tautological, 'material mind' is oxymoronic. By 'material mind' does he mean something like the kind of mind supported by, or associated with, the 'gross material' body, and by 'mental' the kind of mind supported by or associated with the 'subtle' body, and by 'spiritual mind' the kind of mind supported by or associated with the 'causal' body? If so, we are back to the original problem: *How* are the various forms of mind 'supported' by the various forms of body?

---

[17] To be fair, Wilber does not use the term 'mental mind'. But what else would he call the level of mind between 'material' and 'spiritual'? He does, in fact, identify this particular form of mind as 'emotional, *mental*, and higher *mental*' (my italics). So although he doesn't use the term, he does *mean* 'mental mind'.

When we confront this question we can ignore the issue of particular levels of mind and body, and focus on the issue of how *any* form of mind could interact with *any* form of body: the old, familiar mind–body problem. Either way, Wilber's discussion of the mind-body relation adds more tangles to the 'world knot' rather than helping us unsnarl it (Griffin, 1998). I will return to this problem in a moment when I examine Wilber's preferred distinction between 'interior' and 'exterior' domains of reality.

Now let's look at what he means by 'body': 'body is the energetic support of the various states and levels of mind' (IP, p. 12), (i.e., support for the three levels of mind identified in the quote above). These distinctions seem to beg more questions than they answer: For instance, how is the distinction between the 'body/energetic support' and the mind or consciousness not a form of dualism? What does it mean to say that the body is an 'energetic support' for the mind? How is such support achieved — in other words, what is the nature of the mind–body interaction that would necessarily underlie such support? Wilber does not answer these questions. In fact, as we will see, he is quite explicit that he will not attempt to explain *how* mind (interior) and body (exterior) interact. He is content to leave that up to psychics and mystics.

Another difficulty: His interpretation of the 'average person's' common usage of 'body' to mean 'subjective feelings, emotions and sensations of the felt body' (IP, p. 178) does not match what I experience the 'average person' to mean. In fact, I think this is exactly what they don't mean. What Wilber says the 'average person' means for 'body' is, I think, what they typically mean by 'mind'. Wilber describes one aspect of the mind–body problem as an experienced conflict between 'thoughts and beliefs' (cognition) and our feelings. To be sure, this conflict is often real — we do frequently feel this split. But it is more a conflict between different levels of mind (rational and emotional) than a split between mind and body.

The average person does not experience or report a problem in terms of causal efficacy between thoughts and emotions (or vice versa). In fact, the all too often obvious causal relation between these levels of or aspects of mind is what troubles people (Freud spoke of this psychological conflict as the battle between the ego and the id, or between the ego and the superego).

But the real mind–body problem, as Wilber knows, is precisely how the causal interaction between mind and body can be explained. It is a split between the UL quadrant (mind) and UR quadrant (body or brain) — not between two levels of the UL quadrant.

Wilber does seem to be confused about what the mind-body problem is (as identified by philosophers for centuries — e.g., Schopenhauer's 'world-knot' or, more recently, Levine's 'explanatory gap' and Chalmers' 'hard problem'. In IP, he says that at least one aspect of the 'world-knot' is to understand how different levels of consciousness or interiority relate to each other:

> the insuperable problem (the world-knot) has been how to relate this mind to both the body (or the lower interior levels of feeling and desire) and to the Body (or objective organism, brain and material environment) (p. 182).

But this is false — at least the first part is. The 'world-knot' is not about relating higher and lower interior levels, about how reason and feelings or emotions are related. The confusion arises because Wilber uses the word 'body' in two very different senses, which he distinguishes by capitalizing the B in the second sense. But Wilber's 'body' is not at all the same as that in the 'mind–body' world-knot. It is, as he says, really another word for lower *interior levels* such as feeling and desire. However, the real mind–body problem is not to account for how different interior levels relate, it is to *explain how interiors and exteriors are related*. In other words, to explain how mind (in the broadest sense of 'interior') relates to what Wilber calls 'Body', or exteriors.

Wilber says the 'inherent paradox' of the world-knot is 'the body is in the mind, but the brain is in the Body'. But this paradox arises only if we accept his idiosyncratic definition of 'body', and his subsequent recasting of the mind–body problem. For most contemporary mind-body theorists, the statement 'the body is in the mind' would be either meaningless or patently false. Ask any 'average' mind–body theorist to choose between 'mind in body' or 'body in mind' and they will choose the former.[18]

So, to characterize the mind-body problem in terms of a paradox, one part of which states 'the body is in the mind' is to set up a straw man. No mind-body theorists, besides idealists and Wilberesque 'integralists' would accept that premise. And without that premise, Wilber's version of the world-knot paradox dissolves. Wilber says, 'the felt body is in the mind' (IP, p. 179) — but only on his model. For the rest of us, the sentence would be more meaningfully cast as 'the *feelings* of the body are in the mind.' Expressed that way, it is an unproblematic tautology. Of course, feelings are in the mind. That's not a problem. The real mind–body problem is: *How are feelings in the body?'* *That's* the hard problem. That's the world-knot that materialists and dualists have been unable to unsnarl, as Wilber, following Griffin, correctly points out.

There are not 'four mind–body problems' as Wilber says (one for each quadrant). There remains the original one: How are interiors causally related to exteriors — how do mind and body interact? Wilber's 'solution' is a promise of a transrational 'nondual awakening':

> As for the traditional mind-body problem . . . The Left-Hand domains refer loosely to 'mind,' and the Right-Hand domains to 'body.' These are ultimately nondual, but that nonduality can only be realized with causal-to-nondual development, at which point the mind–body problem is not solved, but dissolved: seen to be a product of

[18] Wilber says: 'The felt body is in the mind . . . That is, formop transcends and includes conop, which transcends and includes vital feelings and sensorimotor awareness: the mind transcends and includes the body (which is precisely why the mind can causally operate on the body . . .' (IP, p. 179).

It is clear from this that by 'body' Wilber means 'sensorimotor awareness'. But sensorimotor awareness is an aspect or level of *mind* (or interiority), not the body. Agreed, sensorimotor awareness — such as feelings or Gendlin's 'excocepts' — is *somatic* in the sense that it is preverbal, perhaps even cellular, *awareness*. But this is the body's awareness, not the body *per se*. Wilber appears to confuse the body's awareness with the body itself. A similar sort of confusion exists when new agers talk of 'psychic energy' or consciousness as a form of energy. Consciousness is not energy. Consciousness is what *feels* the energy (de Quincey, 1999b). Similarly, sensorimotor awareness is not the body, it is what *feels* the body.

nescience, ignorance, or nonawakening. Short of that, the mind–body problem cannot be satisfactorily solved (IP, p. 233).

What's Wilber's solution, then? Well, you have to evolve to a higher stage of consciousness beyond the rational mind and its higher visionary-logic stage (the one that creates TOEs). That's a solution? On the one hand, he's telling us that his 'all-level, all-quadrant' model 'substantially handles the mind/body problem', while on the other hand he's telling us the solution will be seen only in 'nondual awakening'. But then he says: 'As for the mind/body problem itself . . . I refer to my position as "interactionist," not so much because I believe that position really solves anything, but as a way to disavow the other "solutions"' (SES/CW, p. 574). This is Wilber's 'now-you-see-it-now-you-don't' mind-body shuffle: There is no sub-mystical solution; but here's a sub-mystical solution anyway.[19] Except it isn't.

I'm not denying that Wilber may be correct to propose that at some transrational level of consciousness we may 'see through' the kind of logical knots that befuddle reason, and that mystics and shamans may indeed be privy to

---

[19] Ironically, although Wilber has done a great service integrating psychology and philosophy, one of his weaknesses shows up in the very area of philosophy intimately related to his topic — philosophy of mind, and particularly the mind–body problem.

Wilber reveals a surprisingly loose grasp of the subtle and key issues in philosophy of mind. For example, in IP, he gives a long footnote listing influential writers on the mind–problem over the last ten years. Heading that list is Nicholas Humphrey, a self-proclaimed materialist (Humphrey, 1992; de Quincey 2000b). Yet in summarizing the current state of thinking on this problem from the perspective of scientific materialism, Wilber says, 'there is no way objective systems could give rise to "mental" properties, and therefore those properties are simply illusory byproducts of complex systems, with no causal reality of their own' (IP, p. 175).

But this is a misrepresentation of the mainstream physicalist (or materialist) approach. Standard materialists do not hold this position — in fact, they take the opposite view. Many materialists (Nicholas Humphrey, John Searle and Gerald Edleman, for example) claim that physical-biological evolution can account for the emergence of mental properties — e.g., subjectivity, qualia — from wholly objective raw stuff, such as nervous systems and brains. Wilber says materialists recognize the impossibility of this, but in fact most of them very definitely do not. What Wilber describes as the materialist position (IP, p. 175), is actually the position of critics of materialism (such as Griffin, 1998b; de Quincey, 1999), or of mysterians (such as McGinn, 1999) who claim that the brain does produce consciousness but that understanding how it produces the miracle remains utterly mysterious.

Materialistically inclined mysterians such as McGinn or Galen Strawson are a small minority in current philosophy of mind, and do not represent the dominant position held by philosophers such as Searle, Dennett and Edelman. It is not the materialists who fuss about the impossibility of subjectivity emerging from wholly objective matter, but panpsychists such as Griffin or myself.

Wilber may have in mind some eliminative materialists (such as Paul and Patricia Churchland) who claim that consciousness, qualia, subjectivity, experience, beliefs, desires, purposes — all interiority in fact — are nothing but 'folk fictions', and therefore should be excised from our vocabulary. The Churchlands believe that once the science of neurobiology advances sufficiently, we will understand exactly how the brain works, and will no longer have any need for such folk fictions. But, again, the Churchlands do not represent the mainstream materialist approach.

Wilber's discussion of the mind–body problem in IP emphasizes the difficulties that materialists and dualists say they have with their own positions. This is a very persuasive move, and highlights the very real difficulties materialists and dualists have in unsnarling the world-knot. But in this discussion, Wilber does not explicitly acknowledge that this very strategy is what David Griffin uses in *Unsnarling the World-Knot* with such impressive force. It is unfortunate that Wilber does not acknowledge in the text the obvious contribution and influence Griffin has had on his thinking about the mind–body problem. It is clear from Wilber's endnotes that Griffin is the source of these ideas, but it would have been only fair for Wilber to have acknowledged Griffin in the text — especially since Wilber advises his readers to first read the main text straight through without bothering with the endnotes.

how mind and body are related. But, unless you are in that higher state or stage of consciousness and can experience the 'solution' for yourself, Wilber's proffered mind–body 'solution' amounts to nothing more than promissory idealism or integralism.[20]

It is, in fact, an idealist counterpoint to the kind of promissory materialism we get from neurophilosophers and eliminativists like the Churchlands, or cognitivists such as Dennett, or evolutionary biophilosophers such as Edleman or Searle. It is, also, an idealist variation of McGinn's 'mysterianism'. But neither mystery nor promises fill the explanatory gap. No filler, no solution.

This is not to single out Wilber. Unless we make a radical departure in our modes of thought, from substance- to process-thinking, it seems highly unlikely anyone will ever 'unsnarl the world knot' (Griffin, 1998). This radical turn is what Alfred North Whitehead attempted, and by many accounts accomplished, in *Process and Reality*.[21] Without something like Whitehead's process approach, Wilber cannot be expected to solve the mind–body puzzle. But by proposing his promissory integralism as a solution, he leaves himself vulnerable to severe criticism from anyone versed in the nuances of the mind–body problem. His claim to have 'resolved' the problem will be dismissed, at best, as naïve, or, worse, as a case of hubris.

I agree with Wilber that a full understanding of the mind–body solution involves a development of consciousness. In de Quincey (1994), I explain why I agree with Colin McGinn that the mind–body problem may remain a mystery, opaque to a reason-only solution — but, I point out, not to an extrarational *process* solution involving, for example, feeling and intuition.

However, I also argue that at the level of rational understanding, the most coherent solution to date, in my evaluation, is that offered by Whitehead. In *Process and Reality*, he reframes the mind–body problem away from discussion in terms of spatial relationships and interaction of substances, and proposes instead a solution in terms of temporal relations between subjects and objects. I think Whitehead has gone a long way, perhaps as far as reason can take us, toward providing a coherent rational solution to the mind–body problem. But precisely because the essence of his solution directs our attention to *time*, it is difficult for reason to fully grasp and hold the relevant abstractions. Reason is not a very effective tool for dealing with *experienced time*, with duration. Whitehead, recognizing this, invented a network of neologisms in an attempt to nudge us out of our habitual grooves of rational, substance-based modes of thought.

Nevertheless, the deep meaning of his solution seems to elude a steady, clear, unambiguous rational understanding. Even with Whitehead's brilliant exposition, we still need to help it along with a shift in our own consciousness, a shift that augments his rational arguments with extrarational feeling and insight.

---

[20] As noted in footnote 5 above, the vitriol and lack of compassion in Wilber's writings casts doubt on whether he has attained the higher stages of spiritual consciousness. And since he himself argues that unless one achieves constancy at a particular stage the kind of knowing associated with that level is not accessible, how would he know that the mind-body problem is 'dissolved' in transrational, mystical awareness? What 'cash-value' should we assign to this integralist promissory note?

[21] See de Quincey (1999b) for a discussion of Whitehead's process solution to the mind–body problem.

Speaking for myself, I understand Whitehead best when I allow myself to embody his concepts, to feel them, preverbally, to let them take root in my cells. So, there is an extrarational, *somatic*, component to the mind–body solution. You have to feel it in your body as well as think it in your mind — which is, perhaps, what we should have expected all along. After all, it is the *mind–body* problem.

But this is not at all to dismiss, as Wilber does, the possibility of providing a rationally coherent solution, albeit infused with some extrarational shafts of wisdom.[22] Whitehead has provided a solution, within the limits of reason. Wilber asks us to wait for when consciousness grows beyond reason. He asks us to have faith in 'promissory idealism' or 'promissory integralism': 'Therefore, the "proof" for this nondual solution can only be found in the further development of the consciousness of those who seek to know the solution' (IP, p. 181).

As I said, this is less a 'solution' to the hard problem than it is an epistemo- logical 'promissory note'. Wilber is clearly aware, however, that his model cannot really deliver on that promise. When it comes to explaining *how* mind and body, or interior and exterior, are related he, not surprisingly, declines to make the attempt:[23] 'It does not matter "how" this [mind–body interaction] happens; that "how," I am suggesting is more fully disclosed at the postrational, nondual waves' (IP, p. 184).

Wilber offers his four-quadrant model — that shows how UL, UR, LL and LR co-evolve, or, as he likes to say, 'tetra-evolve'. But at the crucial point where 'subjective intentionality [UL] and objective behavior [UR] . . . mutually interact', along with cultural worldviews (LL) and social structures (LR) (pp. 183–4), he tells us that it doesn't matter 'how' the interaction occurs. 'It is only necessary to acknowledge that this interaction seems phenomenologically undeniable' (p. 184).

Experientially and phenomenologically he is correct: We are in little doubt that mind and body interact. But the mind–body problem is not about the *fact* of interaction; it is about *explaining* that fact. And telling us they interact through 'will and response' (p. 184) merely restates the problem.

---

[22] To repeat: Wilber's position is that 'the exact relation of interiors to exteriors is disclosed only in the postrational stages of development', and then, rather mildly, 'we can nonetheless understand rationally that every interior has an exterior, and vice versa' (IP, p. 276). His nod in the direction of a rational grasp of the mind–body problem is merely to state the rather obvious point that 'every interior has an exterior'. This is true; it is a truism. But it does not enlighten us (even rationally) about the mind–body problem. Whitehead, in *Process and Reality*, takes us much further along the road of reason toward unsnarling the world-knot.

[23] The mind–body solution shuffle again: On the one foot, Wilber says he will not attempt to say 'how' the interaction occurs. It's just sufficient to know that it does, and the mystery will be solved when we evolve to higher consciousness. However, on the other foot, he also makes the claim that his model does provide a solution: 'At each of those levels [within each quadrant], not only do interiors prehend their corresponding exteriors, they prehend their own past (Griffin would agree with that, I believe). This appears to account not only for Mind–Body (interior–exterior) interaction, but for interior causation, interior inheritance, and mind–body interaction' (IP, p. 278). So here, Wilber is borrowing Whitehead's notion of 'prehension' and applies it to his quadrants. To the extent that Whitehead's process ontology accounts for the relationship between subject (interior) and object (exterior), Wilber's 'prehension-enriched' quadrants can offer a solution for the subject–object relation. But, in that case, it is not Wilber's model that supplies the solution, it is Whitehead's (which Wilber has assimilated into his own).

If we are, rightly I believe, sceptical of promissory materialism, should we be any more credulous of 'promissory integralism', which — from the perspective of rationality — amounts to about the same explanatory currency as 'and then a miracle occurred'?[24]

Panpsychism and Whitehead

Related to his unsatisfactory treatment of the mind–body problem is Wilber's problematic characterization of panpsychism. It is really his own invention, another 'straw man', easy to knock down, but of little practical value because it does not inform us about real panpsychism.

His 'straw panpsychism' is expressed in his most interesting and most lengthy (seven pages) endnote in IP on the mind–body problem. Having just acknowledged that every exterior has an interior all the way down, he says that this 'would appear to involve some sort of panpsychism'. Agreed. But since panpsychism is not Wilber's pet ontology, (not obviously integralism in the form of the Great Chain of Being and the four quadrants), he resorts to his own version of 'panpsychism'.

> Every major form of panpsychism equates 'interiors' with a *particular type of interior* (such as feelings, awareness, soul, etc.), and then attempts to push that type all the way down to the fundamental units of the universe (quarks, atoms, strings, or some such) (p. 276).

And then:

> Most schools of panpsychism take *one* of those interiors — such as feeling or soul — and maintain that *all* entities possess it (atoms have feelings, cells have a soul) and this *I categorically reject* [emphasis added] (p. 277).

The problem with this characterization is that it fails to acknowledge that, for instance, when Whitehead uses 'feelings' or 'prehensions' he means what Wilber means by 'interiors'. The difference is that Whitehead then goes on to propose how feelings/interiority are related to the world of exterior objects. Wilber does not.

If Wilber posits interiors all the way down, and rejects feeling, then either feeling emerges discontinuously, or some trace of feeling must exist in the 'all-way-down' interiors. Here's the dilemma: (i) What could 'interiority' mean if it does not have something of the sense of 'feeling', 'prehension', 'sentience', 'experience',

---

[24] 'Miracles' are a measure or indication of our ignorance. When we don't understand how something could happen, but want to insist that it did happen nevertheless, we invoke the non-explanation of 'miracle'. This is not to say real miracles can never occur. It just means that if they do, they are beyond our ken. Miracles lie beyond the pale of knowledge. As far as epistemology is concerned, the great problem with miracles is this: By what criteria do we decide when to invoke their occurrence? What are the rules of evidence by which we decide when and where to insert a 'miracle' into our explanations, revealing a breakdown in our sequence of reasoning? If miracles are evidence of our ignorance, what prevents us from invoking a miracle every time we are at a loss to explain something? (Science replaced magic as a method of knowledge because it did not accept gaps in explanation — in contrast, magic invoked spirits and miracles when something happened beyond the reach of the knowledge of the time.) If we allow miracles to pepper our explanations, then what's to stop any of us resorting to 'and then a miracle occurred' every time we fail to understand anything? Why bother with seeking any explanations at all? Why not just say 'it's all a miracle' and leave it at that?

'subjectivity'? (ii) If 'interiority' doesn't have any trace of prehension or feeling, etc., then Wilber leaves himself wide open to the kind of 'emergent miracle' that materialists face when claiming that consciousness can emerge from wholly mindless matter. If 'interiority' is *wholly* without anything resembling feeling or prehension etc., then the jump from wholly non-feeling/prehension to even some minute feeling/prehension requires an ontological miracle. If Wilber's critique of materialism is valid (and I believe it is), then he can't have it both ways: the same critique levelled at his ontological emergence is equally valid. (The reverse of this problem faces idealists who claim that pure Spirit [wholly without a trace of anything physical or objective] 'emanates' real objective, real physical matter.) What's happening here is either Wilber engaging in one-upmanship word quibbling, or he is committing the 'emergence fallacy'.[25]

Wilber does not distinguish between 'tokens' and 'types', two key concepts in philosophy of mind. What he calls 'types' are actually 'tokens', so that in one sense 'feelings', 'awareness', 'souls' are all tokens of the same type ('mental', 'experiential', 'interior'), in contrast to 'neurons', 'synapses', 'brains', which are all tokens of the same type (matter, body). In this sense it is true that *tokens* do not go all the way down, but any particular type does — both interiors and exteriors (consciousness and matter) go all the way. This is Whitehead's position, and it is pure panpsychism.

However, in another sense feelings equal interiors, and hence 'feelings' (as used by Whitehead) refer to ontological type. It is in this sense that Whitehead (and Griffin and I) say that feelings (or sentience or experience) go all the way down. This is no different (other than chosen terminology) from Wilber's position on interiors. Hence, he is either splitting terminological hairs, or attacking a straw man.

When he says, 'I am a pan-interiorist, not a pan-experientialist, pan-mentalist, pan-feelingist, or pan-soulist' (IP, p. 276–7), he is word quibbling. This only distracts from the more significant point that, whether you call it 'interior', 'experience', 'feeling', 'prehension', or 'consciousness', the fact remains that that ontological type must go all the way down if we are even to begin to have a coherent, rational solution to the mind–body problem.

Wilber is saying nothing more than what panpsychists such as Whitehead, Hartshorne, Griffin, and I mean when we say the 'tokens' or forms of experience,

---

[25] Wilber's ambiguous position on panpsychism is reflected in another inconsistency. On the one hand, he is explicit that all exteriors have interiors, and that interiors go all the way down (see, for example, *Integral Psychology*), yet on the other hand, he criticizes Aristotle's teleology, for ascribing 'to matter a type of lower-order purpose or telos itself. The error here, as we might now explain it, is that genuinely purposeful or intentional behavior begins only on the biological level, not on the material level' (1982).

  If purpose or intentionality is not present in matter, but is present in biological organisms, then Wilber faces the 'miracle of emergence' problem. How could something wholly without a trace of purpose or intentionality ever give rise to something that did have purpose and intentionality? Wilber's critique of Aristotle is excerpted from his 'forthcoming' *System, Self, and Structure*, and appeared in the December 1982 edition of the *Newsletter* from the Association for Humanistic Psychology. This notion of 'dead' or insentient matter is repeated in *Integral Psychology*: '. . . developmental space that spans *insentient matter* to superconscient spirit' [emphasis added] (2000c, p. 47; see also pp. 276–82).

sentience, or subjectivity show a developmental unfolding — e.g., from prehension to self-reflective consciousness (Whitehead, 1979; Hartshorne, 1968; Griffin, 1998; de Quincey, in press).[26]

Wilber 'categorically rejects' taking any one of those tokens and pushing it all the way down. So do Whitehead, Hartshorne, Griffin and I. Like Wilber, we all recognize that non-objective reality evolves from dim, primitive tokens of that type to higher and higher varieties of it. So, again, Wilber is 'categorically rejecting' not panpsychism, but his own mischaracterization: 'straw panpsychism'.

In IP, he says, 'interior feelings correlate with objective limbic system' (p. 70), as if only creatures with limbic systems could feel (what about worms?). Yet in his four-quadrant graph, he correlates *emotion* with the limbic system (p. 62 graph). Thus, he equates feelings with emotions. Clearly limbic systems do not go all the way down, so given Wilber's correlation of both feelings and emotions with limbic systems, it is not surprising that, for him, neither feelings nor emotions go all the way. But this is not what panpsychists claim: they do not push the kind of feelings or emotions associated with limbic systems all the way down. In the panpsychist view emotions are higher-order tokens of the type 'feelings' (prehension, experience, interiority, it's all the same type).[27] In fact, in his four quadrants, Wilber does place Whitehead's prehension at the base of his system of cognitive development (in UL). For Whitehead, prehension is synonymous with feeling; nevertheless Wilber denies feeling goes all the way down.

Furthermore, Wilber is himself hesitant, reflecting perhaps some confusion, about how far down to 'push' consciousness, sentience, or interiority. On the one hand, in his critique of Whitehead's and Griffin's panpsychism, as we've seen, he is explicit that he does not want to accept that 'feelings' or 'prehensions' go all the way down — only interiors. In a previous chapter, however, he wavers about how far down not only he is willing to 'push' consciousness or sentience, but even interiors:

> How far 'down' you wish to push interiors or consciousness is, of course, up to you. Some people push it down to mammals, others to reptiles, others to plants, others all the way down to atoms. I find this a completely relative issue: however much consciousness one holon has — say, an amoeba — a senior holon has a little more — say, a deer — and its senior has even more — say, a gorilla. The lower on the Great Nest, the less sentience a holon has, until it fades into the shades that we cannot detect (IP, p. 162).

---

[26] I have also developed an evolutionary model that describes the stages of consciousness developing from sentience, to awareness/awakeness, to personal, to reflexive, to interpersonal, to unitive consciousness (de Quincey, in press & 1997).

[27] In Wilber's defence, I should point out that Whitehead does make a case that emotions go as far down as electrons, so that something of the quality we humans associate with, e.g., the experience of the colour green, is also experienced in some inchoate way even by lowly electrons.

But here, again, Whitehead is merely making a case against type-emergence. Something of the *type* that we recognize as emotion must go all the way down — though, of course, different emotional *tokens* (e.g., anger, jealousy, or fear, do not).

If Wilber could keep this distinction in mind, he would see that his position is indeed not only compatible with panpsychism, but is actually a form of panpsychism. Wilber's 'interiors' all the way down and Whitehead's 'prehensions' all the way down are tokens of the same ontological type. And this is the essence of panpsychism.

At this point, Wilber seems to be equating interiors, consciousness, and sentience (as, in fact, I do, too). But in his panpsychism critique he opts to distinguish interiors from sentience, prehension, feeling, and consciousness. Panpsychists would agree with his characterization in the section quoted above that, as we retrace evolution, whatever sentience a holon has it 'fades into the shades' at lower phylogenetic levels. But 'fading into the shades' does not, cannot, mean fading out of existence altogether (otherwise, we face the 'miracle of emergence'). It means, rather, that sentience becomes so dilute, so primitive, so primordial, it hardly resembles anything we are familiar with at the level of human sentience and consciousness. But, even in the 'shades', the light is not completely out — something of the nature of sentience, consciousness, subjectivity is present in trace form even at the level of atoms, electrons, quarks or quanta.[28]

Wilber criticizes Whitehead for being 'monological' — which is Wilber's code for Cartesianism, a 'philosophy of the subject monologically accessing a pregiven world', a philosophy that fails to include 'a dialogical investigation of the intersubjective structures that allow subjects and objects to differentiate and appear in the first place' (EoS, p. 168).

But this critique misses the significance of Whitehead's emphasis on 'concrescence'. Not only does each subject prehend its ancestors as objects ('now subject, then object), each subject is *constituted* by its ancestral objects. As subjects, we are necessarily in dialogue with our own past as objects — in fact, according to Whitehead, with the history of the entire universe. In Whitehead, subjects and objects co-create each other in time.

Critiquing Whitehead, therefore, for not recognizing that every subject arises only in intersubjective space is incorrect. Whitehead's subjects very clearly arise in the intersubjective 'space' of universal concrescence. If each subject is constituted by every other subject, how much more intersubjective can you get? The fact that the 'constituting' ingredients of each new subject are prior 'expired subjects' (Whitehead's 'objects') does not diminish access to the being or knowledge of those 'subjects-become-objects'. Although 'expired' — although each prior subject's moment of experience has passed — the actuality of that subject's being or interiority gains new life as an ingredient of each subsequent subject. The past literally lives on in the present. Past-objects are vital constituents of now-subjects. This 'conservation of experience' (de Quincey, 2000c), this flowing of past subjects into now subjects establishes Whitehead's ontology and epistemology as radically *constitutively intersubjective*. Wilber's critique betrays a limited grasp of the profound implications of Whitehead's process metaphysics.

---

[28] Of course, it is not really a matter of 'fading into the shades that we cannot detect', if by 'detect' we mean empirically measure. We don't have a Chalmers' consciousness meter, so we can't even 'detect' consciousness, sentience, or interiority, in humans, never mind in amoebas or atoms. However, if by 'detect' Wilber means intersubjectively apprehend, then that's a different issue. It is questionable that consciousness/sentience is not detectable 'all the way down'. Not one of Wilber's favourite areas of study, I know, but there is no shortage of reports from shamans (or even others involved in shamanic-type work, or other experiential programmes such as Grof's holotropic breathwork) describing direct, intersubjective 'detection' of consciousness in other animals, in plants, in DNA (Narby, 1998), even in minerals (Grof, 1985).

Whitehead is clear and explicit:

> The subject–object relation takes its origin in the double role of these eternal objects. They are modifications of the subject, but only in their character of conveying aspects of other subjects in the community of the universe. Thus no individual subject can have independent reality, since it is a prehension of limited aspects of subjects other than itself (Whitehead, 1925, p. 151).

For Whitehead, then, all subjects arise in a vast network of interrelated subjects or intersubjects. What Whitehead doesn't have, something essential to Wilber, is the Great Nest or Chain of Being in addition to the Great Network of Being. For that, we would need to augment Whitehead with Aurobindo.

I agree with Wilber that Whitehead's ontology is an 'incomplete holarchy'. The levels of the Great Nest are missing. And if this is what Wilber means by 'monological', then so be it. However, he also uses 'monological' to mean something else: a reduction of all communication to exchanges between Cartesian (individual, isolated) subjects. In this case, the labels can be switched: Wilber is monological (per my critique of his 'intersubjectivity'), Whitehead is dialogical.

Wilber also uses 'monological' to mean 'flatland' — i.e., gross reduction of all levels of reality to the atomistic physical (UR), or 'subtle reductionism' to physical systems (LR). But this most definitely is not what Whitehead does. He does not reduce interiority to the physical — quite the opposite, in fact. Nor does he reduce all interiority to prehension. True, he is not as explicit about the hierarchy of interiors (per the Great Nest) as Wilber is. But this does not mean Whitehead failed to acknowledge the complexity of interiority. In *Process and Reality*, he explicitly emphasizes that the subject–object, or interior–exterior, relationship complexifies with evolution. Whitehead is very clear that the prehension of an electron is qualitatively different (a 'lower grade', to use his term) from human prehension. This is not 'flatland', and it is a serious misreading of Whitehead to say he reduces all interiority to pre-conscious prehension. Whitehead does more than explore a variety of prehensions (conceptual, hybrid, impure, negative, and physical). His philosophy of organism accounts for all the multiplicity of varieties and levels of prehension/experience/sentience/subjectivity/interiority from quanta to human beings . . . and from there to God.

Wilber's critique that Whitehead makes a big jump from humans to God is valid. This is where Whitehead misses out on the perspective of transpersonal psychologists (not surprising, since they hadn't yet appeared on the scene). Whitehead, as Wilber points out, does not account for transrational stages of interiority (except for God). And had he had access to Aurobindo's work, this very well might have rounded out his cosmology. Thankfully, we now have Wilber and others to pick up the task.[29] However, this will happen only if Wilber builds on a fair and accurate interpretation of Whitehead.

Bottom line: Whitehead no more reduces all interiority to prehension than Wilber 'elevates' all interiority to Spirit. Both recognize a spectrum of 'grades' of interiority.

---

[29] Eric Weiss is also working on a major project to integrate the works of Whitehead and Aurobindo (personal communication).

Furthermore, Wilber is on shaky ground when he questions Whitehead's relevance to transpersonal psychology/philosophy because he didn't have transpersonal experiences:

> [A]lthough some theorists (such as John Buchanan) believe that Whitehead fits the bill as the great transpersonal philosopher, I believe Whitehead fails that task in the most essential respects (much as I admire him otherwise). To give only the most obvious examples: in order to actually awaken to the nondual Kosmos, as we have seen, one must attain subject permanence (the unbroken continuity of awareness through waking, dream and sleep states). Without that as an actual yogic or contemplative accomplishment in consciousness, there is no corresponding mode of knowing that will disclose the Real. This yogic injunction, exemplar, or practice is the real transpersonal paradigm, and without it (or something similar to it) you have no authentic transpersonal anything. . . . Whitehead doesn't even come close. This is not a secondary issue; it is the precise heart of the entire matter, a heart that Whitehead completely lacks (EoS, p. 350).

It is speculation to conclude, as Wilber does, that Whitehead had no rigorous spiritual practice just because there is nothing explicit about his 'yoga' in any of his writings or in his biographies. For one thing, Whitehead was, by all accounts, a very religious, even spiritual, man who had a profound sense of the numinous, of divinity in all things. And as for lacking rigorous spiritual practice, it would be very easy to argue that he exemplified as much as anyone the path of 'jana yoga', the yoga of the intellect. To deny this as a spiritual path would amount to very unspiritual 'spiritual snobbishness'. Whitehead's entire speculative cosmology was aimed at integrating the divine and the world of nature — a true evolutionary panentheist.

Whitehead may not have had the distinctions or the language categories that arrived on the scene in the Sixties with the birth of the transpersonal movement, but that doesn't mean he didn't have (what we today call) transpersonal experiences. (In fact, in an essay published in 1948, 'Uniformity and Contingency', Whitehead describes a remarkable lucid dream [pp. 145–6].)[30] Personally, from my readings of Whitehead, I have very little doubt that he did have such experiences — and not just as 'states', but as a 'stage' or 'stages'.

The Human Consciousness Project

Up to this point, my critique of Wilber has focused on some problematic 'details' in his model — important details that, I believe, have ramifications for his cosmology as a whole. I'd now like to focus on the 'big picture', and on the practical implications of his work.

Notwithstanding some of the theoretical and logical difficulties buried in the details of Wilber's vast and comprehensive model, his overall contribution has been immense. More than any other individual, he has pieced together a truly remarkable map of the mind.

---

[30] Thanks to Eric Weiss for drawing my attention to this.

If we learn one unavoidable fact from Wilber, it's that the world of the mind, the interior life, is at least as complex and differentiated and interrelated as the immense complexities of the outer world revealed by physical sciences. Wilber's integral psychology alerts us to the baffling complexity of consciousness.

Whereas modern science tends to simplistically divide the world into outer-physical and inner-mental, and modern philosophy of mind focuses on the mind–body relationship, Wilber, drawing on a wide spectrum of psycho-spiritual disciplines and traditions, has documented and charted the immense complexity of the inner domain — not just the id, ego, and superego of psychotherapy, but a whole host of characters and developmental sets through which we play out our life's dramas (e.g., developmental levels of the self; levels/waves, structures, the navigating self; and each wave with its multiple self-streams [identity, needs, emotion, etc.]).

Wilber highlights the significance of integral psychology by proposing the intriguing idea of the 'Human Consciousness Project' (TOE, p. 7). Based on the mapping of consciousness found in cross-cultural variations of the Great Chain of Being, on the one hand, and the 'waves and streams' of consciousness mapped by Clare Graves, Don Beck and Christopher Cowan, along with Wilber's own formulation of the four quadrants, on the other, we now have a blueprint for an 'all-level, all-quadrant' model of consciousness — equivalent to, if not surpassing in scope and importance, the Human Genome Project.

As an example of the complexity involved in weaving together the Human Consciousness Project, here are just some of the streams of development Wilber identifies (following Don Beck's Spiral Dynamics) — what he calls 'self streams' that evolve through the multiple levels of the Great Chain or Nest:

> We have credible evidence that these different streams, lines, or modules include cognition, morals, self-identity, psychosexuality, ideas of the good, role taking, socioemotional capacity, creativity, altruism, several lines that can be called 'spiritual' (care, openness, concern, religious faith, meditative stages), communicative competence, modes of space and time, affect/emotion, death-seizure, needs, worldviews, mathematical competence, musical skills, kinesthetics, gender identity, defense mechanisms, interpersonal capacity, and empathy (TOE, p. 44).

In an endnote, he goes on to say, 'Individuals can be at a relatively high level of development in some modules, medium in others, and low in still others — there is nothing linear about overall development' (TOE, p. 142).

If we factor in cross-cultural differences, and attempt to map these self-developmental streams as they move, independently, through the many levels, stages, and structures of the Great Nest (Wilber identifies at least seventeen levels on the spectrum of consciousness ranging from prehension at the least developed end — through various levels of sensation, perception, emotion, symbolic, concrete operational, formal operational, to vision-logic, psychic, subtle, causal — all the way up to the nondual consciousness of full-blown enlightenment), *and* recognize that the movement of these streams flows in nonlinear loops and spirals, *and* then multiply this mind-boggling complexity by four (to accommodate the quadrants) we begin to get some idea of the immense task facing the Human

Consciousness Project. Do the math: Without factoring in cross-cultural differences, or loops or spirals, we have at least 31 streams, 17 levels, and 4 quadrants, giving us a *minimum* of 2,108 consciousness variables to track as each individual person develops his or her matrix of 'intelligences' or 'competencies' in life.

The disconcerting question, of course, is how to keep track of all this? No wonder so many of us have difficulty navigating through the maze of cognitive, emotional, behavioural, cultural, and social complexities that face us daily as we try to deal with the vagaries of life. No surprise, then, if many of us suspect that the diagnosis 'multiple personality' refers not merely to a pathology, or even to an anomaly, but to the intrinsic condition of human consciousness. How can we possibly keep up with so many developmental challenges? How can we ever learn to corral this overpopulated society of selves that is each of us? Is such a complex, multi-dimensional typology of consciousness more likely to overwhelm than enlighten us?

Once the Human Consciousness Project gets underway, we will, presumably, have a growing awareness and insight into what makes each of us 'tick' psychologically. We may be able to help individuals assess or diagnose their states and stages of consciousness as it grows and spirals throughout life. Perhaps, we may even devise psychometric tools to monitor periodic (monthly, weekly, daily, hourly?) swings in consciousness — and, even more important, develop an essential curriculum, practices that will enable people to consciously develop their own consciousness in whatever areas of the spectrum appropriate for them at any particular time.

Wilber's *Integral Psychology* (and his *Collected Works* in general) provides an impressive 'first-pass' outline for integrating the multiple disciplines engaged, one way or another, in the study of consciousness. In a manner comparable to how the Human Genome Project gave a specific focus and purpose to genetics, the Human Consciousness Project could give a pragmatic purpose and focus to the broad, and currently fragmented, field of consciousness studies. If such a project ever gets off the ground, Wilber will be, rightly, lauded for his single-minded passion and determination to create an integral foundation for the study of consciousness.[31]

---

[31] With a group of colleagues, Wilber has established a non-profit Integral Institute based in Boulder, Colorado. Interestingly, participants in that institute use the shorthand 'I-I' when referring to it. It strikes me as one of those ironic coincidences that the same acronym should be used both for Wilber's Integral Institute and (by me) for intersubjectivity — especially when the lack of true intersubjectivity is one of the weakest aspects of Wilber's four-quadrants model. It is my hope that I-I (the institute) will include 'I–I' (intersubjective) explorations of consciousness as an essential component of their work. The Boulder gatherings are themselves opportunities for such 'I–I' explorations. First reports from the meeting on Integral Psychology indicate that some awareness of the importance of non-cognitive relationship (including the value of silence) is being incorporated into the group's deliberations.

Recognizing the difference between an 'argumentative universe of discourse' and a 'dialogical universe of discourse' (Patel, 1994; Ferrer, 1998b) is crucial. I believe one of the first — and key — tasks for any rigorous 'I–I' exploration of consciousness is to address the issue of methodology. For example, is the idea of 'metrics' (to measure data or to evaluate propositions) even valid or appropriate in this domain? Native Americans (and other indigenous peoples, as well as Jamaican Rastafarians [see note 12 above]) do not typically engage in dialogue or conversation aimed at uncovering truth–falsehood values, or for getting at factual truth; rather the purpose of such dialogue is to build relationships (through sincere self-expression and genuine acknowledgement and participation in mutuality), often for therapeutic or soteriological purposes. Bohmian dialogue is one of the best modern Western 'methodologies' I'm aware of for facilitating this.

Conclusion

Questions raised in this paper about *details* in Wilber's theory of everything indicate deeper challenges to his model as a whole. To recap: As long as he restricts intersubjectivity to 'only' linguistic exchanges he leaves one quadrant vacant, and the entire structure tilts like a three-legged table. His promissory integralism as a 'solution' to the mind–body problem leaves the causal relationship between the exterior and interior domains of his quadrants an unsolved mystery. We have no idea, from Wilber, how these two fundamental domains of reality interact. His critique of Whitehead and panpsychism, and his 'categorical rejection' of the ontological significance of feeling, begs questions about emergence. We are left wondering how the jump from wholly non-feeling interiors to any kind of feeling at all could ever occur without the intervention of a miracle.

Indeed, Wilber's approach to all three issues — intersubjectivity, mind–body problem, and panpsychism — reveals an underlying problem with feeling. The felt-relational quality of the shared experience of 'We' is missing from his 'intersubjectivity'. The hard problem of explaining how feelings are in the body is left unanswered. And, as just noted, his treatment of panpsychism is founded on a categorical rejection of ontologically fundamental feeling.

As a result, for all its rational magnificence, Wilber's grand edifice has a kind of robotic quality — or, to use a favourite metaphor of philosophers of mind, it comes across as a kind of Zombie World, lacking any felt interiority. Despite Wilber's major emphasis on the importance of including interior domains, we can come away from the four quadrants feeling 'there's nobody home'.

And yet . . .

Remember he says, 'ignored truths actually reappear in the system as an internal and massive self-contradiction . . . [the] denied quadrant will in fact sneak into your system'. Emotion, a lot of it, echoes off the walls of Wilber's grand edifice when he expresses feelings about, for example, self-contradicting postmodernists, regressive Romantics, flatland ecologists, narcissistic Boomers, retro Goddess worshipers, and angry feminists. Clearly, Wilber himself is no zombie. Where, then, does he fit within his own model?

In any case, whether my critique reflects a misreading of his work (which is often his response to critics) or whether the problems I've identified are actual deficiencies in his model, further clarification from him would be a great help. The whole point of this paper is to contribute to a useful exchange and refinement of ideas.

Ken Wilber's contribution is already very valuable. The mere construction of such a magnificent intellectual edifice is itself a worthy enterprise — even if, as is inevitable at some point, cracks appear in the foundations and it begins to fall apart. For, far more valuable than the edifice is the vision that inspired it — a vision for an integral world, a world nurtured by an integral psychology, an integral philosophy and metaphysics, an integral science and spirituality, an integral economics and ecology, an integral aesthetics, an integral medicine, an integral sociology, an integral politics . . . a vision of *inclusion*, a vision of the 'whole' embraced by Spirit.

Acknowledgement

Many thanks to colleagues who read earlier drafts of this manuscript, or parts of it, and who took the time to talk or correspond with me about many of the ideas discussed here. These include: Chris Bache, John Buchanan, John David Ebert, Jorge Ferrer, Sean Hargens, Sean Kelly, David La Chapelle, Michael Mahoney, Kaisa Puhakka, Kenneth Ring, Jeffrey Sanders, RichardTarnas, Keith Thompson, Jenny Wade, and Eric Weiss.

References

Aurobindo, Sri (1939), *The Life Divine* (Pondicherry, India: Centenary Library).

Buber, M. (1970), *I and Thou*, trans. Walter Kaufmann (New York: Charles Scribner's Sons).

de Quincey, C. (1994), 'Consciousness all the way down? An analysis of McGinn's critique of pan-psychism', *Journal of Consciousness Studies*, **1** (2), pp. 217–29.

de Quincey, C. (1997), 'Evolutionary model of consciousness', *Nature of Consciousness Course Reader* (Orinda, CA: John F. Kennedy University).

de Quincey, C. (1998), 'Engaging presence', *IONS Review*, Spring 1998, **45**.

de Quincey, C. (1999a), 'Intersubjectivity: Exploring consciousness from the second-person perspective', in Hameroff *et al.* (1999).

de Quincey, C. (1999b), 'Past matter, present mind: A convergence of worldviews', *Journal of Consciousness Studies* **6** (1) pp. 91–106.

de Quincey, C. (1999b), 'Language, energy, and consciousness' (Scientific and Medical Network: www.cis.plym.ac.uk/SciMedNet/home.htm)

de Quincey, C. (2000a), 'Consciousness: Truth or Wisdom?', *IONS Review*, **51**.

de Quincey, C. (2000b), 'Conceiving the inconceivable: Fishing for consciousness with a net of miracles', *Journal of Consciousness Studies*, **7** (4), pp. 67–81.

de Quincey, C. (2000c), *Deep Spirit. Higher Consciousness: In Search of the Noetic Code* (Santa Clara, CA: MightyWords www.mightywords.com).

de Quincey, C. (in press), *Radical Nature: Consciousness All the Way Down* (Vermont: Marion Foundation Press).

Ferrer, J. (1998a), 'Speak now or forever hold your peace: A review essay of Ken Wilber's *The Marriage of Sense and Soul: Integrating Science and Religion*', *Journal of Transpersonal Psychology*, **30** (1), pp. 53–67.

Ferrer, J. (1998b), 'Beyond absolutism and relativism in transpersonal evolutionary theory', *World Futures*, **52**, pp. 239–80.

Ferrer, J. (in press), *Revisioning Transpersonal Theory: A Participatory Vision of Human Spirituality* (Albany, NY: State University of New York Press).

Gebser, J. (1985), *The Ever-Present Origin* (Athens, OH: Ohio University Press).

Griffin, D.R. (1998), *Unsnarling the World-Knot: Consciousness, Freedom, and the Mind–Body Problem* (Berkeley, CA: University of California Press).

Grof, S. (1985), *Beyond the Brain: Birth, Death and Transcendence in Psychotherapy* (Albany, NY: State University of New York Press).

Hameroff, S., Kaszniak A.W. & Chalmers, D.J. (1999), *Toward A Science of Consciousness: The Third Tucson Discussions and Debates* (Cambridge, MA: MIT Press).

Hartshorne, C. (1968), *Beyond Humanism: Essays in the Philosophy of Nature* (Lincoln, NE: University of Nebraska Press).

Humphrey, N. (1992), *A History of the Mind: Evolution and the Birth of Consciousness* (New York,: Simon and Schuster).

Koestler, A. & Smythies, J.R. (ed. 1969), *Beyond Reductionism. The Alpbach Symposium 1968: New Perspectives in the Life Sciences* (London: Hutchinson).

McGinn, C. (1999), *The Mysterious Flame: Conscious Minds in a Material World* (New York: Basic Books).

Narby, J. (1998), *The Cosmic Serpent: DNA and the Origins of Knowledge* (New York: Tarcher/Putnam).

Patel, K.C. (1994), 'The Paradox of Negation in Nagarjuna's philosophy', *Asian Philosophy*, **4**, pp. 17–32.

Rothberg, D., & Kelly, S. (ed. 1998), *Ken Wilber in Dialogue: Conversations with Leading Transpersonal Theorists* (Wheaton, IL: Quest Books).

Velmans, M. (1993), 'A reflexive science of consciousness', in *Experimental and Theoretical Studies of Consciousness* (New York: John Wiley & Sons).

Whitehead, A.N. (1979), *Process and Reality: An Essay in Cosmology*, corrected edition, ed. D.R. Griffin & D.W. Sherburne (New York: Free Press).

Whitehead, A.N. (1925), *Science and the Modern World* (New York: Free Press).

Whitehead, A.N. (1948), *Science and Philosophy* (New York: Philosophical Library).

Wilber, K. (1977), *The Spectrum of Consciousness* (Collected Works, Vol. 1; Wheaton, IL: Quest Books).

Wilber, K. (1979), *No Boundary: Eastern and Western Approaches to Personal Growth* (Collected Works, Vol. 1; Boulder, CO: Shambhala).

Wilber, K. (1980), *The Atman Project: A Transpersonal View of Human Development* (Collected Works, Vol. 2; Wheaton, IL: Quest Books).

Wilber, K. (1981), *Up From Eden: A Transpersonal View of Human Evolution* (Collected Works, Vol. 2; Wheaton, IL: Quest Books).

Wilber, K. (1982), 'In defense of Descartes', *Newsletter*, December, pp. 7–9, (San Francisco, CA: Association for Humanistic Psychology).

Wilber, K. (1983a), *Eye to Eye: The Quest for the New Paradigm* (Collected Works, Vol. 3; Boston, MA: Shambhala).

Wilber, K. (1983b), *A Sociable God* (Collected Works, Vol. 3; New York: New Press/ McGraw-Hill).

Wilber, K. (ed. 1984), *Quantum Questions: Mystical Writings of the World's Great Physicists* (Boston, MA: Shambhala).

Wilber, K. (1991*), Grace and Grit: Spirituality and Healing in the Life and Death of Treya Killam Wilber* (Collected Works, Vol. 5; Boston, MA: Shambhala).

Wilber, K. (1995), *Sex, Ecology, Spirituality: The Spirit of Evolution* (Collected Works, Vol. 6; Boston, MA: Shambhala).

Wilber, K. (1996), *A Brief History of Everything* (Collected Works, Vol. 7; Boston, MA: Shambhala).

Wilber, K. (1997), *Eye of Spirit: An Integral Vision for a World Gone Slightly Mad* (Collected Works, Vol. 7; Boston, MA: Shambhala).

Wilber, K. (1998), *The Marriage of Sense and Soul: Integrating Science and Religion* (Collected Works, Vol. 8;. Boston, MA: Shambhala).

Wilber, K. (1999), *One Taste: The Journals of Ken Wilber* (Collected Works, Vol. 8; Boston, MA: Shambhala).

Wilber, K. (1999–2000), *Collected Works*, Volumes 1–8 (Boston, MA: Shambhala).

Wilber, K. (2000a), *Integral Psychology: Consciousness, Spirit, Psychology, Therapy* (Boston. MA: Shambhala).

Wilber, K. (2000b), *A Theory of Everything: An Integral Vision for Business, Politics, Science, and Spirituality* (Boston, MA: Shambhala).

Wilber, K., Engler, J. & Brown, D.P. (1986), *Transformations of Consciousness: Conventional and Contemplative Perspectives on Development* (Collected Works, Vol.4; Boston, MA: Shambhala).

James H. Austin

Consciousness Evolves When the Self Dissolves

We need to clarify at least four aspects of selfhood if we are to reach a better understanding of consciousness in general, and of its alternate states.

First, how did we develop our self-centred psychophysiology? Second, can the four familiar lobes of the brain alone serve, if only as preliminary landmarks of convenience, to help understand the functions of our many self-referent networks? Third, what could cause one's former sense of self to vanish from the mental field during an extraordinary state of consciousness? Fourth, when a person's physical and psychic self do drop off briefly, how has conscious experience then been transformed? In particular, what happens to that subject's personal sense of time?

Our many-sided self arose in widely distributed brain networks. Since infancy, these self-oriented circuits have been over-conditioned by limbic biases. Selfhood then seems to have evolved along lines suggesting at least in shorthand the operations of a kind of 'I–Me–Mine' complex.

*But what happens when this egocentric triad briefly dissolves? Novel states of consciousness emerge. Two personally-observed states are discussed: (1) insight-wisdom (kensho-satori); (2) internal absorption. How do these two states differ phenomenologically? The physiological processes briefly suggested here emphasize shifts in deeper systems, and pivotal roles for **thalamo**-cortical interactions in the front and back of the brain.*

Can our waking consciousness lose its strong sense of self? To some readers, this notion may seem counter-intuitive, if not preposterous. Yet, sages have attested to this curious idea for many centuries. And, in a new millennium, scholars from several disciplines are asking: What does happen, and why, when a wide-awake brain shifts suddenly into a major state of 'no-self'?

Journal of Consciousness Studies, **7**, No. 11–12, 2000, pp. 209–30

I: The Self As A Psychological Construct;
A Resource Needing Improvement

The personal imperative thrusts up from deep within. To William James, sensory messages from our head and body were the perceptual nucleus of our private, physical self. As we grow older, we can identify other 'layers' of the self: thoughts, concepts, emotions, and instincts. These layers blend cognitive and urgent affective properties. They seem to fall into a *'psychic'* category, to be *non*-sensory in scope. At the level of descriptive psychology, it helps to over-simplify these physical and psychic themes of our self. For the purposes of our discussion, we can visualize three main interactive components in operation:

I, Me and *Mine*

But this *I–Me–Mine* triad has its vexing, dysfunctional side (Austin, 1998). For yes, our sovereign *I* is (proudly) aware that its physical body exists and acts in space. But its basic attitude remains that of an arrogant 'busy-body.' Prone to meddle and to over-do, in all its doing, it can 'do no wrong'.

In contrast, our *Me* occupies the tender butt-end of the self. This *Me* can get kicked around. It is fearful, easily threatened, and suffers accordingly. Our *Mine* is readily captured by its greedy longings to possess other people and to covet material goods. In addition, it owns firm opinions. And cherishes them.

Zen Buddhism emphasizes an in-depth, insightful approach to understanding this complex, deluded self. The Zen meditative Path begins by sponsoring a clear, composed alertness (Austin, 2001). It encourages introspection, discernment, and a series of lesser realizations. This is a decades-long, incremental training process. But sudden, major, brief, insightful states greatly facilitate it.

Over the years, both agencies of change reinforce each other. Many maladaptive traits of the earlier self fade away. The person's energies are increasingly liberated from unfruitful conditioning and from outworn habit patterns. A lower profile emerges: an i–me–mine. A more genuine self.

If this idealized outcome had to be condensed in elementary *a-b-c* terms, then one might describe the acts of this newly-emerging i as more *a*ware, more *a*uthentic and *a*ccommodating. This evolved me becomes more *b*uoyant, resilient. Slowly, this mine starts to open outward, becoming more *c*ompassionate to others.

II: Some Physiological Sources of Selfhood

Many physiological sub-systems generate our multifaceted self. Elsewhere, we discuss how these systems, when integrated, are associated with selfhood's assets and liabilities (Austin, 1998, pp. 147–290). But this paper begins, for the convenience of the general reader, by surveying only certain brain functions. And it will view them initially from a more familiar perspective: that of the four lobes comprising each cerebral hemisphere (*Figure 1*).

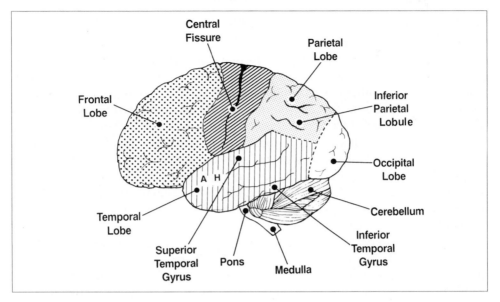

Figure 1. The left cerebral hemisphere, lateral view

The prefrontal cortex occupies most of the convex dotted surface of the frontal lobe. In front of the central fissure, the crosshatched area represents the primary motor cortex; that behind it represents the primary somatosensory cortex. In back, the dotted lines suggest approximate boundaries between the temporal, parietal and occipital lobes. Near the front of the temporal lobe, the letters 'A' and 'H' are used to suggest the deeper sites of the amygdala and hippocampus. Hidden from view are the other limbic regions, thalamus, and basal ganglia, buried deep in each hemisphere. Medulla and pons represent the lowest two regions of the brainstem.

A complexity enters once we turn to alternate states of consciousness. Zen uses the technical terms, *kensho* or *satori*, to refer to the deeper, more advanced of these major 'peak experiences'. The abrupt flash of its insight-wisdom (termed prajna) is symbolized by a sword. Why? Because the old egocentric self seems to have been cut off. Viscerally. Briefly. But for a seemingly timeless interval.

Only a greatly-pruned i–me–mine will first emerge from kensho's brief catharsis of self. And no such 'sword-cut' respects a brain's lobar boundaries. So, why focus here on such brief dissolutions of selfhood, if they prove mostly temporary? For two reasons: (1) the metaphor is accurate; (2) the way these brief dissolutions efface one's rigid old boundaries can shed light on how our human consciousness first develops, on how it awakens, and on how it evolves, suddenly and slowly, during long processes of personal transformation.

Because one cerebral lobe also contains two limbic regions linked to the emotional side of the psychic self, our survey begins with this temporal lobe.

Please note that this paper can cite only two of the temporal lobe's diverse functions: the ways it helps personalize our constructs of space and of time. Soon one wonders: If personal constructs in space and time drop out, how does consciousness change?

A. Temporal lobe contributions to our physical and psychic self, in space

1. The Outer Temporal Cortex. Temporal lobe circuits help recognize and interpret patterns. In short, they respond to questions of the *'What* is it?' variety. Example: *'What* is that person saying to me?' Yet beyond mere words, temporal lobe circuits make other covert comparisons. These help establish a vast conceptual interface. Along it, we keep interpreting our private experiences of 'self' as separate from 'other'. (As if 'wave' escaped from being part of ocean). Our split between self/, and /other, becomes only one of countless dualities. Using such barriers we categorize items and events as being good/bad, young/old, this/that, etc. And, as if this weren't enough, our temporal-limbic circuits invest each pair of dualities with a 'load' of conditioned affective resonances. These emotional polarities (+/−) strongly bias perception. When refracted through the charged layers of such distortions, who sees the real world clearly?

(a) *Some egocentric physiologies.* Up in a monkey's superior temporal gyrus, certain nerve cells fire only when one particular object is viewed, such as the head of another monkey. Moreover, these cells will fire only if this other head is seen from a special perspective: from that point of view which refers its line of sight back to the head of this *observing* monkey (Perrett *et al.,* 1991).

So, the firings of these temporal nerve cells both establish and maintain this *egocentric* construct: their very 'own' observing monkey's head is the standard 'physical' observation site for an implicit self-referent point of view.

Farther down, in the perirhinal cortex of the inferior temporal gyrus are pattern recognition functions. They help the monkey recognize, say, that the fruit it sees is indeed a banana (Buckley and Gaffan, 1998).

2. The Hippocampal Formation. This sensitive limbic region of ancient lineage lies curled up in the innermost part of the temporal lobe. The hippocampus itself is one sub-region of the rest of this formation.

(a) *Egocentric and allocentric systems of orientation.* In the primate hippocampus, special 'place cells' receive messages distilled from much larger perceptual systems (Rolls, 1999). The input from each such system helps localize signals entering from sites in the outside world. But one set of place cells, termed egocentric, uses coordinates based on self-centred criteria. Like some compass needle designed to point internally, the codes of these cells reinforce the sense of a physical self. Why? Because they too relate back to the central physical site and position of the head, eyes and body of the observing monkey.

The contrasting cells and systems are called *allocentric.* (Nothing esoteric. Dictionaries simply define *allo-* as implying that one's interest and attention are centered *outside* oneself.) Note: these 'allo'-place cells seem coded to represent a kind of *selfless,* external 'view'. They process details in 'space *out there*' (Rolls, 1999). Why just out there? Because their larger allocentric networks send them only 'impersonal' sensory cues. These percepts originated just with reference to sites in the external world. Normally, of course, the two categories of associative networks work together. Their egocentric/allocentric blend becomes a kind of biological 'global positioning system' (GPS). This merger underlies our larger sense of inhabiting a distinct personal place within a matrix of 'non-personal' space. The associative links of the 'GPS' also become a framework on which to hang one's memories. And so we remember: It was *this* spot where *that* defining event occurred.

Could some major dissociative event separate these two categories of 'GPS' functions? If so, it might help us realize how much each construct itself brings up to that vast interface along which we still tend at one level or another to regard our own 'inside' self as split off from that 'other' world outside.

3. The Amygdala. Each amygdala is buried farther forward inside the medial temporal lobe. Its limbic nuclei add much to the intimate emotional 'charges' that condition the psychic self. For example, our normal amygdala makes early, major contributions both to: (a) the primary experience of fear (Fish *et al.*, 1993); and (b) to the processes by which we learn to avoid unpleasant consequences [aversive conditioned learning] (Buchel *et al.*, 1998; Morris *et al.*, 1998). It also enters into social judgments. We soon learn to decipher which emotion (+, –) is expressed on another person's face (Adolphs *et al.*, 1998). Paths from the amygdala relay its affective resonances both to the cerebrum and brainstem. Circuits descending from the amygdala comprise the core of our fearfulness and defensive responses. These deeper modules include not only the ventromedial hypothalamus, but the central grey of the brainstem and the norepinephrine-releasing cells of the locus coeruleus in the upper pons (Caldji *et al.*, 1998).

4. The Over-Conditioned Self. What do these various affective and visceral links bring to our self/other interface? A mixed bag. Liabilities, not only assets. For these networks shape our hidden biased opinions, attitudes and expectations. Many links go back, at subconscious depths, to childhood fears and delusions.

Most persons remain unaware of how much their personalities had been shaped by the patterns of these positive (+), and negative (–), affective valences. Meditators learn to examine each specific situation that causes them to blush with shame, flush with anger, glow with pride, blanch with fear, clutch with desire. Unfortunately, our own limbic systems seem designed to amplify these conditioned responses to dysfunctional levels. Do we humans really 'rattle our own cages' so disadvantageously?

During operations, Gloor has studied how patients respond while their temporal lobes are being stimulated. When does a percept 'ring'? When does it really get *intimate*, penetrate internally with compelling experiential immediacy? Not when the electrode stimulates surface sites over the temporal cortex. But only when the deep limbic structures are excited directly, or when they become excited, secondarily, as an evoked seizure discharge spreads (Gloor, 1990).

5. Personal Time. On a galactic time clock, only during the last few seconds have such subjective limbic biases shaped the ways a conscious brain reacts. And, as far as one knows, before nerve networks evolved here on planet Earth, no word label existed that tried to represent the whole Ageless, Ultimate, Universal Reality. Only in recent hominid cultures were brains conditioned to split up their notions about such a cosmic 'Oneness' into seemingly separate abstract categories. Before symbolic language arose here, any inclusive Yahweh-God-Tao-Nature had remained nameless, indivisible, undifferentiated, limitless.

Some capitalized words in the above paragraph might suggest not only an infinite cosmos but also a timelessness, a perpetuity, an eternity. The terms point toward the ways the brain interprets time. This second frame of reference means our personal sense of time, not time in the abstract. It seems not yet fully appreciated that two temporal lobe phenomena (which are very common) can tell us much about how we split our sense of the present from our sense of the past.

6. What Do Déjà vu and Jamais Vu Imply for Our Usual Sense of Time? Most normal people will experience brief illusions of *déjà vu*. Things being seen 'now' seem familiar. The sense is: 'Yes, I've *already* seen this before.' Ordinary déjà vu episodes are eloquent whispers, carrying a threefold message: (a) many potential instabilities reside within the medial temporal lobe; (b) one medial temporal function is to help us respond to the nuances, if any, between events in present time and past time; (c) even some minor cerebral event, such as a little sleep loss, can briefly dissolve that barrier which had once consigned a previous episode to a compartment separate from this present moment.

My temporal lobe used to be vulnerable to the loss of sleep. Sleep loss unveiled its low threshold for déjà vu episodes. However, déjà vu experiences can also occur in patients whose focal seizures start in the temporal lobe. Moreover, stimulating the amygdala or hippocampus also prompts them. Again, sites over the outer temporal cortex are not as productive (Fish *et al.*, 1993).

The 'positive' (yes) resonances of déjà vu have a 'negative' counterpart. This contrasting visual experience is termed *jamais vu*: literally, 'No, I've *never* seen this before.' Things seen now seem unfamiliar, strange. fMRI studies are still untangling the ways we resolve such complex decisions (Henson *et al.*, 1999).

Because complexities reside in the omni-self, we tag an event in time not only based on its exterior context, but on an interior premise: Where *we* were as self-referent observers. This implicit self inserts an autobiographical frame of reference. PET scan studies suggest that some modules of this personal omni-self reside within the temporal lobe, more so on the right (Austin, 1998, pp. 247–53).

7. Can Such Ordinary Temporal Lobe Functions Be Relevant to Brief Extra- Ordinary, Insightful States of Consciousness? Old frameworks of one's pejorative self seem to drop off during a major transformative state. Though our survey of the omni-self has only just begun, yet parts I and II already suggest that aspects of one's personal space and time may be two facets of consciousness vulnerable to change.

(a) Dissolutions of self-in-*space*. Start with those spatial reference systems, coded to represent a personal ego-self placed inside, in relation to the 'other' world outside. Given that each normally draws on an extensive matrix of spatial coordinates distributed throughout many brain regions. Now let us suppose that a deep 'seismic' shift occurs, suddenly releasing a cascade of linked physiological processes. And that such processes could seem to 'dissolve' *only* the usual 'inside' psychic conditionings plus their loosely associated physical referents just from the personalized, egocentric 'inside' of that former space.

The author has undergone one such kensho experience (Austin, 1998, pp. 536–42; 1999). What had become of his usual subliminal premise? An instant before, it appeared to have represented the bulk of his habitual subjective self-image inside his self/other boundary, while it also co-represented the other objective 'allo-world' as having other properties displaced outside it. What was being viewed, if there was no such 'inside'?

In this state of kensho, only the 'other' correlates seemed to occupy his field of awareness. They still expressed the detailed form and content of the 'outside' setting. You might wonder: Didn't this state prompt a psychic identity crisis? True, this residual mental field was 'depersonalized'. Yes, it had lost its central experiencing axis of self, for one timeless moment. But no crisis arose. Why not? Because no longer was this 'other, outside' world — though now *un*-conditioned — being viewed in the same old habitual, mundane manner.

Awareness awakened to THIS world, transfigured. Each and all of its basic elements, now perceived afresh, seemed exempt from any desires and distortions of my old intrusive self. One might speculate: is it just the basic allocentric systems underlying consciousness, when their percepts are unveiled, that yield the impression of being directly in touch with the more intrinsic qualities of 'other' things?

How can a brain's basic level of awareness become so awakened to the sense of 'all things as *they* really are'? When can all things seem fully present, *in themselves*? Not, it would appear, until consciousness drops off the former 'inside' self and all of its subjective attachments. Two key words emphasize the non-subjective, uniquely 'objective' qualities of this awakening.

The first is *anatta*. Buddhists reserve this technical term for an anonymous state of no-self. In Zen, it means *non-I*. And, in the writings of D.T. Suzuki, we find the second word: '*Suchness*'. It refers to this curious sense of 'things as they really are' (Austin, 1998, pp. 549–53). Suchness perceives both the comprehensive scope and the individual threads of THIS world's rich tapestry.

Suzuki concluded that suchness was 'the basis of all religious experience'. It certainly is an essential ingredient of that extraordinary, deeper state of insight-wisdom described as kensho or satori in Zen traditions. Unfortunately for clarity in communication, the deep structure of this impression of non-dual, unconditioned reality can be realized only by directly experiencing this insight.

(b) Dissolutions of self-in-*time*. As noted in item 6, above, brain functions can be vulnerable in the way they estimate 'time' relationships. Let us again suppose that 'seismic' processes closely related to those in (a) above have also dissolved these time-tagging codes that had formerly split personal time into its present/past, now/then pairs. Some readers, still curious, may wonder: During kensho, what did happen to this author's personal memories, his private sense of time past? Solely by way of illustration, let us imagine that you will be invited — more than once — to look 'into' this state of consciousness. Your role will be that of an impartial, outside witness.

So your own consciousness won't be changing. You'll still be peering at the scene through your usual semantic 'window'. It will keep defining your own sense of the 'now' within its normal 'time frame'. And this physiological constraint limits your own sense of 'present time' to a fleeting instant, normally perhaps only three-seconds-or-so wide (Hasse *et al.*, 1998).

As you enter such an alternate state, why would you sense the need to move to a vantage point out on the leading edge of your own present time? And why, once there, would you turn to take a slightly retrospective stance? Because you anticipate you'll need to look back, at an angle, beyond one window frame. Only from this position could you glimpse that marginal region where events of the author's present moment were fading away into his own distant historical past. But remember: kensho is an extraordinary state. Its previous occupant had just been rendered anonymous. What could you bear witness to? What would seem to remain, far off in that reverse direction toward 'then', in this special state which had dropped off his personal past? Nothing. The former occupant's sense of 'time past' had vanished into an indefinable vacancy, an emptiness.

B. Parietal lobe contributions to the sensate constructs of a physical self

Our parietal circuits pay close attention to '*Where?*' questions. For example: '*Where* is that apple?' True, outside stimuli inform many of our parietal visual, auditory and tactile functions. But other circuits, more inturned, address such specific queries as: 'Where are the parts of my own physical body, my hand, my fingers?' Our parietal lobe responds to that last intimate question by attending to personal messages from the 'inside'. It can register the precise positions of our bodies' muscles, joints and tendons. Hence the term proprioceptive stimuli, meaning one's own. The parietal lobe integrates these, our internal, sources of information with sensate data entering from the outside. Now this embodied brain 'knows' how far to reach to grasp that apple on the table.

Farther back, beyond the primary somatosensory cortex, parietal association circuits become even more sophisticated. Here, parietal functions mesh both with visual associations from the occipital lobes and with pattern recognition messages from the temporal lobes. Striking new supra-modal functions emerge from this cross-modal mosaic: topographical skills used to read Braille; cognitive skills that enable us to reconnoitre with the aid of a map, etc.

Anatomists may split the posterior parietal cortex into its superior and inferior divisions (*Figure 1*). Yet, physiologically, their meldings occur seamlessly, and so preconsciously that one takes them for granted. But suppose a person suffers an acute stroke, or a discrete penetrating injury. And this damage is confined just to the uppermost region, also known as the superior parietal lobule.

1. The Superior Parietal Lobule (Area 7 of Brodmann) Let us first inquire: What drops out when this upper lobule is damaged only on the right side? For these patients are no longer aware: (a) of the left side of their own body, and (b) of items outside them in left extrapersonal space. Moreover, neurological examination reveals that the patients have also lost other three-dimensional skills: (a) they can't tell where and how their own left body parts are articulated; (b) they can't locate, re-image and re-construct external objects — now relying on memory — that were once out in their left half of external space.

Detailed neuropsychological tests were recently reported on a rare patient. Her slowly progressive focal damage was limited, on MRI scan, to both posterior superior parietal lobules (Stark *et al.*, 1996). Because right and left lobules were involved, she could reconstruct no accurate representation in three dimensions of any item off in either side of the visual or auditory space outside her body.

Bedside examination also disclosed a marked loss of proprioception. She could not position her own body in space. Nor could she tell where either arm or leg was. The authors concluded that she had suffered a primary loss of her egocentric 'spatial representation system'. She had lost her normal, private topographical 'master map'. It had once informed her precisely where her body's physical parts were articulated. Note: Normally, many sensory messages, before they can rise up to inform a person's superior lobules, must first pass through the 'gates' of the thalamus.

2. The Inferior Parietal Lobule (Chiefly Areas 39 and 40 of Brodmann). Nothing is 'inferior' about this large region of strategic crossroads (*Figure 1*). Here, among the diverse connections of its supramarginal and angular gyri, the brain elaborates upon at least two additional categories of associations. Each is involved in the ways we relate our inside self to the outside world.

(a) Symbolic functions. Among the more obvious are our familiar, left-lateralized language-related skills, as well as the Braille, and map-reading examples cited above. Our many other similar polymodal and supramodal skills seem to proceed automatically, with no conscious effort. However, if such complex functions are to be effective during task situations, we must also keep them 'on line' for many seconds. In this regard, the inferior lobule takes on a crucial role.

(b) Attentive Functions. 'Attention' is a word often used to summarize this second key category of integrative processes. Again, however, it must first be noted that our several skills at 'paying attention' depend on hierarchies of interactive networks. These pathways link brainstem-subcortex-cortex in both directions.

William James once regarded our ability to focus attention as the very root of judgment, character and will. More recently, researchers have monitored a monkey's brain during such an attentive task: here its goal is to focus its vision on just one spot in outside space. At this juncture, specialized nerve cells now fire actively in its inferior parietal cortex. What shapes their firing? Once again, they fire with reference to lines of sight based on self-centered cues. Their egocentric coordinates, in turn, refer back to the positions of both the head and eyes of the observing monkey as it gazes out at this spot. (Anderson *et al.*, 1985). PET scans of humans confirm that this parietal module of 'on-line' external attention also arises within the inferior parietal lobule. Here, the active site lateralizes to the right supramarginal gyrus (in Brodmann area 40). But it also has a 'willing' partner, a frontal lobe correlate. For when a person voluntarily sustains external attention on more complex tasks [now termed 'intention'], PET activity lateralizes to the right middle frontal gyrus (in Brodmann area 46) (Johannsen *et al.*, 1997).

C. Frontal lobe contributions to concepts of the physical and psychic self

Our frontal lobes orient us toward personal time in a different way. They help us respond to such questions as: 'What *should I do* about it?' Noting how frontal functions often seem to help us weigh options at high levels of abstraction and behavior, some suggest that they are 'executive' in nature. Yet again, in any such hierarchical role, one views them as orchestrating the responses of a vast interactive consortium (Austin, 1998, pp. 253–9).

The frontal lobes, extending their reach through subcortical and brainstem regions, exemplify the brain's remarkable 'associative fluency'. Which other useful attributes does this instant flexibility confer? Our normal skills in dividing attention (Johannsen *et al.*, 1997); our facile shifting of mental sets; judgment; intuition; will; impulse control; social conscience; etc. Can we relate these normal 'frontal' lobe nuances to the two big temporal lobe issues that were raised before in 7 (a) and 7 (b): selflessness and timelessness?

There is room here to cite only four pertinent frontal lobe correlates, and to condense these topic areas under the following four headings: 1. Sequencing events in time; 2. Scenarios for action; 3. Self-conscious awareness and introspection; 4. Autobiographical themes at high levels of organization.

1. Frontal Contributions to the Ways We Normally Sequence Recent Events. Time passes swiftly. It seems to move in one direction. Hence the old term, 'the arrow of time'.

Let us adopt this arrow metaphor. But as a model, it will first prove useful to 'aim' it back toward that earlier discussion of temporal lobe functions, as begun in IIA 6. For in those normal decisions of the already?/never? type, each of us is making dynamic retrospective estimates. We ask our own memory stores: 'Does this event in the present moment match an instance in *(my) time past*?'

So, in accord with the model of time's arrow just illustrated above, let us first return to gaze back along the kind of normal now/then interface which everyone shares. Again, we'll be directing our gaze at an angle. In this instance, off to the left. For we're now representing those oldest layers of historical events in our own retrograde memory as being off to the arrow's left. *Normally*, what might we expect to see at this arrow's farthest end, way off in the left distance?

The arrow's notch. Let this notch represent the farthest back anyone can remember. From that remote horizon of our personal time, the scope of our normal viewing could also extend up the arrow-shaft. Each new incident will then 'line up' in a file more to the right, toward the ever-advancing margin of this present moment.

We're poised next to inquire: Can this arrow metaphor also illustrate how our *frontal* lobes render one special kind of decision about time? For they do enable a normal brain to make recency decisions about time sequences (Austin, 1998, pp. 557–60). You might conduct a preliminary test of your own recency judgement skills as follows. Let an arrow whiz past your usual three-second 'window of now'. You watch it fly from left to right, and vanish from sight.

Now consider what you might report, if someone were to ask you: 'Which parts of the arrow did you see *last*, most recently?' Three sites along the rear of time's arrow will figure prominently in your judgments.

Your correct answers will tend to unfold in this sequence: Notch, most recently. Feathers, recently. Rest of shaft, more remotely, etc. This task requests you to assign top priority to 'most recently', not to 'earliest'. 'Recently' implies that you must have filed each fresh, successively most recent detail into its correct position, threaded on some 'time-line' equating subtly with distance. Our frontal sequencing operations are more complex than those easier hunches about then/now, at least the ones which have temporal lobe correlates.

2. Frontal Lobe Contributions to Action Scenarios, with Special Reference to Our Subconscious 'Doing-time'. Now we're getting to the point. For the frontal lobes also go on to project prospective scenarios. These hint at where time's arrowhead might land way off to the right, in our dimension of future time.

Why are the arrow's outlines interrupted as they approach the tip? To suggest that, in fact, our 'future time' sense is *not real*. Still, one feels driven to make plans for this imaginary realm. Here, covert instinctual urges and desires contend with fearful fantasies. Fruitful foresights? These are relatively rare.

(a) Ordinary kinds of '*doing-time*'. Future time has hidden subtleties. The phrase, 'doing-time,' helps conceptualize these silent functions. 'Doing-time' sums up some vital operations of a widely distributed personal clock. It reflects frontal-parietal interactions with subcortical motor systems. What does 'doing-time' accomplish? Over a lifetime, it has made incidental notations. Its files record: *I* can *do* this much in a split-second. We are not aware of this future-oriented file. Not until it surfaces — survival value personified — instantly informing us: Dash this fast across the next wide street, or you'll get run over.

(b) The extraordinary state of kensho: two openings toward timelessness. During the initial discussion of time, back in part IIA 7 (b), you were first invited into one aspect of kensho. You witnessed how the author's vacancy of self-in-time was associated with a *retrograde* time loss. Using the visual metaphor of 'time's arrow', let us now regard that former gap as referable to the back portions of an arrow of time. Under those circumstances, its *left* parts will have vanished.

Now let us suppose that the three, just-cited, future-time functions also drop off. So, not only is there that major gap off to the left, but these three *forward projections* of time have also vanished: its layers of time-sequencing; its prospective scenarios that must keep envisioning plans for future time; its covert measures of doing-time. We had just regarded these normal, prospective correlates of frontal lobe functions as extending off to the arrow's *right*.

You now witness the full extent of this extraordinary state. Its two outer limits have lapsed into timeless vacancies: no notch back there during infancy, and no feathered interval. No markings along a shaft. No arrowhead pointing off into the future. No arrow. No archer. No willful obligation to any destination.

Instantly, the former subjective sense of 'time' has become doubly open- ended. Nothing retrospective on the left. Nothing prospective on the right. And what about the subject's former 'window of now'? It, too, seems to have expanded in both directions. Because those two limiting sides of any 'time-frame' that might once have constrained this interval seem also to have opened out into perpetuity.

What impression remains when every dimension of subjective time dissolves? Various languages substitute mere abstractions for this beginningless past, timeless present, and endless future. In English, the flavour of such (directionless) words points toward:

$$\ldots . e . . t . . e . . r . . n . . i . . t . . y \ldots .$$

3. Frontal Lobe Contributions to Our Ordinary Self-Conscious Awareness and Introspections. Human beings have a remarkable capacity to introspect. The phrase, 'I think, therefore I am', exemplifies concepts that are essentially 'psychic' in nature. How do our usual abstract 'turnings inward' arise? Most similar notions appear to emerge into thought-full elaborations farther forward in the brain. Their high-level exchanges seem to be more intricate than the sensory percepts and physical self-images referable to the brain's back half.

Can such introspections help to diagnose one's errors and resistances, support one's steps toward self-improvement? If so, under what circumstances? During quiet meditative settings, conducive to calmness, clarity, and resolve.

(a) Meditative introspections and intuitions: challenges for the neurosciences. Meditative training helps to encourage more of these quiet pauses. Calm moments of 'letting go' do permit lesser-known facets of the self to drift up, spontaneously, into awareness. Identified in clarity, our dysfunctions can now be responded to more objectively. By an 'evenly hovering attention', as Freud once said. Insights that rise spontaneously from such introspections do become the focal point for our active, constructive, voluntary efforts to change.

In this arena, the neurosciences have yet to live up to their promise. For only a major interdisciplinary agenda can define: (1) the different styles and depths of meditation; (2) the psychophysiological mechanisms underlying our minor introspections and intuitions; (3) their usual cyclic variations; (4) how brain and body, reacting to adversity, shift further into extraordinary insightful states of consciousness; (5) how behavior is subsequently transformed (Austin, 1998).

4. Frontal Lobe Input into Our High-Level Organization of Autobiographical Themes. Consider this situation: Suppose you are now invited to write the story of your life. Which skills would you need? Can you select just the relevant, self-defining moments out of your retrograde memory? Will you stick to your goal? True, your prefrontal cortex would remain active, helping both to keep your best intentions on line and to generate some broad, flexible algorithms. Yet, key historical details require frontal networking through many other modules.

Thus, you might find crucial facets of your omni-self coded among, say: the para-limbic association nuclei in the thalamus; their connections with standard limbic circuitry (Hodges and McCarthy, 1993); the personal memory templates of the anterior and inferior temporal cortex (Austin, 1998, pp. 187, 248, 739); let alone at websites among those egocentric/allocentric frameworks already discussed.

Is one's psychic selfhood so widely represented? Recent reports confirm that, yes, only patients who have certain brain lesions at *several* sites will lose the prior sense of their private identity (Kapur, 1997). In this select group of patients, the disorder of memory takes the form of a dense, only retrograde, autobiographical amnesia.

Several plausible theories arise from such reports. The following comments briefly summarize a few of the normal ways we appear to have developed our self-centred personal memory systems, and then proceed to use them:

(a) We represent the elementary, discrete *features* of each important past event (in a form loosely termed 'engrams' and 'percepts') at local sites chiefly in those particular association regions which closely link our cortex with its thalamic affiliates;

(b) Simultaneously, we also represent each discrete itemized event in terms of its general *context*. To do so, as was discussed above, we employ other codes including those for space, time and affective meaning. These codes specify the overall contextual frames of reference. And among the sites serving to '*index*' these contextual codes are the inferior and anterior parts of the temporal lobe.

(c) Later, we can use interactive retrieval systems to access these various 'feature sites' and their 'index sites for context'. Current concepts suggest that most such retrieval systems will function under the 'direction' of circuits chiefly in the front of the cerebrum (Levine *et al.*, 1998).

III: Could a Thalamic 'Gate' Shut Down Such Contributions to the Self?

Few readers would be inclined to accept, *a priori*, the suppositions and speculations put forth throughout Part II. Lesions aside, the issue is: can any known physiological processes actually divest the omni-self from the vital brain functions just ascribed to our temporal, parietal and frontal lobes? Yet still spare (as kensho does) one's ongoing awareness and memory for this brief experience?

Academicians tend to emphasize 'higher' cognitive functions. And most current neuroimaging technologies also have their higher degrees of resolution still programmed toward functional events that might seem to take place up in 'cortex' *per se*. In Part III, if only to begin to redress any such imbalance, let us now survey a few other dynamic processes that may tend to be neglected. Accordingly, many issues next to be discussed will become oriented toward the thalamus and the deeper '*non*-lobar' systems that interact with cortex, not cortex *per se* (Grenier *et al.*, 1998).

For example, every twenty-four hours, a set of *normal* physiological mechanisms does create a major blockade in our brains. A thin layer of cells, a mere 'cap' on the thalamus, quietly disrupts the otherwise orderly way the thalamus relays its impulses up to cortex (Austin, 1998, pp. 267–71). These pivotal cells are the GABA neurons of the reticular nucleus. Their complex firing properties interact, in a reciprocal manner, with those of the cortex above.

How was this discovered? Neurophysiologists found that a gross sensory blockade developed in the back of the cerebrum each time the normal brain became drowsy, and drifted down toward its state of resting, slow wave sleep. But did this thalamic cap of GABA cells also become 'drowsy' as consciousness waned? No. These reticular nucleus cells now began to fire in very fast, prolonged bursts. Their long bursts blocked incoming sensory impulses, then en route from the deeper sensory relay nuclei, from rising up to reach the cortex. So the back half of the cortex no longer received its usual sensate information coming from the head and body. The thalamic 'gate' had shut down.

Viewed solely in physiological terms, this deep blockade is comparable with a state of sensory deprivation. A state so profound that it could render a person both blind and deaf. A state that would also cut off the subject's parietal lobe from receiving its proprioceptive input. In part IIB, we saw how much this can contribute normally to the sensate impressions of one's *physical* self-image.

This normal descent into sleep is noteworthy for one other reason. Certain of its sensory-deprived aspects resemble internal absorption. Space limits us to merely mention two properties of this second, less-advanced, category of alternate states of consciousness.[1] First, internal absorption serves to remind us that a totally-conscious, meditating subject can also undergo a somewhat similar loss: namely a loss of those *physical* 'sensibilities of self' that have been perceptually-based (Austin, 1998, pp. 503–6). (Note how this preliminary state contrasts with that loss of the *psychic* self which occurs in the later state of kensho). In brief, absorption implies a '*dearth*' of (only) the physical constructs of self. We tend to think of these normal, sensate-based functions as chiefly referable to the back half of the cerebrum (eg: IIB).

Second, absorption's other feature is its distinctive hyper-awareness. It is plausible to consider that absorption's extraordinary excitatory state of awareness reflects an early link in that causal chain of events which can go on to dissolve the subject's usual sense of a physical self-image. Such causal mechanisms, while

---

[1]   A detailed personal account is given elsewhere (Austin, 1998, pp. 469–73)

merely alluded to in parts IIIA 1 and 2, below, are expanded on elsewhere (Austin, 1998, pp. 589–90).

It is an unusual chain of events which links a state of hyperawareness with deafferentation. Indeed, this sequence just proposed for internal absorption seems quite different from the usual permissive chain of events underlying our familiar waking state. For during normal waking, the GABA nerve cells of the reticular nucleus are *less* active and fire relatively slowly. This leaves the thalamic 'gate' more widely open. Now, messages flow up in a more reliable linear manner between the dorsal tier of the thalamic nuclei and their corresponding cortical affiliates farther up in the association cortex (Buchanan *et al.*, 1997). The reticular cap, poised as it is over the medialdorsal nucleus, is ready to modulate many other operations of the whole pre-frontal cortex. How much these interactions can profoundly influence the form and content of human consciousness seems not yet to be fully appreciated (Guillery *et al.*, 1998).

A. Five ways to modify the functions of this thalamic reticular nucleus

The functions of this thin wafer of GABA cells have been shown, over three decades of research, to resonate through thalamo-cortical circuits in a highly complex manner (Steriade *et al.*, 1996). Our survey limits itself to how this large circuitry can function more like a 'shield' than a 'sieve'. For in this regard, the GABA nerve cells also fire — this time in their long, powerful, 'shielding', fast bursting mode — under two additional basic conditions of interest:

(1) at times when when parts of the cerebral cortex are overexcited.
(2) at times when reticular nucleus cells themselves are excited by norepinephrine and/or glutamate. Stressful circumstances increase the release of these neuro-messengers (and many others).

How will these two situations affect the normal conceptual, insightful, psychic, thalamo-cortical functions referable to the *front* half of the human brain? This question still begs for answers. But we also need to focus on these thalamo-cortical circuits while consciousness is undergoing major transitions (Austin, 1998, pp. 311–27). Why during intervals of transition? Because dynamic instabilities are implicit in such rapid transitions. Instabilities invite substates of consciousness first to dissociate, and then to coalesce in novel alternate forms. Which transition periods? Let us list a few ordinary ones. They occur at the commonplace intervals during our normal sleep/waking cycle. For example:

(3) when waking descends toward slow-wave sleep (noted above).
(4) when slow-wave sleep ascends toward active dreaming sleep.
(5) when we rouse from this active (REM) sleep toward waking.

One wonders: Could the same five conditions be relevant to meditative states? For countless observations confirm two conclusions: prolonged meditative training does help to access alternate states of consciousness; drowsy meditators, shifting up and down, often traverse similar sleep transition periods.

B. The role of sudden events that trigger major 'peak experiences'

We need to reach a detailed understanding of thalamo-cortical interactions for one more reason. We need to know how, during these five circumstances, our fast transmitter pathways react to a sudden stimulus, release glutamate and acetylcholine, then set off the next cascade of events. For triggers are well-known precipitants of alternate states. A trigger can be a sensate stimulus: a penetrating sound like the caw of a crow. Or it could be a psychic stimulus: the sudden shock of an unexpected question. In an appropriate setting, seemingly 'minor' triggers can set off seismic events in a human brain.

Once triggering mechanisms are themselves understood, we may begin to comprehend why the flash of kensho's insight-wisdom briefly illuminates only an anonymous, impersonal awareness. Not unless the basic processes releasing such a peak moment suddenly dismantle one's frameworks of selfhood does the experience deeply etch consciousness. And not unless consciousness is deeply penetrated during that flashing insight does the stage seem set for the subsequent, long-range changes in traits of character. As these evolve, they transform that person's attitudes, behaviour and approach to living (Austin, 1998, pp. 314–15, 615–17).

IV: Larger Issues Involved in the Peak Moment of Kensho; The Paradoxical Sense that Consciousness, Though Divested of Self, Is Being 'Unified'

What else registered within this briefly awakened, liberated field of consciousness? More than kensho's lack of my psychic self, although this authentic 'death of self' was awesome when mulled over afterward. And more than the lack of fear. For, while still inside the depths of kensho, the realizations included an affirmative quality: a sense of perfection was infused throughout 'things as they really are'. How can a brain realize the novel scope and depth of such insights, when its former omni-self is absent (Austin, 1998, pp. 593–615)?

A. Potential sources for remarkable 'unifications' within the field of consciousness

Suppose you're looking, through a filmy veil, at a certain unknown object. You see it only partially. How do you recognize what it is? Some perirhinal nerve cells under your temporal lobe respond to its rounded shape. More distant cells, back in the fusiform gyrus, resonate to its red colour. Also stimulated are cell assemblies elsewhere in temporal cortex. They had been coded for patterns that represent different categories of fruits. Without thinking, you draw together all these separate strands. One unified percept leaps to mind. But precisely how did your brain manage to 'bind' together data from such separate loci? How did you instantly conclude: this unknown object is an APPLE?

1. The Role of Synchronized Oscillations. Current research suggests that such normal events of instant recognition correspond with distinct physiological epochs.

During these split-seconds — instants when physiological coherences reach psychological relevance — we synchronize the firing of many distant relevant cell assemblies. The question arises: Could similar processes give rise, selectively, to some of the unique configurations, and comprehensibilities, during kensho's extraordinary state?

While recent reports provide hints in this direction, issues so complex require much more research (Steriade *et al.*, 1996; Sohmiya *et al.*, 1998). Moreover, attentive focus *per se* enters into comprehension, as a crucial ingredient. We need to define its supportive role, if only to avoid confusion (Sokolov *et al.*, 1999).

For example, sometimes fast coherent oscillations are associated with alertness, but sometimes they are not (Steriade *et al.*, 1996). Moreover, current interpretations also suggest that synchronized oscillations might arise at several other frequencies, and in different loci, yet still support interactive processes which are of potential importance to cognition (Basar *et al.*, 1999). Selection implies exclusion. Before selecting that apple, you excluded a tomato.

To be sure, much current interest focuses on oscillations that synchronize at gamma frequencies, say at around 40 cycles per second (Fisahn *et al.*, 1998; Tallon-Baudry *et al.*, 1998). Whereas other studies promote synchronizations arising at lower theta frequencies of only 4–7 cps (Sarnthein *et al.*, 1998). Some theories hint that mental coherence arises because the cyclic peaks of gamma and theta firing rates nestle into phase relationships (Parthasarathy, 1999).

2. A Potential Role for the Small Intralaminar Nuclei of the Thalamus. These tiny nuclei broadcast diffuse messages up to 'recruit' the cortex. How do their gamma firing rates, at 40 cps and faster, influence consciousness? In theory, they could help infuse a diffuse background awareness of form and general context into the matrix of our conscious experience (Austin, 1998, p. 266).

But could variations of such functions alone explain why 'peak' moments differ in their phenomenology? Help explain why some subjects seem impressed by an intimate, inseparable 'union' of witnesser and witnessed, a kind of 'self–other merger', as it were? Whereas others (including this author) perceive anonymously, viewing all details of a field as unified, with all (potential) paradoxes fully reconciled (Austin, 1998, pp. 593–613)? We don't yet know. Whatever the basis for two such different impressions of a moment, the sense afterward is that one's old, divisive polarities had just been briefly dissolved.

3. A Potential Role for Posterior Thalamo-Cortical Unifying Functions. Deep in the back of the brain, two large association nuclei of the thalamus are primed to work in concert with long broad bands of visual association cortex. Two zones of their cortical partners occupy the uppermost regions of visual association cortex (*Figure 1*). High up in this posterior region (in areas 18 and 19 of Brodmann), lie circuits that help bring us a perception of visual texture. To do so, they will blend their functions with those from the adjacent posterior parietal lobule. Residing at dual nearby sites is a second set of thalamo-cortical associative functions. They co-sponsor our grasp, into one coherent meaningful whole, of small visual details that might otherwise seem unrelated. Countless trees now constitute one forest.

A third region of interest lies farther down in the right posterior temporal cortex. It might also help clarify how we unify meaning, for it lends a sense of closure at times when perception might otherwise sense that some visual gap had existed in the spatial aspects of the scenery (Austin, 1998, pp. 593–615).

When we register percepts within these three general regions, it will be the result of a thalamo-cortical partnership (Steriade *et al.*, 1996). This point is raised with reference to a recent EEG study of normal subjects which found 40cps synchronized EEG activity developing over several of these visual association regions (Revonsuo *et al.*, 1997). The EEG epoch arrived suddenly, and on the right side. Moreover, it signaled a prodromal physiological event. In fact, this early gamma EEG activity peaked some 400 milliseconds *before* the subjects' consciousness abruptly underwent a salient shift. So this EEG epoch appeared early, during an interval of '*pre*-consciousness'. Why is such early gamma activity so significant?

Because it anticipated a striking mental change. A novel sense of meaning next transfigured the scene. Some readers will recall, and can appreciate, how it feels when a similar kind of delayed realization breaks through into consciousness: those who have experienced being able to see directly into 'Magic Eye' pictures. This mental shift happens automatically. Instantly, incoherent fragments assemble themselves. A flat, two-dimensional scene transforms itself. The astonished observer beholds a meaningful, textured Gestalt image — in three dimensions.

This EEG study employed surface leads only. So it could not detect the thalamic input from those two large association nuclei deep within the posterior thalamus. In fact, back here, the pulvinar and lateral posterior nuclei are the deep correlates of that perceptual closure which any ordinary EEG study might seem to 'assign' solely to the surface layers of posterior 'cortex'. Yet this implicit thalamo-cortical alliance brings attentive focus, salience, and a literal sense of texture into our everyday, normal grasps of comprehension. Other collateral evidence suggests that thalamo-cortical activities referable to the left frontal lobe may normally help us detect links among fragmented clues, before they somehow seem to leap together intuitively (Austin, 1998, pp. 593–615). Even so, our most 'will-full' frontal intentions block such insights from reaching their automatic closure.

B. Potential sources for the impression of selective deletions from the field of consciousness

By now, the reader can appreciate that to enter kensho implies letting go of selfhood, and being released into a state of no-I, no-time and no-fear. Indeed, only after the author emerged from this brief state could he realize how much it had involved processes of deletion. Moreover, they had dissolved, with some selectivity, the substrates of his self-centred systems.

1. Representative Neuromessenger Candidates for Kensho. The GABA cap of the reticular nucleus is poised, as are countless other inhibitory GABA systems, briefly to block brain functions in the relevant brain regions specified throughout.

In this manner, what we tend to think of as our 'higher' functions of selfhood could appear briefly to 'drop out', 'dissolve' or be 'deleted' from our consciousness.

Acetylcholine systems present several different inhibitory options. So do some slower-acting neuropeptides. Among them are four endogenous opioids: the endomorphins, ß-endorphins, enkephalins and dynorphins. Some unleash excitation indirectly. How? By inhibiting local inhibitory mechanisms (disinhibition). Opioids have subtle indirect effects. In hippocampus they first disrupt the orderly, synchronous gamma oscillations of local GABA neurons. This causes a series of ill-timed, incoherent firing patterns. Finally, these disfirings disrupt the transfer of messages in still more distant circuits (Whittington et al., 1998).

Studies in the 1800s showed that a dose of morphine could dissolve both fear, painful suffering, and motivation (and that it could also induce blissful variations on the themes of euphoria). We are led to wonder: What causes that total 'death of fear' and absolute sense of peace within kensho? Might some of these phenomena, too, reflect an earlier, prodromal release of opioids? And could this then go on (as just cited above) to disrupt some underlying roots of our human angst? (Part II A 3).

Some opioid receptor systems do inhibit the deeper networks of fear. Their reach extends down into the central grey core of the brainstem. Others can dampen primal fear up in the amygdala and the hypothalamus; or in the para-limbic nuclei of the thalamus. These sites, in turn, interact with still higher-order constructs of fear, distributed as far up as the frontal lobes.

On the other hand, if genuine behavioural transformations have evolved and endured, then major trait changes must have taken place. Often, these require one or more of the deep, brief penetrations of self that are more likely to occur when meditators superimpose long retreats on their regular daily-life practice. One may speculate that such enduring, ongoing, long-range attitudinal changes might reflect the cumulative local excitotoxicities of glutamate, nitric oxide or dynorphin (Austin, 1998, pp. 653–9).

2. Could Our Normal Asymmetries of Lobar Functions Be Relevant to States of Insight-Wisdom? With regard to the origins of fear, the two frontal lobes differ. The right appears relatively more interconnected with networks of our fearful selves, at least when such indices are used as EEG activity, elevated adrenal cortisol levels in plasma, and fear-related behaviours (Kalin et al., 1998).

Certain cortical circuits mediating our usual private, self-knowing ('autonoetic') awareness might also draw on frontal-temporal interactions that are more right-sided (Levine et al., 1998). Accordingly, in kensho, when a person briefly enters the state of total fearlessness and loss of the psychic self, some ego-centric networks might be more disengaged on the right side.

V: First-Person Psychological Aspects of the Dissolution of the I–Me–Mine

What does kensho's state of insight-wisdom feel like? My old yearnings, loathings, fears of death, and insinuations of selfhood vanished temporarily. Only after emerging from this state could I appreciate how deep were the visceral roots of all my prior conditioning. Can words express some immediate consequences of this deep wordless loss of the self? *Table 1* is an oversimplified attempt.

THE DISSOLUTION OF	MEANS SUBTRACTING	AND IS EXPERIENCED AS
I	The aggressive 'doing self' Self-concepts in time	Freedom from compulsive doing, from 'shoulds and oughts' Timelessness
Me	The beseiged and fearful self	Fearlessness Deep Peace
Mine	The clutching self that: 1. Had possessed other persons and things 2. Had been captured by its own dualistic attitudes	The world as *it* really is, without self-referent attachments. The world's original diversity, coherence and Unity

Table 1

The table proceeds from one premise: all self-centered subjectivities briefly dissolved. My old personalized limbic valances seemed to have dropped off. No longer could they polarize either side of such opposites as: self/other, now/then. Once all such covert dualities implicit in 'self' disappear, which residual functions could now lend structure to the field of awareness? Allocentric functions.

Allocentric themes are not new. In one sense of that old Zen phrase, they are 'nothing special'. Their circuits have always been implicit in the way we first pay direct attention to bare stimuli, and register them immediately without obvious discriminations.

Then why did the resulting content within awareness seem, in retrospect, so novel? Perhaps in part because, when one's habitual self-centred role abruptly drops out from the scene, this world of 'other' is itself suddenly left free-standing. Now released from subjective attachments, the world revealed is in a form awesomely unburdened and clarified. And only from within such an inconceivably selfless, allocentric mode of perception can consciousness be impressed by its first, all-too-brief glimpse of 'reality': of things as they '*really*' are.

Even so, more is realized within this 'reality' than stark allocentricity. As the table suggests, kensho is also infused by salient impressions that are deeply affirmative in tone. For this novel state of consciousness, now rendered timeless and fearless, also comprehends that all individual items and events share a vast interrelated field. Perfectly unified, it lies beyond all prior categories imposed by personal prejudice and by artificial conventions.

References

Adolphs, R., Tranel, D. and Damasio, A. (1998), 'The human amygdala in social judgement', *Nature*, **393**, pp. 470–4.

Anderson, R., Essick, G. and Siegel, R. (1985), 'Encoding of spatial location by posterior parietal neurons', *Science*, **230**, pp. 456–8.

Austin, J. (1998), *Zen and the Brain. Toward an Understanding of Meditation and Consciousness* (Cambridge, MA: MIT Press).

Austin, J. (1999), 'Six points to ponder', *Journal of Consciousness Studies*, **6** (2–3), pp. 213–16. [Personal descriptions of the two states are also at www.issc-taste.org]

Austin, J. (2001), 'The Path', in *Neuropsychiatry 2000* (Tokyo: Springer-Verlag, in press).

Basar, E., Basar-Eroglu, C., Karakas, S. *et al.* (1999), 'Are cognitive processes manifested in event-related gamma, alpha, theta and delta oscillations in the EEG?', *Neuroscience Letters*, **259**, pp. 165–8.

Buchanan, S., Beylotte, F. and Powell, D. (1997), 'Lesions of the thalamic reticular nucleus or the basal forebrain impair Pavlovian eyeblink conditioning and attenuate learning-related multiple-unit activity in the mediodorsal nucleus of the thalamus', *Psychobiology*, **25**, pp. 48–58.

Buchel, C., Morris, J., Dolan, R. *et al.* (1998), 'Brain systems mediating aversive conditioning: an event-related FMRI study', *Neuron*, **20**, pp. 947–57.

Buckley, M. and Gaffan, D. (1998), 'Learning and transfer of object-reward associations and the role of the perirhinal cortex,' *Behavioral Neuroscience*, **112**, pp. 15–23.

Caldji, C., Tannenbaum, B., Sharma, S. *et al.* (1998), 'Maternal care during infancy regulates the development of neural systems mediating the expression of fearfulness in the rat', *Proceedings of the National Academy of Sciences (USA)*, **95**, pp. 5335–40.

Fisahn, A., Pike, F., Buhl, E. *et al.* (1998), 'Cholinergic induction of network oscillations at 40 Hz in the hippocampus in vitro', *Nature*, **394**, pp. 186–9.

Fish, D., Gloor, P. Quesney, F. *et al.* (1993), 'Clinical responses to electrical brain stimulation of the temporal and frontal lobes in patients with epilepsy,' *Brain*, **116**, pp. 397–414.

Gloor, P. (1990), 'Experiential phenomena of temporal lobe epilepsy', *Brain*, **113**, pp.1673–94.

Grenier, F., Timofeev, I. and Steriade, M. (1998), 'Leading role of thalamic over cortical neurons during postinhibitory rebound excitation', *Proceedings of the National Academy of Sciences (USA)*, **95**, pp. 13929–34.

Guillery, R., Feig, G. and Lozsadi, D. (1998), 'Paying attention to the thalamic reticular nucleus', *Trends in Neurosciences*, **21**, pp. 28–32.

Hasse, V., Dinez, L., Wood, G. *et al.* (1998), 'The temporal structure of conscious mental states', *Journal of the Brazilian Association for the Advancement of Science*, **50**, pp. 153–8.

Henson, R., Rugg, M., Shallice, T. *et al.* (1999), 'Recollection and familiarity in recognition memory: an event-related functional magnetic resonance imaging study', *The Journal of Neuroscience*, **19**, pp. 3962–72.

Hodges, J. and McCarthy, R. (1993), 'Autobiographical amnesia resulting from bilateral paramedian thalamic infarction: a case study in cognitive neurobiology', *Brain*, **116**, pp. 921–40.

Johannsen, P., Jakobsen, J. Bruhn, P. *et al.* (1997), 'Cortical sites of sustained and divided attention in normal elderly humans', *Neuroimage*, **6**, pp. 145–55.

Kalin, N., Larson, C., Shelton, S. *et al.* (1998), 'Asymmetric frontal brain activity, cortisol, and behavior associated with fearful temperament in Rhesus monkeys', *Behavioral Neuroscience*, 112, pp. 286–92.

Kapur, N. (1997), 'How can we best explain retrograde amnesia in human memory disorder?', *Memory*, **5**, pp. 115–29.

Levine, B., Black, S., Cabeza, R. *et al.* (1998), 'Episodic memory and the self in a case of isolated retrograde amnesia', *Brain*, **121**, pp. 1951–73.

Morris, J., Ohman, A. and Dolan, R. (1998), 'Conscious and unconscious emotional learning in the human amygdala', *Nature*, **393**, pp. 467–70.

Parthasarathy, H. (1999), 'Mind rhythms', *New Scientist*, **2210**, pp. 28–31.

Perrett, D., Oram, M., Harries, M. *et al.* (1991), 'Viewer-centred and object-centred coding of heads in the macaque temporal cortex', *Experimental Brain Research*, **86**, pp. 159–73.

Revonsuo, A., Wilenius-Emet, M., Kuusela, J. *et al.* (1997), 'The neural generation of a unified illusion in human vision', *NeuroReport*, **8**, pp. 3867–70.

Rolls, E. (1999), 'Spatial view cells and the representation of space in the primate hippocampus', *Hippocampus*, **9**, pp. 467–80.

Sarnthein, J., Petsche, H., Rappelsberger, P. *et al.* (1998), 'Synchronization between prefrontal and posterior association cortex during human working memory', *Proceedings of the National Academy of Sciences (USA)*, **95**, pp. 7092–6.

Sohmiya, S., Sohmiya, K. and Sohmiya, T. (1998), 'Connection between synchronization of oscillatory activities at early stages and a final stage in the visual system', *Perceptual and Motor Skills*, **86**, pp. 1107–16.

Sokolov, A., Lutzenberger, W., Pavlova, M. *et al.* (1999), 'Gamma-band MEG activity to coherent motion depends on task-driven attention', *NeuroReport*, **10**, pp. 1997–2000.

Stark, M., Coslett, H. and Saffran, E. (1996), 'Impairment of an egocentric map of locations; implications for perception and action', *Cognitive Neuropsychology*, **13**, pp. 481–523.

Steriade, M., Contreras, D., Amzica, F. et al. (1996), 'Synchronization of fast (30-40Hz) spontaneous oscillations in intrathalamic and thalamocortical networks', *The Journal of Neuroscience*, **16**, pp. 2788–808.

Tallon-Baudry, C., Bertrand, O., Peronnet, F. *et al.* (1998), 'Induced gamma band activity during the delay of a visual short-term memory task in humans', *The Journal of Neuroscience*, **18**, pp. 4244–54.

Whittington, M., Traub, R., Faulkner, H. *et al.* (1998), 'Morphine disrupts long-range synchrony of gamma oscillations in hippocampal slices', *Proceedings of the National Academy of Sciences (USA)*, **95**, pp. 5807–11.

Brian L. Lancaster

On the Relationship Between Cognitive Models and Spiritual Maps
Evidence from Hebrew Language Mysticism*

It is suggested that the impetus to generate models is probably the most fundamental point of connection between mysticism and psychology. In their concern with the relation between 'unseen' realms and the 'seen', mystical maps parallel cognitive models of the relation between 'unconscious' and 'conscious' processes. The map or model constitutes an explanation employing terms current within the respective canon. The case of language mysticism is examined to illustrate the premise that cognitive models may benefit from an understanding of the kinds of experiences gained, and explanatory concepts advanced, within mystical traditions. Language mysticism is of particular interest on account of the central role thought to be played by language in relation to self and the individual's construction of reality.

*The discussion focuses on traditions of language mysticism within Judaism, in which emphasis is placed on (i) the deconstruction of language into primary elements and (ii) the overarching significance of the divine Name. Analysis of the detailed techniques used suggests ways in which multiple associations to any given word/concept were consciously explored in an altered state. It appears that these mystics were consciously engaging with what are normally preconscious cognitive processes, whereby schematic associations to sensory images or thoughts are activated. The testimony from their writings implies that these mystics experienced distortions of the sense of self ('I'), which may suggest that, in the normal state, 'I' is constructed in relation to the preconscious system of associations. Moreover, an important feature of Hebrew language mysticism is its emphasis on embodiment — specific associations were deemed to exist between the letters and each structure of the body. Implications, first, for the relationship between language and self, and, second, for the role of embodiment in relation to self are discussed. The importance of the continual emphasis on the Name of God throughout the linguistic practices may have provided a means for effectively replacing the cognitive indexing function hypothesized here to be normally played by 'I' with a more **transpersonal** cognitive index, especially in relation to memory.*

*Based on a paper delivered at the symposium on Cognitive Science and the Study of Religious Experience, Vermont, 1998.

Journal of Consciousness Studies, **7**, No. 11–12, 2000, pp. 231–50

Introduction: Process and Model

> Read the entire Torah, both forwards and backwards, and spill the blood of the lan-
> guages. Thus, the knowledge of the Name [of God] is above all wisdoms in quality
> and worth.[1]

The above is an extract from the work of Abraham Abulafia, an influential
thirteenth-century Jewish mystic, who taught a distinctive form of language
mysticism. As I shall explore later, the suggested value of reading scripture 'both
forwards and backwards' stems not only from the mystics' view of the Torah's[2]
supreme value but also from the rabbinic attitude which holds Hebrew and the
Hebrew letters to be of transcendent significance. As for the Name, it is viewed by
Jewish mystics as conveying, through its letters and their arrangement, the divine
essence itself. These two factors may be said to set the parameters for Hebrew
language mysticism. What is especially distinctive in Abulafia's technique is its
complexity and the intensity with which it was practised. The metaphor, 'spilling
the blood of the languages', is an apt reflection of the fervour with which he and
his disciples attacked their task. My interest concerns the possible psychological
dimension in their practices. To what extent may the phenomena associated with
language mysticism hint at the kinds of psychological processes involved in consciousness and in the generation of altered states?

Whilst a defining hallmark of mysticism is the quest to *experience* a transcendent realm in whatever form the cultural canon allows, we find that probably the
majority of mystical writings relate to the challenge of modelling whatever passes
for *reality*, in both inner and outer aspects. Abulafia's discourses on language
mysticism include 'explanations' of the states he encountered in terms of
kabbalistic imagery and those philosophical concepts, such as *active intellect* and
prime material, which were current in the mediaeval period. In essence, my
approach suggests that contemporary psychological terminology may serve a
similar role in allowing explanatory discourse in our day. Whilst my psychological terminology may have the distinction of being more related to suggested causative brain processes than that used by Abulafia, the central concern remains the
same: namely, to generate explanatory models. We generally claim understanding
of a process to the extent that we can effectively model it, and the terms of our
model constitute the shared knowledge-base of our discipline.

The impetus to generate models is probably the most fundamental point of connection between mysticism and psychology. The various kinds of spiritual maps,
including, for example, mandala images, temple plans, medicine wheels and the
kabbalistic tree of life, are intricate, often beautiful, expressions of this function.
Central to any endeavour to interrelate religious mysticism and psychology is the

---

[1] From the writings of Abraham Abulafia, cited in Idel (1989), p. 27. All cited extracts are from
Abulafia, unless otherwise stated.

[2] In the first place, *Torah* refers to the Five Books of Moses. However, the term has a considerably more
extended meaning in rabbinic thought. It can refer to the entire Hebrew Bible, to authentic teachings
derived from the canon, and, more mystically, to the *World Soul*. The central text of Jewish mysticism,
the *Zohar*, boldly asserts an identity between the Torah and God (*Zohar* II, 60a). In Abulafia's usage
here, it refers to the Five Books as a mystical vehicle for plumbing the depths of God's language.

proposition that such models are expressions of inner, psychological processes. Whatever other, more cosmic, references may be included within the tradition itself, the map may be seen as an expression of the dimensions of human personality and/or the stages operating within psychological processes. The mandala, for example, as emphasised by Jung (1968) and Tucci (1961), is as much a depiction of the relationship between conscious and unconscious realms of mind as it is a representation of a temple, city, or the entire cosmos. Similarly, the kabbalistic tree of life, which is said to depict stages in the emanation of the Godhead as well as the various realms of heavenly influence, is equally an exemplar of stages in the unfolding of thought from its deepest unconscious source through to the level of immediate, phenomenal consciousness. Thus, in the rather cryptic language of the *Zohar*, a primary source of kabbalistic teaching, we read that:

> Thought is the beginning of all. It is within, secret and unknowable. When it extends, it reaches the place where spirit dwells and is then called Understanding, which is not so concealed as the preceding even though it is still secret. This spirit expands and produces a Voice comprising fire, water, and air, namely north, south, and east. . . . When you examine the levels, you find that Thought, Understanding, Voice, and speech are all one, and that thought is the beginning of all — there is no separation (*Zohar* I: 246b).

In this scheme, each *sefirah*,[3] or divine emanation, becomes a different quality of thought in the movement from unconscious ('secret') to conscious, as symbolized by key kabbalistic terms such as Understanding, Voice and the directions of space. Moreover, the same scheme provides the psychological framework for the mystic's quest to gain experience of the higher, divine realm: 'The *sefirot* . . . are both the ontic realities that constitute the divine realm and the psychological paradigms by means of which the mystic visualizes these realities' (Wolfson, 1994, p. 72). This emphasis on modelling the relationship between an unseen realm and that of the seen is very much the focus of all spiritual maps, and it finds psychological expression in the challenge to understand the relation between unconscious and conscious processes.

Given that specifying the relation between unconscious and conscious processes is one of the major challenges facing cognitive neuroscience today (Kihlstrom, 1993; Velmans, 1996), these various models generated, or employed, by mystics may offer a fruitful perspective to complement data generated through the scientific method. Mystical models are by no means straightforward, and some degree of 'decoding', using a broad understanding of the religious and cultural context within which a given model developed, is inevitably needed. The objective here is not simply to 'explain' mystical states in terms of proposed brain states and psychological processes, as has been attempted, for example, by Persinger (1987) and D'Aquili and Newberg (1993). Rather, my approach draws on mystics' experiences and the models they use in order to refine our understanding of psychological processes. Forman (1998) similarly analyses mystical

---

[3] The *sefirot* (plural) represent successive focuses through which the divine essence unfolds from the level of transcendence to that of immanence in relation to the human sphere.

states for their value in our understanding of consciousness, since mystics' descriptions regarding inner awareness may offer 'a kind of ongoing microscope on human consciousness' (p. 187).

In recent works (Lancaster, 1997a; 1997b), I have pursued this goal of integrating mystical and psychological data through an examination of perceptual and thought processes as described in *Abhidhamma* texts of the Buddhist Pali canon. I have argued that integrating the understanding of stages of perception presented in this Buddhist literature with contemporary insights into brain systems can generate an inclusive psychological model. The model emphasizes the role played by two brain systems in particular. First, sensory input is analysed and matched against stored memory images. Neuronal oscillatory systems in sensory cortex and connecting structures are presumed to effect this process of interrelating sensory input with memory systems (Damasio, 1989). Second, a representation of self ('I') is constructed in relation to the most parsimonious match(es) achieved. If, for example, the light reflected from a pen strikes my retina, the first stage will generate a match between the input and neuronal constellations representing previous experience with pens, etc. The second stage would, in this example, eventuate in my experience that I am holding my favourite pen in my hand (or whatever). In this model it is specifically the second stage, whereby an 'I'-connection to other activated cognitive structures is effected, which constitutes conscious recognition of the object (see also Kihlstrom, 1993; 1997). The system identified by Gazzaniga as the *interpreter* (Gazzaniga, 1985; 1988) is hypothesized to play a major role in this second stage by generating the everyday sense of self as subject of whatever experience is ongoing. The various characteristics of this sense of self are products of the drive towards interpretation. Thus, the sense of self is experienced as unified, and as the director of events in the mind. Although it is accordingly experienced as a *unified 'I'*, there are good reasons for thinking that it is neither unified nor the control centre of the mind. It is merely a putative focus of the (conscious) mind (for a similar view, see Baars, 1996, p. 213).

This representation of self is further engaged in memory functions, since it is considered to act as an indexing or 'tagging' device in association with other stored representations (*'I'-tag*). The hypothalamus and related limbic structures are implicated in these indexing operations (Moscovitch, 1994; 1995; Teyler and DiScenna, 1986). Figure 1 presents the model in diagrammatic form, indicating the stages as described in the Abhidhamma in juxtaposition to the proposed cerebral and cognitive operations.[4] Full details of the Abhidhamma stages, together with my arguments for their relationship to cognitive and neural processes may be found in Lancaster (1997a; 1997b). In brief, the generation of a match between sensory input and memory systems is hypothesized to occur during the first four

---

[4] What I have described thus far as a two-stage process is presented in the Abhidhamma as entailing six stages (see Figure 1). However, any seeming inconsistency is minimised when we bear in mind that the Abhidhamma conceives the first four stages as comprising a single block. Any stimulus triggering the stage labelled 'sense' will automatically eventuate in the fourth stage, following which there is a potential break prior to stage five. Thus Abhidhamma stages one to four include the neuro-cognitive processes described above as constituting the first of the two stages in perception.

stages recognized by the Abhidhamma. Following a preliminary response by the sense organ ('sense'),[5] the image is received by the neuronal encoding system ('receive') and a range of neuronal representations is activated through associative mechanisms ('examine'). The principal representation is then determined through the matching process described above ('establish').

The subsequent stage is termed *javana* in Pali. It is said to be the stage at which the conceit of 'I am' arises, and I have argued that it corresponds to the stage during which the Interpreter system generates the sense of a unified 'I'. The final stage in the Abhidhamma system is 'register' and seems to correspond to an updating of memory systems in short-term memory. I relate this stage to my proposals concerning the 'tagging' of memory representations in relation to 'I'.

It is beyond the scope of this paper to give full details of the arguments for the correspondences described here and depicted in Figure 1. As already mentioned, extensive discussion of the model will be found in Lancaster (1997a; 1997b). It has been necessary for me to outline the model here since it provides the foundation for my speculations regarding language mysticism. My major premise is couched in terms of the model, as represented in Figure 1. This premise holds that

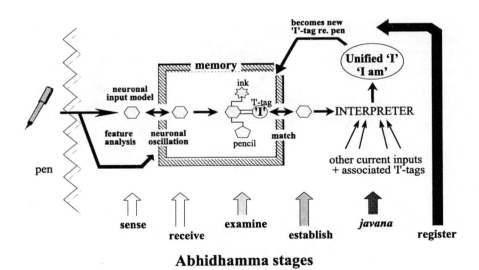

Abhidhamma stages

Figure 1. 'I'-tag model of perception and memory illustrating correspondences with perceptual stages described in Abhidhamma

---

[5]   The words in brackets are translations of the Pali terms given in the discussion of the *Sense-Door* (i.e., perceptual) process.

mystical practices bring about a re-balancing between the stages represented in the model. They shift the emphasis from the end stage, in which the 'I'-connection to neuronal representations is generated, to earlier stages, focusing especially on the stage ('examine') in which associations to the object are explored, normally pre-consciously.[6] This proposition is illustrated in Figure 2, in which two routes to such a shift are emphasized. The first involves detachment from 'I', which is promoted through meditation and, in most traditions, by embracing a variety of precepts which encourage ongoing selflessness. In the model, the sense of 'I' arises in relation to memory images activated by current stimuli (sensations, images and/or thoughts). The felt continuity of 'I' is a product of the brain's interpretative drive, and is consequent on a certain habitual rigidity in the meanings ascribed to those stimuli. Detachment from 'I', then, would be expected to free up the movement of images within the mind, relaxing the rigidity of response and encouraging greater creativity. I consider the *apophatic* goal of pure emptiness as an extreme of this first route, through which the mystic becomes increasingly detached from the movement of images. The second route, bringing about a shift to normally pre-conscious stages, is identified with

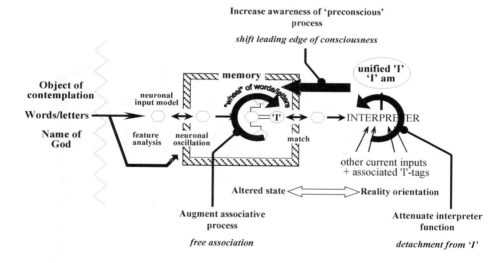

Figure 2. 'I'-tag model of perception and memory illustrating proposed effects of spiritual practice

[6] The term 'pre-conscious' may be misleading due to differences in the use of the term 'consciousness' itself. Typically, psychology and neuroscience refer to the end stage of perception as 'conscious', with preceding stages being seen as 'pre-conscious'. Mysticism tends to regard 'consciousness' as a primary reality, which underlies all stages. In the Abhidhamma, for example, all the stages of the perceptual process, including early ones which an untrained individual would not be aware of, are designated as stages of consciousness. This is not a purely academic distinction, for it bears major implications for our understanding of the extent to which we can bring early stages of perception and thought under the control of the *will*, which in this sense should not be confused with ego-based control. The cultural ramifications of this point are explored in Lancaster (1997b).

kataphatic mysticism, and is hypothesized here to be focused in volitional exploration of the stage labelled *examine* in Figure 1. Wolfson (1994), correctly in my view, refers to such mysticism as *cognitive* and emphasizes the role played by perceptual processes and the imagination. As he notes, although apophatic tendencies are not entirely lacking in mediaeval kabbalistic texts, it is cognitive mysticism which largely defines the mysticism of these texts. A wide variety of imagery-based and contemplative techniques developed within the traditions of cognitive mysticism, and the linguistic mysticism of the kind practised by Abulafia is paradigmatic of this second route. My paper is therefore directed primarily to possible explanations of this *cognitive* form of religious mysticism.

Language Mysticism

To the extent that a goal of mystical practice is that of transcending distinctions and gaining direct experience of the oneness said to characterize ultimate reality, language is often viewed as an impediment on the path, since language specifically compartmentalizes experience. 'Enlightenment is achieved in the letting go of language' (Hayes, 1997, p. 580). Moreover, Forman (1990; 1993) has forcefully argued against the 'constructivist' position (Katz, 1983), which holds that all experience — including mystical experience — is in some sense mediated structurally; that all experience is intentional. Forman offers numerous examples of mystical states which seem to be contentless, and therefore devoid of language. Such pure consciousness events have also been reported by individuals with no interest in mysticism. Sullivan (1995), for example, describes such a state following a road accident:

> There was something, and the *something* was not the nothing [of total unconsciousness]. The nearest label for the *something* might possibly be 'awareness', but that could be misleading, since any awareness I'd ever had before the accident was *my awareness*, my awareness of one thing or another.
>
> In contrast, this *something* . . . had no *I* as its *subject* and no content as its *object*. It just was (p. 53).

I see no reason to contradict the direct evidence of such experiences, and would concur in the view that seemingly contentless conscious states — arising either spontaneously or as a result of mystical practice or injury — need to be incorporated within a meaningful psychology of consciousness. It does not follow, however, that 'language-focused approaches to mysticism' lead to a psychological blind alley, as Mangan (1994, p. 251), for example, implies. Mangan sees the relation between language and mystical experience in a rather starkly dichotomized form: either such experience is 'a distinct phenomenon reflected *by* language' or it is 'a set of propositions imprisoned *in* language' (*ibid*, emphasis original). There is, in fact, at least one alternative, namely, that language can itself provide a means for embracing progressively 'deeper' or 'higher' conscious states, as we find in many traditions of cognitive mysticism. This alternative should be given serious consideration since probably the majority of spiritual traditions have developed schemes of thought and various language-based practices which

reflect it (Katz, 1992). It is probably only in a minority of such cases that the ultimate goal of the practices employed is unequivocally a state of emptiness. The
value to psychology of these traditions, irrespective of any purported spiritual or
therapeutic goals, lies in the detail with which features of the linguistic process
and supposed 'higher' states are described. The insights reported by its practitioners can furnish useful data for the attempts of psychology, and most particularly
cognitive psychology, to model the mind. In discussing the *pure conscious event*,
Forman (1998) rightly concludes that its occurrence implies that 'consciousness
is more than its embodied activities' (p. 193). Beyond the simple statement that
'consciousness *is*', however, there seems little further for the psychologist (as distinct from the metaphysician) to add. When, by comparison, we focus on the detail
of language mysticism — the means rather than the end — we are able to draw on
our understanding of language, and its role in cognitive processing, in order to conceptualize the psychology of the mystics' path.

The notion that language plays a critical role in mundane consciousness[7] finds
expression in three major arguments. First is the view that mundane consciousness is dependent on, or even identifiable with, language. This view, which may
be traced to the thinking of Darwin, has recently been revived by Rolls (1997).
For Rolls, language, defined as the syntactic manipulation of symbols, constitutes
a higher-order thought system which enables reflection on, and possible correc-
tion of, more primary representations. It is this function which he regards as critical for consciousness. The second is the neo-Whorfian view that language
conditions conscious thought (Dennett, 1996). Whilst both of these viewpoints on
language and consciousness may be relevant to issues raised by the phenomenology of language mysticism, it is to a third that I shall refer predominantly in my
discussion below. This is the view which holds language to be a critical determinant of self. It is on account of the suggested centrality for mundane consciousness of the cognitive representation of self (Kihlstrom, 1993;1997; Lancaster,
1991) that this view interrelates language and consciousness.

Bruner (1997) has argued that self arises as a narrative construction; that the
sense of self we may experience in the present is perceived as continuous with a
past state only by virtue of the narrative we construct to connect them. He further
notes that it is effectively impossible to separate the young child's language
development from their process of 'self accounting'. Dennett (1991) similarly
refers to self as the 'centre of narrative gravity', and Sacks (1986) interprets neurological disorders of memory to suggest that, 'each of us constructs and lives a
"narrative", and that this narrative is us, our identities' (p. 105). In the model I
discussed briefly above, the sense of being a unified 'I' is seen as a product of the
drive to interpret events as having a coherent focus. The interpreter, which is

---

[7] I use this term to distinguish it from *pure consciousness*. In their studies of 'consciousness,' psychology and cognitive neuroscience have not been concerned with pure consciousness as such but with the
various ways in which events become available, or accessible (Bisiach, 1988; Block, 1995) to conscious reflection. Central to mundane consciousness is the role played by the representation of self, to
be discussed below. I am not suggesting that there is no continuity between 'mundane' and 'pure' consciousness, but it is important for purposes of explanation to maintain the distinction. See Lancaster
(1993), p. 523 note 2. See also note above.

conceived here as being central to such 'narrative', weaves a coherent image from the multiple strands of 'I' activated by the large array of memory activity at any given time. Indeed, it is conceivable that such a function represents the primary evolutionary value of language, with social communication as a derivative function. Above all, language enables us to construct a sense of ourselves and a view of reality, which we can, secondarily, share with those around us. Postmodernism in particular has emphasized this view of the role played by language in cognition. Krippner and Winkler (1995) offer a series of propositions concerning the impact postmodernism carries for consciousness studies. Their fourth proposition is especially relevant here since it states that,

> Investigators [should] realize that people in each culture construct conscious experience in terms of the categories provided by their own linguistic system, coming to terms with a 'reality' that has been filtered through their language (p. 261).

It is evident that language mysticism relates strongly to these psychological arguments. Whatever else they may be doing at more metaphysical levels, mystics are, at a psychological level, exploring aspects of their linguistically-filtered sense of reality. I consider that the testimony from these mystics can offer a specific window into the ways in which the sense of self and everyday vision of reality become deconstructed.

I remarked above that spiritual maps are invariably concerned with the relationship between the hidden and the revealed. In the movement from inner thought to outer speech, language epitomises this relationship. Language mysticism generally projects this intra-psychic experience onto 'reality'. Thus reality itself takes on the characteristics of language, as in Bonaventura's scheme in which all of creation becomes classified as manifestations of God's language, creatures equating to His nouns, their energy to His verbs, etc. (Cousins, 1992). As Cousins remarks, for Bonaventura, 'at its very apex and centre — on the level of the Absolute — reality is linguistic' (p. 241). Böhme's mysticism similarly venerated language, for he considered God to be 'at the heart of the letters' (Edel, 1996, p. 444). Of course, the biblical underpinnings of these views are crucial. For Christianity, famously, 'In the beginning was the Word . . . .' (John 1:1), a notion which draws its power from the essential biblical premise that the creative work of God arises with His use of language (the 'And God said . . . And it was' formulation of Genesis 1). Indeed, a rabbinic term for God is 'He who spoke and the world came into being'. This religious conception of the power of language becomes a mystical one when language is seen as a medium for direct encounter with the divine, as, for example, in the Sufi *dhikr* meditation which focuses on remembrance of God's Names. Sufism, moreover, considered the letters of Arabic to contain all wisdom, a proposition identical to the Jewish mystics' view of Hebrew. Schimmel (1975) gives numerous examples of the mystical role of the Arabic letters in Sufi thought and practice, noting, for example, that, '[M]ost of the meditations of the mystics were directed toward the letter *alif*' (p. 417).

Distinctive and complex forms of language mysticism may be traced to the earliest phases of Judaism. The intensity with which aspects of language became vehicles for mystical speculation and practice presumably owes something to the lack of other forms of religious imagery available on account of the strict ban on images. But the intrinsic power of language and its immediacy as a medium for exploring the nature of meaning are perhaps more important as positive factors in the rise of language mysticism. Language — and specifically the Hebrew language — becomes not only the medium through which God creates and interacts with His creation, but also the primary means for the mystic to gain access to experience of the divine. The mystic attempts to become closer to God by retracing the movement of His language from its outward expression back towards its inner source.

In Jewish thought, the Torah represents the ground-plan of creation. As the rabbis expressed it in a Midrash,[8] 'The Holy One, blessed be He, gazed into the Torah and created the world accordingly' (*Genesis Rabbah* 1:1). The language of the Torah — Hebrew — is necessarily, therefore, the language by which God created the world (*Genesis Rabbah* 18:4, 31:8). An anonymous Midrash describes the twenty-two letters of the Hebrew alphabet as the 'workmen' necessary for the work of creation (Urbach, 1979, p. 201), and the Talmud concurs in this view that God employed individual Hebrew letters in the act of creation (Talmud, *Ber* 55a). Moreover, the actual form of the Hebrew letters is conceived as being transcendent to the natural order of things (Mishnah *Avot* 5:6) and the letters are, therefore, a kind of window into the infinite.

More elaborate traditions regarding the role of the letters are preserved in two early (dating from the first centuries of the present era) mystical works, the *Sefer Yezirah* and *Shiur Koma* texts. The former details the techniques by which the letters were employed in creation, and the second anthropomorphically analyses the 'body' of God, implying that the letters are in some sense bound up with the very 'structure' of the divine. These works show clear Pythagorean and Hellenistic influences, reflective of the broad base of this whole strand of language mysticism.

These fundamental rabbinic and mystical premises form the mythic background to the development of *Kabbalah* from the twelfth century onwards. Kabbalah is quintessentially a mysticism of language; it is no exaggeration to state that all its major themes are either directly concerned with letters and words, or metaphorically described in relation to the processes involved in generating speech from thought. As Idel puts it, the kabbalists view language as 'the spiritual underpinning of reality' (Idel, 1995, p. 219), and the Hebrew letters as constituting 'a mesocosmos that enables operations that can bridge the gap between the human — or the material — and the divine' (Idel, 1992, p. 43).

The classical talmudic and midrashic texts of the Rabbis adopt a playful but disciplined attitude to the Hebrew of scripture. A teaching is frequently conveyed by adopting a fluid view of the pronunciation of letters so that alternative readings might be introduced:

[8] The term *Midrash* refers to both a style of homiletic interpretation of sacred texts and the corpus of writings to which this style gave rise. Together with the Talmud, the Midrashim (plural) convey the major teachings of the rabbis who taught in the wake of the destruction of the Temple in 70 CE.

Rabbi Elazar said in the name of Rabbi Hanina: Scholars increase peace in the world, as it is said, 'All your children will be learned of the Lord; great shall be the peace of your children' (Isaiah 54:13). Do not read *banayikh* [children] but *bonayikh* [builders; i.e. builders of spiritual learning] (Talmud, *Ber* 64a).

A statement such as this, in which homiletic teachings are conveyed by means of word-play, is not merely an occasional 'poetic' excursion, but a central pillar of rabbinic hermeneutics. The approach is predicated *conceptually* on the Rabbis' view of the 'holiness' of Hebrew, and *practically* on the unpointed (i.e., vowel-less) form of scriptural text.[9] Indeed, this fluidity is itself legitimized from a scriptural text: 'It was taught in the School of R. Yishmael: "Behold, My word is like fire — declares the Lord — and like a hammer that shatters rock" (Jeremiah 23:29). Just as this hammer produces many sparks, so a single verse has multiple meanings' (Talmud, *San* 34a). The rabbinic mind is characterized by a respectful associative tendency with regard to words of scripture, a tendency which, as Handelman (1981; 1985) has argued, displays more than a trivial relation to Freud's approach to interpretation (see also Boyarin, 1990; Faur, 1986; Ouaknin, 1995).

This emphasis on the fluidity in Hebrew constitutes the exoteric dimension to the esoteric practice of language mysticism central to the *ecstatic* kabbalah of Abulafia. Two features in particular seem critical to this esotericism. First, a variety of concentrative techniques were employed, including breath control, visualization, chanting, and body movement as accompaniments to the central work of *permuting* Hebrew letters. Second, the letters were to be continually related to those of the Name of God, thereby imbuing the process with a specific transcendent connection.[10] Whilst features common to many meditative techniques are evident here, the incredible complexity of the linguistic operations themselves marks this mystical practice out from most systems, in which emphasis is placed on simplicity in the object of contemplation (Idel, 1988b). Following preliminaries including fasting and various aspects of religious ritual, Abulafia's technique required the initiate to manipulate letters and words, 'to combine small letters with great ones, to reverse them and to permute them rapidly' (cited in Idel, 1988b, p. 39). Such activity proceeded from writing to chanting to mental imagery alone. The mystic would follow intricate verbal patterns, including various codified means for interconnecting words, letters, numbers, and meanings.

It is beyond the scope of my article to discuss at length the detailed form of these patterns, and the peculiar logic to Abulafia's associative mind. Isolated illustrations are likely to appear singularly bizarre, and the subtlety of the Hebrew

---

[9] Thus, the above quote from the book of Isaiah includes the Hebrew word, BNYKH. It is for the reader to construct a readable word through the addition of vowels, which leads to the kind of ambiguity exploited in the talmudic extract.

[10] In fact, mystics viewed all the letters either as divine Names in themselves or as constituents of divine Names. The major exegete and philosopher, Moshe ben Nachman ('Nachmanides,' 1194–1270), for example, writes in the introduction to his commentary on the Torah that all its letters constitute a divine Name. According to him, the sequence was altered in the 'version' given to Moses in order to portray stories and commandments rather than disclose mystical secrets to all.

is difficult to convey in translation. Consider, as a single example, the following extract from Abulafia's *Chayye ha'Olam ha'Ba*:

> Head and belly and torso, that is, the head, beginning inside the end. The 'head' is the first point that you imagine in it; the 'end' is the purpose of the head, and is like a tail to it, and the belly is likewise like a tail to the head, and is the image of the torso, wherein the heart is located. And the image that you ought to imagine at the time of pronunciation, in order to change within that image the nature of [one] part of the bodies, alone or with others, is: think in your heart the name of that thing, and if it is [composed] of two letters, such as *yam* [sea], and you wish to invert it, and the name of the reversal is *yabasah* [dry land], the companion of *yam* with *yabasah*, and this is 'beginning and end, *yah*.' But the middle is *me-yabes yam*; behold, *Yah meyabes yam* (God makes dry the sea), for He in truth makes the sea into dry land. And pronounce in this image whatever you remember, and thus you will first say *heh*, in the middle of your head, and draw it within your head as if you were contemplating and see the centre of your brain, and its central point in your thoughts, and envision the letter *heh* inscribed above it, which guards the existence of the points of your brain (cited in Idel, 1988b, p. 36).

Here we see Abulafia working with the word for 'sea', blending it with its antonym ('dry land'), and extracting the divine Name (YH, or *Yah*) from the first and last letters of the blended phrase. We may also note the embodied dimension of the process ('Head and belly and torso . . .), and the visualization of the single letter (*Heh*) within the brain. The context of the Hebrew words is the Exodus from Egypt, during which the sea was transformed into dry land (Exodus 14:15–31). The consequent passage of the Israelites through the sea — now dry land — is interpreted kabbalistically as referring to an ascent in spiritual level of being. The mystic ascends individually in parallel to the collective ascent from Egypt and the level of 'slavery'. Psychologically, the sea may be taken as a symbol of the unconscious, and the spiritual path is seen to entail entry into normally unconscious areas. Such interpretations properly belong with the discipline of depth psychology, which lies outside the remit of my article. Nevertheless, the extract serves well to illustrate the cognitive features of Abulafia's approach, and the clear objective — to attain a higher state — itself needs to be accommodated in psychological interpretations of this particular tradition.

It seems clear that the concentrative techniques and bodily accompaniments themselves would be likely to engender an altered state of consciousness. Indeed, Abulafia writes of a variety of effects characteristic of altered states, including warming of the heart, trembling of the body, the feeling of being anointed with oil, and experiencing seemingly out-of-body states. At the same time, the complexity of the linguistic technique presumably ensured that considerable discipline and focus were maintained. I have referred to the state which Jewish visionary mystics sought as one of 'controlled intra-psychic dissociation' (Lancaster, 1991, p. 155). There is a need to 'let go' of normal cognitive control in order that realities outside the range of everyday schemata might be experienced. Such 'letting go' implies a dissociated state in which the role of the ego is weakened. At the same time, descent into purely free play of the imagination is avoided by 'holding on' to the logic and detail of the linguistic practice itself. In the terms

Abulafia himself uses, the imagination is the domain of the *Satan*[11] and must be harnessed in the service of the Active Intellect, that aspect of mind which is shared between God and man.

The Psychology of Language Mysticism: Deconstruction and The Wheel

> Twenty-two foundation letters. He placed them in a wheel, like a wall with 231 gates. The wheel revolves forwards and backwards.... How? He permuted them, weighed them, and transformed them. *Alef* with them all and all of them with *alef; bet* with them all and all of them with *bet*. They continue in cycles and exist in 231 gates. Thus, all that is formed and all that is spoken emerges from one Name.[12]

The *Sefer Yetzirah* describes creation as a process whereby God generates letter combinations from the primary matter of individual letters. A useful modern analogy is provided by the elements of DNA being permuted into forms which generate characteristics when expressed biologically. Abulafia equates this wheel of the letters with the highest sphere of the intellect, seemingly the Active Intellect.[13] Accordingly, the Active Intellect represents both the fount of ideas emanating into manifestation and the level of mind achieved through successful practice of language mysticism. It is the sphere of union with the divine. The goal of Abulafia's language mysticism was indeed the achievement of such union and the consequential experience of *prophecy* which was attributed to the binding of the imaginative faculty to the Active Intellect.

Whether the Active Intellect can be usefully modelled in cognitive terms may be open to doubt. Aside from the problematic reductionism entailed, the concept itself seems to have undergone a number of transformations, especially during the mediaeval period which concerns us here. With this caveat in mind, however, I will return to the model presented in Figure 1. The model assumes that a sensory stimulus triggers multiple representations preconsciously. In the case of spoken polysemous word stimuli, for example, Pynte *et al.* (1984) and Swinney (1979) have demonstrated that a word's multiple meanings are activated simultaneously within 250 milliseconds. Depending on context, a single meaning subsequently enters consciousness, at which point the other, competing meanings seem to be inhibited. An instructive insight into the multiplicity at the preconscious level is also given by the syndrome of synaesthesia, in which sensory modalities become confused — as when someone *hears colours*. On the basis of his analysis of the brain structures involved in the syndrome, Cytowic (1993) argues that it occurs

---

[11] In Jewish thought, *Satan* refers to the force which opposes an individual in their spiritual path. The concept differs somewhat from the more externalized view of Satan, or the devil, propagated through Christian Europe.

[12] *Sefer Yetzirah*, Mishnayot 2:4–5. *Alef* and *bet* are the first two letters of the alphabet, and 231 is the number of two letter combinations which may be generated from the 22 letters of the Hebrew alphabet, ignoring reversals.

[13] In fact, this equivalence is established through the characteristic means of *gematria*, i.e., equating ideas through the numerical equivalence of phrases. *Yesh ra'el* ('There are 231' or 'Israel') = 541 = *sekhel ha-pu'al* ('Active Intellect'). *Gematria* depends on the fact that each Hebrew letter is also a number, *alef* = 1, *bet* = 2, etc.

when the normal multisensory preconscious activities are abnormally extended into consciousness. In other words, the syndrome is evidence for the view that prior to their articulation as stable, meaningful objects and events in consciousness, preconscious images and thoughts are represented in multiple fashion.

In Figure 1, the stage labelled 'examine' depicts this preconscious activation of multiple meanings. In a simplified diagrammatic form, representations connected with the centrally activated image, the pen, are shown to be activated. The image of a *wheel* of associations seems quite apposite to this stage. Normally, such associations will rapidly become inhibited as appropriate 'matches' are achieved, and the dominant image enters consciousness. The figure further conveys the role of 'I' in this process, for it is hypothesized that the dominant image becomes incorporated within the construction of the *unified 'I'*. Indeed, the everyday perceptual process is primarily driven by the need to perceive or think in terms of the categories relating to one's personal world. Contemplation, however, prolongs the 'examine' stage, bringing about consciousness of what are normally preconscious elements and, therefore, of a wider range of multiple meanings or associations (Lancaster, 1991). At the same time, the centrality of 'I' becomes attenuated since the Interpreter module's goal of a single, unified narrative with 'I' as central character is compromised by the multiplicity entering consciousness. As suggested above, the contemplative play of words and letters, as in the example cited from Abulafia, may be particularly effective in this regard on account of the role played by language in structuring the cognitive relationships between schemata.

'What is a "word"?' asks the twelfth-century *Sefer ha-Bahir*. 'That of which it is written, "A word fitly [Hebrew *afenav*] spoken" (Proverbs 25:11). Do not read "fitly" [a*fenav*] but "its wheel" [o*fenav*].' In this answer we see another example of the use of pun to convey a deeper meaning. Whilst we might think of a word as a singularity, a signifier of a specific meaning, this mystical text points rather to the way in which the word opens into a fluidity of meaning. For the Jewish mystic, such fluidity of meaning represents a gateway to the Active Intellect, and therefore to union with the divine. Psychologically, opening to what would normally be preconscious strategies of association might be expected to detach the mystic from habitual lines of meaning. Ouaknin uses the term 'designification' to indicate the distinctive, rabbinic approach to language: 'By "designifying", ideas oppose all semantic actualization and resist becoming object-concepts of a discourse' (Ouaknin, 1995, p. 287). We have here a specific formulation of the more general concept of 'deautomatization' which Deikman (1966) proposes as the psychological foundation of all mystical experience.

The associative nature of Abulafia's technique is well represented by the *wheel* imagery in his descriptions:

> And begin by combining this Name, namely Y-H-V-H, at the beginning alone, and examine all its combinations and move it and turn it about like a wheel returning around, front and back, like a scroll . . . . (cited in Idel, 1988b, p. 21).

In the continuation of this extract, Abulafia refers specifically to the 'rolling about of your thoughts'. However, 'spilling the blood of the languages' is more than mere word association, albeit of sacred words, for the intention is to 'revolve the languages until they return to their prime material state' (cited in Idel, 1989, p. 10), that is, until words no longer convey any cognitive meaning. In this we come to what may be considered especially distinctive in the language mysticism of ecstatic kabbalah, namely the sheer extent of deconstruction of schematic structures involved. Whilst numerous examples of word association, or substitution, may be found in these writings, the major intent was to deconstruct words to their constituent letters — the primary elements of language. This is the central thrust of the *Sefer Yetzirah*, the most important source for all strands of Hebrew language mysticism. Individual letters were to be visualized, and chanted together with other letters, with little or no concern for semantic content. In this sense, language was used effectively to transcend the compartmentalisation of meaning normally ascribed to language.

I noted earlier the relationship between language and self. I suggest that the ecstatic state engendered by the complex of fasting, breath control, visualizations, and associative language techniques would have been likely to bring about alterations in the experience of self. Moreover, reference to the physical body was central to the entire practice since the *Sefer Yetzirah* assigns each letter to a specific bodily part. Given the importance of embodiment for our sense of self, I envisage this embodied dimension of the letters adding critically to the disturbance of the normal self experience (Lancaster, 1997c). Indeed, complex procedures were used whereby specific regions of the body were 'energized' through these correspondences with letters (Ouaknin, 1992). Whilst the given letter was visualized, or chanted, the corresponding body region expanded in the mystic's awareness, pulsing with light or vibrating with the reverberating sound. For Abulafia, however, the emphasis lay on negating the experience of the body. Just as the letters were to be stripped of meaning, so would the mystic's body become void of personal 'ownership'. Abulafia writes of this parallel between deconstruction of language and that of the body:

> Know that all the limbs of your body are combined like that of the forms of the letters combined one with the other. Know also that when you combine them it is you who distinguish between the forms of the letters for in their prime-material state they are equal . . . and with one sweep you can erase them all from a writing board. So too [with] all the moisture of your body and all of your limbs . . . they all return to their prime-material state (cited in Idel, 1989, p. 6).

As noted above, the letters were considered the agents of creation, and the assignation of 'limbs' to letters represents the connection between the mystic's individual body and the collective body of the primordial Adam, that is, the archetypal human form as 'created in the image of the divine'. We find here, then, two aspects to the alterations in bodily self inferred to accompany these mystical practices. The first, parallelling the deconstruction of letter combinations, is a deconstruction of self; and the second, parallelling the ultimate unity of the Name, entails a sense of union with the collective human form.

The encounter with self within this tradition, moreover, appears to have bridged normal bodily boundaries. A testimony left by an anonymous disciple of Abulafia describes reaching a stage 'beyond the control of your thinking' when:

> [T]hat which is within will manifest itself without, and through the power of sheer imagination will take on the form of a polished mirror. And this is 'the flame of the circling sword', the rear revolving and becoming the fore. Whereupon one sees that his inmost being is something outside of himself (Scholem, 1961, p. 155).

Such cases of heautoscopy, whereby an individual sees their self before them (seemingly akin to what are described today as 'out-of-body experiences'), were held to be a defining feature of the prophetic state. Scholem reports an anonymous author who ascribes to Rabbi Nathan the following:

> Know that the complete secret of prophecy is that there arises suddenly before the prophet the form of his self standing before him, and he forgets his [normal] self and it is transported from him (Scholem, 1930, p. 287).

Although it is known that disturbances of the temporal or parietal lobes can trigger hallucinations of the experience of self, the question of what bearing — if any — description of the neural events associated with pathological states has on our understanding of mystical phenomena remains open. I consider that explanatory models focusing on the cognitive basis of these kinds of phenomena offer a more productive approach than those which focus primarily on neural structures since their functional emphasis potentially offers insight into the meaning of the phenomena. In the context of the model presented in this article, I speculate that attenuation of the normal generation of the *unified 'I'* as a habitual constituent of mental activity can dispose the individual to diverse experiences of self, which may range from a loss of self to the kinds of displacement of the bodily location of self indicated in the above extracts. Such outcomes may arise for a variety of reasons and in a variety of frameworks, including ones that are transformational in a positive sense as well as those that are pathological. In the present context, my interest lies in the effects of contemplation and mystical manipulation of language.

In the model presented in Figures 1 and 2, the representations activated during the 'examine' stage are associated with 'I'-tags, which are memory elements depicting the sense of self attaching to previous experience of these various representations. 'I'-tags are, moreover, the memory elements in relation to which the unified 'I' is normally constructed (Lancaster, 1997a; 1997b). It seems reasonable to propose that when a broader range than normal of representations triggered during the 'examine' stage become conscious (through the contemplative process described above), there ensues a hyperactivation of 'I'-tags. Given that the normal organisation of these elements into the *unified 'I'* is attenuated, such hyperactivation of 'I'-tags would eventuate in non-habitual self-related experience — the mystic might indeed see 'his self standing before him'.

The notion that mystical practices alter the experience of self and its relation to the perceived world is hardly surprising. Mystical traditions generally concur in the view that the sense of the individual self constitutes some form of barrier to spiritual 'progress', and that our conventional perception of the world is, at best, selective, and, at worst, delusional. Language is probably the primary tool in maintaining normal reality orientation, by which is meant an everyday sense of the reality of self in its relation to the body and of the physical–spatial world around one. It seems hardly surprising, then, that the deconstruction of language — 'spilling the blood of the languages' — practised over prolonged periods, would eventuate in a deconstruction of the schematic structures through which both the sense of the world and the experience of self are mediated.

It would be a mistake to conclude that Hebrew language mysticism is concerned only with such deconstructive processes, however. An equally forceful emphasis is on the 'reconstructive' use of language. This is evident in the appeals to a higher, or more inclusive, view of language, especially with regard to the divine Name and God's own use of language in creation. I conjecture that by reconnecting deconstructed language elements with the various (and elaborate) permutations of the Name, the mystic is effectively substituting the all-encompassing divine Being into the role normally played by 'I'-tags. Or, to put it another way, the 'I'-tag system becomes subjected to the highest-order indexing system feasible — a kind of *transpersonal* tagging system giving a sense of one's place in the divine mind. Such a proposal is necessarily speculative, but it is perhaps worth elaborating. The one element that is found throughout all strands of Jewish mysticism is contemplation of the Names of God. In the linguistic practices which I have been analysing, working with the letters of the various Names — visualising and chanting them, permuting them and expanding them — continually filled the vacuum left by deconstructing other, mundane, linguistic meanings. My proposal is that whereas in the developing individual the representation of 'I' plays the central role in memory, such that all conscious events or images become indexed by reference to 'I', for these mystics it is their representation of the divine — necessarily linguistic — which takes on such a central indexing function. This may indeed be the enduring psychological consequence of a mystic achieving awareness of the 'I-ness' of God (Idel, 1988a, p. 64).

Ultimately, the attempt to model spiritual meaning in psychological terms reaches the question of *belief*. At the least, and holding a perspective grounded in psychological science, the enlargement of the sphere of meaning implicit in such a transpersonal tagging system might be considered adaptive in a therapeutic sense, since the petty complexes associated with the mundane self system would be transcended (although a cynic might be concerned about possible dogmatic tendencies associated with the mystic's image of the divine). Moreover, the loosening of the bonds of the schematic structure should result in greater creativity.[14] Indeed, Abulafia's extensive elaborations on the associations between words and concepts seem to me to be especially creative. He repeatedly enters into complex

[14] It is relevant to note in this context that the imagery of loosening and re-tying knots is specifically used by Abulafia: 'He must link and change a name with a name, and renew a matter, to tie the loosened and to loosen the tied, using known names, in their revolutions . . . until the one tying and loosening will strip off from the stringencies of the prohibited and the permitted, and dress a new form for the prohibited and permitted' (cited in Idel, 1988b, pp. 136–7).

codified linguistic and numerological systems of thought in order to draw out ideas which are distinctively compelling in their insight into the relationship between the divine and human spheres.

Such putative psychological gains hardly capture the mystics' own religious objective, however. Without doubt these mystics intended to realize their spiritual potential through union with the divine, and language was for them the essential medium for such encounter. A cognitive model cannot fully convey the notion of the human mind somehow extending into the transpersonal, or divine, realm. I am proposing that the preconscious elaboration of possibilities as modelled above, together with the emotional concomitants of entering an altered state of consciousness, may be keys for comprehending the psychology of the kinds of ecstatic states under consideration. However, as William James's studies of religious experience led him to conclude a century ago, there would seem to be a further dimension with which the mind connects in such states:

> The further limits of our being plunge, it seems to me, into an altogether other dimension of existence from the sensible and merely 'understandable' world. Name it the mystical region, or the supernatural region, whichever you choose. So far as our ideal impulses originate in this region . . . , we belong to it in a more intimate sense than that in which we belong to the visible world . . . . (James, 1960, p. 490).

I am inclined to think that the spontaneity in the preconscious fount of associations may be some kind of window into such an 'other dimension'. I envisage trains of activity being generated by each and every image which enters the mind. Simple association ignites connected images which in turn incandesce, triggering ever more connections without the imposition of those limitations which arrive only with the sense of 'I'. It is a ceaseless preconscious effervescence which forms the kernel of the memory process. Perhaps this represents the central dynamic of the Active Intellect, that is, its real *activity*. At root, the spontaneous movement of the psyche — its generation of images and its incessant blending of forms in the fluid quest for meaning — is the essential spark of the divine mirrored within. The mystic seeks a vehicle with which to reach towards that spark, and for the Jewish mystic there is no vehicle equivalent, in terms of transcendent power, to the Hebrew language itself:

> As far as man is concerned, the letters . . . by means of [their] combinations aid the soul to actualise its potential with much greater ease than any other means (cited in Idel, 1989, p. 6).

References

Baars, B.J. (1996), 'Understanding subjectivity: global workspace theory and the resurrection of the observing self', *Journal of Consciousness Studies*, **3** (3), pp. 211–16.

Block, N. (1995), 'On a confusion about a function of consciousness', *Behavioral and Brain Sciences*, **18**, pp. 227–87.

Bisiach, E. (1988), 'The (haunted) brain and consciousness', in *Consciousness in Contemporary Science*, ed. A.J. Marcel & E. Bisiach (Oxford: Clarendon Press).

Boyarin, D. (1990), *Intertextuality and the Reading of Midrash* (Bloomington & Indianapolis: Indiana University Press).

Bruner, J. (1997), 'A narrative model of self-construction', in *The Self across Psychology: Self-Recognition, Self-Awareness, and the Self Concept*, ed. J.G. Snodgrass & R.L. Thompson (New York: The New York Academy of Sciences) (Annals vol. 818).

Cousins, E.H. (1992), 'Bonaventura's mysticism of language', in Katz (1992).

Cytowic, R.E. (1993), *The Man Who Tasted Shapes: A Bizarre Medical Mystery Offers Revolutionary Insights into Reasoning, Emotion, and Consciousness* (New York: Warner Books).

D'Aquili, E.G. and Newberg, A.A. (1993), 'Religious and mystical states: A neuropsychological model', *Zygon: Journal of Religion and Science*, **28**, pp. 177–200.

Damasio, A.R. (1989), 'Time-locked multiregional retroactivation: A systems-level proposal for the neural substrates of recall and recognition', *Cognition*, **33**, pp. 25–62.

Deikman, A.J. (1966), 'Deautomatization and the mystic experience', *Psychiatry*, **29**, pp. 324–38.

Dennett, D.C. (1991), *Consciousness Explained* (Boston, MA: Little, Brown & Co).

Dennett, D.C. (1996), *Kinds of Minds* (New York: Basic Books).

Edel, S. (1996), 'Métaphysique des idées et mystique des lettres: Leibniz, Böhme et la Kabbale prophétique', *Revue de l'Histoire des Religions*, **213–4**, pp. 443–66.*

Faur, J. (1986), *Golden Doves with Silver Dots: Textuality in Rabbinic Tradition* (Bloomington & Indianapolis: Indiana University Press).

Forman, R.K.C. (ed. 1990), *The Problem of Pure Consciousness: Mysticism and Philosophy* (New York: Oxford University Press).

Forman, R.K.C. (1993), 'Mystical knowledge: knowledge by identity', *Journal of the American Academy of Religion*, **61**, pp. 705–38.

Forman, R.K.C. (1998), 'What does mysticism have to teach us about consciousness?', *Journal of Consciousness Studies*, **5** (2), pp. 185–201.

Gazzaniga, M.S. (1985), *The Social Brain* (New York: Basic Books).

Gazzaniga, M.S. (1988), 'Brain modularity: Towards a philosophy of conscious experience', in *Consciousness in Contemporary Science*, ed. A.J. Marcel & E. Bisiach (Oxford: Clarendon Press).

Handelman, S. (1981), 'Interpretation as devotion: Freud's relation to rabbinic hermeneutics', *Psychoanalytic Review*, **68**, pp. 201–18.

Handelman, S. (1985), *The Slayers of Moses: The Emergence of Rabbinic Interpretation in Modern Literary Theory* (Albany, NY: State University of New York Press).

Hayes, L. (1997), 'Understanding mysticism', *The Psychological Record*, **47**, pp. 573–96.

Idel, M. (1988a), *Kabbalah: New Perspectives* (New Haven, CT: Yale University Press).

Idel, M. (1988b), *The Mystical Experience in Abraham Abulafia* (Albany, NY: State University of New York Press).

Idel, M. (1989), *Language, Torah and Hermeneutics in Abraham Abulafia*, trans. M. Kallus. (Albany, NY: State University of New York Press).

Idel, M. (1992), 'Reification of language in Jewish mysticism', in Katz (1992).

Idel, M. (1995), *Hasidism: Between Ecstasy and Magic.* (Albany, NY: State University of New York Press).

James, W. (1902/1960), *The Varieties of Religious Experience: A Study in Human Nature* (London: Fontana).

Jung, C.G (1968), 'The Symbolism of the mandala', in *Psychology and Alchemy CW Vol. 12. 2ⁿᵈ edn*. Originally published 1944.

Katz, S.T. (ed. 1983), *Mysticism and Religious Traditions* (New York: Oxford University Press).

Katz, S.T. (ed. 1992), *Mysticism and Language* (Oxford: Oxford University Press).

Kihlstrom, J.F. (1993), 'The psychological unconscious and the self', in *Experimental and Theoretical Studies of Consciousness*, Ciba Foundation Symposium no. 174. (Chichester, UK: Wiley).

Kihlstrom, J.F. (1997), 'Consciousness and me-ness', in *Scientific Approaches to Consciousness*, ed. J.D. Cohen & J.W. Schooler (Mahwah, NJ: Lawrence Erlbaum).

Krippner, S. and Winkler, M. (1995), 'Postmodernity and consciousness studies', *Journal of Mind and Behavior*, **16**, pp. 255–80.

Lancaster, B.L. (1991), *Mind, Brain and Human Potential: the Quest for an Understanding of Self* (Shaftesbury, UK and Rockport, MA: Element Books).

Lancaster, B.L. (1993), 'Self or no-self? Converging perspectives from neuropsychology and mysticism', *Zygon: Journal of Religion and Science*, **28**, pp. 509–28.

Lancaster, B.L. (1997a), 'On the stages of perception: Towards a synthesis of cognitive neuroscience and the Buddhist Abhidhamma tradition', *Journal of Consciousness Studies*, **4** (2), pp. 122–42.

Lancaster, B.L. (1997b), 'The mythology of anatta: Bridging the East–West divide', in *The Authority of Experience: Essays on Buddhism and Psychology*, ed. J. Pickering (Richmond, UK: Curzon Press).

Lancaster, B.L. (1997c), 'The *golem* as a transpersonal image: 2. Psychological features in the mediaeval golem ritual', *Transpersonal Psychology Review*, **1** (4), pp. 23–30.

Mangan, B. (1994), 'Language and experience in the cognitive study of mysticism — commentary on Forman', *Journal of Consciousness Studies*, **1** (2), pp. 250–2.

Moscovitch, M. (1994), 'Recovered consciousness: A hypothesis concerning modularity and episodic memory', *Journal of Clinical and Experimental Neuropsychology*, **17**, pp. 276–90.

Moscovitch, M. (1995), 'Models of consciousness and memory', in *The Cognitive Neurosciences*, ed. M.S. Gazzaniga (Cambridge, MA & London: MIT Books).

Ouaknin, M-A. (1992), *Tsimtsoum: Introduction à la Méditation Hébraïque* (Paris:Albin Michel).

Ouaknin, M-A. (1995), *The Burnt Book: Reading the Talmud*, trans. L. Brown. (Princeton, NJ: Princeton University Press). Originally published (French) 1986.

Persinger, M.A. (1987), *Neuropsychological Bases of God Beliefs* (New York: Praeger).

Pynte, J., Do, P. and Scampa, P. (1984), 'Lexical decisions during the reading of sentences containing polysemous words', in *Preparatory States and Processes*, ed. S. Komblum & J. Requin (Mahwah, NJ: Lawrence Erlbaum).

Rolls, E.T. (1997), 'Brain mechanisms of vision, memory, and consciousness', in *Cognition, Computation, and Consciousness*, ed. M. Ito, Y. Miyashita and E.T. Rolls (Oxford: Oxford University Press).

Sacks, O. (1986), *The Man who Mistook his Wife for a Hat* (London: Pan Books). Originally published 1985.

Schimmel, A-M. (1975), *Mystical Dimensions of Islam* (University of North Carolina Press).

Scholem, G.G. (1930), 'Eine kabbalistische Erklärung der Prophetie als Selbstbegegnung', *Monatsschrift für Geschichte und Wissenschaft des Judentums,* **74**, pp. 285–90.*

Scholem, G.G. (1961), *Major Trends in Jewish Mysticism* (New York: Schocken Books). Originally published 1941.

Sullivan, P.R. (1995), 'Contentless consciousness and information-processing theories of mind', *Philosophy, Psychiatry, Psychology*, **2**, pp. 51–59.

Swinney, D.A. (1979), 'Lexical access during sentence comprehension: (Re)consideration of context effects', *Journal of Verbal Learning and Verbal Behavior*, **18**, pp. 645–59.

Teyler, T.J. and DiScenna, P. (1986), 'The hippocampal memory indexing theory', *Behavioral Neuroscience*, **100**, pp. 147–54.

Tucci, G. (1961), *The Theory and Practice of the Mandala. With Special Reference to the Modern Psychology of the Unconscious*, trans. A. H. Brodrick (London: Rider & Co). Originally published 1949.

Urbach, E.E. (1979), *The Sages: Their Concepts and Beliefs, Second enlarged edition*, trans. I. Abrahams. (Jerusalem: The Magnes Press).

Velmans, M. (1996), 'An introduction to the science of consciousness', in *The Science of Consciousness: Psychological, Neuropsychological and Clinical Reviews*, ed. M. Velmans (London & New York: Routledge).

Wolfson, E.R. (1994), *Through a Speculum that Shines: Vision and Imagination in Medieval Jewish Mysticism* (Princeton, NJ: Princeton University Press).

Translations from Hebrew and Aramaic sacred texts are the author's own.

English versions are available as follows.

The Bahir, ed. A. Kaplan (New York: Samuel Weiser, 1979)

The Jerusalem Bible (Jerusalem: Koren Publishers, 1992).

The Mishnah ((7 vols.), ed. P. Blackman (New York: Judaica Press, 1963).

The Midrash (10 vols.), ed. H. Friedman & M. Simon (London: Soncino Press, 1961).

Sefer Yetzirah, ed. A. Kaplan (New York: Samuel Weiser, 1990)

The Talmud (18 vols.), ed. I. Epstein (London: Soncino Press, 1961).

The Zohar. Extensive extracts may be found in *The Wisdom of the Zohar*, ed. I. Tishby, transl. D. Goldstein (Oxford: Oxford University Press, 1989).

* I am grateful to my wife, Dr. Irene Lancaster, for her translations of these articles.

Andrew B. Newberg and Eugene G. d'Aquili

The Neuropsychology of Religious and Spiritual Experience

This paper considers the neuropsychology of religious and spiritual experiences. This requires a review of our current understanding of brain function as well as an integrated synthesis to derive a neuropsychological model of spiritual experiences. Religious and spiritual experiences are highly complex states that likely involve many brain structures including those involved in higher order processing of sensory and cognitive input as well as those involved in the elaboration of emotions and autonomic responses. Such an analysis can help elucidate the biological correlates of these experiences and provide new information regarding the function of the human brain.

Introduction

This paper will consider the neuropsychology of religious and spiritual experience. A neuropsychological analysis of these experiences serves several important purposes. It helps to elucidate the biological correlates of these experiences and provides new information regarding the function of the human brain. It provides a new understanding of how and why these experiences have had such an important role in human thought and history. And finally, it leads to an understanding of the relationship between these experiences and human health and psychological well being.

Religious and spiritual experiences such as those associated with meditation, prayer, and ritual have been described in the biomedical, psychological, anthropological, and religious literature. It has been suggested that such experiences became possible with the evolution of various structures in the brain of early primates and eventually of *Homo sapiens* (Laughlin & d'Aquili, 1974). The concatenation of 'religiogenic' brain mechanisms in *Homo sapiens* was accompanied historically by the advent of a number of religious traditions in both Eastern and Western civilizations that have continued to permeate human societies since prehistoric times. More recently, neurobiological and neuropsychological correlates of religious and spiritual experiences have begun to be postulated. By considering the current neuropsychological literature, a more complex model of the

Journal of Consciousness Studies, **7**, No. 11–12, 2000, pp. 251–66

neurophysiological events that occur during religious and spiritual experiences can be developed. Neurophysiological correlates of these experiences also can be considered in relation to the brain's interconnection with other aspects of body physiology that are modulated by the autonomic nervous system as well as the neuroendocrine system. A consideration of this relation between cognitive processes in the brain and the autonomic nervous system may yield a more complete understanding of a variety of spiritual experiences ranging from a feeling of 'awe' to intense unitary states. On the basis of these analyses, a foundation for the development of a neuropsychological model can be considered in order to guide future studies in the neurobiology of religious and spiritual experiences. In addition, the use of state-of-the-art brain imaging techniques such as functional magnetic resonance imaging (fMRI), positron emission tomography (PET), and single photon emission computed tomography (SPECT) have begun to be utilized, in addition to traditional electroencephalography (EEG), to investigate brain function in general and religious and spiritual experiences in particular (Newberg & Alavi, 1996; Newberg et al., 1998). One further point regarding the study of religious and spiritual experiences is that these are subjective states that may have many different aspects and result from a variety of different approaches. We hope to present a relatively general approach to the neuropsychology of these states realizing that individual experiences ultimately must have unique physiological correlates. However, for neuroscience techniques to be useful, we must explore the general characteristics of these states first before proceeding to specific attributes of these states.

Methods of Attaining Spiritual Experiences

In considering a neuropsychological and neuroevolutionary approach to the study of religious and spiritual experiences, it is important to consider two major avenues towards attaining such experiences. These two basic categories are group ritual and individual contemplation or meditation. It must be understood that within these two general categories, there are thousands of possible approaches. Furthermore, there are also 'hybrids' such that individual meditation takes place as part of a group or when ceremonial ritual is performed by an individual. Even hybrid approaches can usually be classified into one category or the other. The major determining factor is whether or not the stimulation is from the external environment (i.e. via interindividual interaction, music, etc.) or whether the experience is being purely internally driven (i.e. via meditation, prayer, etc). However, it is probably helpful to consider these two broad categories rather than focus on highly specific practices if general neurophysiological models of such practices are to be developed. Thus, we do not intend in this paper to relate specific practices and experiences to neuropsychological correlates; instead, we endeavour to develop general principles from which detailed neuropsychological models of specific experiences and practices can be developed. A phenomenological analysis of group and individual practices reveals that they are similar in kind, if not in intensity, along two dimensions: (1) intermittent emotional discharges involving the subjective sensation of awe, peace, tranquillity, or ecstasy; and (2) varying degrees of unitary experience correlating with the emotional discharges just mentioned (d'Aquili & Newberg, 1993). These unitary experiences may consist of a decreased sense or awareness of the boundaries between the self and the external world (d'Aquili & Newberg, 1993; Smart, 1969; 1978; Stace, 1961). The latter dimension can also lead to a sense of oneness with other practitioners thereby generating a sense of community. At the extreme, unitary experiences can eventually lead to a state of undifferentiated oneness with consequent abolition of all boundaries of discrete being (d'Aquili & Newberg, 1993).

It should be noted that the experiences of group ritual and individual meditation have a certain degree of overlap such that each may play a role in the other. In fact, it may be that human ceremonial ritual actually provides the 'average' person access to mystical experience ('average' in distinction to those regularly practising intense contemplation such as highly religious monks). This by no means implies that the mystic or contemplative is impervious to the effects of ceremonial ritual. Precisely because of the intense unitary experiences arising from meditation, mystics may be more affected by ceremonial ritual than the average person.

Brain Function and Structure

It may be helpful to consider the brain as having particular functions by which it interprets sensory input and thoughts (d'Aquili, 1978; 1983). We have previously called these functions cognitive operators. Cognitive operators refer to general methods or functions by which the brain interprets the world. These are not meant to be atomic in the sense that they represent specific, undivided modules of brain function, but rather refer to global functions. Furthermore, the cognitive operators can be attributed to the function of complex neuronal interactions, sometimes involving a number of brain structures. The cognitive operators include the application of quantitation to sensory and cognitive input, the abstraction of generals from particulars, the perception of spatial or temporal sequences in external reality, and the ordering of elements of reality into causal chains giving rise to explanatory models of the external world whether scientific or mythical. It should be mentioned that the cognitive operators are similar to the concept of cognitive modules in that both refer to functions of the brain that are based on certain neural interactions. However, we have usually used to the term cognitive operator to describe very broad or overarching functions while cognitive modules usually refer to more specific functions. For example, what we refer to as the 'quantitative operator' implies the brain's functional ability to manipulate and utilize numbers. Several investigators have demonstrated specific quantitative modules in the brain that perform specific numerical applications (Dahaene, 1997). There is certainly some overlap between the two concepts and the evidence to support one usually could be utilized for the other.

With regards to religious and spiritual experiences, several of the operators we have previously described require consideration. The causal operator refers to the brain's ability to perform causal ordering of events in reality as experienced by sensory perception (d'Aquili, 1978). The ability to derive causality from events in the external world appears to result primarily from the functioning of the inferior parietal lobule in the left hemisphere, the anterior convexity of the frontal lobes, primarily in the left hemisphere, and their reciprocal neural interconnections (Luria, 1966; Pribram, 1973; Mills & Rollman, 1980). This causal function of the brain organizes any set of events in reality into what is subjectively perceived as causal sequences back to some original event. In view of the apparently universal human trait of positing causes for any given event, we postulate that if some original causal event is not given by sense data, the brain automatically generates such an event. The Western scientific method refuses to postulate an initial terminus or first cause for any strip of reality unless it is observed or can be immediately inferred from observation. We propose that when no observational or 'scientific' causal explanation is forthcoming for a strip of reality, some other causative construct is automatically generated by the causal operator. Thus, the brain simply operates spontaneously on reality, positing an initial causal terminus when none is given. This function often constructs various myths filled with personalized power sources (i.e. God, gods, spirits, etc.) to explain the world.

A second operator that has particular significance regarding spiritual experience is the holistic operator. The holistic operator refers to the brain's ability to view reality as a whole or as a gestalt. This operator allows for the abstraction from particulars or individuals into a larger contextual framework. The parts of the brain responsible for holistic operations likely resides in the parietal lobe in the non-dominant hemisphere, more specifically, in the posterior superior parietal lobule and adjacent areas that have been found to be involved in generating gestalt understanding about both sensory input and various abstract concepts (Schiavetto et al., 1999; Gazzaniga & Hillyard, 1971). It is interesting that this area sits opposite to the area in the dominant hemisphere that provides the neuroanatomical substrate for logical-grammatical operations. Thus, the right parietal lobe is involved in the generation of a holistic approach to things and the left parietal lobe is involved in more reductionist/analytical processes.

A Neurophysiological Review

Any understanding of the neuropsychological basis of spiritual experience necessarily requires at least a basic understanding of neurobiology. Therefore, it is helpful to consider here the neurobiological concepts that are particularly relevant to spiritual experience. We will consider some of the major anatomical and functional components of human neurobiology. Furthermore, we will try to build this review using a 'bottom-up' approach, considering the more primitive evolutionary aspects first and finishing with the cerebral cortex.

The autonomic nervous system

The autonomic nervous system is responsible, in conjuction with the rest of the brain, for maintaining baseline body functions. Thus, this system keeps us alive, but also plays a crucial role in the overall activity of the brain as well as in the generation of fundamental emotions such as fear. The autonomic nervous system is traditionally understood to be composed of two sub-systems, the sympathetic and parasympathetic system (Hugdahl, 1996; or for a detailed discussion of the autonomic nervous system please see Kandel *et al.*, 2000). The sympathetic system is responsible for the so-called fight-or-flight response which is the physiological basis of our adaptive strategies either to noxious stimuli or to highly desirable stimuli in the environment (Gellhorn, 1967; Gellhorn & Loofbourrow, 1963). Since the functions of the sympathetic nervous system are involved in the expenditure of the body's energy and metabolism, the total of the sympathetic system with its associated brain structures has been called the ergotropic system (Lex, 1979).

The parasympathetic system, on the other hand, is responsible for maintaining homeostasis (Gellhorn, 1967; Gellhorn & Loofbourrow, 1963). Since the functions of the parasympathetic nervous system are involved with the conservation of body energy and the maintenance of baseline metabolism, the total of the parasympathetic system with its associated brain structures has been called the trophotropic system (Lex, 1979).

The ergotropic and trophotropic systems have often been described as 'antagonistic' to each other, but they can be complementary to each other under certain conditions. Normally, the increased activity of one tends to produce decreased activity in the other. Each system is designed to inhibit the functioning of the other under most circumstances. However, studies have shown that if either system is driven to maximal stimulation, one can induce 'reversal' or 'spillover' phenomena (Gellhorn & Keily, 1972; Hugdahl, 1996). This spillover phenomenon occurs when continued stimulation of one system to maximal capacity begins to produce activation responses (rather than inhibitory) in the other.

We have proposed, in a previous work (d'Aquili & Newberg, 1999), five basic categories of ergotropic/trophotropic events and their sensorial concomitants which may occur during extraordinary phases of consciousness. The Hypertrophotropic State in which trophotropic activity is exceptionally high, may result in extraordinary states of quiescence. This activity can occur during normal sleep but may occur during deep meditation, prayer, or other related activities. The Hyperergotropic State occurs when ergotropic activity is exceptionally high. This results in an extraordinary state of unblocked arousal and excitation and is associated with keen alertness and concentration in the absence of superfluous thought and fantasy (Czikszentmihalyi, 1975).

The next two autonomic states involve hyperactivation of one system with spillover into excitation of the other system. Thus, the Hypertrophotropic State with Ergotropic Eruption is the state when trophotropic activity is so extreme that 'spillover' occurs and the ergotropic system becomes activated (Gellhorn & Kiely, 1972). During certain types of meditation, for example, we have proposed that as the hypertrophotropic state creates a sense of oceanic bliss, the ergotropic eruption results in the experience of a sense of a tremendous release of energy. The Hyperergotropic State with Trophotropic Eruption occurs when ergotropic activity is so extreme that 'spillover' occurs and the trophotropic system becomes activated. This may be associated with the experience of an orgasmic, rapturous, or ecstatic rush, arising from a generalized sense of flow and resulting in a trance-like state.

There is recent evidence of unusual autonomic fluctuations during meditative states in which there was a significant increase in heart rate oscillations during both Qigong meditation and Kundalini Yoga meditation (Peng et al., 1999). The authors concluded that there is a complex pattern of autonomic activity, involving both sympathetic and parasympathetic systems, that is occurring during these meditative practices.

The fifth and final state involves maximal stimulation of both the ergotropic and trophotropic systems (d'Aquili & Newberg, 1993). We have postulated that this state is likely associated with the most intense forms of mystical experience and may lie at the heart of compelling spiritual experiences, meditative states, near death experiences, and other types of human experiential phenomena (d'Aquili & Newberg, 1993; Newberg & d'Aquili, 1994). While, it is difficult to test such a hypothesis due to the difficulty of isolating these experiences, we can utilize what studies have actually been performed to consider how such experiences might occur.

Brain structure and function

The brain itself is divided into a number of subdivisions. The first subdivision separates the brain into a left and right hemisphere. The cerebral hemispheres are generally regarded as the seat of higher level cognitive and emotional functions. It is known that the cerebral cortex likely underlies the development of complex thought, language, religion, art and culture.

In addition to the cerebral cortex, there are a group of structures near the base of the brain that are called the limbic system. The limbic system is associated with the more complex aspects of emotions and is involved with assigning emotional feelings to various objects and experiences and directing these emotions outward via behaviour (Damasio, 1994;1999). The limbic system is also interconnected with the ergotropic and trophotropic components of the autonomic nervous system via the hypothalamus. The limbic system has also been implicated as having a major role in religious and spiritual experiences (d'Aquili & Newberg, 1993; Saver & Rabin, 1997; Joseph, 2000).

The hypothalamus is one of the most ancient structures in the brain from an evolutionary perspective. The medial part of the hypothalamus is an extension of the trophotropic system into the brain while the lateral hypothalamus seems to be an extension of the ergotropic system into the brain (Smith et al., 1990). The amygdala is more recently developed evolutionarily than the hypothalamus and is preeminent in the control and modulation of higher order emotional and motivational functions, particularly those pertaining to arousal or fear (Morris et al., 1996). In addition to emotional and motivational functioning, the amygdala is also involved in attention, learning, and memory. The function of the amygdala is complex and although it has primarily an ergotropic function, it also has some functions usually attributable to trophotropic activity (Davis, 1992).

The final structure of the limbic system that requires discussion is the hippocampus. A number of investigators have assigned a major role to the hippocampus in information processing, including memory, new learning, cognitive mapping of the environment, and focusing attention. The hippocampus is greatly influenced by the amygdala, which in turn monitors and responds to hippocampal activity (Halgren, 1992). The hippocampus and amygdala complement each other and interact in regard to attention and generation of emotionally linked images, as well as in regard to learning and memory. The hippocampus also partially regulates the activity in another structure that connects the autonomic nervous system to the cerebral cortex called the thalamus (Green & Adey, 1956). Since the thalamus is a major relay between a variety of brain structures, the hippocampus can sometimes block information input to various brain structures via the thalamus. It is important to note that while the amygdala may enhance information transfer between brain regions, the hippocampus usually tends to do the reverse. Through interconnections with the amygdala and the hypothalamus, the hippocapmus can also prevent emotional extremes (Redding, 1967). This ability to inhibit the transfer of information from one region to another, in addition to its control over emotional responses will prove to be very important in generating certain experiences related to religious and spiritual experiences.

Association areas

As we return to the cerebral cortex with its structures involved in higher cognitive, sensory, and emotional functioning, we note that there are four association areas that integrate neuronal activity from various other areas in the brain. These cortical regions are the posterior superior parietal lobule (PSPL), the inferior temporal lobe (ITL), the inferior parietal lobule (IPL), and the prefrontal cortex (PFC).

The PSPL is heavily involved in the analysis and integration of higher order sensory information. Through the reception of auditory and visual input, the PSPL is also able to create a three dimensional image of the body in space (Lynch, 1980). There is some difference in function between the PSPL on the right and the PSPL on the left. It has been observed that the right parietal lobe appears to play an important role in generalized localization and the sense of spatial coordinates, whereas the left PSPL exerts influences in regard to objects that may be directly grasped and manipulated (Mountcastle, 1976). That some neurons in the left PSPL respond most to stimuli within grasping distance, and other neurons respond most to stimuli just beyond arms reach suggests that the distinction between self and other may, in part, arise from the left PSPL's ability to judge these two categories of distances. Thus, it seems probable that the self-other dichotomy is a left PSPL function that evolved from its more primitive division of space into the graspable and the non-graspable.

The ITL neurons scan the entire visual field so as to alert the organism to objects of interest or motivational importance through its interconnections with the limbic nuclei. Brain imaging studies using PET have also shown that the ITL and PSPL are involved in the visual perception and learning of complex geometric patterns (Roland & Gulyas, 1995).

The IPL is located at the confluence of the temporal, parietal, and occipital lobes. The IPL is an association area of association areas, and maintains rich interconnections with the visual, auditory, and somaesthetic association areas. This area is generally regarded as responsible for the generation of abstract concepts and relating them to words.

The prefrontal cortex is the only area that receives afferent fibres from all sensory modalities, as well as from the other association areas (Fuster, 1997). The prefrontal cortex is involved in mediating concepts via its rich interconnections with the inferior parietal lobe (Stuss & Benson, 1986). Also, and importantly for our concerns here, the prefrontal cortex of each hemisphere is connected to the prefrontal cortex of the other by connecting nerve fibres (Stuss & Benson, 1986).

In humans, the loss of the ability to concentrate is a characteristic feature of any prefrontal disorder, as is the loss of the ability to plan and to orient oneself to future behaviour (Frith *et al.*, 1991). Patients with prefrontal lesions not only lose the ability to plan and orient themselves to future activity, but they also suffer a severe deficit in carrying out complex perceptual and conceptual tasks. Patients with prefrontal disorders also exhibit flatness of affect and apathy and tend to have difficulty controlling emotion (Fuster, 1997; Stuss & Benson, 1986). To put it bluntly, a great part of what one sees with this disorder is a loss of will or of the capacity to form intention. If any part of the brain can be said to be the seat of the will or of intentionality it is certainly the prefrontal cortex (Frith *et al.*, 1991).

Deafferentation

One other aspect of brain function that may play an important role in spiritual experience is the ability of certain brain structures to block input into other structures. This blocking of input into a brain structure is called deafferentation. There is much evidence of such phenonena arising from natural (i.e. stroke or neuronal degeneration) or induced lesions in various parts of the brain (Baron *et al.*, 1986; Gilbert & Peterson, 1991; Jeltsch *et al.*, 1994; Kataoka *et al.*, 1991). Deafferentation of a brain structure also can occur via the activity of inhibitory fibres from other nervous system structures. For example, it has been shown that one hemisphere can be prevented from knowing what is occurring in the opposite hemisphere by the inhibitory or deafferenting actions of the frontal lobes (Hoppe, 1977). There is similar evidence that intrahemispheric information transmission can be partially or totally prevented via impulses originating in the prefrontal cortex and passing via the hippocampus (Green & Adey, 1956; Joseph *et al.*, 1981).

When a brain structure that ordinarily processes input has been deafferented to a significant degree, the structure is required to function upon its own random neural activity (Lilly, 1972). For example, a deafferented area of the brain that normally functions to analyse visual input will tend to interpret any neural activity as visual input resulting in a visual hallucination. Such hallucinations occur in patients with cortical blindness in which the association areas and primary visual areas are disconnected.

Neurophysiological Studies of Spiritual Experiences

A number of different types of studies have been performed to try to specifically investigate the neurophysiological correlates of spiritual experiences. Originally, studies analysed the relationship between electrical changes in the brain (measured by electroencephalography) and meditative states. Corby, Roth, Zarcone, & Kopell (1978) showed that during Tantric yoga meditation, proficient practitioners had increased alpha and theta amplitudes compared to baseline. These changes were associated with increased autonomic activation. Banquet (1972) found an increased intensity of a frontal alpha pattern during the early stages of meditation. Another study found hemispheric asymmetries in alpha and beta activity associated with Buddhist g *Tum-mo* yoga meditation (Benson *et al.*, 1990). Unfortunately, EEG is limited in its ability to distinguish particular regions of the brain that may have increased or decreased activity.

For this reason, more recent studies of meditation have utilized brain imaging techniques such as single photon emission computed tomography (SPECT) and positron emission tomography (PET). We have previously presented data from SPECT images measuring cerebral blood flow (which correlates with activity) obtained on highly proficient Tibetan Buddhist meditators during a form of *vajrayana* meditation (Newberg *et al.*, 1997a,b). Baseline and meditation scans were compared with regions of interest (ROIs) drawn around specific brain structures. The activity in these ROIs were compared to determine the relative changes that occurred during meditation. Our preliminary results showed significant increases in brain activity in the region comprising the PFC consistent with focusing attention on a visualized image during meditation. We have also observed relatively decreased activity in the area of the PSPL possibly consistent with deaferentation the PSPL. Interestingly, there was also a strong inverse correlation between activity in the PFC and in the PSPL. This might indicate that the more active the PFC is, the more the PSPL is deafferented. These results, although preliminary, are consistent with the model for the neurophysiological basis of meditative experiences presented in this chapter, which was developed and published before these brain imaging studies were embarked upon. Further, our results corroborate an earlier PET study of a yoga meditative relaxation technique that showed an increased frontal:occipital ratio of cerebral glucose metabolism (Herzog *et al.*, 1990–91). A more recent study demonstrated changes in the temporal lobes, frontal lobes, and parietal lobes associated with yoga relaxation techniques (Lou, 1999).

In all, these studies can provide a starting point to develop a more detailed model of the neurophysiological correlates of religious and spiritual experiences. This kind of model can also be utilized as the hypothesis for future investigations of such experiences.

A Neurophysiological Model for Religious and Spiritual Experiences

It appears that there are a variety of spiritual experiences which, although they seem to be fundamentally different, actually have certain neuropsychological similarities. In terms of spiritual experiences, unitary states appear to play an important role. In fact, we might consider spiritual experiences to lie along a 'unitary continuum' with multiple discrete being at one end and complete unitary experiences at the other.

A neurobiological analysis of mysticism and other spiritual experiences might elucidate the continuum of these experiences by allowing for a typology based on the underlying brain functions. In terms of the effects of ceremonial ritual we, along with other colleagues, have proposed that rhythmicity in the environment drives either the ergotropic or trophotropic system to maximal capacity (Lex, 1979; Iwanaga & Tsukamoto, 1997) with the possibility of spillover and simultaneous activation of the other system creating unusual subjective states (Gellhorn & Kiely 1972; d'Aquili, 1983; Bernston et al., 1991; d'Aquili & Newberg, 1993; Hugdahl, 1996). For the most part, this neurophysiological activity occurs as the result of the rhythmic driving of ceremonial ritual. We have postulated that this ultimately results in a progressive deafferentation of certain parts of the right PSPL, creating an increasing sense of wholeness progressively more and more dominant over the sense of the multiplicity of baseline reality. Ceremonial ritual may be described as generating these spiritual experiences from a bottom-up approach, since it is through rhythmic sounds and behaviours that ritual eventually drives the ergotropic and trophotropic systems. It should also be mentioned that the particular system initially activated (ergotropic or trophotropic) depends upon the type of ritual. Rituals themselves might therefore be divided into 'slow' and 'fast' ritual (d'Aquili & Newberg, 1999). Slow rituals might involve calm, peaceful music and soft chanting to generate a sense of quiescence via the trophotropic system. Fast rituals might utilize rapid or frenzied dancing to generate a sense of heightened arousal via the ergotropic system.

However, activation of the holistic operator (the right PSPL and adjacent structures) and the attainment of ecstatic and blissful unitary states can also be achieved via other mechanisms. For example, meditation approaches the situation from the opposite direction as that of ceremonial ritual (d'Aquili & Newberg, 1993). Meditation appears to utilize a 'top-down' mechanism using cognitive/emotional activity to drive the ergotropic / trophotropic systems to maximum activation. This appears to occur via a complex mechanism of neural interactions.

A detailed mechanism for the neurophysiological basis of meditative experiences has been previously described (d'Aquili & Newberg, 1993). However, it may be helpful to review some of the major components of that model in order to develop a better understanding of the spiritual continuum. Some forms of meditation begin with the subject willing or intending to focus either on a mental image or on an external physical object. This initially results in activation of the right PFC which activates the right PSPL via the thalamus which functions as a relay. These impulses are correlated with the person subjectively focusing their attention on a visual object. This object, presented by the ITL, is oriented by the PSPL. Thus, there is a relative increase in stimulation between the right PFC, the ITL, and the PSPL.

We postulate that continuous fixation on the image presented by the right ITL begins to stimulate the right hippocampus, which in turn stimulates the right amygdala. The result is a stimulation of the lateral portions of the hypothalamus generating a mildly pleasant, alert sensation. Impulses then pass back to the right amygdala and hippocampus recruiting intensity as they go along. This then feeds back to the right PFC reinforcing the whole system with progressively intense concentration upon the object. Thus, a reverberating loop is established.

In our model, the circuit continues to reverberate and to augment in intensity until the stimulation of the hypothalamic ergotropic centres (lateral part) reaches maximum thus leading to a 'spillover' such that maximal stimulation of the hypothalamic trophotropic centers (medial part) occurs. At this point, there would be maximal stimulation feedback through the limbic structures to both the left and right PFC. This then results in instantaneous maximal stimulation of the left PFC with immediate total blocking of input into the left PSPL which may be associated with the obliteration of the Self–Other dichotomy. In the right hemisphere, there is already an ongoing, powerful stimulation system from the right PFC to the right PSPL which blocks the ability of the right PFC to deafferent the PSPL. This stimulation has been reinforced by a constant feedback loop going through the right ITL (the neurophysiological basis of 'focusing on an object').

Therefore, the inhibitory ability of the right PFC, although at maximum, must fight against a pre-existent, and very strong, facilitatory or stimulating system that is generated by fixating and focusing upon the original object. Since the meditating subject is still intending to focus on the object of meditation, this system continues to be reinforced even in the presence of ecstatic feelings generated by the limbic system and the progressively stronger activity of the inhibitory system. Throughout the period of time when there is conflict in the right hemisphere between facilitatory and inhibitory mechanisms there has been total instantaneous blocking of input into the left PSPL. Thus, the Self–Other dichotomy has been obliterated during a period of time, perhaps fairly long, when the image still remains a focus of meditation. We would suggest that this is the period of time when the subject feels absorbed into the object or describes a sense of becoming one with the object of meditation. Eventually, in the face of maximal ergotropic and trophotropic activity, either the meditator surrenders, or possibly even against his/her will, the inhibitory influences take over and total blocking of input into the right PSPL occurs. Since the left PSPL has already been totally blocked, the Self–Other dichotomy has been obliterated for some time. Thus, the endpoint of the meditation is maximal stimulation of the ergotropic and trophotropic systems with total blocking of input into both the right and left PSPL, resulting in the most profound unitary state attainable. The period of time from spillover to the final assertion of dominance of the inhibitory neurons of the right prefrontal cortex is the period of absorption of the meditator into the object of meditation.

It should be mentioned here that there is a distinction between the experience associated with a totally deafferented right PSPL and a totally deafferented left PSPL. Total deafferentation of the left PSPL is likely associated with the obliteration of the self/other dichotomy and we believe that the resulting experience is a sense of union between the self and the object of meditation which is often God, Brahman, etc. The important point is that deafferentation is associated with the sense of union with something outside of the self. On the other hand, total deafferentation of the right PSPL is most likely associated with the loss of usual orientation with regards to space and time. Since all input into this structure is blocked, it results in an orientation towards nothing. We have previously suggested that this may be experienced as a sense of complete nothingness, or possibly infiniteness. Thus, experiences in which both the left and right PSPL are totally deafferented should result in the sense of a merging of the self with all that is (e.g. emtiness experiences).

In returning to a comparison of ceremonial ritual with meditation, the end result can be the same in both situations (d'Aquili and Newberg, 1993). In other words, both methods can result in simultaneous activation of the ergotropic and trophotropic systems as has been described above, with concommitant deafferentation of the left and right PSPL. This results in the experience of bliss and ecstasy as well as in profound unitary states. It should be noted that the most profound unitary states are unlikely to occur in ceremonial ritual since it is very difficult to maintain the level of rhythmic activity necessary for the continued driving of the ergotropic system to result in simultaneous maximal activity of both the ergotropic and trophotropic systems. However, ceremonial ritual still can result in powerful unitary experiences.

While it is difficult to define what makes a given experience spiritual, the sense of having a union with some higher power or fundamental state seems an important part of spiritual experiences. To that end, this union helps reduce existential anxiety as well as provide a sense of control over the environment (d'Aquili, 1978; Smart, 1969). The bottom line in understanding the phenomenology of subjective religious experience is to understand that every religious experience involves a sense of the unity of reality at least somewhat greater than the baseline perception of unity in day to day life (d'Aquili & Newberg, 1999). This is another way of saying that a more intense application of the holistic operator to incoming stimuli, over and above its baseline function, coupled with the limbic or emotional stimulation that accompanies such increased functioning, results in experiences which are usually described as religious or spiritual.

We are proposing that the unitary continuum is based upon the activation of this holistic operation with the subsequent experience of greater senses of unity within the sensorium. As there is an increasing sense of unity, there is the perception of ever greater approximations of a more fundamental reality (d'Aquili & Newberg, 1999). The more the holistic operator functions in excess of a state of balance with the analytic functions of the left hemisphere, the stronger will be the associated emotional charge. Thus, in any perception such as a piece of music, a painting, a sculpture, or a sunset, there is a sense of meaning and wholeness that transcends the constituent parts. In aesthetic perceptions such as those just described, this transcendence may be slight to moderate. We would locate the overarching sense of unity between two persons in romantic love as the next stage in this spiritual continuum. The next stages proceed through a sense of numinosity or religious awe to the state of religious exaltation which Bucke has called Cosmic Consciousness (Bucke, 1961). This state is characterized by a sense of meaning and wholeness extending to all discrete being whether subjective or objective. The essential unity and purposefulness of the universe is perceived as a primary datum despite the perception and knowledge of evil in the world. During this state, there is nothing whatsoever that escapes the mantle of wholeness and purposefulness. But this state does not obliterate discrete being, and it certainly exists within a temporal context.

In the most profound unitary states, a person looses all sense of discrete being and even the difference between self and other is obliterated. There is no sense of the passing of time, and all that remains is a perfect timeless undifferentiated consciousness. However, it is important to realize that the limbic system is intimately involved in the perception of these experiences (Saver & Rabin, 1997). Thus, when such a state is suffused with positive affect there is a tendency to describe the experience, after the fact, as personal. Such experiences are often described as a perfect union with God (the *Unio mystica* of the Christian tradition) or else the perfect manifestation of God in the Hindu tradition. When such experiences are accompanied by neutral affect they tend to be described, after the fact, as impersonal. These states are described as the Absolute of a number of philosophical/mystical traditions. There is no question that whether the experience is interpreted personally as God or impersonally as the Absolute it nevertheless possesses a quality of transcendent wholeness without any temporal or spatial division whatsoever.

We have postulated that these rare states of undifferentiated unity are attained through the 'absolute' functioning of the holistic operator (d'Aquili, 1982; d'Aquili & Newberg, 1993). As described in the model above, the neurological substrate for the holistic operator involves the function of the right PSPL. However, there also would be an intense activity of structures in the left cerebral hemisphere associating with that wholeness the intense consciousness of the reflexive ego associated with normal left hemispheric functioning. Thus, the state of undifferentiated unity may actually be experienced as one of intense consciousness.

Conclusion: Proof of the Model

Clearly, one of the most important aspects of a neuroscientific study of spiritual experiences is to find careful, rigorous methods for empirically testing hypotheses. One such example of empirical evidence for the neurophysiological basis of spiritual experiences comes from the studies already described which have measured neurophysiological activity during religious and spiritual experiences. Meditative states comprise perhaps the most fertile testing ground because of the predictable, reproducible, and well described nature of such experiences. Studies of meditation have evolved over the years to utilize the most advanced technologies for studying neurophysiology. Such techniques include EEG, fMRI, SPECT, and PET imaging. While the initial findings are promising, more studies, with improved methods will be necessary to further elucidate the neuropsychology of religious and spiritual experiences. Furthermore, different spiritual experiences might be studied to compare and contrast the phenomenology with specific physiological states. That the underlying neurophysiology of extreme spiritual states can be considered at all allows for the eventual conceptualization of a neuropsychology of religious and spiritual experiences.

References

Banquet, J.P. (1972), 'EEG and meditation', *Electroencephalography and Clinical Neurophysiology*, **33**, pp. 454.

Baron, J.C., D'Antona, R., Pantano, P., Serdaru, M., Samson, Y. and Bousser, M.G. (1986), 'Effects of thalamic stroke on energy metabolism of the cerebral cortex. A positron tomography study in man', *Brain*, **109**, pp. 1243–59.

Benson, H., Malhotra, M.S., Goldman, R.F., Jacobs, G.D. and Hopkins, J. (1990), 'Three case reports of the metabolic and electroencephalographic changes during advanced Buddhist meditation techniques', *Behavioral Medicine*, pp. 90–5.

Berntson, G.G., Cacioppo, J.T. and Quigley, K.S. (1991), 'Autonomic determinism: the modes of autonomic control, the doctrine of autonomic space and the laws of autonomic constraint', *Psychological Review*, pp. 459–87.

Bucke, R.M. (1961), *Cosmic Consciousness* (Secaucus, NJ: Citadel Press).

Corby, J.C., Roth, W.T., Zarcone, V.P. and Kopell, B.S. (1978), 'Psychophysiological correlates of the practice of Tantric Yoga meditation', *Archives of General Psychiatry*, **35**, pp. 571–7.

Czikszentmihalyi, M. (1975), *Beyond Boredom and Anxiety* (San Francisco, CA: Jossey-Bass).

Damasio, A.R. (1994), *Descartes' Error: Emotion, Reason, and the Human Brain* (New York: Avon Books, Inc.).

Damasio, A.R. (1999), *The Feeling of What Happens: Body and Emotion in the Making of Consciousness* (New York: Harcourt Brace & Company).

d'Aquili, E.G. (1978), 'The neurobiological bases of myth and concepts of deity', *Zygon*, **13**, pp. 257–75.

d'Aquili, E.G. (1982), 'Senses of reality in science and religion', *Zygon*, **17** (4), pp. 361–84.

d'Aquili, E.G. (1983), 'The myth-ritual complex: A biogenetic structural analysis', *Zygon*, **18**, pp. 247–69.

d'Aquili, E.G. and Newberg, A.B. (1993), 'Religious and mystical states: a neuropsychological model, *Zygon*, **28**, pp. 177–200.

d'Aquili, E.G. and Newberg, A.B. (1999), *The Mystical Mind: Probing the Biology of Religious Experience* (Minneapolis, IN: Fortress Press).

Davis, M. (1992), 'The role of the amygdala in fear and anxiety', *Annual Review of Neuroscience*, **15**, pp. 353–75.

Dehaene, S. (1997), *The Number Sense* (New York: Oxford University Press).

Frith, C.D., Friston, K., Liddle, P.F. and Frackowiak, R.S.J. (1991), 'Willed action and the prefrontal cortex in man. a study with PET', *Proceedings of the Royal Society of London*, **244**, pp. 241–6.

Fuster, J.M. (1997), *The Prefrontal Cortex: Anatomy, Physiology, and Neuropsychology of the Frontal Lobe*, 3rd Edition (Philadelphia, PA: Lippincott-Raven).

Gazzaniga, M.S. and Hillyard, S.A. (1971), 'Language and speech capacity of the right hemisphere', *Neuropsychologia*, 9, pp. 273–80.

Gellhorn, E. and Loofbourrow, G.N. (1963), *Emotions and Emotional Disorders: A Neurophysiological Study* (New York: Norton).

Gellhorn, E. and W.F. Kiely. (1972), 'Mystical States of Consciousness: Neurophysiological and Clinical Aspects', *Journal of Nervous and Mental Disease*, **154**, pp. 399–405.

Gellhorn, E. (1967), *Principles of Autonomic-Somatic Integration: Physiological Basis and Psychological and Clinical Implications* (Minneapolis, IN: University of Minnesota Press).

Gilbert, M.E. and Peterson, G.M. (1991), 'Colchicine-induced deafferentation of the hippocampus selectively disrupts cholinergic rhythmical slow wave activity', *Brain Research*, **564** (1), pp. 117–26.

Green, J.D. and Adey, W.R. (1956), 'Electrophysiological studies of hippocampal connections and excitability', *Electroencephalography and Clinical Neurophysiology*, **8**, pp. 245–62.

Halgren, E. (1992), 'Emotional neurophysiology of the amygdala within the context of human cognition', in *The Amygdala*, ed. J.P. Aggleton (New York: Wiley-Liss).

Herzog, H., Lele, V.R., Kuwert, T., Langen, K-J., Kops, E.R. and Feinendegen, L.E. (1990–91), 'Changed pattern of regional glucose metabolism during Yoga meditative relaxation', *Neuropsychobiology*, **23**, pp. 182–7.

Hoppe, K.D. (1977), 'Spilt brains and psychoanalysis', *Psychoanalytic Quarterly*, 46, pp. 220–44.

Hugdahl, K. (1996), 'Cognitive influences on human autonomic nervous system function', *Current Opinion in Neurobiology*, **6**, pp.252–8.

Iwanaga, M. and Tsukamoto, M. (1997), 'Effects of excitative and sedative music on subjective and physiological relaxation', *Perceptual and Motor Skills*, **85**, pp. 287–96.

Jeltsch, H., Cassel, J.C. Jackisch, R., Neufang, B., Greene, P.L., Kelche, C., Hertting, G. and Will, B. (1994), 'Lesions of supracallosal or infracallosal hippocampal pathways in the rat: behavioral, neurochemical, and histochemical effects', *Behavioral and Neural Biology*, **62** (2), pp. 121–33.

Joseph, R. (2000), *The Transmitter to God: The Limbic System, the Soul, and Spirituality* (San Jose: University Press California).

Joseph, R., Forrest, N., Fiducis, D., Como, P. and Siegal, J. (1981), 'Behavioral and electrophysiological correlates of arousal', *Physiological Psychology*, **9**, pp. 90–5.

Kandel, E.R., Schwartz, J.H. and Jessell (2000), *Principles of Neural Science* (New York: Elsevier Science Publishing Co., Inc).

Kataoka, K., Hayakawa, T., Kuroda, R., Yuguchi, T. and Yamada, K. (1991), 'Cholinergic deafferentation after focal cerebral infarct in rats', *Stroke*, **22** (10), pp. 1291–6.

Laughlin, C.D. and d'Aquili, E.G. (1974), *Biogenetic Structuralism* (New York: Columbia University Press).

Lex, B. (1979), 'The neurobiology of ritual trance', in *The Spectrum of Ritual: A Biogenetic Structural Analysis*, ed. E.G. d'Aquili, C.D. Laughlin Jr. and J. McManus (New York: Columbia University Press).

Lilly, J.C. (1972), *The Center of the Cyclone* (New York: Julian Press).

Lou, H.C., Kjaer, T.W., Friberg, L., Wildschiodtz, G., Holm, S. And Nowak, M. (1999), 'A ^{15}O-H$_2$O PET study of meditation and the resting state of normal consciousness', *Human Brain Mapping*, **7**, pp. 98–105.

Luria, A.R. (1966), *Higher Cortical Functions in Man* (New York: Basic Books).

Lynch, J.C. (1980), 'The functional organization of posterior parietal association cortex', *Behavioral and Brain Sciences*, **3**, pp. 485–99.

Mills, L. and G.B. Rollman. (1980), 'Hemispheric asymmetry for auditory perception of temporal order', *Neuropsychologia*, **18**, pp. 41–7.

Mountcastle, V.B. (1976), 'The world around us: neural command functions for selective attention', *Neurosciences Research Progress Bulletin*, **14**, pp. 1–47.

Morris, J., Frith, C.D., Perrett, D., Rowland, D., Young, A.W., Calder, A.J. and Dolan, R.J. (1996), 'A differential neural response in the human amygdala to fearful and happy facial expressions, *Nature*, **383**, pp. 812–15.

Newberg, A.B. and Alavi, A. (1996), 'The study of the neurological disorders using positron emission tomography and single photon emission computed tomography', *Journal of the Neurological Sciences*, **135**, pp. 91–108.

Newberg, A., Alavi, A., Baime, M. and d'Aquili, E. (1997a), 'Cerebral blood flow during intense meditation measured by HMPAO-SPECT: A preliminary study', American College of Nuclear Physicians Annual Meeting, Palm Springs, California.

Newberg, A., Alavi, A., Baime, M., Mozley, P. and d'Aquili, E. (1997b), 'The measurement of cerebral blood flow during the complex cognitive task of meditation using HMPAO-SPECT imaging', *Journal of Nuclear Medicine*, **38**, pp. 95P.

Newberg, A.B., Alavi, A., Bhatnagar, A., Baime, M. and d'Aquili, E.G. (1998), 'The neurophysiological correlates of meditation: Implications for neuroimaging', *Journal of the Indian Academy of Clinical Medicine*, **3**, pp. 13–18.

Newberg, A.B. and d'Aquili, E.G. (1994), 'The near death experience as archetype: A model for 'prepared' neurocognitive processes', *Anthropology of Consciousness*, **5**, pp. 1–15.

Peng, C-K., Mietus, J.E., Liu, Y., Khalsa, G., Douglas, P.S., Benson, H. and Goldberger, A.L. (1999), Exaggerated heart rate oscillations during two meditation techniques', *International Journal of Cardiology*, **70**, pp. 101–7.

Pribram, K.H. (1973), 'The primate frontal cortex — Executive of the brain', in *Psychophysiology of the Frontal Lobes*, ed. K.H. Pribram and A.R. Luria (New York: Academic Press).

Redding, F.K. (1967), 'Modification of sensory cortical evoked potentials by hippocampal stimulation', *Electroencephalography and Clinical Neurophysiology*, **22**, pp. 74–83.

Roland, P.E. and Gulyas, B. (1995), 'Visual memory, visual imagery, and visual recognition of large field patterns by the human brain: functional anatomy by positron emission tomography', *Cerebral Cortex*, **5**, pp. 79–93.

Saver, J.L. and Rabin, J. (1997), 'The neural substrates of religious experience', *Journal of Neuropsychiatry and Clinical Neurosciences*, **9**, pp. 498–510.

Schiavetto, A., Cortese, F. And Alain, C. (1999), 'Global and local processing of musical sequences: An event related brain potential study', *Neuroreport*, **10**, pp. 2467–72.

Smart, N. (1969), *The Religious Experience of Mankind* (London: Macmillan).

Smart, N. (1978), 'Understanding religious experience', in *Mysticism and Philosophical Analysis*, ed. S. Katz (New York: Oxford University Press).

Smith, P.H., DeVito, J.L. and Astley, C.A. (1990), 'Neurons controlling cardiovascular responses to emotion are located in the lateral hypothalamus-perifornical region', *American Journal of Physiology*, **259**, pp. 943–54.

Stace, W.T. (1961), *Mysticism and Philosophy* (London: Macmillan).

Stuss, D.T. and Benson, D.F. (1986), *The Frontal Lobes* (New York: Raven).

Robert H. Sharf

*The Rhetoric of Experience and the Study of Religion**

The exercise of thought cannot have any other outcome than the negation of individual perspectives. — Georges Bataille

I

One might expect an essay on the term 'experience' to begin with a definition, but immediately we confront a problem. To define something entails situating it in the public sphere, assuming an objective or third-person perspective *vis-à-vis* the term or concept at issue. The problem with the term 'experience', particularly with respect to its use in the study of religion, is that it resists definition by design; as we will see, the term is often used rhetorically to thwart the authority of the 'objective' or the 'empirical,' and to valorize instead the subjective, the personal, the private. This is in part why the meaning of the term may appear self-evident at first, yet becomes increasingly elusive as one tries to get a fix on it. (Gadamer places experience 'among the least clarified concepts which we have', 1975, p. 310.)

In spite of (or perhaps owing to) the obscurity of the term, experience as a concept has come to play a pivotal role in the study of religion. The meaning of many religious symbols, scriptures, practices, and institutions is believed to reside in the experiences they elicit in the minds of practitioners. Moreover, a particular mode (or modes) of experience, characterized as 'religious', 'spiritual', 'visionary' or 'mystical', is thought to constitute the very essence of religion, such that the origin of a given tradition is often traced to the founder's initial transcendent encounter, moment of revelation, salvation, or enlightenment. This approach to religious phenomena is not confined to academic discourse alone; many lay adherents feel that the only *authentic* form of worship or scriptural study is one that leads to a personal experience of its 'inner truth'. Consequently, scholarship that does not attend to the experiential dimension of religious practice is dismissed by many as reductionistic.

* This paper originally appeared under the title 'Experience' in the volume *Critical Terms in Religious Studies*, ed. Mark C. Taylor (Chicago: The University of Chicago Press, 1998), pp. 94–116.

Some scholars go further. Not content with limiting the range of the term 'experience' to particular individuals, they go on to speak of the 'collective experience' of an entire community or culture. Attention to the collective or 'lived' experience of a religious community is touted as one way of overcoming cultural bias — our tendency to view the beliefs and actions of people different from ourselves as backward, foolish, or bizarre. If we can bracket our own presuppositions, temper our ingrained sense of cultural superiority, and resist the temptation to evaluate the truth claims of foreign traditions, we find that their *experience* of the world possesses its own rationality, its own coherence, its own truth. This approach, sometimes known as the phenomenology of religion, enjoins the 'imaginative participation in the world of the actor' in order to arrive at 'value free' and 'evocative' descriptions (Smart, 1973, pp. 20–1).

This use of the concept 'religious experience' is exceedingly broad, encompassing a vast array of feelings, moods, perceptions, dispositions, and states of consciousness. Some prefer to focus on a distinct type of religious experience known as 'mystical experience', typically construed as a transitory but potentially transformative state of consciousness in which a subject purports to come into immediate contact with the divine, the sacred, the holy. We will return to the issue of mystical experience below. Here I would only note that the academic literature does not clearly delineate the relationship between religious experience and mystical experience. The reluctance, and in the end the inability, to clearly stipulate the meaning of such terms will be a recurring theme in the discussion below.

II

It is not difficult to understand the allure of the rhetoric of experience in the modern period. Both Western theologians and secular scholars of religion found themselves facing, each in their own way, a host of challenges that, for the purposes of this essay, I will group under the two headings of *empiricism* and *cultural pluralism*.

By empiricism I refer to the notion that all truth claims must be subject, in theory if not in fact, to empirical or scientific verification. This was a potential problem for modern theologians, as many essential elements of theological reflection are simply not amenable to empirical observation or testing. By emphasizing the experiential dimension of religion — a dimension inaccessible to strictly objective modes of inquiry — the theologian could forestall scientific critique. Religious truth claims were not to be understood as pertaining to the objective or material world, which was the proper domain of science, but to the inner spiritual world, for which the scientific method was deemed inappropriate.

Unlike the theologian, the secular scholar was not necessarily invested in the truth claims of any particular religious tradition. However, scholars of religion do have a vested interest in the existence of irreducibly *religious* phenomena over which they can claim special authority. That is to say, other academic disciplines — history, anthropology, sociology, or psychology, for example — could (and sometimes did) claim to possess the requisite tools for the analysis of religion, a claim that threatened to put the religion specialist out of a job. By construing religion as pertaining to a distinct mode of 'experience', the scholar of religion could argue that it ultimately eludes the grasp of other more empirically oriented disciplines.

The second challenge for both theologians and secular scholars was that of cultural pluralism. By the twentieth century it had become difficult for Christian theologians to simply ignore the existence of non-Christian traditions, much less to smugly assert Christian superiority. But to take other traditions seriously entailed the risk of rendering Christianity merely one of several competing systems of belief. In privileging religious experience theologians could argue that all religious traditions emerged from, and were attempts to give expression to, an apprehension of the divine or the ultimate. Differences in doctrine and forms of worship are to be expected due to vast differences in linguistic, social, and cultural conditions. What is key, however, is that as a response to a fundamentally human (and thus pan-cultural and ahistorical) sense of the transcendent, all religious traditions could lay *some* claim to truth. This allowed Christian theologians to affirm the validity of Christian revelation without necessarily impugning their non-Christian rivals.

Cultural pluralism was no less a problem for secular scholars of religion, who had to contend with the knowledge that the category 'religion' was itself a cultural product. Many, if not most, non-Western traditions lacked an indigenous lexical equivalent for 'religion' altogether, and attempts to define or stipulate the nature of religion were often tainted with Western presuppositions. Like the theologian, the scholar of religion found the very existence of his ostensible subject of expertise open to question. By appealing to non-tradition-specific notions such as the 'sacred' or the 'holy' — notions that blur the distinction between a universal human experience and the posited object of said experience — the scholar could legitimize the comparative study of religion even while acknowledging the specifically Western origins of the category itself. The scholar could then argue that if places such as India or Japan or pre-Columbian America lacked an indigenous term for religion it was not because they lacked religious experience. On the contrary, every aspect of their life was so suffused with a sense of the divine that they simply did not distinguish between the secular and the sacred.

III

The ideological aspect of the appeal to experience — the use of the concept to legitimize vested social, institutional, and professional interests — is most evident when we turn to the study of mysticism. As mentioned above, mystical experience is generally construed as a direct encounter with the divine or the absolute, and as such some scholars claim that the 'raw experience' itself is not affected by linguistic, cultural, or historical contingencies. Obviously, a given individual's understanding and articulation of such an experience will be conditioned by the tradition to which he or she belongs. Thus a Christian might talk about witnessing the Holy Spirit, a Hindu about absorption into Brahman, a Buddhist about the extinction of the self. But if one is able to see beyond the superficial, culturally determined differences between these accounts one discovers a single unvarying core. Or so goes the argument advanced by William James (1961/1902), Rudolf Otto (1958/1917), Aldous Huxley (1946), W.T. Stace (1960) and Robert Forman (1990), among others. Needless to say there are important differences in the views of these scholars, but all more-or-less agree that it is possible to distinguish between a core experience (or core experiences) proper, and the divergent culturally conditioned expressions of that core. Such a position led naturally to attempts to isolate the universal features of mystical experience through the analysis of 'first-hand reports'. William James, for example, proposed four such features, namely, noetic quality, ineffability, transiency, and passivity (1961); Rudolf Otto speaks more loosely of 'creature feeling', awefulness, overpoweringness, energy, and fascination (1958). Others reject the essential features approach altogether in favour of a looser 'family resemblance' model, and several scholars argue that not one but two or more primary experiences exist, distinguishing, for example, between 'introvertive' and 'extravertive' types (Stace, 1960).

This understanding of mystical experience, sometimes known as the 'perennial philosophy' (a term popularized by Huxley's 1946 book of that title), proved quite influential among scholars of religion. But how is one to make conceptual sense of such an experience? One popular explanation goes as follows: logically we can, and indeed must, distinguish the object of consciousness from the *knowing* of that object; otherwise, we would be indistinguishable from insentient robots or automatons that are able to respond to stimuli without being conscious of them. There is, in other words, a residue in all conscious experience that cannot be reduced to the content of consciousness alone. This knowing factor, variously referred to as pure consciousness, prereflective experience, the true self, the *cogito*, and so on, is the proper object of a mystic's self-knowledge. Mystical experience consists in the direct, though somewhat paradoxical, apperception of, or absorption into, the knowing subject itself. Since this experience of pure subjectivity is free of individuating ego, mystics are led to speak of being one with the world, or one with the absolute. (If some theistically oriented mystics avoid explicitly monistic language, it is due to the doctrinal constraints imposed by their respective dualistic traditions.)

This is, of course, a highly simplified account of the perennialist position, and its defenders do not speak with a single voice. Be that as it may, in the past few decades this approach to mysticism has come under concerted attack from a number of scholars, notably Gershom Scholem (1969), Steven Katz (1978; 1983; 1992), Wayne Proudfoot (1985) and Grace Jantzen (1995). The objections are manifold. To begin with, critics note that we do not have access to mystical experiences *per se*, but only to texts that purport to describe them, and the perennialists systematically misconstrue these texts due to their *a priori* commitment to the perennialist position. Read impartially, there is little internal evidence to indicate that these very disparate accounts are actually referring to one and the same experience.

Besides, the very notion that one can separate an unmediated experience from a culturally determined description of that experience is philosophically suspect. According to Katz, 'neither mystical experience nor more ordinary forms of experience give any indication, or any grounds for believing, that they are unmediated' (1978, p. 26). In other words, mystical experience is wholly shaped by a mystic's cultural environment, personal history, doctrinal commitments, religious training, expectations, aspirations, and so on.

Yet another problem with the perennialist position emerged as scholars turned to the intellectual genealogy of the category 'religious experience' itself. The concept turns out to be of relatively recent, and distinctively Western, provenance. Wayne Proudfoot traces the roots of the idea to the German theologian Friedrich Schleiermacher (1768–1834), who argued that religion cannot be reduced to a system of beliefs or morality. Religion proper, claimed Schleiermacher, is predicated on a feeling of the infinite — the 'consciousness of absolute dependence' (see, for example, Schleiermacher, 1928). According to Proudfoot, this emphasis on feeling was motivated by Schleiermacher's 'interest in freeing religious doctrine and practice from dependence on metaphysical beliefs and ecclesiastical institutions' (1985, p. xiii; see also Jantzen, 1995, pp. 311–21). Schleiermacher's strategy proved fruitful: the notion of religious experience provided new grounds upon which to defend religion against secular and scientific critique. The 'hermeneutic of experience' was soon adopted by a host of scholars interested in religion, the most influential being William James, and today many have a difficult time imagining *what else* religion might be about. Yet prior to Schleiermacher, insists Proudfoot, religion was simply not understood in such terms, and it is thus incumbent upon us to reject the perennialist hypothesis in so far as it anachronistically imposes the recent and ideologically laden notion of 'religious experience' on our interpretations of premodern phenomena.

IV

The claim that religious experience is a relatively late and distinctively Western invention might strike the reader as dubious at best. Did not mystical experience play a central role in the religions of Asia since time immemorial? We read repeatedly that Asian mystics have charted the depths of the human psyche, explored a vast array of altered states of consciousness, and left behind detailed maps so that others may follow in their footsteps. Hinduism and Buddhism, to pick the two best-known examples, are often approached not as religions, philosophies, or social systems, but rather as 'spiritual technologies' intended to induce a transformative experience of the absolute in the mind of the practitioner. Thus, while the emphasis on experience might be relatively new in the West, this is clearly not the case in the East. Or so one might suppose from the plethora of writings on the subject.

But not so fast. The notion that Asian religions are more experientially rooted than their Western counterparts is one of those truisms so widely and unquestioningly held that corroboration of any kind is deemed superfluous. But when we turn to premodern Asian sources the evidence is ambiguous at best. Take, for example, the many important Buddhist exegetical works that delineate the Buddhist *marga* or 'path to liberation' — works such as 'Stages on the Bodhisattva Path' (*Bodhisattvabhumi*), 'The Stages of Practice' (*Bhavanakrama*), 'Path of Purity' (*Visuddhimagga*), 'The Great Calming and Contemplation' (*Mo-ho chih-kuan*), 'The Great Book on the Stages of the Path' (*Lam rim chen mo*), and so on. These texts are frequently construed as descriptive accounts of meditative states based on the personal experiences of accomplished adepts. Yet rarely if ever do the authors of these compendiums claim to base their expositions on their own experience. On the contrary, the authority of exegetes such as Kamalasila, Buddhaghosa, and Chih-i, lay not in their access to exalted spiritual states, but in their mastery of, and rigorous adherence to, sacred scripture (Sharf, 1995a). This situation is by no means unique to Buddhism: premodern Hinduism was similarly wary of claims to authority predicated on personal experience (Halbfass, 1988).

The notion that meditation is central to Asian religious praxis might seem to support the thesis that Asian traditions exalt personal experience. But here too we must be cautious: contemporary accounts of Asian meditation typically *presume* that they are oriented toward meditative experience, and thus such accounts must be used with considerable caution. Besides, while meditation may have been esteemed in theory, it did not occupy the dominant role in monastic and ascetic life that is sometimes supposed. (This point is often overlooked by scholars who fail to distinguish between prescriptive and descriptive accounts.) Even when practised, it is by no means obvious that traditional forms of meditation were oriented toward the attainment of extraordinary 'states of consciousness'. Meditation was first and foremost a means of eliminating defilement, accumulating merit and supernatural power, invoking apotropaic deities, and so forth. This is not to deny that religious practitioners had 'experiences' in the course of their training, just that such experiences were not considered the goal of practice, were not deemed doctrinally authoritative, and did not serve as the reference points for their understanding of the path (Sharf, 1995a). Indeed, as we will see below, personal experience, no matter how extraordinary, *could not* serve as such a reference point precisely because of its ambiguous epistemological status and essentially indeterminate nature — a point appreciated by not a few medieval Buddhist exegetes.

The complementary notions that Asian religious traditions are predicated on mystical experience, and that meditation is a means to induce such experience, are so well ingrained that it might be useful to pause for a moment to consider their provenance. The valorization of experience in Asian thought can be traced to a handful of twentieth-century Asian religious leaders and apologists, all of whom were in sustained dialogue with their intellectual counterparts in the West. For example, the notion that personal experience constitutes the heart of the Hindu tradition originated with the prolific philosopher and statesman Sarvepalli Radhakrishnan (1888–1975). Like his European and American predecessors, Radhakrishnan argued that 'if philosophy of religion is to become scientific, it must become empirical and found itself on religious experience' (1937, p. 84), and 'it is not true religion unless it ceases to be a traditional view and becomes personal experience' (1937, p. 88). Thus in a single stroke Radhakrishnan could associate true religion with both personal experience and the empirical method. Radhakrishnan did not stop there, however, but went on to place the rhetoric of experience in the service of Hindu nationalism. He argued that if 'experience is the soul of religion,' then Hinduism is closest to that soul precisely because it is not historical, but based directly on the 'inward life of spirit' (1937, pp. 89, 90).

Radhakrishnan's intellectual debt to the West is no secret. Although he was educated in India, he was steeped in Western philosophical and religious thought from an early age, and his specific interest in experience can be traced directly to the works of William James (1842–1910), Francis Herbert Bradley (1846–1924), Henri Bergson (1859–1941), and Baron F. von Hügel (1852–1925), among others (Halbfass, 1988, p. 398). Radhakrishnan held numerous academic posts in India and England, including the Spalding Professor of Eastern Religions and Ethics at Oxford, and his writings are filled with appreciative references to a variety of American and European thinkers popular at the time, from Evelyn Underhill (1850–1941) to Alfred North Whitehead (1861–1947). What is curious is not that he should have placed his synthesis of Western and Indian philosophy in the service of an overtly apologetic and nationalist project, but that given this project he is nevertheless considered by many to be a credible 'native source' on the subject of traditional Hinduism.

One can, perhaps, find antecedents of Radhakrishnan's hermeneutic in the writings of Debendranath Tagore (1817–1905), an early leader of the Western influenced Hindu reform movement Brahmo Samaj, who held that the teachings of the Vedas may be affirmed through one's own experience. However, Tagore, like his predecessor Rammohun Roy (1772–1833), was intimately acquainted with Western thought in general, and Christian critiques of Hinduism in particular. His exegetical writings, and his work for the Brahmo Samaj, were directed toward the 'purification' of Hinduism so as to stay the growing influence of Christian missionaries and their converts. In the end there is simply no evidence of an indigenous Indian counterpart to the rhetoric of experience prior to the colonial period (Halbfass, 1988).

Western conceptions of 'Asian spirituality' are equally indebted to the writings of that indefatigable proselytizer of Zen Buddhism, D.T. Suzuki (1870–1966). According to Suzuki, religious experience is not merely a central feature of Zen, it is the whole of Zen. In his voluminous writings Suzuki advanced the notion that Zen eschews all doctrine, all ritual, all institutions, and is thus, in the final analysis, not a religion at all. Zen is pure experience itself, the experiential essence lying behind all authentic religious teachings. Zen is associated, of course, with particular monasteries, forms of worship, and works of literature and art, but these are all mere 'fingers pointing at the moon'. The moon is none other than the unmediated experience of the absolute in which the dualism of subject and object, observer and observed, is transcended. This view of Zen has become so well established that many hesitate to speak of Zen at all for fear of being censured as insufficiently experienced.

Suzuki, like Radhakrishnan, places this understanding of Zen in the interests of a transparently nationalist discourse. Suzuki insisted that Zen is the wellspring of Japanese culture, and that the traditional arts of Japan — tea ceremony, monochrome painting, martial arts, landscape gardening, Noh theatre, etc. — are all ultimately expressions of Zen gnosis. Japanese culture naturally predisposes the Japanese toward Zen experience, such that they have a deeply ingrained appreciation of the unity of subject and object, human being and nature. This is in marked contradistinction to the excessively materialistic and dualistic traditions of the West.

Suzuki's musings on the 'Japanese mind' must be understood in the context of Japan's sense of technological and scientific inferiority *vis-à-vis* the Occident in the earlier part of this century. In the final analysis, Suzuki, like Radhakrishnan, attempts nothing less than the apotheosis of an entire people. And like Radhakrishnan, Suzuki's emphasis on experience owes as much to his exposure to Western thought as it does to indigenous Asian or Zen sources. In fact, Suzuki's qualifications as an exponent of Zen are somewhat dubious. Suzuki did engage in Zen practice at Engakuji during his student days at Tokyo Imperial University, and he enjoyed a close relationship with the abbot Shaku Soen (1859–1919). But by traditional standards Suzuki's training was relatively modest: he was never ordained, his formal monastic education was desultory at best, and he never received institutional sanction as a Zen teacher. This is not to impugn Suzuki's academic competence; he was a gifted philologist who made a lasting contribution to the study of Buddhist texts. In the end, however, his approach to Zen, with its unrelenting emphasis on an unmediated inner experience, is not derived from Buddhist sources so much as from his broad familiarity with European and American philosophical and religious writings (Sharf, 1995c).

Suzuki's early interest in things Western was wide-ranging, and included such fashionable quasi-religious movements as Theosophy, Swedenborgianism, and the 'Religion of Science'. The latter doctrine was the brainchild of the German-American essayist Paul Carus (1852–1919), who worked as editor at the Open Court Publishing Company in La Salle, Illinois. Carus was convinced that once the 'old religions' were purified of their superstitious and irrational elements, they would work in conjunction with science to bring humankind to the realization that there is no distinction between the immaterial and the material — between mind and matter. Carus was particularly attracted to Buddhism, which he felt was close in spirit to his own philosophy.

Suzuki was initially drawn to Carus after reading *Gospel of Buddha*, a compendium of Buddhist teachings compiled by Carus and published in Open Court's 'Religion of Science' series in 1894 (see Carus, 1915). Carus had taken available European translations of Buddhist scriptures and, through the use of careful selection, creative retranslation, and outright fabrication, managed to portray the teachings of the Buddha as humanistic, rational, and scientific. Suzuki, who had been asked to translate the *Gospel* into Japanese, was so impressed with Carus's work that he arranged to travel to America to study under his tutelage. Suzuki was to remain in La Salle for some eleven years, and it was toward the end of this period that he became familiar with the writings of William James.

Suzuki appears to have been responsible for introducing James' work to his high-school friend Nishida Kitaro (1870–1945). It was through Nishida, who was to emerge as Japan's leading modern philosopher, that the notion of a distinctively religious mode of experience took hold in Japan. Nishida's first philosophical monograph, published in 1911 under the title *Zen no kenkyu* ('A Study of the Good', see Nishida, 1990), was dedicated to the elucidation of *junsui keiken*, or 'pure experience', a notion culled directly from James. But the context of Nishida's 'pure experience' was much removed from that of James. James sought to overcome the substance ontology that continued to infect classical empiricism, and to this end he proposed a pragmatic account of experience that avoided the reification of either subject or object. Nishida, on the other hand, was interested in integrating Western philosophy with his understanding of Zen, and consequently his notion of pure experience seems to function both as an ontological ground that subsumes subject and object, and as a psychological state of heightened self-awareness.

Suzuki seized upon Nishida's notion of pure experience and made it the central element in his exposition of Zen. And it proved to be an effective hermeneutic strategy, for here was an approach to Zen that was both familiar and attractive to Suzuki's Western audience. The irony of the situation is that the terms used by the Japanese to render 'experience' — *keiken* and *taiken* — are both modern neologisms coined in the Meiji period (1868–1912) by translators of Western philosophical works. (As far as I have been able to determine, *keiken* was first used to render the English 'experience', while *taiken* was used for the German *erleben* and *Erlebnis*.) There simply is no premodern Japanese lexical equivalent for 'experience'. Nor, I would add, is there a premodern Chinese equivalent. Chinese translators borrowed the Japanese neologisms in their own renderings of Western texts.

The interest in religious experience among twentieth-century Asian intellectuals is not difficult to fathom. Like their Western counterparts, Asian apologists were forced to respond to empiricist and pluralist critiques of their religious heritage. But Asian intellectuals had another threat with which to contend as well, namely, the affront of Western cultural imperialism, sustained as it was by the West's political, technological, and military dominance. Asian intellectuals, many of whom were educated in Christian missionary schools, were deeply aware of the contempt with which Occidentals viewed the religious culture of Asia. Castigated as primitive, idolatrous, and intellectually benighted, Asian religion was held responsible for the continent's social, political, and scientific failings. This is the context in which we must understand the Asian appropriation and manipulation of the rhetoric of experience. Men like Radhakrishnan and Suzuki would not only affirm the experiential foundation of their own religious traditions, but they would turn around and present those traditions as more intuitive, more mystical, more experiential, and thus 'purer' than the discursive faiths of the West. In short, if the West excelled materially, the East excelled spiritually. This strategy had the felicitous result of thwarting the Enlightenment critique of religion on the one hand, and the threat of Western cultural hegemony on the other.

The polemics of Radhakrishnan, Suzuki, and their intellectual heirs has had a significant impact on the study of religion in the West. Few Western scholars were in a position to question the romanticized image of Asian mysticism proffered forth by these intelligent and articulate 'representatives' of living Asian faiths. Besides, the discovery of common ground offered considerable comfort. The very notion that religious experience might function as a universal in the study of world religions evolved, in many respects, out of this cross-cultural encounter. In time the dialogue grew into a veritable academic industry, complete with its own professional societies, its own journals, and its own conferences and symposia, all devoted to the comparative study of 'Western' and 'Eastern' thought. The striking confluence of Western and Asian interests prevented those on both sides from noticing the tenuous ground on which the exchange had been built.

V

Seemingly oblivious to matters of historical context, arguments continue over the nature of mystical experience to the present day with no resolution in sight. The issues have not changed: scholars disagree over the extent to which mystical experiences are shaped by prior culturally mediated expectations and presuppositions, over whether one can separate a mystic's description of her experiences from her interpretations, over the existence of so-called 'pure consciousness' devoid of intentional objects, over competing schemes for typologizing mystical states, and over the philosophical and ethical significance, if any, of mystical experience. (The *Journal of the American Academy of Religion* alone has, of late, seen fit to publish an article a year on the topic; see Barnard, 1992; Forman, 1993; Shear, 1994; Short, 1995; and Brainard, 1996.) What is curious in these ongoing discussions is not so much the points of controversy as the areas of consensus. Virtually all parties tacitly accept the notion that terms such as 'religious experience', 'mystical experience', or 'meditative experience' function referentially, that is, their signification lies in the signifieds to which they allegedly refer. Hence scholars of mysticism are content to focus on the distinctive characteristics and the philosophical implications, if any, of religious or mystical experiences without pausing to consider what sort of thing 'experience' might be in the first place.

What exactly *do* we mean by experience? The dictionaries provide several overlapping definitions, but for our purposes we can focus on two more-or-less distinct usages. The first is to 'participate in', or 'live through', as one might say 'I have combat experience' or 'I have experience with diesel engines'. This use of the term is relatively unproblematic; it does not elicit any particular epistemological or metaphysical conundrums since the referent of the term would seem to lie in the social or public sphere. The second more epistemological or phenomenological meaning is to 'directly perceive', 'observe', 'be aware of', or 'be conscious of'. Here there is a tendency to think of experience as a subjective 'mental event' or 'inner process' that eludes public scrutiny. In thinking of experience along these lines it is difficult to avoid the image of mind as an immaterial substrate or psychic field, a sort of inner space in which the outer material world is reflected or re-presented. Scholars leave the category experience unexamined precisely because the meaning of experience, like the stuff of experience, would seem to be utterly transparent. Experience is simply given to us in the immediacy of each moment of perception.

This picture of mind clearly has its roots in Descartes and his notion of mind as an 'immaterial substance' (although few today would subscribe to Descartes' substance ontology). And following the Cartesian perspective, we assume that in so far as experience is immediately present, experience *per se* is both indubitable and irrefutable. (While the *content* of experience may prove ambiguous or deceptive, the fact that I am experiencing *something* is beyond question.) The characteristics of immediacy and indubitability galvanized the 'hermeneutic of experience'. Experience, construed as the inviolable realm of pure presence, promised a refuge from the hermeneutic and epistemological vagaries of modern intellectual life. Just as some scholars of literature would invoke 'authorial intent' as a way to overcome ambiguity in the interpretation of literary works (see esp. Hirsch, 1967), the notion of experience promised to ground the meaning of religious texts and performances through an appeal to the experiences to which they refer. (The analogy is more than fortuitous: 'authorial intent' and 'religious experience' both occupy the same highly ambiguous but ultimately unassailable 'ontological space'.)

Yet the problem is unavoidable: if talk of 'shamanic experience', 'mystical experience', 'enlightenment experience', or what have you is to have any sort of determinate meaning we must construe the term 'experience' in referential or ostensive terms. But to do so is to objectify it, which would seem to undermine its most salient characteristic, namely, its immediacy. So we are posed with a dilemma: experience cannot be determinate without being rendered a 'thing'; if it is a thing it cannot be indubitable; but if it is not a thing then it cannot perform the hermeneutic task that religious scholars require of it — that of determining meaning. We will return to this point below.

But first I must respond to the following inevitable rebuke: the fact that a scholar such as myself should have a difficult time 'situating' the locus of religious experience merely attests to his own spiritual impoverishment. If only I had a taste of the real thing I would quickly and humbly forgo my rueful attempt to explain away such phenomena. Indeed, I would sympathize with the difficulty mystics have in expressing themselves. Do not mystics repeatedly allude to precisely this problem, that is, the problem in conceptualizing that which transcends all concepts?

This objection would seem to rest on an appeal to ethnographic evidence, to the witness of real mystics or religious adepts with first-hand experience of nonconceptual states. Of course, the problem is exacerbated by the fact that, according to the historical critique summarized above, the category 'experience' is itself of recent provenance, and thus the testimony of mystics of old, who talk in rather different terms (not to mention in dead languages), is going to prove ambiguous at best. So let us keep things simple and select a contemporary religious community that (1) unquestionably valorizes religious experience, and (2) possesses a sophisticated technical vocabulary with which they describe and analyze such experience.

Vipassana or 'insight' practice (also known as *satipatthana* or 'foundations of mindfulness') is a Buddhist form of meditation that is popular in Theravada communities in Southeast Asia. (It is also influential among Buddhist enthusiasts in the West.) It must be noted that the specific techniques propagated today under the *vipassana* rubric, with their unequivocal emphasis on exalted meditative states, cannot be traced back prior to the late nineteenth century, and thus they are an unreliable source for the reconstruction of premodern Theravada. (The techniques were reconstructed in the modern period on the basis of scriptural accounts; see Sharf, 1995a). Be that as it may, contemporary adepts believe that their experiences in meditation tally with the 'descriptions' of progressive soteriological stages found in Buddhist scriptures. They thus treat the ancient scholastic terms pertaining to stages of Buddhist practice as if they designated discrete experiences accessible to contemporary practitioners. The claim that adepts in *vipassana* can clearly recognize and reproduce the various stages mentioned in canonical sources has encouraged some scholars to treat Theravada meditation theory as a sort of empirical phenomenology of altered states of consciousness that can be applied to non-Buddhist as well as Buddhist phenomena (Sharf, 1995a, p. 261).

On closer inspection, however, we find that the scriptures upon which the *vipassana* revival is based (primarily the two *Satipatthana-sutta*s and the *Visuddhimagga*) are often ambiguous or inconsistent, and contemporary *vipassana* teachers are frequently at odds with each other over the interpretation of key terms. For example, Buddhist sources categorize the range of available meditation techniques under two broad headings, *samatha* or 'concentration', and *vipassana* or 'insight'. Judging from scriptural accounts, one would presume that it would be difficult to confuse the two; both the techniques and the goals to which the techniques are directed differ substantially. *Samatha* practices, which involve focussing the mind on a single object, are supposed to result in an ascending series of four 'material absorptions' (or 'trances', *rupa-jhana*) and a further series of four (or five) 'immaterial absorptions' (*arupa-jhana*), that bestow upon the practitioner various supernatural powers. *Vipassana*, on the other hand, involves the disciplined contemplation of seminal Buddhist doctrines such as impermanence or nonself, and leads directly to nirvana or full liberation. Nirvana is achieved in four successive stages known as the 'noble attainments' (*ariya-phala*), the first of which is called *sotapatti* or 'entry into the stream'. While *samatha* is an effective means to acquire specific spiritual powers, such as the ability to levitate or to read minds, only *vipassana* leads to enlightenment proper. Since the soteriological ramifications of *samatha* and *vipassana* differ so markedly, one would suppose that the experiential states with which they are associated would be easy to distinguish on phenomenological grounds.

All contemporary Theravada meditation masters accept the canonical categories outlined above. But curiously, despite the fact that these teachers have 'tasted the fruits' of practice, there is little if any consensus among them as to the application of these key terms. On the contrary, the designation of particular techniques and the identification of the meditative experiences that result from them are the subjects of continued and often acrimonious debate. More often than not the categories are used polemically to disparage the teachings of rival teachers. Since all agree that *vipassana* leads to liberation while *samatha* does not, *samatha* is used to designate the techniques and experiences promoted by one's competitors, while *vipassana* is reserved for one's own teachings. Other teachers may *think* they are promoting authentic *vipassana* and realizing stages of enlightenment, but in fact they are simply mistaking *jhanic* absorption for *sotapatti*, the first stage of enlightenment achieved through *vipassana*.

I do not have the space to explore the *vipassana* controversies in detail here (see the full account in Sharf, 1995a). Suffice it to say that there is simply no public consensus in the contemporary Theravada community as to the application of terms that allegedly refer to discrete experiential states. Not surprisingly, the same is found to be true in Japanese Zen. Again, it is important to remember that, pace much of the popular literature on Zen, premodern Zen masters rarely emphasized exotic experiential states, and terms such as *satori* ('to understand' or 'apprehend') and *kensho* ('to see one's true nature') were not construed as singular 'states of consciousness'. Be that as it may, some contemporary Zen teachers, notably those associated with the upstart Sanbokyodan lineage, do approach Zen phenomenologically. In other words, they unapologetically present Zen practice as a means to inculcate *kensho*, which they understand to be an unmediated and transitory apprehension of 'nonduality.' Some Sanbokyodan masters go so far as to present certificates to students who achieve *kensho* to validate and celebrate their accomplishment.

Even if the Sanbokyodan understanding of *kensho* does not accord with classical models, one might suppose that it is nevertheless an identifiable and reproducible experience. After all, it is verified and certified by the masters of the school. But once again the ethnographic evidence points in another direction. One quickly discovers that eminent teachers from other living Zen traditions (Rinzai, Soto, Obaku) do not accord legitimacy to Sanbkydan claims of *kensho*. This might be dismissed as mere sectarian rivalry or sour grapes. But even within the Sanbokyodan itself there has been a long-standing controversy surrounding the verification and authentication of *kensho* experiences that has threatened to result in schism (Sharf, 1995b). In modern Zen, as in Theravada, eminent meditation masters prove unable to agree on the identification of a 'referent' of terms that supposedly refer to specific and replicable experiential states.

The lack of consensus among prominent Buddhist teachers as to the designation not only of particular states of consciousness but also of the psychotropic techniques used to produce them (*samatha* versus *vipassana*) belies the notion that the rhetoric of meditative experience, at least in Buddhism, functions ostensively. Critical analysis shows that modern Buddhist communities judge 'claims to experience' on the basis of the meditator's particular lineage, the specific ritual practice that engendered the experience, the behaviour that ensued, and so on. In other words, a meditative state or liberative experience is identified not on the basis of privileged personal access to its distinctive phenomenology, but rather on the basis of eminently public criteria. Such judgments are inevitably predicated on prior ideological commitments shaped by one's vocation (monk or layperson), one's socioeconomic background (urban middle-class or rural poor), one's political agenda (traditionalist or reformer), one's sectarian affiliation, one's education, and so forth. In the end, the Buddhist rhetoric of experience is both informed by, and wielded in, the interests of personal and institutional authority.

The modern Theravada and Zen reform movements discussed here are of particular import, as both claim to possess an elaborate technical vocabulary that refers to a set of exotic but nonetheless verifiable and reproducible experiences. Clearly, if these experiential states are not determinative, then the baroque visions, ineffable reveries, and exotic trances associated with various other mystical traditions inspire even less confidence that the rhetoric of experience functions ostensively.

VI

At this point the reader may well be growing impatient. Surely, even if mystics and meditation masters cannot always agree among themselves as to the designation or soteriological import of their experiences, it is clear that *something* must be going on. Those Buddhist meditators are clearly experiencing *something* in the midst of their ascetic ordeals, even if they cannot ultimately agree on whether it should be called *jhana*, *sotapatti*, *kensho*, or whatever. The vigorous and often exuberant language used by mystics the world over to describe their visions, trances, and states of cosmic union must refer to *something*.

This objection attests once again to our deep entanglement in the Cartesian paradigm, to the lingering allure of what Richard Rorty has called the 'glassy essence' or 'mirror of nature' view of mind (1979). This is not the place to plunge into the hoary controversies waged under the auspices of 'philosophy of mind'. Rather, I will defer once again to an ethnographic case that underscores issues of immediate relevance to the study of religion.

Consider, for a moment, a distinctly contemporary form of visionary experience: reports of alien abduction. There are now hundreds if not thousands of individuals from across America who claim to have been abducted by alien beings. A number of apparently reputable investigators have found the abductees' stories compelling, in large part because of the degree of consistency across the narratives (e.g. Mack, 1995; Bryan, 1995). For example, many of the abductees 'independently' report encountering the 'small greys' — short hairless humanoid beings with large heads, big black eyes, tiny nostrils, no discernible ears, and a thin slit for a mouth which is apparently little used. (The small greys communicate telepathically.) Their torsos are slender, with long arms and fingers but no thumb, and they sport close-fitting single-piece tunics and boots (Mack, 1995, pp. 22–3). After being transported to the alien craft, abductees report being subject to various medical examinations and procedures, many of which focus on the reproductive system. The abductees are then returned, usually to the place from which they were first spirited away.

The vast majority of the abductees have no initial recall of the episode at all. They may be aware only of an unaccountable gap of a few hours or so, and a lingering sense of anxiety, confusion, and fear. They are able to fill in the blanks and reconstruct the details of their abduction only with the help of therapy and hypnosis.

The abductees, known among themselves and in the literature as 'experiencers', come from a wide variety of economic and social backgrounds. According to investigators, as a population the abductees show no significant prior history of, or propensity toward, psychopathology. Many of the abductees insist that prior to their alien encounter they had no interest in, or exposure to, reports of abductions, UFOs, or other 'new age' phenomena. In fact, the one thing on which both believers and sceptics agree is that the abductees are on the whole sincere; they are not consciously fabricating the narratives for personal fame or profit. On the contrary, the abductees are convinced that their memories accord with objective events, and they stand by their stories even when ridiculed or ostracized by neighbours and relatives. Investigators sympathetic to the abductees' plight report that they manifest the sort of confusion, stress, and chronic anxiety characteristic of 'post-traumatic stress syndrome'. In fact, the psychological disorders suffered by the abductees, and their own steadfast belief in their stories, constitute the closest thing we have to empirical evidence for the abductions.

Despite the pleas of a few prominent investigators such as John Mack, most scholars are understandably sceptical. Sceptics can cite the striking absence of corroborating physical evidence, as well as the questionable methods used by investigators. As mentioned above, many abductees have no memory of the event until it is 'recovered' by therapists who have made a speciality out of treating victims of alien abductions. Finally, folklorists are able to trace the origins of many central elements and motifs in the abduction narratives — the physiognomy of the aliens, the appearance of their spacecrafts, the ordeal of the medical examination, and so on — to popular science fiction comics, stories, and films of the past fifty years. The scholarly consensus would seem to be that the abductions simply did not take place; there is no *originary event* behind the memories.

The notion of originary event is crucial here. Clearly, we will not get far by denying the existence of the memories themselves. Our scepticism is rather directed at what, if anything, may lie behind them. We suspect that the abductees' reports do not stem from actual alien encounters, but that some other complex historical, sociological, and psychological processes are at work. Whatever the process turns out to be (and we are a long way from an adequate explanation of the phenomenon), it is reasonable to assume that the abductees' memories do not faithfully represent actual historical occurrences.

One might argue that scepticism with regard to the existence of aliens does not imply that there is no *other* determinate historical event at the root of the memories. The memories must refer back to *some* previous incident, even if the nature of this incident is systematically misconstrued by the credulous abductees. Memory is fickle.

This has been the approach of some psychoanalytically oriented observers, who treat the alien encounters as 'screen memories' that cloak an early repressed trauma such as childhood sexual abuse. The problem with this hypothesis is that the epistemological problems raised by postulating repressed memories turn out to be, in many respects, of the same order as those associated with alien abductions. Childhood trauma has been the *etiology du jour*, and is typically only 're-covered' in a therapeutic encounter with a specialist whose training and institutional investments predispose him to this specific diagnosis. In the end childhood trauma is as elusive a beast as the aliens themselves (see Hacking, 1995).

Several scholars have drawn attention to the religious patterns and motifs running through the abduction narratives. The reports are reminiscent, for example, of tales of shamanic trance journeys, in which the subject is transported to an alien domain populated by otherworldly beings with inconceivable powers and ambiguous intentions. Many abductees are entrusted with important spiritual messages to be propagated among the human race, messages about the importance of peace, love, and universal brotherhood (Whitmore, 1995). Moreover, the role of the therapists who help to elicit and shape the abduction narratives is analogous to the role played by priest or preceptor in more established religious traditions. The question is unavoidable: is there any reason to assume that the reports of experiences by mystics, shamans, or meditation masters are any more credible as 'phenomenological descriptions' than those of the abductees?

It should now be apparent that the question is not merely whether or not mystical experiences are constructed, unmediated, pure, or philosophically significant. The more fundamental question is whether we can continue to treat the texts and reports upon which such theories are based as referring, however obliquely, to determinative phenomenal events at all.

VII

But I have felt so many strange things, so many baseless things assuredly, that they are perhaps better left unsaid. To speak for example of the times when I go liquid and become like mud, what good would that do? Or of the others when I would be lost in the eye of a needle, I am so hard and contracted? No, those are well-meaning squirms that get me nowhere.

— From *Malone Dies* by Samuel Beckett.

Consider the taste of beer. Most would agree that beer is an acquired taste; few enjoy their first sip. In time many come to enjoy the flavour. But what has changed? The flavour, or merely our reaction to it? More to the point, how could one possibly decide the issue one way or the other? Something seems fishy about the question itself.

This is one of a series of illustrations and anecdotes used by the philosopher Daniel Dennett to undermine the concept of *qualia* (1992; see also Dennett,

1991). Qualia (the singular form is *quale*), is a term proposed by philosophers to designate those subjective or phenomenal properties of experience that resist a purely materialistic explanation. (The notion is an attempt to capture that aspect of consciousness that, say some, could never be reproduced by a 'thinking machine'.) In short, qualia refer to the way things *seem*. 'Look at a glass of milk at sunset; *the way it looks to you* — the particular, personal, subjective visual quality of the glass of milk is the *quale* of your visual experience at the moment. The *way the milk tastes to you then* is another, gustatory *quale*' (Dennett, 1992, p. 42). As it is never possible to communicate exactly how things appear to us (how could we ever know whether your experience of red is precisely the same as mine?), qualia are construed as essentially private, ineffable, and irreducible properties of experience.

Dennett thinks the whole notion of qualia is wrong-headed, and employs a series of 'intuition pumps', such as his musings on the flavour of beer, in order to undermine our confidence in the existence of intrinsic properties of experience. 'If it is admitted that one's attitudes towards, or reactions to, experiences are in any way and in any degree constitutive of their experiential qualities, so that a change in reactivity *amounts to* or *guarantees* a change in the property, then those properties, those 'qualitative or phenomenal features', cease to be 'intrinsic' properties and in fact become paradigmatically extrinsic, relational properties' (Dennett, 1992, p. 61). And if these most salient aspects of experience are in fact extrinsic and relational, one must relinquish one's picture of experience as a determinate *something* that occurs someplace 'inside the brain', in what Dennett calls the 'Cartesian theater' (Dennett, 1991). In short, one must give up what, in the Cartesian view, is a fundamental attribute of experience: its privacy.

In a somewhat similar spirit I have suggested that it is ill conceived to construe the object of the study of religion to be the inner experience of religious practitioners. Scholars of religion are not presented with experiences that stand in need of interpretation, but rather with texts, narratives, performances, and so forth. While these representations may at times assume the rhetorical stance of phenomenological description, we are not obliged to accept them as such. On the contrary, we must remain alert to the ideological implications of such a stance. Any assertion to the effect that someone else's inner experience bears some significance for *my* construal of reality is situated, by its very nature, in the public realm of contested meanings.

Before we throw out experience altogether, however, we must take stock of what is at stake. The appeal of the rhetoric of experience lay in its promise to forestall the objectification and commodification of personal life endemic to modern mass society. By objectification I refer to the projection of the 'subject' or 'self' into a centreless physical world of 'objective facts' amenable to scientific study and technological mastery — a projection that threatened to efface subjectivity altogether (Nagel, 1986). The flip side of objectification has been the rampant alienation that characterizes modernity — the sense of being rootless and adrift, cut off from tradition and history. Into this vacuum rushed the experts — sociologists, psychologists, anthropologists, and even scholars of religion — who claimed to understand *my* memories, *my* dreams, *my* desires, *my* beliefs, *my* thoughts, better than I. We are understandably reluctant to cede such authority to a guild of specialists, no matter how enlightened or well intentioned they may be. Our last line of defence has been the valorization of the 'autonomous self', construed as a unique and irreducible centre of experience.

This raises a host of complex political and philosophical issues concerned with the modern notion of selfhood and self-determination, issues that, for lack of space, I am unable to pursue here. As students of religion, our more immediate theoretical concerns are hermeneutic: How are we to understand people very different from ourselves without somehow effacing the very differences that separate us? Scholars have become acutely aware of the methodological problems entailed in using *our* conceptual categories and theoretical constructs to comprehend the world of others. In addition, recent post-colonial and feminist critiques have forced us to focus on the asymmetrical relationship between the investigator and his or her subjects. We are wary of the intellectual hubris and cultural chauvinism that often attends scholars as they claim insight into the self-representations of others, especially when those others are at a political and economic disadvantage. And again, the one defense against the tendency to objectify, to domesticate, to silence and eviscerate the other has been to sanction the other's singular and irreducible experience of the world.

Therein lies the rub. We believe it politically and intellectually essential to respect diverse 'worldviews', but at the same time we are hesitant to abandon the hermeneutic suspicion that is the mark of critical scholarship. We want to valorize the self-representations of others, yet we balk when 'respect for others' places undue demands upon our own credulity. Most draw the line, for example, when it comes to acceding the existence of the small greys. And well we should; a critical investigation of the abduction phenomenon can only begin once the decision has been made to look for alternative explanations — explanations that do not involve the existence of interloping aliens.

One strategy to negotiate this impasse has been to empower experience by affirming the truth of the experience narrative, but only to the one doing the narration. This strategy, which is closely allied with the phenomenological approach to religion mentioned above, tends to fragment reality into 'multiple objective worlds' (Shweder, 1991) — a consequence that does not seem to trouble many scholars of religion. In her book on near-death experiences, for example, Carol Zaleski engages in a critical historical analysis of the sociological and mythological factors that have contributed to near-death narratives in both medieval and modern times. But, somewhat incongruously, she concludes her sophisticated contextual analysis by insisting on the inherent truth value of the experiences themselves. Zaleski manages this by identifying the 'other world' described in the near-death accounts with the 'inner psychological world' of the subjects themselves. This allows her to valorize the near-death experiences as a 'legitimate imaginative means through which one can instill a religious sense of the cosmos' (1987, p. 203). Zaleski is thus able to countenance the experiences without subscribing to the fantastic cosmologies — the baroque views of heaven, hell, and everything between — that attend them.

Felicitas Goodman, in her study of spirit possession, goes a step further, assuming a decidedly agnostic stance toward the existence of the spirits reported by her subjects.

> The experience of [the] presence [of spirits] during possession is accompanied by observable physical changes. We should remember that whether these changes are internally generated or created by external agencies is not discoverable. No one can either prove or disprove that the obvious changes of the brain map in possession or in a patient with a multiple personality disorder, for that matter, are produced by psychological processes or by an invading alien being (Goodman, 1988, p. 126).

Goodman's agnosticism is but a small step away from John Mack's qualified acceptance of the existence of alien abductors.

This methodological stance is made possible by the peculiar nature of claims to experience, particularly religious experiences that are, by definition, extraordinary. Reports of mystical or visionary experiences can be likened to reports of dreams in so far as it is difficult, if not impossible, to separate the report of the experience from the experience itself. In a philosophical examination of dreams Norman Malcolm argues that the dream report is indeed the *only* criterion for the dream, and thus to report that one has dreamed *is* to have dreamed; there is simply no other criterion for the dream's existence (Malcolm, 1959). Malcolm concludes that dreams are therefore not experiences, a claim that has more to do with how he stipulates the meaning of 'experience' than with the nature of dreaming itself.

Scholars such as Zaleski and Goodman (as well as Steven Katz and other 'constructivists') tacitly, if not explicitly, adopt a similar perspective toward religious experience. They acknowledge that there is no way to tease apart the representation of a religious experience from the experience itself. Malcolm would argue that if the two cannot be separated — if the only criterion for the 'experience' is the report itself — then one cannot claim to be dealing with an experience at all. But Zaleski and Goodman move in a different direction, treating the reports as if they provided unmediated access to some originary phenomenal event. The constructivists seem to assume that since the historical, social, and linguistic processes that give rise to the narrative representation are identical with those that give rise to the experience, the former, which are amenable to scholarly analysis, provide a transparent window to the latter.

While we might laud the humanistic impulse that motivates this line of reasoning — the desire to countenance a diversity of 'worldviews' — it fails to grasp the rhetorical logic of appeals to experience. The word 'experience', in so far as it refers to that which is given to us in the immediacy of perception, signifies that which by definition is nonobjective, that which resists all signification. In other words, the term experience cannot make ostensible a *something that exists in the world*. The salient characteristic of private experience that distinguishes it from 'objective reality' is thus its unremitting indeterminacy. At the same time, the rhetoric of experience tacitly posits a place where signification comes to an end, variously styled 'mind', 'consciousness', the 'mirror of nature', or what have you. The category experience is, in essence, a mere place-holder that entails a substantive if indeterminate terminus for the relentless deferral of meaning. And this is precisely what makes the term experience so amenable to ideological appropriation.

Again, I am not trying to deny subjective experience. (Indeed, how would one do that?) I merely want to draw attention to the way the concept functions in religious discourse — in Wittgenstein's terms, its 'language game'. I have suggested that it is a mistake to approach literary, artistic, or ritual representations as if they referred back to something other than themselves, to some numinous inner realm. The fact that religious experience is often circumscribed in terms of its nondiscursive or nonconceptual character does not mitigate the problem: that nothing can be said of a particular experience — that is, its ineffability — cannot in and of itself constitute a delimiting characteristic, much less a phenomenal property. Thus while experience — construed as that which is 'immediately present' — may indeed be both irrefutable and indubitable, we must remember that whatever epistemological certainty experience may offer is gained only at the expense of any possible discursive meaning or signification. To put it another way, all attempts to signify 'inner experience' are destined to remain 'well-meaning squirms that get us nowhere'.

References

Barnard, G.W. (1992), 'Explaining the unexplainable: Wayne Proudfoot's *Religious Experience*', *Journal of the American Academy of Religion*, **60** (2).

Brainard, F.S. (1996), 'Defining "mystical experience"', *Journal of the American Academy of Religion*, **64** (2).

Bryan, C.D.B. (1995), *Close Encounters of the Fourth Kind: A Reporter's Notebook on Alien Abduction, UFOs, and the Conference at M.I.T* (New York: Arkana).

Carus, P. (1915), *The Gospel of Buddha* (Chicago, IL: The Open Court Publishing Company).

Dennett, D.C. (1991), *Consciousness Explained* (Boston, MA: Little, Brown).

Dennett, D.C. (1992), 'Quining qualia', in *Consciousness in Contemporary Science*, ed. A.J. Marcel and E. Bisiach (Oxford: Oxford University Press).

Forman, R.K.C. (1993), 'Mystical knowledge: Knowledge by identity', *Journal of the American Academy of Religion*, **61** (4).

Forman, R.K.C. (ed. 1990), *The Problem of Pure Consciousness: Mysticism and Philosophy* (New York: Oxford University Press).

Gadamer, H. (1975), *Truth and Method*, trans. Joel Weinsheimer (New York: Crosssroad).

Goodman, F.D. (1988), *How About Demons? Possession and Exorcism in the Modern World* (Bloomington, IN: Indiana University Press).

Hacking, I. (1995), *Rewriting the Soul: Multiple Personality and the Sciences of Memory* (Princeton: Princeton University Press).

Halbfass, W. (1988), 'The Concept of experience in the encounter between India and the West', in *India and Europe: An Essay in Understanding* (Albany, NY: SUNY Press).

Hirsch, E.D. (1967), *Validity in Interpretation* (New Haven: Yale University Press).

Huxley, A. (1946), *The Perennial Philosophy* (London: Harper and Brothers).

James, W. (1961/1902), *The Varieties of Religious Experience: A Study in Human Nature* (New York: Collier).

Jantzen, G.M. (1995), *Power, Gender, and Christian Mysticism* (Cambridge: Cambridge University Press).

Katz, S.T. (1978), 'Language, epistemology, and mysticism', in *Mysticism and Philosophical Analysis*, ed. S.T. Katz (New York: Oxford University Press).

Katz, S.T. (1983), 'The "conservative" character of mystical experience', in *Mysticism and Religious Traditions*, ed. S.T. Katz (New York: Oxford University Press).

Katz, S.T. (1992), 'Mystical speech and mystical meaning', in *Mysticism and Language*, ed. S.T. Katz (New York: Oxford University Press).

Mack, J.E. (1995), *Abduction: Human Encounters with Aliens*, Revised ed. (New York: Ballantine Books).

Malcolm, N. (1959), *Dreaming: Studies in Philosophical Psychology* (London: Routledge and Kegan Paul).

Nishida, K. (1990), *An Inquiry into the Good,* trans. M. Abe and C. Ives (New Haven: Yale University Press).

Nagel, T. (1986), *The View from Nowhere* (Oxford: Oxford University Press).

Otto, R. (1958/1917), *The Idea of the Holy: An Inquiry into the Non-Rational Factor in the Idea of the Divine and its Relation to the Rational,* trans. J W. Harvey (London: Oxford University Press).

Proudfoot, W. (1985), *Religious Experience* (Berkeley and Los Angeles: University of California Press).

Radhakrishnan, S. (1937), *An Idealist View of Life*, The Hibbert Lectures for 1929, Revised 2nd ed. (London: Allen and Unwin.)

Rorty, R. (1979), *Philosophy and the Mirror of Nature* (Princeton: Princeton University Press).

Schleiermacher, F.D.E. (1928), *The Christian Faith,* trans. H.R. Mackintosh and J.S. Stewart, 2nd ed. (Edinburgh: T & T Clark).

Scholem, G.G. (1969), *On the Kabbalah and Its Symbolism,* trans. R. Manheim (New York: Schocken Books).

Sharf, R.H. (1995a), 'Buddhist modernism and the rhetoric of meditative experience', *Numen*, **42** (3).

Sharf, R.H. (1995b), 'Sanbokyodan: Zen and the Way of the New Religions', *Japanese Journal of Religious Studies*, **22** (3–4).

Sharf, R.H. (1995c), 'The Zen of Japanese Nationalism', in *Curators of the Buddha: The Study of Buddhism Under Colonialism*, ed. Donald S. Lopez, Jr. (Chicago, IL: University of Chicago Press).

Shear, J. (1994), 'On mystical experiences as empirical support for the perennial philosophy', *Journal of the American Academy of Religion*, **62** (2).

Short, L. (1995), 'Mysticism, mediation, and the non-linguistic', *Journal of the American Academy of Religion*, **63** (4).

Shweder, R.A. (1991), *Thinking Through Cultures* (Cambridge: Harvard University Press).

Smart, N. (1973), *The Science of Religion and the Sociology of Knowledge: Some Methodological Questions* (Princeton: Princeton University Press).

Stace, W.T. (1960), *Mysticism and Philosophy* (London: Macmillan).

Whitmore, J. (1995), 'Religious dimensions of the UFO abductee experience', in *The Gods Have Landed: New Religions from Other Worlds*, ed. J.R. Lewis (Albany, NY: SUNY Press).

Zaleski, C. (1987), *Otherworld Journeys: Accounts of Near-Death Experience in Medieval and Modern Times* (Oxford: Oxford University Press).